Gender in Latin America

SYLVIA CHANT
with NIKKI CRASKE

Latin America Bureau
LONDON

First published in Great Britain in 2003
by Latin American Bureau
1 Amwell Street
London EC1R 1UL

ISBN 1 899365 53 2 (paper)

A CIP catalogue record for this book is available from the British Library.

Editing: Jean McNeil
Cover Design: Andy Dark
Cover Image: José Zuñiga, Cazador de Amantes, 1971, Col Museo de Arte Moderno
del Centro Cultural D.I.F.O.C.U.R.
Culiacán, Sinaloa, Mexico, Serie de la Pintura Mexicana, Ediciones AMAPAL.
Design and typesetting: Kate Kirkwood
Manufactured in the United States of America

CONTENTS

LIST OF TABLES, BOXES AND FIGURES

TABLES

BOXES

FIGURES

ACRONYMS

AIDS	Acquired Immunodeficiency Syndrome
AMNLAE	Asociación de Mujeres Nicaraguënses Luisa Amanda Espinoza
BWI	Bretton Woods Institutions
CCSS	Caja Costarricense de Seguridad Social
CEDAW	Convention on the Elimination of all Forms of Discrimination Against Women
CEFEMINA	Centro Feminista de Información y Acción (Costa Rica)
CEPAL	Comisión Economica para América Latina
CEPSS	Centro de Educación y Prevención de Salud Social (Chile)
CHA	Comunidad Homosexual Argentina
CIESAS	Centro de Investigaciones y Estudios Superiores en Antropología Social (Mexico)
CMD	Common Mental Disorders
CNDM	Conselho Nacional dos Direitos de la Mulher (Brazil)
CNM	Consejo Nacional de la Mujer (Argentina)
COMIBOL	Corporación Minera Boliviana
CONAMU	Consejo Nacional de la Mujer (Ecuador)
CONAPO	Consejo Nacional de Población (Mexico)
DF	Distrito Federal (Mexico)
DFID	Department for International Development (UK)
DIF	Desarrollo Integral Familiar (Mexico)
DGAG	Dirección General de Asuntos de Género (Bolivia)
DGPM	Dirección General de Promoción de la Mujer (Dominican Republic)
DINAMU	Dirección Nacional de la Mujer (Panama)
EBAIS	Equipos Básicos de Atención Integral en Salud (Costa Rica)
ECLAC	Economic Commission for Latin America and the Caribbean
EOI	Export-oriented Industrialisation
ESF	Emergency Social Fund
FMC	Federación de Mujeres Cubanas
FMLN	Frente Farabundo Martí para la Liberación Nacional (El Salvador)
FSLN	Frente Sandinista de Liberación Nacional (Nicaragua)
FWCW	Fourth World Conference on Women
GAD	Gender and Development
GATT	General Agreement on Trade and Tariffs
GDI	Gender-related Development Index
GDP	Gross Domestic Product
GEM	Gender Empowerment Measure
GLLU	Gay and Lesbian Latinos Unidos (USA)
GNP	Gross National Product
HAI	HelpAge International
HDI	Human Development Index
HIPC	Highly Indebted Poor Countries
HIV	Human Immunodeficiency Virus
HPI	Human Poverty Index
IADB	Inter American Development Bank
IAFA	Instituto Sobre el Alcoholismo y Farmacodependencia (Costa Rica)
ICCPR	International Covenant of Civil and Political Rights
ICESCR	International Covenant of Economic, Social and Cultural Rights
ICPD	International Conference on Population and Development
ILANUD	Instituto Latinamericano de las Naciones Unidas para la Prevención y Tratamiento del Delincuente
ILGA	International Lesbian and Gay Association (USA)

IMAS	Instituto Mixto de Ayuda Social (Costa Rica)
IMF	International Monetary Fund
INAMU	Instituto Nacional de las Mujeres (Costa Rica)
INFM	Instituto de la Famila y de la Mujer (Uruguay)
INIM	Instituto Nicaragüense de la Mujer
IPPF	International Planned Parenthood Federation
ISI	Import Substitution Industrialisation
IT	Information Technology
IUD	Intra-uterine Device
LEA	Lesbianas En Acción (Chile)
LU	Lesbianas Unidas (USA)
MINDESP	Ministerio de Desarrollo Sostenible y Planificación (Bolivia)
NAFTA	North American Free Trade Agreement
NBFI	Non-bank Financial Institution
NGO	Non-governmental Organisation
NHE	New Household Economics
NIDL	New International Division of Labour
NIE	New Institutional Economics
NPA	New Poverty Agenda
OASIS	Organización de Apoyo a una Sexualidad Integral Frente al SIDA (Guatemala)
OECD	Organisation for Economic Cooperation and Development
OIM	Organización Internacional de Migración
ONAM	Oficina Nacional de la Mujer (Guatemala)
PAHO	Pan-American Health Organisation
PAN	Partido Acción Nacional (Mexico)
PHC	Primary Healthcare
PLN	Partido Liberación Nacional (Costa Rica)
PPF	Partido Peronista Femenino (Argentina)
PRD	Partido Revolucionario Democrático (Mexico)
PRI	Partido Revolucionario Institucional (Mexico)
PROGRESA	Programa de Educación, Salud y Alimentación (Mexico)
PROMUDEH	Ministerio de Promoción de la Mujer y del Desarrollo Humano (Peru)
PRONASOL	Programa Nacional de Solidaridad (Mexico)
PUSC	Partido Unido Social Cristiano (Costa Rica)
SAP	Structural Adjustment Programme
SEDESOL	Secretaría de Desarrollo Social (Mexico)
SERNAM	Servicio Nacional de la Mujer (Chile)
SF	Social Fund
SIDA	Sindrome de Inmunodeficiencia Adquirida
SIPAM	Salud Integral Para la Mujer (Mexico)
SPHC	Selective Primary Health Care
SSA	Secretaría de Salubridad y Asistencia (Mexico)
STD	Sexually Transmitted Disease
UN	United Nations
UNAM	Universidad Nacional Autónoma de México
UNO	Unión Nacional Opositora (Nicaragua)
UNCHS	United Nations Centre for Human Settlements
UNDP	United Nations Development Programme
UNICEF	United Nations Children's Fund
VIH	Virus de Inmunodeficiencia Humano
WHO	World Health Organisation
WID	Women in Development

GLOSSARY OF LATIN AMERICAN TERMS

All terms are Spanish unless otherwise indicated.

Albañil Construction worker

Ajuste estructural Structural adjustment

Arpillera Embroidered picture. During the Pinochet dictatorship in Chile, *arpilleras* often had political content

Asilo Old people's home

Barrio Low-income neighbourhood

Bracero Labourer, generally used in context of Bracero Programme of 1942-1964, which originally admitted Mexican workers into the United States to ease labour shortages during the Second World War

Cabeza Head/head of household

Cachapera Derived from '*cachapa*', a Chilean word for a maize pancake which literally means 'pancake-maker', but is used as a term for lesbian

Cacique 'Strong man'/feudal-type leader

Caja popular Savings cooperative

Calle Street

Cantina Bar or saloon (traditionally male-only)

Caudillo Leader or political boss

Carnaval Brazilian word for carnival

Carne Meat/flesh

Casa House

Casera Adjective to decsribe a woman who is 'home-loving' and/or 'housebound'

Chicano/a Person of Mexican descent who was born or is living in the United States

Cochón Colloquial Nicaraguan term for man who is penetrated in anal intercourse. Used in relation to a heterosexual man means 'unmanly', 'sissy'

Colectivo Collective (as in group or organisation), but also a term for mini-bus in some countries (for example, Argentina)

Compadre/Comadre Co-parent, used to describe relationship between child's father/mother, and godfather/godmother

Compañero/a Term used in many parts of Latin America to describe sexual partner (usually cohabiting). Can also mean companion or political colleague/ally

Concupiscencia Brazilian term for sin of unfettered sexual desire

Conquistador Conqueror/soldier

Criollo Creole

Cuerpo Body

Culero Colloquial Honduran term for homosexual man who is penetrated in anal intercourse

Curandero/a Traditional healer

Cupo Quota

Derecho Right

Derechos humanos Human rights

Desfile March or parade

Dominar To dominate

Empoderamiento Empowerment

Encuentro Encounter/meeting

Entendido Self-referential term for gay man in various parts of Latin America

Entendida Self-referential term used by lesbian women in various parts of Latin America

Evangélico Evangelical – generic term given to Pentecostal-Charismatics in Latin America

Familia Family

Feminista Feminist

Fiesta Party/Festival

Folclor Folklore

Frente Front (political)

Guadalupismo Idealisation of women as virgins and/or mothers, deriving from the Virgin of Guadalupe

Gringo/a Term used in Latin America mainly to describe people from the United States, but can also be applied to other foreigners, or very Hispanicised Latin Americans. In Argentina, for example, the term can refer to someone of Italian, Polish or Russian descent

Hembra Term to describe the female of any animal species, but also used for women in certain contexts

Hembrismo Cult of female power, strength and sensuality (Cuba)

Hogar Household

Hombre Man

Homem Man (Brazil)

Homem-machão 'He-man' (Brazil)

Hombre-hombre Very manly

Iglesia Church

Jefe/a de hogar Chief/head of household

Jineterismo Term to describe 'hustling' in Cuba

Joto/a Term roughly equivalent to 'queer', used by Mexican gay men to describe gay men in general – note there is masculine and feminine version of the term

Latino/a Person of Latin American descent living in United States

Lesbiana Lesbian

Ley Law

Macehualtin Term to describe 'the masses' in Nahuatl, the language of the Mexican Aztecs.

Machete Large knife used mainly for agricultural work and wood-cutting

Machismo Cult of 'manliness' emphasising bravery, strength, sexual potency, and power over women and other men. Often associated with exaggerated masculinity, male chauvinism and/or a male supremacist ideology

Machista Adjective pertaining to actions, attitudes or persons (male or female) who display traits of (or who subscribe to ideals of) *machismo*

Macho Male (animal or human), but is also used in certain contexts (e.g. Mexico) to describe a man, an action or an attitude with traits of *machismo*

Macho marica Colloquial term for 'manly homosexual' or 'butch queen' (Argentina)

Marimacha 'Masculine Mary'. Term used to describe butch lesbian in various parts of Latin America

Madre Mother

Mancha Stain or mark, sometimes used in relation to loss of a girl's virginity prior to marriage

Mandilón Literally 'apron-wearer'. Mexican colloquial term for man who is 'under his wife's thumb'

Maquila/ Maquiladora Assembly production/assembly production unit, usually in multinational export manufacturing

Marianismo Cult of the 'Virgin Mary', idealising motherhood, and chaste and decorous behaviour in women

Maricón Pejorative term for gay man, effeminate man, or 'sissy', used in many parts of Latin America

Maricona Queer woman. Often used pejoratively by 'outsiders', but now noted to have been subverted and 'reclaimed' by lesbians in various parts of Latin America

Maternidad Motherhood

Matrimonio Marriage or married couple

Mestizo/a Person of Spanish and indigenous descent

Mestizaje Intermixing of Spanish and indigenous New World peoples

Mujer Woman

Mulato/a Person of African and Portuguese descent. The Anglicised version is spelt mulatto/a

Mulher Portuguese word for woman

Muliplicadora Term used for community educator, trainer and/or facilitator in community projects in various parts of Latin America

Neoliberalismo Neoliberalism

Nosotras We (women)
Padre Father
Partera Midwife
Partido Party (political)
Paternidad Paternity
Patria potestad Legal term for rights over children
Peón Unskilled worker in agriculture or construction
Píldora Contraceptive pill
Píldora poscoital Morning after pill
Pinguero Term used for Cuban men who perform the penetrative role in commercial anal intercourse
Pipiltin Nahuatl term for 'nobility'
Plaza de toros Bull ring
Pobreza Poverty
Poder Power
Pollerón Pejorative term for man who 'hangs onto his wife's skirts' (Argentina)
Praia Beach (Portuguese)
Preta Portuguese term for black woman
Puta Pejorative term meaning 'whore'
Puto/Putonesco Gay/gayish, often used derogatorily
Promotora Woman who promotes preventive health within her community, often trained in local clinic
Raza 'Race'
Red Network
Sacanagem Brazilian term for transgressive sexual interaction
Salud Health
Sangre Blood
Sendero Luminoso Shining Path
Sexualidad Sexuality
SIDA AIDS
Sociedad de convivencia Civil union (Mexico)
Sol Sun (also in Portuguese)
Suar Sweat (Portuguese)
Supermadre Supermother
Temporera Female agricultural worker on temporary contract
Tercer Edad 'Third Age', as in relation to elderly people
Tortilla Staple foodstuff, like pancake, made out of wheatflour or maize. Also used as colloquial term in Mexico to refer to gay men who both penetrate and are penetrated in anal intercourse
Tortillera Literally 'pancake maker', but colloquial term for lesbian in various parts of Latin America
Travesti Transvestite (also in Portuguese)
Union libre/ Union consensual Cohabiting relationship (without legal marriage)
Varonilla Colloquial term for butch lesbian (literally 'little [feminine] man' or 'little male/female')
Vejez Old age
VIH HIV
Verão Summer (Portuguese)
Vestida Colloquial term for transvestite (Mexico)
Vida digna 'Dignified life'
Violencia Violence

PREFACE AND ACKNOWLEDGEMENTS

This book would probably not have seen the light of day had it not been commissioned! The massive and on-going expansion of work on gender in Latin America is such that even making a stab at the task (which is all this book can hope to do) would have been much less likely without the inspired and encouraging suggestions of a publisher. For this, we owe huge gratitude to Marcela López Levy at the Latin America Bureau, and to Jean McNeil who oversaw the copy-editing and publication process when Marcela took maternity leave. The contributions of Silvia Posocco at the London School of Economics to translation and indexing are also warmly appreciated.

While the book aims to provide something of a 'state-of-the-art' review of gender in Latin America at the start of the twenty-first century, the themes selected and our approaches to the task inevitably reflect our disciplinary backgrounds in Geography (Chant) and Politics (Craske), and our particular research interests – in employment, migration, households, poverty and livelihood strategies, and in politics, citizenship and corporatism respectively. Financial support to explore these research topics, all of which are drawn upon in the present volume, have come from different bodies. Chant would like to thank the Nuffield Foundation, ESRC, Leverhulme Trust, the Central Research Fund and the London School of Economics for funding various research projects in Mexico and Costa Rica between 1986 and 1999. Craske's gratitude goes to the British Academy for supporting research in Argentina and Chile in 1995, and to the Universities of Belfast and Liverpool for funding fieldtrips to Mexico, Peru and Chile in 1999 and 2000. Chant also gratefully acknowledges the field assistance given by Cathy McIlwaine and Sarah Bradshaw in Costa Rica in 1989 for her ESRC project on Gender and Migration (Award no. R000231151), by Carlos Borge in 1997 for the project on Men, Households and Poverty jointly funded by the Nuffield Foundation (SOC/100[1554]) and ESRC (Award no. R000222205), and by Wagner Moreno in

1999 for the Nuffield financed pilot study on Youth, Gender and 'Family Crisis' (SGS/LB/0233).

Thanks are due to the following for their immensely valuable comments and assistance as the text emerged: Matthias Rohrig Assuncão (University of Essex, UK); Kevin Burchell (London School of Economics, UK); Andrew Canessa (University of Essex, UK); Mariana Cervantes (Council for Ethnic Minority Volunteer Organisations, UK); Anna Coates (London School of Economics, UK); Andrea Cornwall (Institute of Development Studies, Sussex, UK); Andrew Davies (University of Liverpool, UK); Agustín Escobar Latapí (Centro de Investigaciones y Estudios Superiores en Antropología Social del Occidente, Mexico); Txema Espada Calpe (Universidad Complutense de Madrid, Spain); María del Carmen Feijoó (Consejo Nacional de Investigaciones Científicas y Técnicas and Dirección General de Cultura y Educación, Provincia de Buenos Aires, Argentina); Jasmine Gideon (Birkbeck College, University of London, UK); Mercedes González de la Rocha (Centro de Investigaciones y Estudios Superiores en Antropología Social del Occidente, Mexico); Matthew Gutmann (Brown University, USA); David Hojman (University of Liverpool, UK); Rosaleen Howard (University of Liverpool, UK); Haydea Izazola Conde (Universidad Autónoma Metropolitano – Xochimilco, Mexico); Hazel Johnstone (London School of Economics, UK); David Lehmann (University of Cambridge,UK); Cathy McIlwaine (Queen Mary College, University of London, UK); Carl McLean (London School of Economics, UK); Maxine Molyneux (Institute of Latin American Studies, University of London, UK); Abel Pérez-Zamorano (London School of Economics, UK); Diane Perrons (London School of Economics, UK); Anne Phillips (London School of Economics, UK); Silvia Posocco (London School of Economics, UK); Eugenia Rodríguez (Universidad de Costa Rica); Helen Safa (University of Florida, USA); Cecilia Tacoli (International Institute for Environment and Development, UK); Goran Tadic (Islington Council, UK); Jim Thomas (London School of Economics, UK); Penny Vera-Sanso (University of Kent at Canterbury, UK), and Katie Willis (University of Liverpool, UK).

Last but not least, we owe special gratitude to those closest to us – especially Chris – for their forebearance and support throughout.

Sylvia Chant
Nikki Craske

London/Liverpool, UK
2001–2

FOREWORD

MERCEDES GONZÁLEZ DE LA ROCHA

Despite the difficulties of writing about gender in a region as diverse as Latin America, Chant and Craske provide an admirable overview that respects particularities and variations in the region's economic, political, demographic and cultural characteristics. Besides diversity, Chant and Craske capture the complex panorama of social change. The transformations experienced by Latin America in recent times have been, without doubt, profound and multitudinous. From changes in its demographic profile, to processes of democratisation that have been incubated and advanced to different degrees in different countries, through transformations in economic and social relations within the family and domestic groups, and in gender relations, Latin America presents itself to the world as an extremely dynamic region. The impact that these changes have had on the behaviour of national economies, the structures of employment and the lives of individuals and their families, has been great. The present book by Chant and Craske leads us to reflect upon gender relations and their very many facets and complexities, which in everyday life have been integrally and fundamentally bound up in the repercussions of broader social change.

Gender in Latin America is an important book for many reasons. First, because it covers such a broad spectrum of themes and issues – representing different elements of gender relations and dynamics in a remarkably balanced fashion. Second, because to this thematic breadth and balance is added a meticulous concern for detail. Were this not enough, the authors strive to cover all parts of the region, despite the fact that, as with all scholars working in the area, they have not been able to do their own fieldwork in more than a few countries.

Chant and Craske prioritise the analysis of social change over a span of twenty to thirty years, from the 1970s to the present. They highlight some of the political shifts that have marked social life in the different countries as much as incipient legislative changes. The authors show that even if gender differences in the realm of politics and in legal apparatuses have not disappeared, they have started to change, giving ground to greater female participation in public office and in positions characterised by greater equality of rights and duties between women and men.

Of the many issues developed in the book, there are three on which I would like to comment briefly here. First, I would like to highlight the significance of economic change and its impact on households where, of course, women have been crucial agents in the struggle for survival. Second, it seems appropriate to emphasise the importance of demographic change for women's lives and their negotiations with men. Third, and leading on from these points, it is important to focus on shifts in intimacy and gender relations within the household. By reflecting on these three important aspects of social change, and the interrelations among them, we can better understand how macroeconomic adjustments generate private adjustments.

Transformations in economic structures have been profoundly associated with changes in the urban and rural distribution of populations in Latin America. The majority of countries in the region went from being predominantly rural to largely urban societies within the space of a few decades. During the 1960s and 1970s, Latin America experienced accelerated economic growth that translated into a rise in employment opportunities, the transformation of occupational structures and a substantial increase in manufacturing activities and services. In spite of the vertiginous process of economic growth, poverty continued to be one of the central traits of Latin America's burgeoning cities as well as of the countryside – the latter being the site of increasingly neglected and deteriorating farming activities. In the first part of the 1970s, 40 per cent of the Latin American population was considered poor. Although in 1980 this proportion had diminished, estimates from the Economic Commission for Latin America and the Caribbean (ECLAC), suggested that it was in the region of 35 per cent. The so-called 'lost decade' of Latin America followed, years in which ordinary people dedicated their everyday lives to struggles for survival. Some of these struggles were of a silent nature, developed in the privacy of home and household; others were more organised and reached the streets and other public spaces. After the lost decade came the decade of economic restructuring and the implementation of neoliberal economic reforms, which continued to exact high costs on family budgets and engender important changes in the social organisation of domestic groups. The challenge for many studies of the region has been to understand and explain these processes of social change, as well as the survival mechanisms of low-income sectors in towns, cities and rural areas. The social organisation of families and households, the survival and work strategies of low-income populations, unequal relations within domestic environments and in the workplace in terms of gender, race and age, have all gained ground in the research agendas of Latin America from the late twentieth century onwards.

Chant and Craske are sensitive to the dramatic transformations of models of development in the region. The changes that produced the foreign debt crisis and the decline of so-called Import Substitution Industrialisation are the basis of ample reflection by the authors. Gender relations, as dynamic and changing, that intersect with questions of class, ethnicity, migration and the life course, are the leading themes that the authors weave through the complex processes of change in Latin America. They discuss the emergence – and consolidation – of programmes of neoliberal economic restructuring which entailed deregulation of markets, export-led industrial production and general opening up of economies. Crucial themes such as global competition, the rise of unemployment and occupational insecurity, and the withdrawal of the state from economic life, social protection and provision of services are all highlighted by Chant and Craske in their accounts of the social impacts of recent developments. On the basis of the evidence analysed by the authors, these processes have produced a considerable increase in poverty in the region and have left the majority of the population in a situation of increased vulnerability and resource scarcity.

However, increased precariousness and poverty in the lives of the majority of Latin Americans has not affected all the population in the same way. The research that has been carried out in the region, including that of Sylvia Chant and other scholars specialising in the subject, has shown that the erosion of household income necessary for survival impacts particularly on low-income women. Unequal burdens have been documented with women's responsibilities intensifying alongside the diminution of periods dedicated to rest and leisure. In the research currently being carried out and coordinated by Agustín Escobar and myself at CIESAS Occidente in Guadalajara on the effects of the Mexican social programme PROGRESA,[1] we have seen that the poorest women have to bear a complex burden of tasks and functions (to which PROGRESA has added), which maintain them in a situation of work overload and exhaustion.

Gender differences and inequalities are at the core of Chant and Craske's review. However, far from focusing on these inequalities with a static and monolithic vision, the authors consider the many directions in which changes have led. A particularly relevant aspect of their perspective is the recognition that change is rarely unidirectional. As part and parcel of this, they deal with the analysis and discussion of what we might call the 'costs and benefits' that broader economic and social transformations have brought to the lives of women in Latin America. Before addressing this point – which is central to the book that we now hold in our hands as much as to the work of all of us committed to the study of gender relations – I would like to dedicate a section to some aspects of change in the structures of Latin America's populations that Chant and Craske have incorporated.

To their analysis the authors add the complex panorama of population dynamics in Latin America, and their links with gender relations. Although it is true to say that Latin America as a whole is undergoing what population experts define as a 'demographic transition', there are important variations among countries (and among regions within countries) with regard to morbidity and mortality, life expectancy for men and women, and fertility. The demographic transition has differential implications in terms of gender that the authors recognise and discuss. It is an established fact, for instance, that declining population growth in Latin America has been achieved mainly through the use of birth control, in which women have played a crucial part as the main targets of population programmes. Although fertility rates in countries such as Argentina, Cuba, Uruguay, and to a certain extent Chile were already low during the 1970s, there is now a very significant decrease across the whole region, which has occurred in a relatively short period of time. Chant and Craske focus on a number of factors relevant to our understanding of the social and gender implications of demographic dynamics: the differentiated role of men and women in family planning and gendered dimensions of ageing. And although it is clear that female bodies have been the object of population policies in ways that we may oppose (forced sterilisation and other socio-bio-technological aggressions, for example), it is also necessary to highlight the gains that result from some demographic processes. Above all, it appears that women with fewer children command more time and freedom to engage in waged activities. As has been widely noted, the decrease in fertility is strongly linked with rising rates of female labour force participation.[2] Second, women's use of contraceptive methods has marked the beginning of greater negotiation with their partners with respect to sexuality and reproduction. And although the negotiation of gender is crucial in the gains and failures of national population policies, the control that women may exercise over reproductive technologies is equally important. Women who are less subordinated to the desires and decisions of men are women who can not only access, but also use reproductive methods and techniques more effectively.

As indicated previously, major social changes do not have a homogeneous impact across different social groups. The gender-differentiated burdens provoked by broader economic change have been the subject of systematic research and analysis by academics of different disciplinary and theoretical perspectives. Private adjustments, as responses to the use and deterioration of the resources available for survival, have been documented for a long list of countries not only in Latin America but also in other regions.[3] In the wake of material hardship generated by shifting development models, what has actually happened to flesh-and-blood women and men and to gender relations?

We know that greater numbers of women in Latin America now participate in the labour markets in exchange for a wage. During the era of Import Substitution Industrialisation, women workers were in large part childless single women with relatively high education. Yet, as has been widely documented, the 1980s were a watershed in terms of female employment. The economic necessities created and augmented during economic crisis pushed women into work in greater numbers, including those who were married, had children and/or possessed little formal education. The determinants of women's work[4] changed as a result of growing unmet needs and the growing poverty of households. What changes might be expected – in terms of gender relations and hierarchies within households – to ensue from such a process? Many efforts have been made to find answers to this question. In the case of Mexico, for example, studies undertaken during the 1980s and the early 1990s revealed that working women often had little chance to improve their situation within households, characterised as they were by acute poverty, asymmetrical and violent relations, and the unequal distribution of resources. Benería and Roldán,[5] in their now classic study of industrial subcontracting and assembly home working in Mexico City, stressed the existence of male control over female income. García and Oliveira (op. cit.) observed that the households where women – with co-resident husbands – obtained the greatest income for the economy of the family were those where domestic violence was most evident, and men, without being breadwinners, still imposed their authority and control through physical, verbal and psychological abuse.

Debates emanating from those years remained inconclusive, yet, as Chant and Craske suggest, despite the less than favourable economic context which has evolved in Latin America, it is possible to glimpse an anticipated process of increased 'gains' for women. The Caribbean experience documented by Helen Safa[6] and others, for example, has shown, *inter alia*, that workforce participation has been associated with rising female autonomy, increased capacity for negotiation between men and women, and female resistance to patterns of patriarchal authority. In turn, women come over, in the present book, endowed as it is with carefully analysed evidence, as extremely important actors in social change. *Gender in Latin America* contributes impressively to our understanding of the transformation of women's condition as a fundamental trait of the structural change that contemporary Latin American societies are experiencing. The mass entry of women in the labour market, the decrease in fertility and the rise of their educational levels seem to be fundamental aspects of such a transformation. As I have written elsewhere, the fact that a growing number of Latin American women see themselves as indispensable providers or co-providers for the sustenance of domestic groups is not an insignificant detail in the social life of Latin America. This has led, gradually and through difficult negotiations and painful experiences, to the weakening of patriarchal domestic arrangements and to the transformation of the traditional model of the family. The rise of separation and divorce, as a product of female decision-making, and the rise of female headed households in the last decades are phenomena that are undoubtedly associated with the fact that many women can now command their own income, and that this enables them to opt for different forms of life. Can we – or should we – now talk of an incipient crisis of masculine identity? Chant and Craske argue that this deserves attention given that men's identities, as with those of women, have been destabilised by changes in many of the aspects that defined and sustained them.

Gender in Latin America is a book that considers the different gender configurations of contemporary Latin American societies with reference to their social, political, economic, demographic and cultural contexts and dimensions. It makes connections between spheres that are fundamental for understanding and explaining change in Latin American societies. It is about men and women in transition, who have transgressed norms and values in their everyday practices. It is about women and men who, through the gender confrontations and negotiations which have emerged out of their new realities, currently find themselves in the process of rewriting their scripts, while weaving new social relations.

Translation by Silvia Posocco

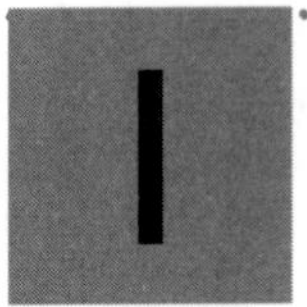

INTRODUCTION Gender in a Changing Continent

SYLVIA CHANT

This book explores configurations of gender in key social, political, economic and demographic aspects of contemporary Latin American societies. The themes covered – politics, legislation, social movements, poverty, population, migration, employment, health, sexuality, families and households – interrelate in important ways. We elaborate on these connections at various points in the book, as well as indicating how issues pertaining to gender in Latin America are informed by, and themselves inform, wider international debates on theory and policy.

The volume focuses on the last fifty years, with particular emphasis on the last three decades of the twentieth century. During this period many countries in Latin America have emerged from the shadows of authoritarian regimes, whether civilian or military, in which there was limited scope for civil society activity among women or men. In the case of military dictatorships, particularly in Central America and the Southern Cone, state terrorism was frequently deployed in the attempt to paralyse all kinds of 'subversive' action, including feminism (see Feijoó and Gogna, 1990; Fisher, 1993; Molyneux, 2000; Rivera Puentes, 1996b). While women still managed to be active in exile as well as to contribute to the transition to democracy in many parts of the continent, the initially high expectations that women would participate fully in national political life thereafter were less than satisfied (see Craske, 1999; Fisher, 1993:2; Jaquette [ed], 1994). In addition, since the early 1980s most countries in Latin America have fallen under the shroud of crippling external debt crises and long-term programmes of neoliberal economic restructuring. The latter have included greater opening up to global competition, deregulation of labour markets, and a 'rolling back' of the state from economic life, and from social protection and provision. In many cases these moves have been associated with deepening poverty (especially in urban areas), rising precariousness in people's livelihoods, and particular hardships for low-income women. Paradoxically perhaps, these trends have formed the backdrop to the most intense period of feminist organising in Latin American history, and the introduction throughout the region of state apparatus and legislation oriented to advancing the cause of gender equality and/or women's rights. If it is surprising that so many gains have been made by and for Latin American women in this 'generally unfavourable economic milieu' (Deere and León, 2000b:31), it was precisely women's efforts which played a part in creating the conditions to make them happen. As Molyneux (2000:64–5) notes:

> The collapse of military rule in the 1980s and the return of civilian governments to power were accompanied by a deepening of the restructuring process, but in the context of a greater commitment to social justice and "good governance"…. Partly under the influence of the international women's movement, partly due to the greater self-confidence and organisational strength of national women's movements, and partly in an effort to present a modern face to the world, newly elected democratic governments recognised women as a constituency that required representation in the state.

While gender is inherently dynamic, whatever the historical juncture, a number of important changes have accompanied the growth of institutional support for women in Latin America in the late twentieth century. Prominent among these are the interrelated trends of a general (if differentiated) decline in fertility across the continent, rising levels of education and employment among women[1], a weakening of patriarchal household arrangements (linked, *inter alia*, with upward trends in divorce and growing numbers of female-headed households), and, in some quarters, a brewing 'crisis' of masculine identity (see Chant, 1997a, 2000; Escobar Latapí, 1998; González de la Rocha, 1994, 1995; Güendel and González, 1998; Kaztman, 1992; Safa, 1995a,b). Alongside these processes, it is possible to discern diminishing gaps in 'quantitative' indicators of gender inequality, including literacy and educational attainment, and male–female headcounts in formal politics, even if, in most contexts, women's shares of GDP per capita and of managerial and professional employment continue to lag far behind those of men (see Tables 1.1 and 1.2).[2] Our main concerns in the light of these transitions is to examine what they signify for gender at the start of the twenty-first century. Are gender inequalities in Latin America lessening over time, or simply changing in nature? How far is gender a more important basis of inequality than other axes of difference such as class, 'race' and sexuality? How do these combine with one another, and with what effects? What kinds of strategies might be advanced to create conditions for greater gender equality in Latin American societies in the new millennium?

While we hope to go some way to answering these questions in the following chapters, it is critical to emphasise that a book of this kind can never be exhaustive, and that much historical and geographical texture is sacrificed in the interests of providing a general overview. This problem is greatly compounded in a region such as Latin America, given immense variations in the economic, political, demographic, social and cultural characteristics of its constituent countries. Adding to complexity

Table 1.1 Latin America: Gender-related Development Index (GDI)

	Gender-related development index (GDI) 1998*		Life expectancy at birth (years) 1998		Adult literacy (% age 15 & above) 1998		Combined primary, secondary & tertiary gross enrolment ratio (%) 1997		GDP per capita (PPP US$) 1998**		HDI rank minus GDI rank§
	Rank	Value	Female	Male	Female	Male	Female	Male	Female	Male	
Argentina	35	0.824	76.9	69.8	96.6	96.7	82	77	5553	18,724	–1
Bolivia	96	0.631	63.6	60.2	77.8	91.3	64	75	1217	3334	0
Brazil	66	0.736	71.2	63.3	84.5	84.5	82	78	3830	9483	–3
Chile	39	0.812	78.4	72.4	95.2	95.6	76	78	4011	13,660	–3
Colombia	58	0.760	74.5	67.6	91.2	91.3	71	70	4079	7979	2
Costa Rica	46	0.789	79.1	74.4	95.4	95.3	65	66	3126	8768	–1
Cuba	—	—	78.2	74.3	96.3	96.5	73	70	—	—	—
Dominican Republic	73	0.720	73.3	69.2	82.8	82.9	72	68	2333	6787	2
Ecuador	78	0.701	72.7	67.5	88.7	92.5	72	75	1173	4818	–1
El Salvador	83	0.693	72.7	66.7	75.0	80.8	63	64	2779	5343	3
Guatemala	100	0.603	67.6	61.7	59.7	74.9	43	51	1614	5363	0
Honduras	94	0.644	72.5	67.7	73.5	73.4	59	57	1252	3595	1
Mexico	50	0.775	75.7	69.7	88.7	92.9	69	71	4112	11,635	–1
Nicaragua	97	0.624	70.9	66.1	69.3	66.3	65	61	1256	3039	1
Panama	52	0.770	76.5	71.9	90.8	92.1	74	72	3034	7421	0
Paraguay	71	0.723	72.2	67.7	91.5	94.0	64	65	2058	6481	–2
Peru	70	0.723	71.2	66.2	84.3	94.2	77	79	2104	6493	–2
Uruguay	37	0.821	78.2	70.7	98.0	97.2	81	74	5791	11,630	0
Venezuela	56	0.763	75.9	70.2	91.4	92.6	68	66	3281	8302	2

Source: UNDP (2000: Table 2)

Notes: — = no data. * Rank of GDI is out of 143 countries of world for which GDI had been computed as of 1998. ** PPP = Purchasing Power Parity. This is a measure whereby one dollar in the relevant country has the same purchasing power over domestic GDP as the US dollar has over US GDP. This allows a standard comparison of real price levels between countries. § A positive figure indicates that the GDI rank is higher than the HDI (Human Development Index) rank, a negative, the opposite. The HDI incorporates life expectancy at birth, adult literacy, combined primary, secondary and tertiary enrolment and GDP per capita.

Table 1.2 Latin America: Gender Empowerment Measure (GEM)*

	Gender empowerment measure (GEM)**		Seats in parliament held by women (as % of total) (2000)	Female administrators & managers (as % of total)	Female professionals & technical workers (as % of total)	Women's GDP per capita (PPP US$)[§]
	Rank	Value				
Argentina	—	—	21.3	—	—	—
Bolivia	54	0.422	10.2	24.9	42.6	1217
Brazil	—	—	5.9	—	62.0	—
Chile	51	0.440	8.9	22.4	50.5	4011
Colombia	37	0.510	12.2	40.4	44.6	4079
Costa Rica	24	0.553	19.3	29.5	45.1	3126
Cuba	—	—	27.6	18.5	—	—
Dominican Republic	39	0.505	14.5	30.6	49.4	2333
Ecuador	43	0.481	14.6	27.5	46.6	1173
El Salvador	30	0.527	16.7	34.9	44.3	2779
Guatemala	—	—	8.8	—	—	—
Honduras	48	0.460	9.4	54.4	48.5	1252
Mexico	35	0.514	18.0	20.7	40.2	4112
Nicaragua	—	—	9.7	—	—	—
Panama	46	0.470	9.9	33.6	48.6	3034
Paraguay	57	0.406	8.0	22.6	54.1	2058
Peru	50	0.446	10.8	26.9	41.6	2104
Uruguay	45	0.472	11.5	24.0	63.1	5791
Venezuela	20	0.597	28.6~	24.3	57.6	3281

Source: UNDP (2000: Table 3)

Notes: — = no data

* Except for data on seats in parliament held by women, all data in this table relate to the latest available year before publication of the UNDP 2000 Human Development Report.

** Rank out of 70 countries for which GEM has been computed.

§ PPP = Purchasing Power Parity. This is a measure whereby one dollar in the relevant country has the same purchasing power over domestic GDP as the US dollar has over US GDP. This allows a standard comparison of real price levels between countries.

~ Data refer to the Legislative National Commission of Venezuela.

is the fact that people's experiences and negotiations of gender are cross-cut by myriad, interwoven axes of difference such as ethnicity, class, migrant status, urban/rural residence, family and household characteristics, sexual orientation and stage in the life course. Set against the increasingly rapid changes linked with globalisation in the continent, it is clearly difficult to do justice to all possible permutations of contemporary Latin American diversity. One of the principal shortfalls in the present volume, for example, is that of uneven attention to different sectors of the Latin American population. Although there are growing bodies of gender-sensitive literature on 'minority' groups such as indigenous peoples, gays and lesbians, and on sections of the populace who have not conventionally been the object of dedicated feminist study (men, upper-income groups, the elderly and so on), the bulk of gender research to date has concentrated on low-income, *mestiza* women in urban areas. This has somewhat inevitably impacted upon *who* we write about most in the book.

A second caveat pertains to geography, with *where* we write about most in Latin America being influenced by uneven intra-regional coverage in the literature. Countries such as Paraguay, Uruguay, Panama, Guatemala and Venezuela, for example, do not figure as prominently in respect of internationally accessible work on gender as, say, Peru, Ecuador, Brazil, Nicaragua, Costa Rica, Mexico, Chile, and Argentina. Accordingly, more examples are drawn from this latter group than the former. The fact that our respective fieldwork has taken place in the last four countries is another reason why they feature more frequently in case study sections than those for which our knowledge has come through secondary sources.

As for *what* we write about in the book, our choice of themes is also governed partly by our own research interests. More significant still, however, is that these reflect the topics of some of the most extensive work on gender in the region, both by Latin Americans and by the wider diaspora of Latin Americanists. Indeed, the very nature of the present enterprise emerges out of a rich and ever-expanding body of feminist scholarship in Latin America. Current theory and knowledge owe a large debt to the groundbreaking efforts of academics, practitioners and activists working at a time when gender was an unfamiliar and often deeply unpopular concept, not to mention personally and politically dangerous. Accordingly, we consider it vital to dedicate some discussion, albeit brief, to the development of gender research in and on Latin America over time, and to highlight issues which have become hallmarks in debates on gender in the region, both internally and internationally.

Research on gender in Latin America: a brief retrospective

Although isolated studies on gender in Latin America have a long history, dedicated research and writing on the subject took off on a grand scale only in the 1970s. This was the era of the United Nations Decade for Women (1975–1985) which provided two major impetuses to research and action on gender. First, it highlighted how little was actually known about women in any region of the world. Second, in galvanising international interest in 'the position of women', it created an environment in which networks of individuals and organisations felt moved and encouraged to 'de-invisibilise' women. Latin America was no exception in this regard, with the years following the launch of the UN Decade in Mexico City being marked by an unprecedented number of feminist conferences, encounters, campaigns and writings on the part of academics, activists, planners and policy-makers (see Nash, 1986).

Themes and approaches in gender research in Latin America

Early research on gender in Latin America, as in other parts of the world, was predominantly conducted on, by and for women. This is hardly surprising given the feminist groundswell of the 1970s, and the predominance of the 'Women in Development' (WID) paradigm in academic and policy circles. In some respects, WID concern with 'integrating' women into development policy and practice also skewed thematic emphasis towards 'tangible', 'material' and/or 'measurable' aspects of women's lives, such as their economic well-being, their position in the labour market, their fertility and health status, and their representation in politics and public life. Another reason for a focus on the practical aspects of women's lives, especially among low-income groups, was the legacy of theories of Dependency and Internal Colonialism which had emphasised the importance of class in Latin American inequalities (see Scott, 1994). Yet as noted by Melhuus and Stølen (1996:11 *et seq.*), other more culturalist veins of analysis ran concurrently in work on gender in Latin America, and have steadily assumed a more important place in the literature (for examples see Balderston and Guy [eds], 1997; Coates, 2001; Harvey and Gow [eds], 1994). While many of the material concerns around gender which characterised research in the 1970s continue to preoccupy researchers and activists today – gender segmentation in employment, gender inequalities in access to resources and basic services, and gender disparities in political participation, for example – the contemporary scene is one in which far more explicit acknowledgement is made of gender imagery, symbolism and representations (Melhuus and Stølen, 1996:14). Lest it might be imagined that there have been distinct 'camps' in gender scholarship on Latin America, it should be emphasised that much of the early work on women's 'productive roles' recognised that gender inequalities could not be explained by materialist analyses alone (see for example, Nash, 1986; Nash and Safa [eds], 1980; Scott, 1986c). Indeed, this is one important reason why 'the family', representing a complex confluence of both material and non-material aspects of gender, has long been such a prominent element in gender analysis in Latin America. Although treatment of 'the Latin American family' in Eurocentric overviews of world family patterns, and in economistic policy analyses, has often been characterised as stereotyped, monolithic and gender blind, in feminist writings on Latin America families have seldom been dealt with in ways other than which reflect them as non-uniform, dynamic and as encompassing highly variegated gender relations (Chant, 1991; Cicerchia, 1997; Dore, 1997; González de la Rocha, 1986; Kuznesof, 1989; Jelin [ed], 1991).

Representing gender in Latin America

Accepting that in the early literature on Latin America seeds had already been sown about the multi-dimensionality of gender, and the need for holistic theoretical approaches, the pluri-vocal nature of gender research on the region has arguably been more overlooked. At first glance it might appear that gender research on Latin America was primarily the domain of 'outsiders'. Just over fifteen years ago, for example, exiled Argentinian academic and activist Marta Zabaleta wrote about the irony embedded in Latin American women reading about themselves through the writings of North American academics, and in a language (English) other than their own. This, she charged, placed them in the 'strange position of making their own acquaintance though the medium of an internationally projected, internationally recognised image of themselves which they played little part in constructing' (Zabaleta, 1986:97). While we do not deny the veracity of this statement, nor the fact that in the early days authors and editors of 'mainstream' (English) texts on gender in Latin America were overwhelmingly European and North American women, *inside* these volumes Latin Americans featured extensively in citations and bibliographies, not to mention as contributors of chapters (for examples see Harris [ed], 1982; Nash and Safa [eds] 1980, 1986).[3] This, in turn, foregrounded an unprecedented rise from the mid-1980s onwards of Latin American authored and/or co-authored publications on gender available to readers outside the continent (for example, Benería and Roldan, 1987; Bose and Acosta-Belén, [eds], 1995; González de la Rocha, 1986; Jelin [ed], 1990, 1991; Nash and Fernández-Kelly [eds], 1983; Ruiz and Tiano [eds], 1987). Although Latin Americans have progressively claimed more visible leadership in what is written about their region, what has possibly changed to an even greater degree is not *who* is writing about Latin America, but who is getting *published in English* about gender in Latin America. On one hand, the rise in Latin American-authored 'international' texts can be interpreted as a positive sign of receptivity towards other voices in a heavily Northern-dominated academic 'mainstream'. As Molyneux (2001:9) notes 'the countries seen as occupying the "periphery" have moved from the margins to occupy at least an honorific place within contemporary social science'. Yet questions clearly remain about why Latin Americans have to be translated into English to 'count' in any substantial way, and why so many Northern Latin Americanists fail to devote time to writing in the language of the region they study. These issues await more satisfactory resolution in the twenty-first century if terms such as 'globalisation' and 'international feminism' are to have the same resonance in reality as in rhetoric.

From women to gender

Having noted that revisiting early work on gender in Latin America reveals more in the way of continuity than change in both themes and authorship, there has undoubtedly been a progressive shift from a focus on *women* to *gender* over time. This is partly a result of wider developments in feminist theorising, and, within the policy sphere, a move (in principle at least) from a WID to a GAD (Gender and Development) approach (see Chant and Gutmann, 2000; Pearson, 2000a). The transition from women to gender embodies two important analytical developments that pertain not only to Latin America but to other regions. The first of these might be summed up as a shift from 'woman' to 'women', insofar as the growing currency of gender as a dynamic social construct demanded greater interrogation of women's differentiation on account of class, age, 'race' and so on. Even if on the surface the roles that women performed in different cultures happened to 'look' similar, the nature and meanings of these roles needed to be scrutinised in context, and not from a single (and more particularly Euro-American) vantage point. The second main aspect of the shift from women to gender has been the greater attention given to the practical as well as theoretical dimensions of gender as a relational concept, not only in respect of other social criteria, but also with regard to public and private interactions and negotiations over gender among men and women. Brief sketches are given of these developments in the context of Latin America in the following sections.

DIVERSITY AMONG WOMEN

While the idea that women were not an undifferentiated group existed from the very beginning in work on gender in Latin America, less primacy was given to differences among women in the 1970s than it is now. There are several likely reasons for this: first, that the interest in making women visible in a male-dominated world called for a strength in numbers that was probably best served by binding women under the banner of a unitary gender identity. Women's struggle for equality was construed primarily as one which had to be waged alongside other women against structures of patriarchy. The idea of women's 'interests' as differentiated on grounds of class, 'race', age and so on was potentially diversionary and could undermine solidarity and momentum. Second, information on women (not only in Latin America) was so deficient that this scarcely allowed for general conceptual formulations, let alone ones which catered to difference and to the complex interactions of gender with other identities. Third, the fact that the 'epicentre' of feminist scholarship and development policy-making lay in the North led, at times, to an homogenisation of the experiences of women in regions of the South. In short, while there may have been substantial recognition of diversity among women *within* Latin America, this was less apparent in 'global reviews'. Instead, in the interests of codifying a complex range of emerging data, 'international' analyses sometimes fell back on reactive monolithic stereotypes which tended not only to mask difference, and to 'exoticise' Latin American women's experiences (see Jaquette, 1994:3), but did so through a lens which privileged issues that accorded with preoccupations about gender oppression among Northern feminists. Explanations for 'gender subordination' held to be categorically evidenced by factors such as high fertility and lack of labour force participation, for example, were often reduced to 'culture' and 'tradition', with 'motherhood' commonly signalled as one of the biggest stumbling blocks to women's emancipatory possibilities.

FROM 'SUFFERING MOTHERS' TO 'SUBVERSIVE MOTHERS'? CHANGING DISCOURSES OF MOTHERHOOD

'Motherhood' has always loomed large in images and representations of women in Latin America This is partly a reflection of the importance of motherhood in the realities of women's lives. There is absolutely no question that – in *mestizo* Latin America at least – motherhood has been both privately and publicly venerated, expressed in the form of monuments or in vast and elaborate celebrations of 'Mother's Day' which have tended to persist as a public exaltation of private, and often heavily essentialised, 'female virtues'.

In the context of Euro-American perspectives on feminism in the 1970s, this exaltation of the private sat uneasily with agendas for women's 'liberation' which stressed that only the 'public' really counted, and which in parts of Europe drew on a tradition whereby women had striven to 'individuate themselves from the family in matters of identity and rights' (Molyneux, 2001:169). The latter figured less promininently in feminist thought in Latin America (ibid.), besides which, from the outside, stereotypical projections of motherhood, conceived as entrapped by Catholic *diktat* and thereby linked with high levels of fertility, domesticity and self-sacrifice, were construed as presenting major obstacles to women's progress. It was around this time that *marianismo*, a compensatory complex to that of *machismo* (see later), emerged as one of the pegs on which the ills of Latin American women's sub-ordination were hung.

The first appearance of *marianismo* in the gender literature is normally associated with Evelyn Stevens (1973), who claimed that the seeds of the syndrome lay in Old World cultures, travelled to the New World with the *conquistadores*, and thereafter came to their fullest expression in *mestizo* Latin America. While noting that *marianismo* is not a religious practice, Stevens (1973:91) argued that Marianism (or Mariology), a movement within the Roman Catholic Church which venerated the Virgin Mary, has 'provided a central figure and a convenient set of assumptions around which the practitioners of *marianismo* have erected a secular edifice'. This hybrid complex of idealised femininity offered a series of beliefs about women's spiritual and moral superiority to men that acted to legitimate their subordinate domestic and societal roles. As described by Stevens (1973:94):

> Among the characteristics of this ideal are semidivinity, moral superiority, and spiritual strength. This spiritual strength engenders abnegation, that is an infinite capacity for humility and sacrifice. No self-denial is too great for the Latin American woman, no limit can be divined to her vast store of patience with the

> men of her world. Although she may be sharp with her daughters – and even cruel to her daughters-in-law – she is and must be complaisant toward her own mother and her mother-in-law for they too, are reincarnations of the great mother. She is also submissive to the demands of the men: husbands, sons, fathers, brothers.

Aside from idealising women's virtues of chastity and nurturance (Bunster-Burotto, 1986:299), given the common notion that children were a 'gift from God', women's connection with childbirth gave them a 'unique opportunity to fulfill God's will' (Martin, 1990:478). This, in turn, allowed mothers to 'bridge the natural and supernatural worlds, as well as the sacred and the profane' (ibid.). While these ascriptive entitlements may well have helped women see themselves through moments of particular difficulty in their lives, the emphasis on women's roles within the family, and on the significance of their 'personally fulfilling sphere of spiritual authority and action in the home' sealed off their access to public power, even within the Church (Drogus, 1997:57; see also Cubitt, 1995:111).

That *marianismo* never received the same attention as *machismo* in the bulk of empirically grounded studies of gender in Latin America is undoubtedly because the term was not in common parlance. Another reason, pointed out by Melhuus and Stølen (1996:12) is that: 'Placing the burden of their situation on women themselves was not politically correct at the time!' (exclamation in original). By the same token, Melhuus and Stølen note that Stevens set another agenda in 'focusing on the role of the individual in the shaping of their own life situation, and emphasising aspects of ambiguity and complexity in gender relations'. Stevens is also accredited by the same authors as having raised important, if 'awkward', questions about the part played by women themselves in maintaining oppressive gender relations (ibid.).

These latter issues continue to have resonance three decades on. None the less, it is vital to point out that while discussions continued, mainly in Euro-American quarters, over the 'obstacle' of motherhood both at home and abroad, an alternative discourse was in the making, and one in which some elements of *marianismo* were discernible. This alternative discourse took the standpoint that motherhood was a source of power, and more particularly a basis for political participation, identity, resistance and/or transformation.

Various strands can be pulled out of the literature on 'maternalist/motherist politics' in Latin America (see Craske, 1999, 2000b; Jaquette [ed] 1994; Molyneux, 2001; Stephen,1997), but one is the idea that it is precisely women's private virtues as mothers (including their purportedly inherent moral superiority and concern for others) which has provided them with a route into political life. In the context of her study in Morelos, Mexico, for example, Martin (1990:478), argues that women gained 'considerable symbolic power because of their association with the redemptive power of childbirth', and that their altruistic maternalism garnered them a place in local politics. The basic tenets of this argument resonate more widely across the region and are perhaps most dramatically epitomised in the figure of Eva Perón in Argentina, who identified herself as 'the loyal wife of the great leader and mother of the "great Peronist nation"' (Molyneux, 2001:170). Eva Perón had wide appeal to a broad cross-section of women, many of them working class, whom she exhorted to 'support their men (who were supporting Perón), by minding hearth and home' (ibid.). Although Eva Perón also supported the enfranchisement of women (in 1947), and encouraged the mobilisation of women, this was very much within the confines of the traditional gender order (see Bianchi, 1993). As summed up by Molyneux (2000:58):

> Eva's discourse invoked older arguments about women's special feminine attributes in an effort to direct them into the service of the state. She spoke of the need to moralise political life through women's participation – referring to her own role in politics as the heart, whereas Perón, in a predictable binary, was the head.[4]

Another perspective on motherhood is that it has given Latin American women a space to act *against* the state and/or in subversive ways (see for example, Alvarez, 1990; Chuchryk, 1989; Puar, 1996; Rivera Fuentes, 1996a; Schirmer, 1993). While the role of maternalism has been noted in relation to various types of movement, such as urban protests against increased costs of living, it has perhaps been most applicable to political and human rights mobilisations in repressive Latin American dictatorships. One of the most famous examples is that of the Mothers of the Plaza de Mayo in Argentina, which started off as a small group in 1977 and grew to gain international recognition within and beyond the region for its role in both the fight for democracy and for human rights (Fisher, 1993:104). The *Madres* (Mothers) were women whose children had 'disappeared' under the military regime, and who not only wanted to know what had happened to their children, but to have them returned alive. In a context in which Christian family values were not only exalted but lent moral legitimacy to those in power (Fisher, 1993:109), motherhood gave women a more 'legitimate' reason to mobilise insofar as this was not overtly 'political' (Craske, 2000b:2 & 5). As noted further by Molyneux (2000:62): 'The status of motherhood conferred a degree of protection from annihilation'. Indeed, one of the reasons why women mobilised was precisely because it was deemed too dangerous for their male relatives to do so (Fisher, 1993:109). As summed up by Feijoó with Nari (1994:113):

> Because of the cultural and ideological conceptions of motherhood, which is the basis of Argentine feminine identity, motherhood might be expected to offer more security as a basis for political action than alternative roles. Although subsequent events proved that the notion that women as mothers would be safe from repression was only a myth, the legitimacy of the maternal appeal at least allowed a symbolic refuge.

Even if it has been argued that the strategic political use of maternalism was not an explicit rationalisation for the *Madres'* actions but rather 'reconstructed after the fact' (Feijoó with Nari, 1994:113), as suggested above, some mothers did not escape the excesses of military rule. In Guatemala, violence and rape were systematically used against the wives and mothers of 'subversives' in the 1970s and 1980s (see Tuyuc, 1994). In the countries of the Southern Cone, women were frequently arrested on account of the 'transgressions' of their menfolk, and sometimes made to face their torturers in 'chapels' installed in the detention camps, where they were beaten in front of the self-same symbols of idealised motherhood, such as icons of the Virgin Mary (see Bunster-Burotto, 1986:299; also Hollander, 1996; Jelin, 1997:78; Molyneux, 2000:62). Subjected to the horrors of gang rape, bestiality, and threatened violations of daughters, Bunster-Burotto (1986:307) asserts that one of the essential ideas behind the sexual slavery of women in torture was 'to teach her that she must retreat into the home and fulfill the traditional role of wife and mother'. Even in situations where the lives and fundamental human dignity of women and their families have not been at stake, Chaney (1979), amongst others, has argued that motherhood places an ultimately constraining set of boundaries around women's political participation. Straying too far from concerns that are deemed to belong within a particular patriarchal construction of motherhood jeopardises women's claims on the political arena, and, in turn, the prospects for securing gains for women as *women* (as opposed to mothers).[5] As echoed by Feijoó with Nari (1994) with reference to the Mothers of the Plaza de Mayo, while the task of defending life was 'forced out of the private sphere of the household and into the autonomous space of public and political expression' (ibid.:113), in analytical terms, this approach to the defence of human rights reinforced the gender division of labour, and through the links to 'feminine emotionality' constituted a 'paradoxical vicious circle' (ibid.:121). This said, using motherist politics as a way of introducing *women* to ideas of *women's* rights remains important (Craske, 2000b: 17). Indeed, in various contexts, such as in El Salvador and Guatemala, 'motherism' has been a crucial entry point for women to protest about the disappearance and massacre of their relatives. Thereafter, through their cumulative political experiences and actions, women have moved beyond this paradigm to challenge not only traditional constructions of 'femininity', but mothering itself (Schirmer, 1993:31; also Ibarra, 1993 on Mexico).

While debates about motherhood, power and politics continue, it is important to point out that these have contributed to a more general tendency over time for most people to be more circumspect about how different aspects and constructions of motherhood 'aid' or 'abet' women's struggles for gender equality in Latin America. This, in turn, has also been a product of the changing context and content of motherhood among many groups in Latin America in the last thirty years. Despite the assertion that 'Motherhood has always had a public identity in Latin America, at least for many women engaged in it' (Stephen, 1997:274; see also Cubitt and Greenslade, 1997), it is also true that women nowadays much more visibly straddle the arbitrary divide between the public and private domain. For example, women in all sectors of Latin American society currently engage in greater shares of 'productive' (i.e. paid or income-generating) work than in the past (see García and de Oliveira, 1997; Lagarde, 1994:26; McClenaghan, 1997; Moser, 1997). They are increasingly raising their children without men, and their daughters are (generally) spending longer in education and delaying marriage and/or childbirth (see Chant, 1997a; Datta and McIlwaine, 2000; González de la Rocha, 1999a,b; Willis, 2000). Women are also much more visible in different strands of political and institutional life (see Craske, 1999; Craske and Molyneux [eds], 2002; Jaquette [ed], 1994; Jelin, 1990b,1997). Although these issues and their ramifications are explored in a number of the chapters in the book, we feel it is important to underline here that however much a more considered and cautious reflection on motherhood and its diversity is to be welcomed, we should not forget the concern that is felt within as well as beyond the region about the oppressive social relations in which motherhood is situated. As the Mexican feminist anthropologist Marcela Lagarde (1994) has argued, motherhood is heavily conditioned by men and patriarchal states, so that disrupting the link between women and motherhood (which is often so strong that even women without children are affected by it), is crucially important in the gender struggle. In Largarde's view, one of the most pressing contemporary challenges is to 'dematernalise women, and to maternalise society' (ibid.:34, my translation).

MEN AND MASCULINITIES

The shift from women to gender has not only embodied greater interrogation of and theorisation about diversity among women, but is also associated with an emerging body of work on masculinities in Latin America, based on work *with* men, and frequently *by* men.

One of the major problems with analysing men *through* women writers and informants was that it arguably produced representations of men that were stereotypical, under-problematised, narrow and unhelpful (Gutmann, 1996; Scott, 1994: 94). The common dismissal of poor urban men as 'violent and drunken' (Lehmann, 1994:6), for example, is asserted to have led to a certain pathologisation of Latin American men, and to tendencies for analyses of household dynamics to be 'sidetracked into a denunciation of the consequences of male misbehaviour' (ibid.).

As in other parts of the world, research on men and masculinities in Latin America has gathered considerable momentum over the last ten years, highlighting how men are no more a unitary category than their female counterparts (see Gomáriz, 1997; Gutmann, 1996; Lancaster, 1992). One major outcome of research grounded in detailed fieldwork at the grassroots has been the dismantling of stereotypical images of men as 'irresponsible husbands' and 'distant fathers'. Although it remains true that in many parts of Latin America fathers are not expected to spend much time with children (nor do they), that the link between mothers and children is privileged socially, symbolically and emotionally, and that men are responsible for high levels of abuse towards children as well as wives (see Chant, 1997a; Engle, 1995; Ennew, 1986; Lomnitz, 1977; Martin, 1990; McIlwaine, 2001), it is also increasingly argued that for many men, children are a critically important part of their lives and identities (see Engle, 1997; Engle and Breaux, 1994; UNICEF, 1997). Gutmann (1996), for example, is one of many whose close scrutiny of men in a low-income community in Mexico City reveals that in contrast to the image of the 'typical Mexican man' as a 'hard-drinking philandering *macho*' (ibid.:2), men hold their children, play with their children, have a particularly important role in raising sons, and view fatherhood as a lifetime commitment. Although there continue to be both normative and substantive differences in parenting responsibilities between men and women, Gutmann (1996:88) argues that undifferentiated and essentialising concepts of motherhood and fatherhood are unfounded and misleading:

> We should revise our beliefs that all men in Mexico today and historically have little to do with children. Instead, more active and less active parenting by men seems to correspond more to other factors such as class, historical period, region, and generation. For numerous, though not all, men and women in Colonia Santo Domingo, Mexico City, in the 1990s, active, consistent and long-term parenting is a central ingredient in what it means to be a man, and in what men do.

Work on men has also helped to break down reactive monolithic stereotypes which have either associated men with power, and women with powerlessness or at least with less visible, 'public' powers as men. It has also served to help illustrate how gender relations are actually negotiated at the micro-scale (see Gutmann, 1996; Pineda, 2000; Sternberg, 2001). Another of the more salient contributions of work on masculinities has been more dedicated interrogation of the cultural complex of *machismo*.

MACHISMO

Melhuus and Stølen (1996:14) argue in their introduction to *Machos, Mistresses and Madonnas* that: 'If there is one term which is unambiguously associated with Latin America, it is the term *macho*, and its derivatives *machismo* and *machista*'.

Referring in broad terms to a 'cult of exaggerated masculinity', characterisations of *machismo* have overwhelmingly concurred that among its central tenets lies the assertion of power and control over women, and over other men (see for example, Cubitt, 1995:111; Pescatello, 1976; Sternberg, 2001). Another important strand is that of virility, with Nencel (1996:57) asserting that 'In Latin America, the symbolic representation of masculinity and male sexuality merge in the concept of *machismo*' (see also Stevens, 1965). At the same time, the roots of the complex remain the subject of debate. Mirandé (1997) points to the existence of three main views, one being that it developed out of the humiliation suffered by indigenous men not only at their own defeat, but at the rape of their women by the Spanish conquerors:

> Native men developed an overly masculine and aggressive response in order to compensate for deeply felt feelings of powerlessness and weakness. *Machismo*, then, is nothing more than a futile attempt to mask a profound sense of impotence, powerlessness and ineptitude, an expression of weakness and a sense of inferiority (Mirandé , 1997:36; see also Stavans, 1998).

A variant interpretation is that *machismo* was introduced into the New World by the Spanish whose culture was deeply patriarchal, predicated on the primacy of male 'honour', on the inherent inferiority of women, and on the need for strict sexual control and domination of wives, concubines and daughters (Mirandé, 1997:45; also Pescatello, 1976). These beliefs became exaggerated as the *conquistadores* engaged in brutalising sexual exchange with indigenous women whose 'race' conferred upon them an even lower status than their Iberian counterparts. This laid the groundwork for an extreme form of male supremacy reinforced by a patrilineal kinship system, and an ideology of female domesticity, chastity, fidelity and subservience set down by Church and State (Elmendorf, 1977; Scott, 1986b, 1990).

A third, and less popularised view is that *machismo* was a pre-Columbian, and specifically Aztec trait (Mirandé, 1997:49). Like the Spanish, the Aztecs were a warring, military society in which men dominated women, so it is not entirely inconceivable that this legacy passed into the conquest period and beyond. Indeed, while *machismo* is widely argued to derive from the Spanish term, '*macho*' for male, it is also mooted that it may have come from the classical Nahuatl language whereby '*macho*' meant 'image' or 'reflection of myself' (Mirandé, 1997:142). Although at some level *machismo* must be regarded as an Old and New World hybrid, the pertinence of this last interpretation is tempered by the fact that the Aztecs were only one of a number of indigenous groups conquered by the Spanish, and as Cubitt (1995:111) notes, studies of twentieth-century indigenous communities indicate less evidence of *machismo* than *mestizo* society (see also Buenventura Posso and Brown, 1997; Ennew; 1986; Scott, 1986b; Stevens, 1973; Wolf, 1959).

Machismo has long been recognised as encompassing the notion of competition between men (see Cubitt, 1995:111), but it is probably true to say that in early work on gender in Latin America, more emphasis was given to its implications for women. For example, writers in the 1970s and 1980s drew attention to the fact that *machismo*'s emphasis on male primacy, belief in men's rights to control women, and a strong emphasis on male strength and sexual prowess contributed to a polarisation of gender roles and provided cultural legitimation for the abuse of women (see Arizpe, 1982; Bromley, 1982; Stevens, 1973). The negative outcomes of *machismo* such as violence, financial irresponsibility and sexual infidelity were also seen to be intensified in situations of poverty, thereby leading to the construction of a class-contingent gendered male subject (see Chant, 1985; Harris, 1982; Moser, 1989).

While *machismo* has often become embroidered and reified as it has moved into increasingly global usage (Cornwall and Lindisfarne, 1994:12 *et seq.*),[6] it is important to remember that stereotypes usually have some grounding in practice (Scott, 1986a:22–3). Indeed, to deny the existence of a cult of 'exaggerated masculinity' in Latin America would be inappropriate, when there is so much evidence of male domination and/or mistreatment of women, and where women and men in every-day life refer to *machismo* as denoting particular modes of male behaviour, some of which are construed as positive as well as negative. Indeed, accepting that masculinity is something that men are not born with, but must constantly earn, there are numerous spaces in Latin America in which men are expected to cultivate and/or reaffirm *machista* modes of 'manliness'. In Costa Rica, for example, these range from permanent spaces such as the *cantina* (male-only bar or saloon), where men drink and socialise with other men away from 'domesticating influences' of women and children, to more temporary, but ritual, spaces such as the bull-ring, which, during the *fiestas* held annually in the villages of Guanacaste, becomes an arena in which men publicly display their nerve, wit, stamina and skill in the spectacles of bull-baiting and bull-riding. This second example highlights the significance of *machismo* as a performance which is as much, if not more, validated by the approval of other men, and which has tended to receive more attention as work on men has expanded. As asserted by Roger Lancaster, one of the foremost writers on men and masculinities in Latin America:

> *Machismo* ... is not exclusively or even primarily a means of structuring power relations between men and women. It is a means of structuring power between and among *men*. Like drinking, gambling, risk-taking, asserting one's opinion, and fighting, the conquest of women is a feat performed with two audiences in mind: first, other men, to whom one must constantly prove one's masculinity and virility; and second, oneself to whom one must also show all the signs of masculinity. *Machismo*, then, is a matter of constantly asserting one's masculinity by way of practices that show the self to be 'active' not 'passive' (as defined by a given milieu) (Lancaster,1992:235) [emphasis in original].

Recent work on men, masculinity and *machismo* in Latin America has drawn attention to the fact that women's socialised expectations (and in some cases aspirations) that their men should 'act like men' plays a part in fuelling the complex. Moreover, women themselves can be labelled as *machista* where they foment aggressive behaviour among their spouses and sons, and/or where their own behaviour is 'manly' (see Chant, 2000; also Lancaster, 1992). Another contribution of recent work has been to highlight the oppression imposed by *machista* norms on men who fail to measure up to ideals of manhood such as courage, the ability to provide financially, and/or be virile and sexually dominant (see Kaztman, 1992; Escobar Latapí, 1998; Jiménez, 1996). Additional emphasis on *machismo's* implications for men has also come through work on sexuality where discussions have drawn attention to the fact that it is not so much that a rejection of homosexuality is integral to *machismo* (see Sternberg, 2001:61), but that homosexuality itself is defined by the notions of power embedded in the *machismo* complex. As long as one is 'dominant' in sexual relations (read crudely as taking the penetrator's role), then one can still fend off the label of homosexual (which equates to weak or 'unmanly'), regardless of whether the object of the sexual encounter is male or female (see also Cornwall, 1994:119). While various of these issues are taken up in subsequent chapters, the point in need of emphasis here is that the move from 'women to gender' has brought in its wake a much broader, as well as more nuanced, set of perspectives to the study of gender identities and gender relations. Even if, at an empirical level, men continue to be responsible for a very large share of the problems faced by women, analytically, work on men has given us greater insight into how these problems arise and what might be done to destabilise some of the structures which underpin them. While there is clearly much more to be done, with three decades of feminist scholarship behind us we are in a better position to interrogate and appreciate gender in Latin America at the start of the twenty-first century than was the case in 1970.

Organisation of the book

In terms of the organisation of the volume, the bulk of the chapters deal with specific themes, and each commences with an introduction to core issues, debates and theoretical work in the relevant field. Chapter 2 deals with gender, politics and legislation, detailing the place of women and men under different political regimes in Latin America across space and through time. In particular it points to arguments mounted in support of gender inclusiveness as a *sine qua non* of 'democratisation'. It also discusses the question of gender in legal structures, and the issues which have restrained women's encroachment into the upper echelons of formal politics.

Some of these themes, particularly around politics, are taken further in Chapter 3, which examines gender, poverty and social movements. Core issues within this review are the gender-differentiated effects of recession and structural adjustment, and the ways in which strategies of mobilisation on the part of women at the grassroots have interacted with political, social and economic changes brought about by neoliberal reform in Latin America from the 1980s onwards.

Chapter 4 deals with gender in relation to population, drawing particular attention to two main trends: one, the decline in birth rates since the 1970s, and two, the increase in demographic ageing. In respect of declining fertility, the chapter considers the role of family planning programmes, and how, as is the case at the global level, these have predominantly targeted women. This, in turn, is a major factor in explaining men's traditionally limited participation in fertility management, even if there are some signs of change both at grassroots and policy levels. There are also important gender dimensions to demographic ageing. Not only does women's longer life expectancy mean that women outnumber men among the elderly, but experiences of old age often differ according to gender. In turn, caring for the elderly is an overwhelmingly female, rather than male domain.

Maternal health is obviously a critical issue within health more generally, which is the subject of Chapter 5. This reviews gender differences in physical and mental health, in access to medical attention, and in the provision of preventative health care at the grassroots. Among the most pressing contemporary health problems with significant gender dimensions in Latin America are violence and HIV/AIDS. For both positive and negative reasons, the emergence of the latter has drawn significant political, policy and academic attention to sexuality in general, and to homosexuality in particular. This forms part of the discussion in Chapter 6, which examines the close interactions between constructions of sexuality and constructions of gender, draws attention to the historical influences bearing upon the evolution of sexualised and racialised hierarchies, and notes many of the continuities in heteronormativity in the region to the present day.

Chapter 7 reviews contemporary diversity in household organisation in Latin America and also discusses the decline in patriarchal household arrangements over time. It considers the processes behind these trends, and the implications for gender. It also examines how state organisations and civil society groups have reacted to increasing household plurality.

Changing patterns of work are critically important in understanding household trends, and Chapter 8 provides a detailed review of the evolution of Latin American labour markets over the last few decades, particularly in urban areas. Attention is paid to the factors accounting for steadily rising female labour force participation, and to how men's employment has fared during neoliberal economic restructuring. This chapter also examines current and prospective gender divisions in employment, and their wider social and economic corollaries.

Labour is a critically important motive for migration in Latin America, whether internal or overseas, as discussed in Chapter 9, which reviews the gender dimensions and implications of the movement of men and women in different types of migration stream. The gender dimensions of migrant links with source areas also comes under focus here.

The final chapter offers a brief overall commentary on recent changes in gender in Latin America, and identifies key areas for future research and policy.

2 Gender, Politics and Legislation

NIKKI CRASKE

Introduction

This chapter deals with the formal political sphere of laws and procedures, which both reflects and shapes gender relations. Historically, legislation restricted women's behaviour relative to men's, but it also offered women special protection in some areas. In Latin America, as elsewhere, these gender distinctions in law have been eroded over time, but they have not yet disappeared. Some aspects of contemporary legislation and policy remain grounded in differentiated gender roles, which they can also reinforce. Although social relations can be slow to change, there have been important developments during the course of the twentieth century in response to women's changing roles in public life through work, changing population and migration patterns, social campaigning, feminism and the shifting international environment. Yet, despite these important advances in the 'engendering' of politics and citizenship in Latin America,[1] the region faces further challenges in the search for gender equity, which itself is an integral part of the continuing democratisation process.

The analysis begins with a brief introduction to key conceptual issues in the literature on gender and politics in Latin America. This is followed by discussions of the political context of Latin America and the region's constitutions and civil codes, where much gendered legislation is encoded. We then go on to assess how women have struggled to gain, and subsequently to engender, citizenship in order to make it more responsive to their own needs, interests and experiences. Finally, we discuss women's participation in congresses and executives and the degree to which women have promoted gender-sensitive legislation in the region.

Conceptual perspectives on gender and politics in Latin America

Politics has traditionally been a man's world in which women have been marginalised. Engendering politics necessitates a reformulation of practices to enable and encourage more women to participate. Along with affirmative action such as gender quotas (see below), this includes placing issues of greater interest to women at the centre of political debates and encouraging greater recognition of the gender-differentiated impact of policy in all areas. This struggle for change has accelerated during the last hundred years. As Phillips (1998: 1) argues, however: 'Feminism is politics. Yet, judging from its impact on either theory or practice, feminism has been less successful in challenging "malestream" politics than in the near-revolution it has achieved elsewhere.' In the context of the Latin American 'malestream', three debates around engendering politics have been particularly pertinent: first the relationship between engendering politics and deepening the quality of democracy; second, the tensions surrounding arguments for increased political participation on the grounds of either women's difference from, or their equality with, men; and third, the relationship between women and the state.

Engendering politics and democratisation

Democracies are systems in which sovereignty is, in principle, held 'by the people'. In contemporary systems this sovereignty is exercised through elected representatives. Increasingly, the quality of representation has been called into question and greater emphasis has been placed on the need for elected representatives to reflect the composition of society. Encouraging decision-making arenas to be inclusive and thereby incorporate social diversity is seen as central to improving the quality of democracy; consequently, a political system's democratic credentials are weakened if one half of the population is under-represented in these arenas.[2] As discussed below, the period of rapid political change which occurred in Latin America during the 1980s provided an opportunity for rethinking how politics is 'done'. This involved making the democratisation process more than a question of electoral politics by considering the substantive quality of democracy. The Latin American women's movement has been a highly significant actor in the push for political change at many levels (Craske, 1999; Jaquette [ed], 1994; Miller, 1991; Vargas, 2002; see also Chapter 3). As the post-authoritarian political systems became consolidated, however, parties have re-emerged as the major political protagonists and they remain male-dominated. Women's notable participation in social movements has not been translated successfully into institutional and major decision-making arenas. The gender imbalance in formal politics is testament to the need to deepen the democratisation process.

Within the democratisation struggle, attention has been drawn to questions of identity and the 'authentic' voice of women, where the category of 'women' itself is a contested idea. The degree to which women in power will identify with gender issues where these conflict with identities and/or interests based on class, 'race' and geography is a moot point. As Mexican feminist Marta Lamas has argued, '*cuerpo de mujer no garantiza consciencia de género*' ('a women's body does not guarantee gender consciousness') (cited in Stevenson, 1999:79). Similarly, Peruvian feminist Virginia Vargas has argued that authoritarian women, who supported President Alberto Fujimori (1990–2000), do not represent her any better than authoritarian men.[3] Even with higher numbers of female politicians, arenas of power remain largely white and elitist.

These debates on representation are evident within the women's movement itself. As argued in Chapter 1 there is a perceived greater sensitivity to diversity and the ever-evolving nature of gender constructions. As women's and men's lives change in response to economic and social developments (discussed further in Chapter 3), their needs and interests shift. Despite this recognition of diversity and plurality, there have been tensions among organised women in Latin America about priorities and the terrain of struggles, and over the nature of 'real' feminism. As such, this diversity sometimes makes it difficult to find common ground and can exacerbate tensions among women. Different perspectives and interests, as well as heated debates, were evident in the series of feminist meetings that took place across the region against the backdrop of democratisation during the 1980s and 1990s (see Sternbach *et al.*, 1992). These meetings grew from fairly small affairs, where women who identified themselves as 'feminist' came together to discuss strategies, into massive congresses with parallel sessions and ever-increasing demands to include all women regardless of their identification with a particular understanding of feminism. This growth has presented positive and negative elements (ibid.: see also Craske, 1999:180–5).

In the women's mobilisation that formed part of the democratisation struggle in Latin America, a distinction between 'feminine' and 'feminist' movements could be detected (Alvarez, 1990, 1998; Churchryk, 1994; cf. Molyneux, 1998). These have sometimes appeared to suggest a hierarchy where women's 'real' issues are feminist rather than feminine, but, as Molyneux (1998) argues in relation to practical and strategic gender interests, such distinctions should not be read as fixed either/or dichotomies, but rather serve as tools to help us to understand social complexities. These issues underline the problems of romanticising women's political participation and viewing 'women's interests' in a unitary fashion.[4] Despite these tensions, increasing the number of women in politics raises the likelihood of gender issues becoming more prominent on political agendas (see below). Democracy is aided not just by having more representative decision-making, but also by broadening the political agenda to include issues not previously thought of as 'political' because they were deemed to be part of the 'private' and domestic arena. Challenging such exclusionary aspects of politics itself helps deepen democracy. Furthermore, increasing the numbers of women in politics is likely to have an impact on the style and practice of politics, particularly the adversarial style, the long working hours and 'old boy networks'. Women's encroachment on a variety of political terrains has increased the awareness that such practices do require change, even if there is little evidence to date that the process has begun, either in Latin America or elsewhere. All these issues point to ways in which political institutions have been gendered due to male bias, intentional or otherwise (cf. Elson [ed] 1991 on development). The gendered nature of citizenship is accordingly a result of the masculine assumptions that underpin it, sometimes legally but more often than not in practice.[5]

Equality and difference

In debates over gender and politics, two main arguments have been used to push for the inclusion of women in political life (including their enfranchisement). The first was based on equality: women have the same capacity as men and therefore should have equal rights and responsibilities before the state. The other was predicated on purportedly inherent gender differences.[6] Some feminist theorists have argued that women's difference, particularly in relation to their maternal and nurturing roles, gives them a unique perspective that should be incorporated into political practice and not sidelined as private or intimate (Darcy de Oliveira, 1998; Elshtain, 1998). This claim, unsurprisingly, has proved to be contentious (Dietz, 1998). In Latin America, 'difference' has, on occasions, been interpreted as moral superiority based on women's 'natural instinct' to care for others and place family interests first, indicating a lack of self-interest (particularly when compared with men). As such women's nurturing and caring character renders their political participation a necessity, improving the moral conduct of politics by their participation.[7]

As Miller (1991) argues, the particular valorisation of women's mothering role in Latin America has made sensitivity to difference paramount. Equality feminism has often been perceived as being 'anti-family' and thus 'un-Latin American'. Some have feared that equality feminism is aimed simply at making women conform to masculine models of political participation. Many Latin American women emphasise the complementarity of the sexes to underplay any divisiveness linked to campaigning for women's rights.[8] In reality, equality feminism has been a greater challenge to masculine politics than its stereotype suggests. Although the two approaches of equality and difference seem to be in conflict, in practice they can work together. Molyneux (2001:187) observes that '[t]he central question which feminism from its inception had posed of citizenship was that of whether, and if so how, its universal principles could accommodate difference, but without sacrificing equality.' Lister (1997) suggests that there is a continuum between the polar positions of those who believe in an essential difference between women and men and those who strive for complete, undifferentiated equality. The experience of contemporary Latin America indicates that individual campaigns can engage with arguments of difference and equality simultaneously, as Friedman (2002) demonstrates in her study of the Venezuelan Labour Code. Here women's right to work on equal terms with men was considered compatible with the special provisions required for pregnant women and nursing mothers because women activists promoted the reform as protection for mothers of future generations of workers. Importantly, the protection was justified by recognising simultaneously that not all women workers are mothers and that motherhood is a function for society generally, not just a private issue for the families concerned (ibid.:66). In this way both gender difference and gender equality were recognised. The success of campaigns such as this often relies on strategies of conjunctural, or temporary, alliance building among activists with different perspectives, which entails negotiation and compromise (Alvarez, 1998; Craske, 2000a). In such cases, the language of difference may be strategically useful to generate support, rather than reflecting a belief in essential differences between women and men. Some Latin American feminists who focus their attentions on the state have seen the advantages of difference being employed strategically in the struggle towards greater equality (Craske, 2000a: 21). Thus, while tensions between the two approaches may not be overcome entirely, it is possible to form alliances where both perspectives can be used simultaneously on specific campaigns.

Gender and the state

A key contemporary debate in Latin America among women activists is their relationship with, and the role of, the state (Alvarez, 1997; Molyneux, 2001). Given the repressive history of the state in the region (see below) it is unsurprising that, in the past, distance and autonomy have been dominant strategies, not just for women's organisations but for many other civil society groups. With the 'new democracies', state–civil society relations have changed and this has had a direct impact on women. This is notable in the increase of state initiatives on gender issues, such as establishing women's offices to coordinate gender planning, highlighting gender impacts of poverty alleviation programmes (see Chapter 3) and promoting the use of quotas (see below). At the same time, a significant institutionalisation of the women's movement has also occurred, particularly through NGOs (Alvarez, 1998). These changes have presented new opportunities, but there are many who remain wary of close contact with the state. Autonomous Feminists eschew all contact with the state and are critical of the contractual relationship that many feminist NGOs have cultivated with the state and the conversion of activism into a 'job' (Craske, 2000a; cf. Schild, 1998). Concern is also expressed by feminists who have engaged with the state whether, given the continued problems of authoritarianism and populism in Latin America, states can work to advance gender interests while remaining undemocratic (Vargas, 2002; see also Craske, 2000a:37). For most, interaction with the state is central, especially if their goal is to engender citizenship and legislation, but the challenge remains to avoid cooptation by the state. As such, the issue for many of the region's feminists is not an ideological problem with state intervention *per se*, but the need for a critical approach to engaging with the state given the history of clientelism, corruption and repression. Generally speaking, in Chile, where the state is not perceived to be particularly corrupt and clientelistic, its relations with organised women are well developed. This is much less the case in Peru and Mexico (Craske, 2000a; Vargas, 2002). Whether the state is good or bad for women is not limited to the Latin American women's debate (Pringle and Watson, 1998; Stetson and Mazur [eds], 1995; Staudt [ed], 1997), but, given the particular history of the region's politics (see below), it has special weight.

Latin American political contexts and gender

Latin America experienced great political upheaval and a range of state forms during the twentieth century, including revolutionary states, dictatorships, corporatism, populism and multi-party systems. Even in those countries where enduring party systems were established, this was often preceded by high levels of political violence. Yet over the last thirty years the region generally has undergone a process of democratisation and political liberalisation. By the late 1980s most countries had become liberal democracies, albeit minimalist states that aim to reduce government responsibilities. Cuba remains the notable exception and both Peru and Venezuela experienced a resurgence of populism in the 1990s.[9] The shift to liberal democracies has had an impact on the development of political identities with a move from collective, corporate identities (e.g. 'worker', 'peasant') to a greater focus on the rights and responsibilities of the individual. These different state forms have presented different opportunities for the construction of gender identities. State-led development, whether corporatist or revolutionary, tended to formalise women and men's participation through specific state-endorsed arenas. This offered women a guaranteed political space less evident in more liberal, multi-party systems (until the rise of women's offices in the 1980s – see below).

Corporatism and populism

Corporatism and populism were common in the region in the mid-twentieth century and were manifestations of the developmental state in which governments played a central role in organising and directing socio-economic development. Their challenge was to combine economic development and political stability. Corporatism and populism were designed in part to incorporate the increasingly organised working classes. Given the corporate identities central to this state form, gender and ethnic identities also tended to be delineated and certain gender relations, particularly paternalism, were reinforced. As such, the designated role for women was primarily to support their male leaders. Eva Perón, the wife of the Argentine president Juan Perón, used such imagery in her speeches, even if in reality she exercised considerable influence and leadership (Deutsch, 1991). Women were specifically mobilised in support of the Peronist project through the *Partido Peronista Femenino* (PPF/ Women's Peronist Party) and, as a consequence, in the 1950s Argentina had one of the highest percentages of female legislators in the world. This 'sectoralisation' of women, however, corralled them into a range of areas deemed 'suitable' for women with the Peronist project mobilising ideas of women's destiny being that of homemaker.[10] This 'organic' view of society where there is a natural order, which is gendered and racialised,[11] is evident in other countries where corporatist structures were present, notably Bolivia, Brazil, Mexico and Peru. It was in Mexico that the corporatist system endured the longest. The corporatist sections, including those for women, were organised largely through the government party, the PRI (*Partido Revolucionario Institucional*, Institutional Revolutionary Party) and from the 1930s succeeded in creating political peace, much needed after almost two decades of political violence. Yet the system also depended on graft and clientelism, and economic downturn in the late 1970s made the model increasingly unviable. This gave way to the slow process of democratisation and after seventy-one years in power the PRI lost the presidency in 2000, by which time the centralised corporatist bodies were greatly weakened.

Although these corporatist systems constrained the scope for women's participation, in a limited fashion women did enjoy officially sanctioned political space and access to decision-making arenas. The key issue for questions of representation, however, is that these systems were 'top-down', where channels of representation, for both women and men, were decided and regulated by the ruling elite. Autonomous political activity was limited and the range of political identities restricted. It also encouraged rather monolithic views of identity as people were represented as either women, or peasants, or workers and so forth, rather than as people with multiple identities. This said, the reformist social agendas that accompanied these corporatist and populist systems arguably provided better standards of living than might have been offered otherwise.

Party systems

While some countries were experiencing these authoritarian systems in the mid-twentieth century, others were developing party systems. Chile and Uruguay developed multi-party electoral systems early on until their demise in the 1970s and it is generally accepted that they re-emerged as the most stable and institutionalised party systems in the region in the 1990s. Venezuela and Colombia succeeded in creating relatively stable elite party systems in the late 1950s. In Colombia's case this was after a brutal civil conflict (*La Violencia*, 1948–53), which resulted in the two major parties (Liberals and Conservatives) agreeing to share power for sixteen years in a pact (the National Front, 1958–74). Although this reduced violence for a few years, during the 1990s violence re-emerged as leftist guerrillas challenged the elite settlement and violence continues to dominate the country (Moser and McIlwaine, 2000). Despite this, one of the more dramatic symbolic gestures in relation to gender came on Women's Day in 2001 when the mayor of Bogotá declared a curfew on men, resulting in the city (including police and fire stations) being peopled exclusively by women.[12] In Venezuela, the modern party system also emerged in 1958 after the dictatorship of Marcos Pérez Jiménez. This party system was also dominated by two parties and was bankrolled by oil revenues. By the 1980s, high levels of corruption brought disenchantment and eventually, after an attempted coup, the election of General Hugo Chávez in 1998. Costa Rica emerged as a 'model' democracy in the aftermath of the 1948 Civil War and has subsequently enjoyed 'honest, competitive elections in the context of a basic respect for human and civil rights' (Yashar, 1995:72).

These party systems were generally elite-dominated and women played a minor role in the formal political arena for much of the twentieth century. In particular, there were few women congressional representatives or executive office holders. Indeed, these party systems generally experienced lower levels of female representation than their corporatist neighbours (Craske, 1999:64, Table 4.2) and it is only with the generalised process of democratisation that women have become more visible (see below). Before 1980, when Latin America as a whole (with the exception of Cuba) began its return to elected governments, only one women in the region had been president: Juan Perón's third wife, Isabel, after he died in office in 1974. Where women did participate they tended to conform to normatively 'feminine' areas (Chaney, 1979). Formal democracy, therefore, does little in itself to guarantee women's representation in decision-making arenas and, as party systems re-emerged in the 1980s and 1990s, women had to struggle hard for their voices to be heard.

Military regimes

Whatever the limitations of corporatism, populism and early party systems, a darker period took hold in many Latin American states during the 1960s and 1970s.

Between 1964 and 1976, seven countries suffered military *coups d'état* (Argentina, Bolivia, Brazil, Chile, Ecuador, Peru and Uruguay), while a further seven endured military-supported dictatorships (Dominican Republic, El Salvador, Guatemala, Honduras, Nicaragua, Panama and Paraguay).[13] The military regimes in Peru and Ecuador were reformist, but others were highly repressive states adhering to the US-sponsored Doctrine of National Security where all notions of the rights of citizens were suspended or ignored.[14] Although not all countries engaged in state terror to the same degree, autonomous civil society was demobilised and repressed. Paradoxically, it was during this period that women became more active politically through grassroots social movements (see Chapter 3).

While women could mobilise 'apolitical' identities of mother and carer, men, given their 'public' identities, were the main targets of repressive tactics. This is not to suggest that women were not victims of state terrorism; but they were victims in smaller numbers than men. The military states had conservative social agendas emphasising their commitment to patriotism and Christianity, which also included a conservative gender agenda. Although women had mobilised against the government of Salvador Allende, the Marxist president of Chile (1970–73), General Augusto Pinochet recognised the importance of female political activism and sought to channel it through state bodies that placed a discursive emphasis on the traditional role of women (Miller, 1991). This rhetoric on gender allowed women some room for manoeuvre in repressive states, whether it was the *Madres de la Plaza de Mayo* (Mothers of the Plaza de Mayo) in Argentina (Fisher, 1993), Relatives of the Detained and Disappeared in Chile (Chuchryk, 1994) or activists in Uruguay (Pirelli, 1994). Yet military understandings of gender roles meant that, initially, they did not place the same importance on women's collective action as they did on men's, tending to ignore it since they did not see it as political or particularly 'threatening' (Bouvard, 1994; Fisher, 1993; Jelin, 1997). It is unsurprising, then, that women chose to use these traditional discourses as a place from which to engage in protest activities. The popular protest organisations began to engage in a discourse of rights where their demands became linked to the struggle for democracy (Foweraker, 1999). It was through these social movements that many women developed both an understanding of their citizenship and an awareness of the gendered nature of that citizenship, which had hitherto left women at the margins in more formal political arenas.

Democratisation

Since the late 1970s a process of democratisation has taken place in Latin America, not just in military-controlled states, but also in civilian regimes such as Mexico, Peru (in the early 2000s) and Venezuela (although this has stalled somewhat since the election of Hugo Chávez in 1998).[15] Widespread female mobilisation, alongside

Table 2.1 Gender and Formal Politics in Latin America

Country	Year of women's suffrage	% female deputies (Date of election)	Date of signing CEDAW	State women's agency	Date established[a]
Argentina	1947	30.7 (2001)	15 July 1985	Consejo Nacional de la Mujer (CNM)	1992 (1987)
Bolivia	1952	11.8 (1997)	8 June 1990	Dirección General de Asuntos de Género (DGAG)	1997 (1972)
Brazil	1932	6.8 (1998)	1 February 1984	Conselho Nacional dos Direitos de la Mulher (CNDM)	1995 (1985)
Chile	1949	12.5 (2001)	7 December 1989	Servicio Nacional de la Mujer (SERNAM)	1991 (1949)
Colombia	1954	12 (2002)	19 January 1982	Consejería Presidencial para la Equidad de la Mujer	1999 (1980)
Costa Rica	1949	31.6 (2002)	4 April 1986	Instituto Nacional de las Mujeres (INAMU)[b]	2000 (1974)
Cuba	1934	27.6 (1998)	16 July 1980	Federación de Mujeres Cubanas (FMC)[c]	1960
Dominican Republic	1942	16.1 (1998)	2 September 1982	Dirección General de Promoción de la Mujer (DGPM)	1982 (1979)
Ecuador	1929	14.6 (1998)	9 November 1981	Consejo Nacional de la Mujer (CONAMU)	1997 (1970)
El Salvador	1950	9.5 (2000)	19 August 1981	Instituto Salvadoreño para el Desarrollo de la Mujer (ISDEMU)	1996 (1989)
Guatemala	1945	8.8 (1999)	12 August 1982	Oficina Nacional de la Mujer (ONAM)	1981
Honduras	1955	5.5 (2001)	3 March 1983	Instituto Nacional de la Mujer	1994 (1991)
Mexico	1953	16 (2000)	23 March 1981	Instituto Nacional de Mujeres (INMUJERES)	2000 (1974)
Nicaragua	1955	20.7 (2001)	27 October 1981	Instituto Nicaragüense de la Mujer (INIM)	1987 (1982)

Panama	1946	9.9 (1999)	29 October 1981	Dirección Nacional de la Mujer (DINAMU)	1998 (1980)
Paraguay	1961	2.5 (1998)	6 April 1987	Secretaría de la Mujer	1992
Peru	1955	17.5 (2001)	13 September 1982	Ministerio de Promoción de la Mujer y del Desarrollo Humano (PROMUDEH)	1996 (1974)
Uruguay	1932	12.1 (1999)	9 October 1981	Instituto Nacional de la Familia y de la Mujer (INFM)	1987 (1975)
Venezuela	1947	9.7 (2000)	2 May 1983	Instituto Nacional de la Mujer	1992 (1989)

Sources: CEPAL <www.eclac.cl/espanol/investigacion/series/mujer/directorio/>; IPU http://www.ipu.org/wmn-e/classif.htm; UN http://www.unhchr.ch/pdf/report.pdf; Valdés and Gomáriz (1995:159).

Notes: a: Date the current state women's organisation was established and date of first state body in parenthesis.
b: The Executive Director, Gloria Valerín, is also Minister for the Condition of Women (Condición de la Mujer) and minister without portfolio.
c: The FMC converted into an NGO before the Beijing Conference in 1995.

developments within the political class and the rise of feminism, had an impact on post-authoritarian settlements. The contemporary Latin American state has done much to ensure that gender is foregrounded in new legislation and state duties. This process has been reinforced by a number of interrelated factors. The 'transition and consolidation' of democracy has included states demonstrating their commitment to modernity, democracy and internationalism. As such, the support for gender-sensitive legislation has to be understood within the context of wishing to emphasise that these countries have broken with the authoritarian past and are indeed modern, democratic members of the 'international community'. The immediate post-authoritarian political reforms included tackling obvious discriminatory laws, such as changing *patria potestad* (which gave men sole rights over children) to *patria potestad compartida* (shared custody) and removing some gender-differentiated elements of divorce laws. Attention to women's rights and equality was reinforced by the growth of United Nations conferences and conventions during the 1980s and 1990s. The first World Conference on Women, held in Mexico in 1975, acted as a catalyst for establishing a number of women's offices. The formulation in 1979 of the Convention on the Elimination of All Forms of Discrimination Against Women (CEDAW) encouraged some countries to consider gender issues, even if most countries labouring under repressive governments were not signatories until elected governments were in power (see Table 2.1). Cuba was the first country in the region to sign (1980), quickly followed by El Salvador, Mexico, Nicaragua, Panama and (more surprisingly, given that it was still under military rule) Uruguay in 1981. Chile was the last country to sign in 1989. International agreements have been an important part of the democratisation process and are discussed in greater detail below. Another important international dimension has been the feminist meetings mentioned above. These have helped consolidate regional civil society networks, which represents one of the important developments in gender campaigning of recent times.

Different political systems and state forms have contributed to the development of gender constructions across Latin America, which, in turn, help shape the political systems. The importance of women's participation in the democracy struggles, together with developments in feminist theorising and new international developments, has resulted in the past two decades being an important period for furthering the engendering of politics at the institutional level, although significant imbalances remain.

Legal structures

Democratic states are subject to the rule of law. Such laws are embodied in penal and civil codes whilst rights are enshrined in constitutions. Latin American countries have written or codified constitutions which lay out a citizen's rights, responsibilities and freedoms within a given territory. Civil codes should be compatible with constitutions and, importantly, are the places where everyday life is legislated in codes on marriage and divorce, domestic violence, family, property rights and maternity rights.

Constitutions

Constitutions incorporate different bodies of citizenship rights: civil, political, economic, social and cultural. They define the relationship between the state and its citizens, thus defining states' responsibilities and the limits of their powers. The basic right of citizenship is the vote, even if some rights for women may have been acquired long before enfranchisement. The recent democratisation process has tended, in principle at least, to mitigate the worst excesses of gender bias. Despite positive changes, however, there are many gendered premises in constitutions which give rise to rights that in reality are practised differentially depending on whether the subject is female or male.

Although most Latin American constitutions declare equal rights, Chile's states that 'Men are born free and equal in rights and dignity' (art. 1). Many constitutions also give a special place to the family, such as that of Bolivia where article 193 declares that 'Matrimony, the family and maternity are under the protection of the state'. These sentiments are repeated almost verbatim in the Cuban (art. 35) and Panamanian (art. 52) constitutions. In Chile, article 1 also declares 'The family is the fundamental nucleus of society....' Similar pronouncements are found in the constitutions of Ecuador (art. 37), Nicaragua (art. 70), Paraguay (art. 49), Uruguay (art. 40) and so forth. Article 19 of the Chilean constitution has particular impact on women since it declares that 'The law protects the life of those about to be born' ('*La ley protege la vida del que está por nacer*'). This makes abortion unconstitutional and not merely illegal (see also Chapter 4).

Whilst these constitutions do not legislate specifically on rights of members within the family, their articles frequently interact with cultural norms about the rights and responsibilities of family members. Given cultural expectations about the roles of wives and mothers, and of 'male breadwinners' (see Chapters 1 and 7), they can appear to legitimise certain gender roles. Furthermore, these constitutional articles not only place great emphasis on the family but also reinforce heterosexuality by stressing matrimony or 'the stable union between a man and a woman' (Ecuadorian Constitution art. 38; see also, Bolivia art. 193; Costa Rica art. 52; Nicaragua art. 72; Panama art. 53; Paraguay art. 52; Peru art. 4; Venezuela art. 77) (see also Chapter 6). It is also worth noting that until recently women have been explicitly linked to the family in some Latin American state agencies for women (something that continues to be the case in Uruguay's *Instituto de la Familia y de la Mujer*/National Institute for the Family and Women: see Table 2.1).

Civil codes

If constitutions generally do not differentiate between the rights of women and men within the family, civil codes often do. Many of Latin America's current civil codes date back to the nineteenth century and reflect the Napoleonic legal system that was introduced across the region after Independence. In these regimes, married women were treated as minors. As Molyneux (2000:43) explains:

> they had virtually no rights in the family: if employed, they were required to hand over their earnings to their husbands and enjoyed no automatic rights to marital property. They were not allowed to testify in court or hold public office, and they enjoyed no authority over or claim to their children under the rulings of *patria potestad.* Women were regarded as lacking in rationality, as too weak and impulsive to be treated as the equals of men. They were therefore regarded as 'outside citizenship' and as such were in need of protection, like children.

Civil codes stipulate whether women are 'legally capable'. Valdés and Gomáriz (1995:141) show that a surprising number of Latin American states do not recognise women's full legal capacity. In a number of countries women can be limited in their choice of paid labour, generally on the grounds of it being prejudicial to their domestic role. For example, article 110 of the Guatemalan civil code addresses responsibilities within marriage, conferring upon the wife the 'special right and obligation' to care for dependent children and the home. Article 113 provides that a married woman may only exercise a profession or maintain employment where this does not prejudice her role as mother and homemaker (see Steiner and Alston, 1996:890).[16] In the case of Venezuela there are gender disparities in relation to commercial transactions where women can only pledge conjugal property with the husband's consent, whereas men can pledge such property without the wife's consent. In Nicaragua, women are required to accept the husbands' domicile on marriage (Valdés and Gomáriz, 1995:143). All these examples demonstrate the legacy of women's lack of legal subjectivity in nineteenth-century civil codes which, despite being anachronistic, continue to govern citizens differently.

The ownership and control of property are also gendered. In the case of Latin America, Deere and León (2001a) observe that women actually lost property rights between the early colonial period and the reforms of the civil codes during the nineteenth century, and only regained them in the late twentieth century. Nevertheless, there are important differences across the region in the rights of women to inherit land or to claim equal shares of conjugal goods. Despite some variations, gender-biased codes on property rights make women particularly vulnerable in the case of divorce and 'very dependent on their husbands' goodwill' (Deere and León: 2001a:55). This vulnerability is exacerbated by women's lack of knowledge of their rights over property they brought into the marriage or property that was acquired by the couple during marriage. Given the traditions of men having complete control over material goods, many do not question what are now illegal practices (ibid.).

There have been attempts by revolutionary governments to legislate gender equality. Cuba did this with its 1975 Family Code, which was based on the East German model. In this Code, women and men were mandated to take on equally domestic tasks of social reproduction and childcare (Deutsch, 1991; Molyneux, 2001: Chapter 4). Although difficult to implement, this at least gave symbolic support to the notion of equality within the home. During the Sandinista period in Nicaragua (1979–90), there were also many attempts to improve women's status, including an attempt to outlaw the use of sexist imagery in advertising. Cultural change and the restructuring of traditional gender relations were more difficult, however, especially given the influence of the church (Chinchilla, 1994; Molyneux, 1985).

Penal law

Divorce law forms part of civil codes and, with the exception of Chile, is now legal across the region (see also Chapter 7). Yet one aspect is legislated in penal law: adultery. In the past, adultery has been understood quite differently for women and men in that the former have been judged much more harshly. Moreover, Venezuelan law continues to show this gender bias; for a woman, adultery is committing sexual intercourse with a man other than her husband, but for men this only applies where he 'has sexual intercourse with a concubine in the marital home or outside it, *if* the fact is notorious' (Valdés and Gomáriz, 1995:148, my emphasis). A major tension in divorce for women is that while, on the one hand, it is deemed crucial for women's autonomy, on the other, women are generally left worse off after divorce, particularly in more conservative social groupings where the status of divorcée is perceived as problematic.[17] It remains difficult in many countries to secure alimony payments and support for children. With little viable legal remedy, women's rights in practice are severely undermined.

Another important aspect of penal law regards sex crimes. In many countries, should the perpetrator of rape, sexual abuse or abduction marry the victim, this mitigates the crime. Similarly, the woman's 'honour' is often taken into account: if a woman is not considered to be chaste or honourable, the act is less likely to be regarded as a crime (see Valdés and Gomáriz, 1995:147–9). The struggle for legal abortion has often been couched in terms of the rights of women to enjoy bodily integrity. We can see from these examples, however, that the issue of bodily integrity and the right to consent are not simply issues of reproductive rights but go much further. It also brings into question the contentious issue of citizenship. Jelin (1996) discusses the tensions between women's control over their bodies and their status as citizens. She highlights that there has long been a wish to control women's bodies and that the ideals of freedom and self-determination are limited by public policies and cultural norms; consequently, women's autonomy and their ability to control their lives remains constrained in practice (ibid.:188; cf. Johnson, 2002:118; Willmott, 2002).

Gender and citizenship

The term 'citizenship' is often used exclusively in relation to the right to vote. In this discussion we assess the development of rights more broadly prior to examining Latin American women's suffrage. We conclude the section by analysing the impact on the international arena of women's political participation in the region and *vice versa*.[18]

The question of rights

In the abstract, citizens enjoy certain rights that are perceived to be legitimate and are granted and defended by the state. In principle, citizens have a voice in the decision-making process, whether directly or, more commonly, indirectly through elections. The notion of who and what is included in citizenship has been contested over centuries and the concept is in a continuous and dynamic process of change as new groups challenge existing formulations. Rights have generally expanded to include more issues and more sectors of society. In the twentieth century, one of those challenges has been to engender citizenship and latterly the issues of 'race' and ethnicity have provided new areas of contestation. The continued development of citizenship does not rely merely on absorbing more categories of people and assuming that they will identify with, or be assimilated into, the white, masculine model. It requires that the content and meaning of citizenship change to be inclusive, plural and sensitive to different experiences. Engendering citizenship, therefore, does not rely on women conforming to the male norm but on ensuring that citizenship becomes more inclusive of women's needs, interests and perspectives. This is a fraught process since those struggling for change have different perspectives on the process and nature of change (see Hola and Portugal [eds] 1997; Phillips [ed] 1998).

Rights are central to citizenship and are organised in different 'bodies'. Human rights are generally understood to be basic and universal and above the nation-state:

for example, the right to life, to be free from torture, to trial, to be free from slavery.[19] Many of these are codified in the 1948 International Declaration of Human Rights and also endorsed by national constitutions. Other bodies of rights – civil rights, political rights, economic rights, social rights and cultural rights – are more dependent on the local political context and therefore vary from nation-state to nation-state. Although the 1948 Declaration incorporates elements of all bodies, the multi-faceted nature of rights was recognised when, in the 1960s, separate UN conventions on civil and political rights (ICCPR/ International Covenant of Civil and Political Rights) and economic, social and political (ICESCR/International Covenant of Economic, Social and Cultural Rights) were drawn up. Foweraker and Landman (1997) argue that the philosophical underpinnings of these two bodies of rights are essentially different in that the first is designed to limit and contain the state, while the second is designed to increase the state's field of action. Also, the state both polices rights (being the guarantor of formal rights) and is subject to them. Despite these tensions, Beetham (1995) argues that socio-economic rights and civil and political rights are indivisible, when considering the quality of democracy.[20] There are assumptions that socio-economic rights follow civil and political rights, reflecting Marshall's (1950) influential analysis of the British experience. In Latin America, Roberts (1995:185–6) argues that this is neither obvious nor desirable. Given the development of the Latin American state in the first half of the twentieth century, the concepts of civil and political rights were not as deeply grounded as socio-economic rights; particularly under populism when social welfare was expanding but the regimes remained politically authoritarian. Despite this, they were only tenuously 'rights' since they were an integral part of a clientelist system that was predicated on an unequal exchange of favours. Accordingly, socio-economic benefits were frequently tied to voting. Contemporary neoliberal states have prioritised civil and political rights over socio-economic ones in an attempt to shrink their responsibilities. The latter, however, are of fundamental importance to women since economies are gendered structures (Gideon, 2002) and the impact of structural adjustment has fallen disproportionately on women (see Chapter 3). Consequently women have a particular interest in maintaining Beetham's notion of indivisibility.[21]

Female suffrage

Most Latin American women achieved suffrage during the middle decades of the twentieth century (see Table 2.1). Arguments for the extension of suffrage to women were often based on the grounds of women's difference: that their unique 'nurturing' qualities would make a positive contribution to politics. At the same time, there were many assumptions regarding women's 'conservative nature' that underpinned the debates men were conducting about women's franchise (see Alvarez, 1990:20). The struggle for the vote led to important collective action that occurred at the national, regional and international levels (Miller, 1991). The supposed conservatism of women was a contributory factor in the enfranchisement of Ecuadorian women in 1929 and the refusal to enfranchise Mexican women in 1917. In revolutionary Mexico, women were feared as anti-revolutionary and overly influenced by the Catholic church; consequently, at the same time as codifying the constitution, a special constituent assembly was convened in 1917 to exclude women from being 'citizens'.[22] The last country to start enfranchising women was Paraguay (1961) and in Ecuador full suffrage was not granted until 1967.[23] Although across Latin America the vote for women was won, it was often a hollow victory, given both the limited democracy at the time and the state repression that subsequently occurred in many countries. Indeed, the attainment of the vote sometimes led to a decline in female activism in the immediate aftermath. This was particularly noticeable in Mexico where the struggle for the vote was a long, drawn-out affair that finally came to a successful conclusion in 1953 (Ramos Escandón, 1996).

It also became clear that gaining the vote did not necessarily change much in practice. Few women became important actors in party hierarchies and political systems were not more sensitive to women's issues as a result of the vote. Although the vote was an intrinsic part of engendering citizenship, the struggle has continued in relation to other rights.[24] In contemporary Latin America activists pay much attention to women's rights in practice; as such, they seek to promote equal opportunities and legal changes, including quotas for congresses and domestic violence laws, to make existing rights more effective. Campaigns for legal change, however, are only part of the struggle. It is important to make these rights and laws known, which has led some feminist advocacy groups to engage with the task of promotion (Macaulay, 2002). But there still needs to be recognition about how women's domestic responsibilities limit their ability to participate as full citizens, and how this is mediated by class and age. Furthermore, women's reproductive labour often makes up for the shortfall in public services (particularly caring for the sick and elderly) and allows states to continue to view socio-economic rights as aspirational (see also Chapters 3, 4 and 5).

Latin American women and international initiatives

Despite continued challenges, there is currently much greater acceptance of the need for the 'advancement of women', which the United Nations has also promoted albeit in a rather institutionalised fashion (see Molyneux and Craske, 2002). The focus on women, which began in 1975 with the First World Conference on Women in Mexico, was followed by three more conferences, Copenhagen (1980), Nairobi

(1985) and Beijing (1995). Although these dealt specifically with women's gender issues, there were other fora in which gender issues were raised within a more general context: the Human Rights Conference (Vienna, 1993), the Population Summit (Cairo, 1994) and the World Social Summit (Copenhagen, 1995). These conferences have often provided spaces in which gender issues, particularly unequal access and discrimination, can be discussed. Beijing was particularly important for reiterating the need for women to be included more fully in countries' political life. It also provided the impetus for states and civil society organisations to concentrate on gender issues. Latin American governments were keen to be seen to be promoting women's rights as evidence of their new role as 'modern' states. The Peruvian president, Alberto Fujimori, went as far as attending in person – the only president to do so. This conference was a great stimulus to NGOs which participated in great numbers, although some Latin American activists complained that all other activities were swept away in the organisation (Alvarez, 1998). The Vienna conference was important for clarifying that women's rights were part of human rights and not subordinate (see Box 2.1). The Population Summit in Cairo brought to the fore the thorny issue of reproductive rights, which included not just contraception and safe motherhood, but also whether women ultimately had the right to 'bodily integrity' and thus legal abortion (see Box 2.2). Veteran Mexican feminist Marta Lamas regards the discourse on reproductive rights as a much more effective tool for the struggle for legalised abortion, since it can be seen as part of a broader package.[25] Nevertheless, access to legal abortion remains severely restricted in most countries and the health repercussions are significant (see Chapter 4). At the regional level, the 1994 Belem do Pará convention on domestic violence helped strengthen the push for legal reform, with many countries introducing new legislation and, in some cases, providing state resources to help women and children subjected to domestic violence.[26] Yet elements of the legislation remain contentious. Some countries legislate on issues of domestic violence, while others prefer the notion of 'intrafamilial' violence. Some feminists reject the latter, arguing that it underplays the gendered aspects of the violence by implying that all members of a family are equally likely to be perpetrators and victims of violence, rather than acknowledging the gender dimensions (the fact that most perpetrators are adult men)[27] (see also Chapters 5 and 7).

International conventions focus attention on the issues in a more than transitory way: countries that become signatories are obliged to produce periodic reports, at least every four years, to demonstrate how they are complying with their commitments.[28] These are often accompanied by alternative reports written by relevant national NGOs who make their own assessment regarding their government's actions. This monitoring process is an important part of the process and helps international agreements to filter through to the grassroots. Transparency and accountability are part of the wider process of democratisation. International mechanisms can therefore offer another opportunity for pressuring for change, but this requires active movements in civil society and sympathetic people within bureaucracies.

BOX 2.1

Vienna Declaration 1993

Art. 18. The human rights of women and the girl-child are inalienable, integral and indivisible part of universal human rights. The full and equal participation of women in political, civil, economic, social and cultural life, at national, regional and international levels, and the eradication of all forms of discrimination on grounds of sex are priority objectives of the international community.

BOX 2.2

1994 Cairo Population Summit: Reproductive Rights

Chapter VII: Reproductive rights embrace certain human rights that are already recognised in national laws, international human rights documents and other relevant UN consensus documents. These rights rest on the recognition of the basic right of all couples and individuals to decide freely and responsibly the number, spacing and timing of their children and to have the information and means to do so, and the right to attain the highest standard of sexual and reproductive health. They also include the right of all to make decisions concerning reproduction free of discrimination, coercion and violence. Full attention should be given to promoting mutually respectful and equitable gender relations and particularly to meeting the educational and service needs of adolescents to enable them to deal in a positive and responsible way with their sexuality.

Chapter VIII: Women's health and safe motherhood. Complications related to pregnancy and childbirth are among the leading causes of mortality for women of reproductive age in many parts of the developing world, resulting in the death of about half a million women each year, 99 per cent of them in developing countries. The age at which women begin or stop childbearing, the interval between each birth, the total number of lifetime pregnancies and the socio-cultural and economic circumstances in which women live all influence maternal morbidity and mortality. Although approximately 90 per cent of the countries of the world have policies that permit abortion under varying legal conditions to save the life of the mother, a significant proportion of the abortions carried out are self-induced or otherwise unsafe, leading to a large fraction of maternal deaths or to permanent injury to the women involved.

Gender and representation

The formal arena of politics has been dominated by men and the struggle to engender decision-making arenas is a priority for many organisations interested in women's rights (see Fig 2.1). Women need to be represented in all areas of government (the executive, the legislature and the judiciary), as well as in state bureaucracies.

Figure 2.1 Promoting women's political participation, Guatemala. Cartoon in pamphlet entitled *Nosotras las mujeres y Nuestros Derechos Políticos* produced by the Associación Mujer Vamos Adelante (AMVA), Guatemala. The caption reads: 'All of us [women] have the right and the responsibility to participate in political activities'. (Reproduced with kind permission from the Junta Directiva de AMVA, Guatemala.)

Electing women: recent developments

In Latin America over the past decade there has been a rapid expansion of quota laws to ensure greater gender equality in legislatures. Some parties, mainly on the left, had made earlier attempts to incorporate their own gender quotas to encourage greater female representation.[29] In 1991, however, Argentina became a pioneer by introducing a quota law into its electoral code which obliged all parties to comply. It states that women should make up at least one-third of candidates and be placed no lower than third on party lists (second if only two candidates are listed – see Box 2.3). Since 1991 the reach of such principles has expanded. Within the country many local electoral bodies, including the City of Buenos Aires council, have incorporated gender quotas. More radically, however, the province of Córdoba has increased its quota to fifty per cent. At a regional level, Latin America has embraced quotas as a mechanism for attacking gender disparities in the legislature. There are now twelve countries which have passed quota laws but the impact depends on the nature of the electoral system. In a systematic study of the laws, Htun and Jones (2002:37–40) demonstrate that placement in a closed list system, particularly where district magnitudes are on the larger side (high numbers of legislators per electoral district), is important in making quotas effective. The impact of quotas has been less significant in open list systems. Argentina, Bolivia, Costa Rica, the Dominican

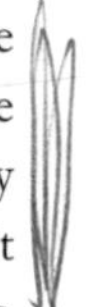

BOX 2.3

The Argentine *Ley de Cupos* (Quota Law) Law 24.012, Promulgated 29 November 1991

Art. 60 The [party] lists which are presented should have women standing as candidates in a minimum of thirty per cent of the electoral positions in proportions where they have the possibility of being elected. Any list which does not comply with these requirements will not be authorised.

Presidential Decree

Art. 2 The thirty per cent stipulated for women's quotas should be understood as a minimum quantity.

Art. 5 In the case where the political party, confederation or transitional alliance renews two posts, at least one of the candidates should be a woman.

Art. 7 Political parties [and] confederations … should change their respective internal norms so that their compliance with the established rules of law 24.024 is made possible before the elections of 1993.

Republic, Mexico, Paraguay and Venezuela use closed lists with Brazil, Ecuador, Panama and Peru using open list systems. Only Argentina and, latterly, Costa Rica say anything about placement of candidates (ibid.:39).

While women do not necessarily act with a gender consciousness when elected as representatives, they do tend to propose whatever 'gender legislation' is passed (Htun and Jones, 2002; Stevenson, 1999:71). Consequently, having more women is important for developing new laws, which will continue the struggle for engendered citizenship. As Htun and Jones (2002) demonstrate, women deputies in Argentina have tended to participate more in committees dealing with 'traditional women's interests'. Similarly they found that 33 per cent of the deputies made legalisation proposals in the area of 'women's rights' but note that 58 per cent of female deputies made no proposals at all in this area. So whilst the majority do little to advance women's rights, the ones who are active are very committed. Consequently the authors conclude, 'by getting more women into Congress, [it helps] to place gender-related issues on the legislative agenda' (ibid.:47).

At present women are still heavily under-represented in the region's legislatures (see Table 2.1). Despite this, three countries, Costa Rica, Cuba and Argentina, rank in the top fifteen countries worldwide in relation to proportions of female legislators, although Cuba has yet to reach the 30 per cent that is the basis for most quotas and is often suggested as the figure needed for 'critical mass' (it has 27.6 per cent). The least-engendered congress in the region is Paraguay's where only 2.5 per cent of representatives are women, ranking the country 112th globally. Brazil has only 6.8 per cent female representation, despite the fact that Brazilian women have been very active in grassroots politics for a number of years. It is clear, then, that although a number of countries in Latin America have played a pioneering role in legislating to encourage greater gender equity in decision-making arenas, they have a long way to go to convert this effectively into practice. Furthermore, the use of quotas is itself controversial. For many women, including significant numbers of feminists, the state remains a problematic entity which has traditionally offered women only a subordinate role, both legally and culturally. Given the history of corruption, authoritarianism and continued problems of clientelism in Latin America, it is unclear that electoral quotas offer the best way forward for women. For some feminists, quota campaigns reintroduced the spectre of corporatism by encouraging the 'sectoralisation' of women.[30] Others remain concerned that it plays on particular views of women's political role where their 'moral superiority' is emphasised.[31] It appears to date that quotas have done little to encourage women from grassroots organisations to become involved in electoral politics, while women from the elite have benefited by gaining access to the decision-making arena. Quotas may be a useful tool but only when used as part of a wider process of effective democratisation which encourages the participation of all women.

Latin American women and the executive

If legislatures suffer from gender imbalance, executives are much more problematic. Despite encouragement from feminist organisations for women to aspire to political leadership (see Fig. 2.2), only three countries have had women presidents: Argentina (Isabel de Perón: 1974–76), Bolivia (Lydia Gueiler Tejada: 1979–80) and Nicaragua (Violeta de Chamorro: 1990–96).[32] Of these three women, only one (Chamorro) was elected and only one (Gueiler Tejada) had previously been an activist. Women have, however, been much more visible within cabinets over the last fifteen years. Although women were originally concentrated in 'appropriate' ministries of education, health and welfare and then later in ministries such as justice, human rights and the environment, they have also made some inroads into 'male' areas such as industry and mines, foreign affairs and finance. In Guatemala, Ana Ordoñez de Molina was appointed Finance Minister in 1994, Liliana Canales Novella was Minister of (amongst other things) International Trade Negotiations for Peru in 1992–94, and, in Venezuela, Eglée Iturbe de Blanco was Finance Minister as early as 1989.[33] Foreign ministries have proved to be particularly difficult to penetrate; Mexico did not appoint a female Foreign Secretary (Rosario Green) until the Zedillo administration (1994–2000) and Chile's first female Minister for Foreign Affairs (Soledad Alvear Valenzuela) was appointed in 2000. Defence ministries have also been difficult to access.[34] It is increasingly the case, however, that it is no longer possible to ignore women in executive positions and their 'right' to be there is much more readily accepted that even ten years ago.

One executive appointment that almost everywhere has been the exclusive preserve of women is that of Minister for Women (or its national equivalent). As noted earlier, all Latin American countries now have state women's agencies and Bolivia even has an office for gender issues (see Table 2.1).[35] Although not all of these positions are ministerial, they often have ministerial status. Their importance lies in guaranteeing a space for gender debates in government, to help provide an impetus to policy formation in relation to gender, and to promote the engendering of legislation emanating from other ministries (remembering, too, that many other state departments have gender programmes and projects). These state bodies are useful tools in the continued struggle for gender equity since they have the resources to present bills to congress that have a high chance of being passed. Blofield and Haas (2001) demonstrate that in Chile gender legislation put forward by SERNAM, the state agency for women, has a higher possibility of becoming law than bills on gender issues presented by members of congress. Being sponsored by a state body gives bills more weight. Although this can offer a strategy for incorporating gender legislation into congress, it also has to fit with government priorities. Furthermore, state machinery for the promotion of women is constrained by its very position as

Figure 2.2 Promoting women's political leadership, Guatemala. Cartoon in pamphlet entitled *Nosotras las mujueres y Nuestros Derechos Políticos* produced by the Associación Mujer Vamos Adelante (AMVA), Guatemala. The captions read: 'A woman can be President of Guatemala' and 'There are already female deputies in the Congress of the Republic'.

(Reproduced with kind permission from the Junta Directiva de AMVA, Guatemala.)

a state body. Staying with the example of Chile, Matear (1996) has highlighted the compromises necessary to have a women's office at all, given that the *Concertación* alliance, in power since the demise of Pinochet, is dominated by the Christian Democrats. They have close ties with the Catholic Church, which has a highly conservative social agenda, and this has stalled any reform of divorce law or discussion on the legalisation of abortion (Blofield and Haas, 2001).

Although women's representation at nation-state level is important, regional and local-level politics are also arenas where women are active. The legal capacity of the regions depends on whether the state is federal (where regions have their own legislatures) and how big these are *vis-à-vis* the federation. Mexico, for example, is a federal state and the government of Mexico City (the Federal District has a population of about 9.5 million) acts as an important counterweight to the power of the president. There are assumptions that local politics are more compatible with women's gender interests. Indeed, in Chile women were granted the vote at the municipal level first on these grounds. Despite this supposed affinity, in percentage terms, women are not highly represented among municipal presidents. Massolo's (1998a:19) work on women's representation in municipal politics in Mexico and Argentina shows that in 1996 only 84 of Mexico's 2,412 mayors were women: this represents less than 3.5 per cent at a time when women deputies at national level represented 14.1 per cent. Although this is lower than the regional norm, few countries have achieved higher than ten per cent. Massolo further comments that the limited pluralism that was part of the country's slow democratisation process did not favour women: in 1996 women mayors governed only three per cent of opposition municipalities but seventy of the PRI's 1,542 town halls (4.5 per cent) (Massolo, 1998b:41), thus the decline of the PRI may disadvantage women. With regard to Latin America as a whole, in the early 1990s women represented less than 15 per cent of mayors with the exception of Uruguay (Valdés and Gomáriz, 1995: 163). Although these figures are low, some women have governed capital cities or municipalities within them; perhaps most notably Rosario Robles (1999–2000), who took over as Head of the Government of the Federal District in Mexico when Cuauhtémoc Cárdenas stepped down. The low levels of women's participation in municipalities presents something of a paradox insofar as women are often highly active in grassroots social movements, as discussed elsewhere in the book (see especially Chapters 3 and 5), but remain marginal to the local institutional arena.

While increased use of quotas means that women are achieving much higher levels of representation at the national level, which is clearly important, it remains necessary to have good representation at the local level because this is where most women gain access to state services and have the potential to enter a useful 'training ground' for national politics. The greater engendering of the political system has to be carried out at all levels of government to be effective. Chilean feminists coined the phrase 'Democracy in the country and in the home' to highlight the indivisibility of the democratisation process. By implication the engendering of rights has to be more than a formal device and has to percolate through a variety of spheres. This linkage between democracy and women's rights remains a central element of women's activism. In Peru, the view of some feminists used to be 'What isn't good for women isn't good for democracy'. In the light of recent experiences, they have now inverted this to 'What isn't good for democracy isn't good for women' (Vargas, 2002:217).

Conclusion

Latin American political systems have gradually become more engendered over time, particularly in the past two decades, as part of the broader process of democratisation across the region. Against this backdrop, the discussion in this chapter has focused on the institutional and formal aspects of politics, indicating that positive developments have occurred in eliminating gender bias in national constitutions and, to a lesser extent, in civil codes. The challenge remains, however, to make these rights engendered in practice. The legacy of sexist civil codes and conservatism in society makes cultural changes difficult to effect. Nevertheless, the existence of state machineries for women has acted as an impetus for rethinking women's role in politics and has often helped promote quotas to encourage greater gender equality in congresses. International factors have also played their part in supporting the process. The increased participation of women in decision-making arenas has facilitated greater gender awareness in the legislative process and made it easier to pass new laws, such as those combating domestic violence. This does not presuppose that all women in political life act with a gender consciousness, but that a critical mass of women means a greater likelihood that gender agendas will develop. Although women have increased their participation in national legislatures substantially over the past few years, they are still heavily under-represented and generally more so at the local level. The women who are engaged in representational politics tend to be members of the elite, with many remaining highly sceptical of institutional political participation. Power and politics are undoubtedly more engendered today in Latin America, but gender equity is still a goal for the future, as explored in the context of economic and social change in the next chapter.

3 Gender, Poverty and Social Movements

NIKKI CRASKE

Introduction

As noted in the previous chapter, Latin American countries have been undergoing major processes of neoliberal economic restructuring since the 1980s.[1] Restructuring has not occurred uniformly across the region and there are notable differences in the speed and depth of reform. Nonetheless, all economies, including that of Cuba, have become more externally oriented. In some countries, particularly the Southern Cone and Mexico, these changes represent a significant break with past state–civil society contracts, where political quiescence has been rewarded with social welfare benefits in the shape of pensions, food subsidies, state provision of health care and other services. These benefits by no means reached the majority of the population (see Mesa-Lago, 1997), but signalled a particular view of the appropriate responsibilities of the state. The radical reforms promoted by the Bretton Woods Institutions (BWI) of the World Bank and the International Monetary Fund (IMF) in the 1980s were often imposed on debtor countries without their full costs being assessed adequately. The impact of the structural adjustment programmes was to deepen the recession and exacerbate the debt crisis. It subsequently became apparent that programmes would have to be introduced to ameliorate the worst excesses and to support the vulnerable in the transition phase. By the 1990s the New Poverty Agenda was being promoted which included the provision of 'safety nets', although to date these appear to have been insufficient in dealing significantly with the problems of poverty currently experienced by millions of people in both rural and urban Latin America.

In this chapter we examine the major elements of neoliberal restructuring, focusing in particular on the impact on poverty and the development of social funds. This is followed by an assessment of their gendered impacts. The 'double crisis' of debt and recession frequently acted as a catalyst for grassroots organising and the emergence of social movements where women have played a notable role. This development will be assessed in the third section of the chapter, which also considers the possibilities for empowerment resulting from such activities. Structural adjustment has had significant repercussions on many aspects of daily life and these have been gendered. To date it appears that women have adapted their lives to respond to these conditions to a greater extent than men. States have also relied on women's ability 'to cope' to help soften some of the impact of economic reform. New opportunities have opened up to women as a result of these changes, but so, too, have burdens increased.

The context and characteristics of post-1980 economic change

Economic change in Latin America since the 1980s can be viewed in a number of stages: first, the debt crisis combined with stagnant growth, which was then exacerbated by the recession brought on by structural adjustment; second, increasing awareness of the rising social costs of adjustment and the growth of poverty; and finally, the rise of social funds or 'safety nets'.

The double crisis of debt and recession

The 1980s have often been termed the 'lost decade' for Latin America as countries suffered from the double crisis of severe debt and adjustment-related recession. The debt crisis, which took hold in the early 1980s, was both a fiscal and a balance of payments problem. Governments were overspending relative to income and domestically produced goods and services were not competitive. Import substitution industrialisation (ISI), which had previously been the dominant economic strategy in the region, had produced high growth rates during the 1960s, but by the 1970s this had begun to stagnate. Growth declined, unemployment and underemployment grew rapidly, prices rose often at hyper-inflation levels, and private banks and international institutions refused to extend or renew loans as governments' ability to pay either service or capital charges declined. These conditions ushered in a period of restructuring. Ramos (1997:16) highlights three reasons why radical measures were introduced: the heavy macro-economic imbalances resulting from external debt crisis, the stagnation of ISI and disquiet in Latin American neoliberal circles about the supposed inefficiency of state interventionism, and concerns about attempts to create a modern welfare state on the basis of a weak economic structure. Although the first two reasons dictated the need for structural reform, it was the latter that determined the shape it was to take.

Restructuring developed in stages. First came austerity measures which were designed to stabilise the economy. When the depth of the recession which these austerity measures generated became apparent, a new phase of restructuring was introduced, with human development placed higher on the agenda. The questioning of the benefits of a growth-led recovery came from neostructuralists and feminist economists. The first stages of restructuring were promoted by supranational institutions, particularly the BWI, and often referred to as the 'Washington Consensus'. Loans that the countries needed to tide them over the crisis were made on condition that structural reforms were put in place, so governments had little choice but to follow the basic tenets of neoliberalism.

NEOLIBERAL ORTHODOXY

Neoliberals believe that growth is the cornerstone of stable economies and thus 'sound economic policies' should be introduced in order to encourage long-term growth. It is only through stable, long-term growth that broader questions of development and equity can be addressed. In essence, growth will 'trickle down' to benefit all. Not all countries in Latin America followed identical economic restructuring policies, but Box 3.1 provides a general outline.[2] The initial impact of these policies was to drive economies into recession as they contracted sharply, with significant reductions in standards of living as a result. Unemployment grew, forcing changes in income generation patterns (see Chapter 8) and the reduction in both state services and subsidies had a serious impact on poor and middle-income families, especially on women, as discussed in detail later. Over time, the results of some of these policies were positive in that they halted the decline in growth. Indeed, by the end of the 1990s most countries in the region had managed to achieve positive growth, albeit at low annual rates of around three per cent. There have also been successes in controlling inflation, with most countries now registering rates of less than 10 per cent (although there are notable exceptions like Ecuador and Venezuela: see Table 3.1). After a sharp rise in unemployment, this, too, has declined and the debt crisis has been brought under control. Yet, although there has been improvement since the height of the debt crisis in the early 1980s, it is still the case that for many countries the amount of debt relative to their GDP is alarmingly high. The most extreme example is that of Nicaragua, which owes nearly three times what it produces (see Table 3.2).

Compared with the relatively modest advances in economic regeneration, the social costs of adjustment have been high. In a survey of eight countries Mesa-Lago (1997:501) suggests that that they have been particularly acute in Peru, high in Chile and Cuba, medium in Colombia, Argentina and Mexico, with only Uruguay and Costa Rica registering low or very low costs. These latter are also two of the most democratic countries and this evaluation tallies with Ramos's (1997) arguments about the ameliorative effects of democratic government.[3] Although annual growth

BOX 3.1

General Policies of Economic Restructuring

REDUCTION IN STATE EXPENDITURE

- Privatisation of some social welfare services (social security, pensions, some health and education services)
- Elimination of most subsidies
- Privatisation of public enterprises (with the exception of some strategic natural resources) and public utilities (natural monopolies such as electricity and telecommunications)
- Efforts to secure fiscal balance

TRADE LIBERALISATION

- Deregulation of main markets (especially capital and foreign exchange and to a lesser extent the labour market)
- Generalised elimination of most non-tariff barriers
- Radical and rapid reduction of customs tariffs (a reduction from around 100 per cent in the 1980s to about 20 per cent)
- Reduction in the number of tariff brackets (from an average of 60 to about three)
- Liberalisation of prices

Source: Ramos (1997:16)

in the region has reached three per cent on average since the inception of trade liberalisation, this is almost half the 5.6 per cent per annum registered in the years 1945–80. Even when calculating solely from the period after inflation was brought under control, it only reaches 4.4 per cent (Ramos, 1997:17). Furthermore, economic statistics do not say much about the quality of recovery and how people's lives have been affected by crisis and adjustment.

TRENDS IN POVERTY IN LATIN AMERICA

The impact of adjustment on poverty has been particularly noticeable (see Table 3.3). For the region as a whole, poor households grew from 35 per cent of the total in 1980 to 41 per cent in 1990. By 1997 the proportion had declined slightly to 36 per cent, but, despite positive growth rates, it was still one per cent higher than in 1980 (CEPAL, 1999: 36). Indigent or destitute households represented 15 per cent of total households in both 1980 and 1997, although this figure had reached 18 per cent in 1990 (ibid.). In Chile, the country that experienced the most radical restructuring, the results were severest on the very vulnerable in society. Between 1973 and 1990 the

Table 3.1 GDP Growth and Inflation in Latin America, Annual Percentage Rates

	GDP Growth per capita			Inflation		
	1971–80	1981–90	1991–97	1984	1990	1997
Argentina	1.0	–2.4	4.3	627.5	2315.5	0.5
Bolivia	2.0	–2.0	2.0	1300.0	17.1	4.7
Brazil	6.1	0.3	2.0	196.7	2937.7	7.5
Chile	0.8	1.7	6.9	20.3	26.6	6.3
Colombia	3.3	1.7	2.5	16.1	29.2	17.7
Costa Rica	2.7	–0.7	1.3	12.0	19.0	13.2
Dominican Republic	4.6	0.1	2.2	27.1	50.4	8.3
Ecuador	6.3	–0.6	1.5	31.3	48.6	30.7
El Salvador	—	–2.5	3.3	11.5	24.1	4.5
Guatemala	2.9	–1.4	1.4	3.4	41.2	9.2
Honduras	2.0	–0.9	0.4	4.7	23.3	20.7
Mexico	3.5	0.1	1.0	65.5	26.7	20.6
Nicaragua	–2.9	–3.5	–0.5	35.4	7485.2	8.9
Panama	4.0	1.5	3.7	1.6	1.0	2.0
Paraguay	5.4	0.6	0.0	20.3	38.2	7.0
Peru	1.2	–2.8	2.7	110.2	7482.6	8.6
Uruguay	2.8	0.3	3.6	56.8	112.6	19.9
Venezuela	0.5	–1.9	1.7	12.2	40.8	50.0

Sources: IADB (www/iadb/int/sta/ENGLISH/staweb/index.htm#bsed); IADB (1993:Table F-2; 1998:Table B-2 and Table F-2).
Note: — = no data.

Table 3.2 The Debt Burden in Latin America

	Total debt ($US billions)			Debt to GDP ratio		
	1982	1990	1998	1982[a]	1990	1998
Argentina	43.6	62.8	144.1	49.5	44.4	48.3
Bolivia	3.3	4.3	6.1	59.1	87.8	71.2
Brazil	92.2	119.9	232.0	33.8	25.8	29.7
Chile	17.3	19.2	36.3	77.4	63.4	49.9
Colombia	10.3	17.2	33.3	30.4	36.7	33.5
Costa Rica	3.6	3.8	4.0	99.6	52.3	28.6
Dominican Republic	2.5	4.4	4.5	55.1	61.8	28.1
Ecuador	7.9	12.1	15.1	68.1	113.3	76.8
El Salvador	1.4	2.1	3.6	28.5	40.3	30.4
Guatemala	1.2	3.1	4.6	16.0	40.3	24.1
Honduras	1.5	3.7	5.0	40.0	122.1	95.3
Mexico	57.4	104.4	160.0	35.1	39.7	38.0
Nicaragua	2.2	10.7	6.0	68.1	482.0	280.7
Panama	3.0	6.7	6.7	60.8	125.7	73.1
Paraguay	1.0	2.1	2.3	18.9	40.0	26.8
Peru	10.0	20.1	32.4	30.9	59.2	51.6
Uruguay	1.7	4.4	7.6	20.1	47.4	33.8
Venezuela	29.3	33.2	37.0	50.6	68.3	38.9

Sources: IADB (www/iadb/int/sta/ENGLISH/staweb/index.htm#bsed); IADB (1990:Table B-1; Table E-1).
Note: a: calculated by author using IADB (1990: Tables B-1and E1).

Table 3.3 Poverty and Income Distribution in Latin America

	Poverty (% households below poverty line)			Income distribution (Percentage share of income or consumption Highest quintile/Lowest quintile)		
	1980	1990	1997	1970[a]	1980[a]	1995
Argentina	9	16[b]	13	50.3/4.4	—	—
Bolivia	—	47 (u)	44 —	—	—	48.2/5.6
Brazil	39 (1979)	41	29 (1996)	66.6/2.0	62.6/2.4	64.2/2.5
Chile	17 (1970)	33	20 (1996)	51.4/4.4	—	61.0/3.5
Colombia	39	—	45 —		53.0/4.0	61.5/3.1
Costa Rica	22 (1984)	24	20	54.8/3.3	54.5/3.3	51.8/8.8
Dominican Republic	—	—	32	—	—	55.7/4.2
Ecuador	—	56 (u)	50	—	—	52.6/5.4
El Salvador	—	—	48	—	—	54.4/3.7
Guatemala	65	63 (1989)	—	—	55.0/5.5	63.0/2.1
Honduras	65 (1970)	75	74	67.8/2.3	—	58.0/3.4
Mexico	32 (1977)	39 (1989)	43	57.7/2.9	—	58.2/3.6
Nicaragua	—	—	66 (u)	—	—	55.2/4.2
Panama	36 (1976)	36 (1991)	27	—	—	60.4/2.3
Paraguay	—	37 (u)	40 (u)	—	—	62.4/2.3
Peru	46 (1979)	—	37	61.0/1.9	51.9/4.4	51.2/4.4
Uruguay	11 (1981)	12 (u)	6 (u)	—	—	—
Venezuela	22 (1981)	34	42	54.0/3.0	50.6/4.7	51.8/4.3

Sources: CEPAL (1995: Table 31; 1998: Table 2); World Bank (1980: Table 24; 1990: Table 30; 2000b: Table 5).
Notes: a: approximate year
b: Greater Buenos Aires
(u) urban areas
— = no data.

proportion of poor families rose from 30 to more than 40 per cent (Ramos, 1997: 18). Crisis and restructuring have also produced widening gaps in income distribution, resulting in Latin America as a whole having one of the most polarised profiles in the world. In the late 1990s the region's richest decile of the population received 45 per cent of income while the poorest quintile received just four per cent (Helwege, 2000:194). Particularly unequal distribution can be found in Brazil (Gini index 60.1)[4] and Mexico (Gini index 53.7) (World Bank, 2000a: Table 5). Growth may benefit the poor but it benefits the rich even more and the rise in income disparities as a result of structural adjustment has exacerbated the significant inequalities that already existed.

Disappointing trends, not only in income poverty but also in other quality of life indicators such as education, employment, job security and health care (discussed later in this chapter and elsewhere in the book – see Chapters 5 and 8), led some to question the Washington Consensus approach to economic recovery. In the 1990s, the 'New Poverty Agenda' (NPA) emerged (see, for example, World Bank, 1990), which recognised the need for social programmes to facilitate the transition, even if growth was still seen as a cornerstone for tackling poverty (Sen, 1999:685–6; cf. McIlwaine, 2002). For critics, however, it is not possible to 'add on' social policies to models which emphasise 'sound economics'; rather, there needs to be a rethink about the very nature of such reforms (Elson and Çağatay, 2000). Elson and Çağatay (2000:1352) argue that the problem is that BWI look at the social *impact* of macroeconomic reform rather than at social *content*. This tends to gloss over the fact that the results are not benefiting people, except a few at the top. Per capita GDP may be improving, for example, but, as noted, income disparities are getting worse. Increasing numbers of people are excluded from basic welfare services or the services that do exist are so meagre and/or depleted by the 'double crisis' that they are of little benefit. These systems, largely modelled on the European experience, have been forced to reform along with the rest of the economy (Mesa-Lago, 1997). Even Uruguay, a country with traditionally low income disparities, has seen the situation deteriorate, partly as a result of welfare targeting (González de la Rocha, 2001:292), discussed in further detail later.

Defining poverty

There are many ways of considering the impact of structural adjustment, yet the issue of poverty remains central to criticisms of BWI strategies. There are two main approaches to defining poverty: first, to view it as a simple matter of income and purchasing power, and, second, to take a more qualitative and subjective approach that encompasses the poor's own perceptions of poverty (McIlwaine, 2002). Stewart (1995:13–17) points to five distinctions in relation to definitions of poverty which illustrate the complexities of the issue (see Box 3.2). At first glance, using a quantitative approach may appear more straightforward, but even within this there are various problems such as how and where to set poverty lines. Alongside issues of definition, there are also distinct typologies. In Latin America, various types of poverty have been identified: 'structural poverty' which is embedded and responds little to changes in the economy; 'new poverty' resulting from structural adjustment; 'poverty of the marginalised' where lack of access to goods and services over time passes from one generation to another, and 'regional poverty' resulting from unequal development within a country (McIlwaine, 2002). Understanding such distinctions goes some way in developing projects to overcome poverty.

Although there is presently greater acknowledgement of the diverse ways of understanding of poverty (see, for example, World Bank, 2000a, b), proponents of the 'conventional' income approach argue that it can take into account the 'intangibles', such as clean air, dignity or autonomy, by creating 'shadow' prices. Others argue that this is ineffective and that 'shadow' prices cannot translate effectively the value of non-market goods (Razavi, 1999:411). In more qualitative

BOX 3.2

Definitions of Poverty

1 *Absolute versus relative poverty:* Absolute poverty refers to the numbers living without access to one or more basic survival needs (e.g. food, shelter). Relative poverty pays more attention to income disparities and defines poverty in relation to wealth and inequality. Absolute poverty has a relative dimension 'since the amount of income needed to achieve given objectives (e.g. education, nutrition) is greater in richer societies because the nature of the commodities available and the relative price changes'.

2 *The dimension in which poverty is to be measured:* Is the problem lack of income or access to basic needs, goods and services, or is it an issue of the quality of life and the capability to achieve it? The income-based poverty line, whereby poor people and/or households fall below it, is a relatively easy measurement to use because data are available. More orthodox economists also prefer it for its 'objectivity'. However, it fails to examine how income is distributed within households and assumes that income is the sole factor in explaining lack of access to goods and services and basic needs, rather than more complex power relations.

3 *The cut-off point of poverty lines:* Calculating numbers of the poor depends on how this cut-off point is determined. The poverty line can be set at the amount needed to maintain consumption at a given calorie level (which can be a rather narrow calculation given different peoples' needs). Alternatively it can be set at the point below which poverty certainly would occur. This can offer stratification of poor people as destitute or merely poor. Access to basic services can also be used to determine the poverty line, although attainment is more problematic and difficult to measure.

4 *Using the poverty line:* Should there be a headcount of people living below the poverty line or should the gap between poor people and the poverty line be the main concern? The latter is more sensitive and useful. When assessing the poverty gap different methods of calculation exist which offer different levels of sensitivity. Aggregate measures, such as the headcount, estimate the magnitude but not the depth of the problem. Increasingly the impact of structural adjustment has led to a new classification between the 'chronic' or long-term poor and the 'new' poor who have dropped below the poverty line as a result of the double crisis. Given that measuring the poor concentrates on current income it does not take into account those who fall temporarily below the poverty line. The new poor are generally better off than the chronic poor and are often the recipients of targeted welfare programmes.

5 *Weighting multi-dimensional approaches to poverty:* The UNDP's Human Development Index and Human Poverty Index (HPI) aggregate three measures of well-being: income, life expectancy and literacy. Whilst these still have problems of arbitrariness, they also have the advantage of moving away from the unidimensional GNP per capita measure.

Sources: Stewart (1995:13–17); UNDP (1997)

terms, research indicates that looking only at income misses other potentially more important issues, such as access to land and/or home ownership (McIlwaine, 2002). Another important factor is vulnerability and the ability to withstand economic shocks. Some poor people are more able to weather such difficulties without their standards of living dropping significantly, while others, particularly seasonal and migrant workers, are much more vulnerable to such changes. Along with gender, ethnicity is a factor in vulnerability (González de la Rocha, 2001).

In trying to understand these other dimensions of poverty, social exclusion has become a popular concept, particularly in policy-oriented analyses, due to its supposed greater sensitivity to the cultural context of people's lives (McIlwaine, 2002). In a study of Central America (Costa Rica, El Salvador and Guatemala) social exclusion was measured using 'direct indicators' (including income poverty, child malnutrition, illiteracy and territorial isolation), and 'indirect indicators' (such as economic precariousness, discrimination [ethnic, linguistic, cultural and political], women's marginality, lack of access to healthcare and sanitation and social abandonment). Using these indicators, Guatemala emerged as suffering the most exclusion, followed by El Salvador and then Costa Rica (McIlwaine, 2002). The United Nations has attempted to capture the multi-dimensional aspects of poverty through quantitative methods, particularly the Human Development Index and Human Poverty Index (see Chapter 1).

Understanding that poverty is a dynamic and shifting concept that is more than a lack of income is key. As Benería and Mendoza (1995:74) observe it is 'not just an economic problem, but is also a historical, political and cultural issue' (see also McIlwaine, 2002:6; Razavi, 1999:424). Although this is increasingly recognised, it is still the case that poverty is generally discussed at the national or regional level in relation to income-based indicators and there remains scepticism towards more qualitative approaches.[5] Nevertheless, there is acknowledgement among politicians and economists at all levels that poverty needs to be addressed; the problem remains that the radical redistribution methods needed to tackle it run contra to the globally dominant neoliberal approach.

Poverty alleviation strategies

Some Latin American countries have a relatively long history of social welfare provision. Roberts, B. (1995: 185) sees the rise of welfare provision, particularly social insurance, as part of attempts by authoritarian states to co-opt the rising working classes in the 1940s and 1950s (see also Chapter 2). The level of provision across the region has always varied greatly as has the quality of the services provided and the percentage of the population covered. In Brazil, for example, the poorest 37 per cent of the population in 1990 received only 9 per cent of social security, while the top 27 per cent garnered 42 per cent (Helwege, 2000:196).[6] Whatever the systems in place, they have not been able to cope with the changing economic situation, resulting in their own reform in recent years (Mesa-Lago, 1997). By the late 1980s it had become clear that growth would not immediately follow the implementation of structural adjustment and the failure of existing systems to respond to the crisis increased the need for 'safety nets' to protect those adversely affected (Cornia, 2001:2; Vivian, 1995:2–3). Social funds (SFs) have proliferated across the region. Designed to alleviate the impact of structural adjustment, they have generally been aimed more at the 'new poor' than the 'chronic' or old poor, who are actually in greater need, although this has changed over time (Cornia, 2001: 2). A key element of social funds is that they are targeted rather than universal and so access to the benefits is not a right (Lloyd-Sherlock, 2000: 109). This recasts the meaning and content of citizenship (see Chapter 2; also Chapter 7 on the targeting of female-headed households in poverty alleviation programmes).

There have been two main approaches within SFs: emergency employment programmes, mainly on public works schemes, which offer an income to the poor; and programmes that provide consumer subsidies. Bolivia was one of the first countries to establish a social fund, the Emergency Social Fund (ESF), in 1985, as a temporary measure to protect the needy, although it gradually became a more permanent fixture as the programme was repeatedly renewed. Originally, the Fund encompassed a two-pronged approach: short-term employment programmes for those most affected by adjustment and, second, basic services provision that the government could not provide. The programme as a whole covered four main areas: economic infrastructure, social infrastructure, social assistance and productive support (Graham, 1994:60).[7]

A common element of social funds is a participatory methodology, which is often managed in a semi-autonomous fashion by the private sector and civil society and with some independence from state bureaucracy (Cornia, 2001: 8). There has been a notable participation of NGOs and often funding is external (from international aid), which adds to the independence from public administrations.[8] Some programmes are demand-led and supposedly respond to the wishes of the target population. As Cornia (2001: 9) observes:

> All in all, SFs distinguished themselves from traditional social programmes because they had a strong *short-term* anti-cyclical component; were mostly *multi-sectoral* (as opposed to the 'vertical programmes' of line ministries); emphasised *employment generation* through public works and *human capital formation* (and less food subsidies), and the expansion of social insurance and assistance; often exhibited *high cost per capita* for both wage and non-wage items; focused mainly on the *social groups affected by adjustment* and not on the structural poor; counted on much *greater external support* than the usual government programmes, and mostly

> relied on *demand-driven* (as oppose to state-initiated) schemes; and were run by temporary *autonomous bodies* possessing administrative flexibility needed to ensure fast programme implementation [emphasis in original].

Greater independence from public administration and traditional political actors was seen as important to make funds less susceptible to the usual political co-optation and more efficient. There have been some attempts to circumvent this by developing parallel bureaucracies and by using external funding, which has been a common characteristic (Vivian, 1995:7). Nevertheless, government attitudes to the implementation of poverty alleviation strategies can also depend on the political cycle (González de la Rocha, 2001:297) and, in some cases, SFs were designed to 'improv[e] the political viability of adjustment programmes, and creat[e] new social infrastructure and institutions able to improve the efficiency and effectiveness of social service delivery' (Vivian, 1995:2). Other programmes were more overtly political. Mexico's PRONASOL (*Programa Nacional de Solidaridad* National Solidarity Programme, 1988-94) may have dislodged some entrenched political interests but also aided some and created new ones in an attempt to garner support for the government (Craske, 1994; Dresser, 1991). Furthermore, the problem of clientelism in Latin America has not been eradicated with neoliberal adjustment and Roberts, K. (1995:91) argues that targeted programmes can reinforce it (see also Craske, 1994). Given that the aim is often more to 'keep people quiet' than provide serious poverty alleviation (Benería and Mendoza, 1995:73), it is unsurprising that SFs should be susceptible to such practices.

There are a number of key elements that are of interest in looking at SFs in Latin America: the target audience, the decision-making process and the efficiency of the programmes. Those most affected by structural adjustment are often not the poorest: as Ravallion (1997:635) notes, 'higher initial inequality protects the poor from negative growth'. This is partly due to the fact that when you have little, there is little to take away. Consequently, as a number of studies on Latin America have shown, poverty alleviation strategies generally do not reach the poorest (Moguel, 1990; Raczynski [ed], 1995) and some argue that targeting 'benefits the poor less' (Draibe and Arretche, 1995:133). Consequently, targeting the 'new poor' rarely attacks long term inequalities. The decision-making process is often demand-led, but Benería and Mendoza (1995:60) note that, despite the best intentions, such approaches are not always successful. They also observe that the 'participatory' element is not always as deep as it could be: 'community participation in the design, implementation and supervision phase is still not seriously contemplated' (ibid.:63). Furthermore, these processes are often skewed in favour of the most organised, again by-passing the poorest and traditionally marginalised (Vivian, 1995:7).[9] In programmes where public services are provided through an alliance between the resource provider and the community, the ability to participate either economically or in kind is often part of the strategy to aid community building. There are many, particularly women, who are unable to participate on these terms. This strategy can reinforce the exclusion of the poorest who are already by-passed by targeting (Helwege, 2000:196). Furthermore, the percentage of the population benefiting is often very small (Vivian, 1995:11) and rarely those in more remote rural (and frequently poorest) areas.

For particular communities there have been notable benefits where services have materialised, but the evidence that such programmes are more efficient is patchy (cf. Lloyd-Sherlock, 2000:115 on the privatisation of welfare services generally). There are advantages to demand-led projects: they respond better to the needs of the clients rather than being dictated by professional decision-makers and can aid the development of civil society, as Draibe and Arretche (1995:104–5) argue in the case of Brazil. But if efficiency and effectiveness are paramount, they have not proven to be better at reaching the poor. In political terms, decentralisation, which has been seen as a complement to the process, has been insufficient and there has been a lack of the necessary training at the municipal level to make SFs more effective (Benería and Mendoza, 1995:62; cf. Draibe and Arretche, 1995:131; Martínez Nogueira, 1995:49). For the most indebted countries of the region (HIPC – heavily indebted poor countries), the only effective solution to poverty and stagnation is probably to write off a significant proportion of foreign debt and remove the stringent conditions which have so far characterised the BWI HIPC Initiative (see Esquivel *et al.*, 2001 on Nicaragua and Honduras).

Gendered impacts of structural adjustment

Structural adjustment has had a significant impact on Latin Americans in general, but particularly on women. In the sphere of social reproduction, for example, privatisation of state services and rising pressures on income have resulted in a greater burden for women who, according to the prevailing gender division of labour, are responsible for domestic care and provisioning. As with approaches to solving poverty generally discussed above, there are tensions among experts about how to tackle female poverty. The neo-classicists argue that growth will erode women's inequality over time, although acknowledging that this change can be slow. The Women in Development (WID) approach is sympathetic to this position, but questions the role that gender inequalities have within the struggle for growth, arguing that in some stages, such strategies can make inequalities worse especially where patriarchal relations are strong. The Gender and Development (GAD) perspective is much more critical, arguing that economic growth alone does little to improve women's status and that structural adjustment may be particularly harmful (see Forsythe, Korzeniewicz and Durrant, 2000 for discussion of these positions). While Chapter 8 deals with the gender impacts of post-1980 changes in employment and labour markets, here we examine the effects of restructuring on three issues related to the domestic domain: the 'feminisation of poverty'; the intensification of reproductive responsibilities; and the gender dimensions of social funds.

The 'feminisation of poverty'?

Whether women are particularly vulnerable to poverty has been a much debated topic in recent years. The idea that 'women are poorer than men' has become something of a truism, often based not only on women's low share of earned income relative to men (see Tables 1.1 and 1.2), but on the prevalence of households with female heads which fall below the poverty line (Fukuda-Parr, 1999: 99). There are a number of factors contributing to this scenario: women on average are paid less than men; they are concentrated in low-income, low-status and frequently irregular jobs; they have less access to traditional welfare benefits, such as pensions, which have generally been linked to the formal sector (see Chapters 4 and 8); and poverty alleviation strategies often pay minimal attention to gender issues (addressed below). Seguino (2000) argues that women's low income is often seen as a stimulus to investment, particularly in semi-industrialised countries where women are concentrated in export industries; a common feature in Latin America. But these features are not static. Women in Latin America have shifted their work patterns significantly in recent decades and, in some export processing zones, have become major earners and are challenging the 'myth' of the male breadwinner (Safa, 1995a; see also Chapters 7 and 8). Poverty, as we have seen, however, is not just a matter of access to income and material goods. Women's disadvantage in respect of benefits, limited choice of work, heavier domestic burdens and lower educational attainment can be greater handicaps. As feminist scholars have emphasised, women and men experience poverty differently (Lind, 1997: 1216; Razavi, 1999: 410 and *et seq.*).

That women on average earn less income than men is not in doubt, but assumptions about female-headed households being synonymous with poor families is very much in question. While this is discussed in more detail in the context of households in Chapter 7, female-headed households are varied and do not conform to one stereotype of the 'poorest of the poor' (see Box 3.3). This stereotype rests on two beliefs: 'that they form a disproportionate number of the poor in the majority of societies worldwide and [...] that women-headed households are prone to experience greater extremes of poverty than male-headed

BOX 3.3

Challenging the 'Poorest of the Poor' Stereotype

- By 'unpacking' the household and understanding that it is not a unitary structure, we are better able to understand the power relations and competing interests inside. It allows us to understand that households are not necessarily benevolent, altruistic entities but that different household members fare differently within them. Women in male-headed nuclear households may experience greater poverty than women who are heads of household, even where the latter earn less income than the former. This highlights the power dimensions of poverty, since the poverty of powerlessness may be considered a worse state by women than material poverty.
- Moving beyond identifying poverty solely with income and consumption allows us a better understanding of women's poverty. In particular it is important to be sensitive to the how the poor both obtain and command resources. It is important to understand poverty and vulnerability as processes. Low income need not be a problem if people have adequate shelter and access to basic services. If female-headed households have these assets they may not be as vulnerable as other, apparently more wealthy, households.
- Acknowledging that female-headed households are as diverse as male-headed units, and that generalisations should be avoided, also helps challenge the stereotype. Female-headed households often enjoy more than one income and are multi-generational or consolidated households which allows them great flexibility in response to poverty.
- Per capita assessments of family incomes give a better estimation of real income poverty levels: male-headed households may have more income but they may also have more people and thus per capita levels are not necessarily higher than in female-headed homes.

Source: Chant (1997b)

units' (Chant, 1997b: 27; see also Moghadam, 1997). Female-headed households emerge for different reasons and households cannot be divided into 'comfortable male'-/'poor female'-headed (Razavi, 1999:413). Although men generally earn more money than women, there is no guarantee that this money contributes to family welfare. Feminist scholars in particular have demonstrated the need to investigate the power relations within households to understand better how poverty might affect members of the household differently. In examining a number of studies, Chant (1996a:14) notes that there is evidence to suggest that men in Guadalajara, Mexico can retain as much as 50 per cent of their income for personal expenditure, while in other Mexican cities and Honduras they contribute only 68 per cent of their income to family expenditure. Women, on the other hand, retain little, so even where women earn less than men, the family unit may be better off. Indeed, it is often as a result of 'female altruism' that women are seen as 'development panaceas' and 'an effective means for increasing welfare' (Razavi, 1999:410; cf. Molyneux, forthcoming).

Women often engage in different income-generation strategies (in both formal and informal sectors) and it is generally other female household members (for example girls and elderly women) who take up the slack in domestic chores (some of which also yield small amounts of income). Although informal sector work has many disadvantages (see Chapter 8), it does tend to be flexible, thereby allowing women to develop a variety of coping mechanisms. Furthermore, it should not be assumed that female-headed households have only one wage earner (Chant, 1997b:40). For some women, the 'loss' of a partner can actually bring stability should they be alcoholics or abusive, and can also bring better standards of living for the women if distribution of goods (including food) had been skewed towards the male 'head of household' (ibid.:41). Indeed, many women prefer to remain single after the disappearance of the man since it gives them more freedom and autonomy (see Chant, 1997a; Safa, 1995b:43). Women's increased participation in paid labour generally has helped remove some of the stigma associated with work, especially outside the home, and has encouraged the acknowledgement that male-headed households can rarely survive on a man's income alone (if they ever did) (see Chapter 7).

These qualifications about female household headship should not detract from the fact most women are at an above-average risk of poverty. Furthermore, some are particularly vulnerable: elderly women face special hardships (see Chapter 4) and CEPAL (2000) also highlights the problems facing indigenous women who suffer from ethnic as well as gender discrimination. Women also encounter disadvantages in land ownership which can affect their poverty levels. In the past, with the exception of Cuba, Mexico and Nicaragua, landholding identified ownership with male producers to such an extent that women were simply not recognised as landowners (CEPAL, 2000:36). CEPAL (ibid:37) also highlights the ambiguous gendered impact of neoliberal reforms which have liberalised the land ownership market: 'on the one hand women have direct access to land ownership, while on the other they cannot always purchase it owing to lack of earnings'.

Despite these difficulties, women have generally shown themselves to be eminently able to cope with crisis; however, this ability is finite. Whether this can be sustained in the face of long-term poverty is questionable (see González de la Rocha, 1997), especially given that their efforts to generate income have been undertaken alongside heavier burdens of work in the home.

The intensification of reproductive labour

Women's burdens of reproductive labour have increased due to shifts in state responsibilities resulting from economic restructuring. Sen (1999:689) notes that anti-poverty strategies have an unintended impact of increasing women's workload because insufficient acknowledgement is made of the 'care economy' (see also Safa, 1995b:45). Women spend more time cooking to save money, care more for sick and elderly to avoid medical costs and sometimes reduce their own calorie intake to protect that of their children (see also Chapter 5). In many Latin American countries at the height of the crisis women engaged in communal strategies to cope with rising food costs as subsidies were withdrawn and income reduced (see below). The fall-back on domestic provisioning to economise means particularly heavy workloads for low-income women whose conditions of labour in poorly serviced neighbourhoods often make the most routine household tasks highly time-consuming (see Figs 3.1 and 3.2; also Chapter 5). This disproportionate burden of restructuring on women's reproductive labour remains largely unrecognised. Safa (1995b:44) observes in the case of Cuba that not only do men not take on more domestic work, 'their wives do not encourage them to do so'. In these terms, gender roles are not greatly affected (cf. Pearson, 1997: 699; Pitkin and Bedoya, 1997: 38; see also Chapter 7).

Women's preparedness to absorb these costs of adjustment allows states to withdraw services while minimising social unrest. As Seguino (2000: 1212) argues in relation to women's lower pay: 'inequality is less likely to produce social conflict if the burden is born by women, a group traditionally socialised to accept gender inequality as an acceptable outcome'. Without recognition that invisible reproductive labour is essential to the productive economy, women's true contribution is ignored and male bias reproduced. In Cuba, expansive public welfare provision and rationing had guaranteed a basic minimum, but the radical decline in the ability of the state to provide these has had massive impacts on women's lives, from increased income generation, to long shopping hours to secure food, and more attempts to mend and adjust clothes. As one woman comments, 'Shopping is much more work: before everything arrived once a month – but now food comes in dribs and drabs. I have to go everyday and queue for everything' (Pearson, 1997:684). Again it is women who have borne the brunt of this reorganisation although men have also contributed (ibid.: 13n).

Women's increased domestic labour has been central to the viability of structural adjustment, but it is unclear that women can maintain these strategies indefinitely or what might happen in the face of further economic shocks. As Pearson (2000b:221) summarises:

> the re-negotiation of responsibility for reproductive work between the public and the private sphere (that is, between the state and the household) has not been

Figure 3.1 Woman grinding maize, Santa Cruz, Costa Rica

(Photograph by Sylvia Chant)

Figure 3.2 Washing clothes, Puerto Vallarta, Mexico. Women returning uphill with their washing from the Rio Cuale

(Photograph by Sylvia Chant)

> accompanied by a re-negotiation of responsibility between men and women within the household, and … the traditional reliance on women to provide the necessary services to ensure reproduction at different levels of the economy and society is no longer proving an efficient mechanism.

Moreover, although women have been central to survival, they have not been a key constituency in the region's social funds.

Gender and social funds

Social funds in Latin America have not generally been gender-sensitive. Despite women suffering more from the impacts of structural adjustment, the primary beneficiaries of SFs are men, particularly in terms of employment programmes (CEPAL, 2000:35; Vivian, 1995:10). In Honduras, Benería and Mendoza (1995:58) refer to a gender bias in the employment programmes, which may not be deliberate but which illustrates a lack of gender awareness. This skewing of employment projects towards men also demonstrates a 'male breadwinner bias' that assumes that male employment is more important. Moser *et al.* (1993) (cited in Gideon, 1998:309) found that women are targeted in their reproductive role and only men are targeted as producers, thus reinforcing gender stereotypes.[10] The participatory methods, discussed above, of some programmes do not encourage women to take part, often because they are less able to do so through lack of skills, or the structure of the meetings is not sensitive to gender constraints such as mobility and time (Craske, 1998). Indeed, women's voices may be misheard or not heard at all (Sen, 1999:690). This lack of gender sensitivity is pervasive: in an assessment of SFs in Honduras, Mexico and Nicaragua, Benería and Mendoza (1995:65) found that:

> the invisibility of women's poverty and women's needs remains a constant throughout the conceptualisation and operationalisation of the ESIFs (emergency social investment funds). Programmes are addressed mainly to men because women's poverty is not conceptualised separately from men's – the assumption is made that a reduction of men's poverty will automatically help women.

This said, there are some projects that are aimed specifically at women. In Mexico, PRONASOL's programme *Mujeres en Solidaridad* (Women in Solidarity) was aimed at helping women with small-scale production and social projects 'to facilitate the performance of women's daily work and so contribute to improving the quality of life of the family and community'.[11] But, little was done to tackle unequal gender roles and it was not a major element in the project's budget (Benería and Mendoza, 1995:71). Under President Zedillo (1994–2000) a new poverty alleviation programme, PROGRESA (*Programa de Educación, Salud y Alimentación*, Education, Health and Food Programme) was introduced. A clear distinction between PRONASOL and PROGRESA is that the former stressed communal responses, community building and co-responsibility (Craske, 1994; Dresser, 1991), while the latter focused on the individual.[12] With regard to women, the direct financial benefit that an individual received relied on her complying with her obligations to ensure the children were at school and that she attended nutrition and health courses.[13] Along with managing family welfare in extremely difficult conditions, women now had to bear the burden of 'solving' the problem by attending workshops which were an extra load (cf. Molyneux, forthcoming). This lack of gender awareness remains an issue and will continue to limit the effectiveness of policies to combat poverty.

Economic restructuring has had significant gendered impacts which have required that women in particular adjust their lives to cope with crisis. In the following section we see how economic restructuring has also generated popular movements and, in some cases, led to the strengthening of civil society.

Social movements

The strong presence of social movements was a generalised phenomenon across Latin America from the late 1970s and into the early 1990s. Since then they have been less visible, although they remain active. There were a number of reasons for the emergence of social movements at this juncture and they developed in different ways depending on the local political terrain, the experience of the actors involved, and the possibilities of horizontal linkages and alliances among different groups. There were two main catalysts for social movements: human rights abuses and economic crisis.[14] Economic crisis was the spark for both urban riots (Mesa-Lago, 1997:503; Walton and Shefner, 1994:107) and grassroots consumption-based mobilisations. These movements have been important in a number of ways. They have provided a 'voice' for people, particularly women. They have allowed people in many cases to reconsider gender constructions, particularly in relation to decision-making at the local level. Finally, they have brought to the fore questions of rights and entitlements. For states they are also a source of potential 'social capital', which has been used successfully by some in SF participatory projects. Central to social capital are trust and reciprocity which are fostered by family relations, schools and voluntary activity. Whitley (2000:450) defines it as 'the willingness of citizens to trust others including members of their own family, fellow citizens, and people in general'.[15] Such capital can be an important asset in economic development since it encourages collective responses to challenges and aids the diffusion of economic benefits. Accordingly social movements can be interpreted as a tool for poverty alleviation.

Consumption-based mobilisations

A range of consumption-based organisations and initiatives sprang up in response to economic crisis, especially in urban areas where organising tended to be easier.[16] Across the region, the range of community-level initiatives was impressive and often reflected pre-existing community reciprocity networks. Communal kitchens emerged in many neighbourhoods where people, mostly women, pooled their resources to maximise returns. In Peru these became so crucial to survival that a law was passed in 1988 to regularise them and to create a support fund (Lind, 1997: 1210). Cañadell (1993:50) reports that in 1986 there were 1,383 popular organisations in Santiago, Chile, and Lind (1997:1206) mentions more than 2,000 in Lima, Peru. In Mexico there were *Caja Populares* or saving cooperatives where groups pooled money to offer short-term loans to members[17] and in Brazil there were health cooperatives (Machado, 1993). Other communal initiatives included neighbourhood kindergartens, small sewing groups which, in Chile, made *arpilleras* (embroidered pictures) that illustrated political repression. The communal kitchens in Peru and Chile are perhaps the best known although they emerged in different conditions. In Peru, the government was corrupt and in crisis, and the activities of the guerrilla organisation *Sendero Luminoso* (Shining Path) made grassroots organising particularly difficult. In Pinochet's Chile, social movements laboured under highly repressive conditions. The important element of these organisations is that although they may have begun as a means to combat crisis, they often became political entities where people learned how to work together, develop democratic structures, deal with authority, plan and organise.[18] Given the nature of the tasks (caring for the sick and children, cooking, shopping) and the fact that women are also at the centre of reciprocal community networks, women have dominated these groups (Logan, 1990; Rodríguez, L., 1994; Vincent, 1998). This has offered women a distinctive opportunity to develop skills, especially in group management.

Social movements have been peopled by those who, generally, have not been political actors, in traditional terms of parties, unions, local government and so on. Many participants, particularly women, have not previously had much activity in 'politics' and do not necessarily think of their activities as falling within this realm. Some women have used what has been termed 'feminine consciousness'[19] as the basis for their activities and others, particularly in the past, have avoided more overtly political identification given the levels of repression in some countries (see also Chapter 2). For many, however, these grassroots organisations have been important for giving them a voice and a more mainstream political visibility (see

Daines and Seddon, 1994). This new visibility is evident in the way that parties and governments in the post-authoritarian period have attempted to court women, albeit frequently in the capacity of valiant, caring mothers. We can point to the establishment of SERNAM in Chile and *Mujeres en Solidaridad* in Mexico as evidence of this. Maintaining this presence has not been easy. For individual women the 'triple burden' (see below) has become too heavy and for women in general gains may be made but sometimes institutionalised in ways that depoliticise the content (Barrig, 1997; Craske, 1998). Nevertheless, it can be argued that the significant role played by women in the democratisation process, not least through social movements, placed pressure on new civilian governments to establish national women's offices and increase the visibility of women at least rhetorically.

The new visibility of women has itself contributed to the continued democratisation process by opening up the political arena to more actors. Social movements have also been a place to learn democratic practice. Often, the extent of their impact relied on the ability to construct horizontal linkages to enable groups to pool strength and resources to become more than isolated movements (on Mexico see Foweraker, 1989). This was easier to do in some countries than in others. Lind (1997) argues that horizontal linkages were more successful in Peru than in either Ecuador or Mexico, suggesting that in Peru people turn to collective action more quickly in comparison with the more 'privatised' responses found in Ecuador and Mexico.[20] Although researchers point to the relationship, albeit difficult, between the voluntary-activist arena and the more formal political terrain as being crucial to long-term success, there is no magic recipe to achieve this. It is also unclear how success might be measured: in terms of longevity, the impact on policy, the impact on participants – female and male? Social movements generally have been part of a resurgent civil society in the region; however, it is a civil society that remains weak and susceptible to cooptation by the state, individual populist leaders and political parties (cf. Benería and Mendoza, 1995:64; Molyneux, forthcoming). For the most part, however, social movements have not fared well under civilian governments (Taylor, 1998; Waylen, 1994), partly as a result of continued clientelism but also because institutional political actors have been privileged as 'voices' in decision-making arenas. This has meant that political parties have re-emerged as the main channels of representation in many countries and NGOs have increasingly replaced social movements and, in some cases, the state.[21] With the re-establishment of parties and executives, women are more likely to be excluded given their weaker presence in these arenas (see also Chapter 2).

By campaigning around consumer issues, women are defending social and economic rights and particular notions of citizenship by demanding that the state should be responsible for supporting a 'dignified life' ('*vida digna*') of its inhabitants. More particularly, from a gender perspective, these movements offered women a space 'to acquire elements of a gender-specific culture of citizenship. This form of political learning involves challenging pre-established boundaries of appropriate feminine behaviour and is lived by women as learning to experience themselves as confident, competent beings and acting accordingly' (Schild, 1994:64).[22]

In the literature there is some debate over whether these movements are 'feminist' or 'feminine' (Alvarez, 1990; Corcoran Nantes, 1993; Craske, 1999; Stephen, 1997). Whether these distinctions are useful remains a bone of contention, but it is the case that participating in social movements has encouraged women to consider their gender position and the constraints they face in a sexist society. Individual women and some groups gained immeasurably from their experience, but translating this into improving the status of women *per se* is much more difficult and dependent on structural changes (see Kabeer, 1999:461). Furthermore, in many cases social movements actually reinforced and institutionalised traditional gender roles, albeit politicising them (see Lind, 1997:1210–11), through the continued gender division of labour (Craske, 1993).

Women's double/triple burden

As noted above, economic restructuring has reinforced the double burden of women as they try to increase incomes while maintaining, and often increasing, their domestic responsibilities. Consequently, greater community participation can create a triple burden. Under these conditions, groups often fold due to lack of time. An added problem is the institutionalisation of crisis management and ' "self-reliance" and "community provisioning" are often euphemisms for reliance on the unpaid labour of women' (Vivian, 1995:19; cf. Lind, 1997:1207; Molyneux, forthcoming; see also Chapter 5). These conditions limit the transformatory potential of collective action. In some cases, women become community leaders and gradually make their way through various levels to become national politicians, as in the case of Benedita da Silva who began campaigning for basic services for her neighbourhood and went on to become a senator in Brazil.[23] Such examples, however, are rare and even in da Silva's case the personal costs were sometimes high. When paid labour, domestic work and community participation are combined, the hours worked by women are extremely long. With labour continuing to be the 'asset of the poor' (Razavi, 1999:431), it is difficult to see how poor women can escape the added burdens. Similarly, to what extent can grassroots participation 'empower' under such circumstances? To date it appears that women's lives have changed massively as a result of the social, political and economic changes of the last twenty years, while men's lives have remained more constant in terms of the balance between different responsibilities. Along with the extra burdens on time, women have had to face other obstacles. Women's participation in social movements causes resentment in some men and can lead to, or increase, tension and domestic violence (Craske, 1993:128; Stephen, 1997:48). In some cases, it has been possible to use social movements as a forum to discuss such problems (Rodríguez, L., 1994:42) but in others, women choose to withdraw from activism.[24] On the positive side, community participation can also lead to the development of political subjectivity where people become actors rather than remain objects of the political process. This is particularly important for women who often lack the spaces that some men have traditionally gained through trade unions and political parties.[25] Social movements have also been considered to aid the process of empowerment, especially when they were at their peak in the 1980s.

Women's 'empowerment'

The personal developments that come about as a result of collective action are a much debated topic. To what extent do women become 'empowered'? Is this process permanent? How does it have an impact on political and social structures around them? How do we *know* if women are empowered? These are all difficult questions to answer. The notion of empowerment dominated development literature, both academic and practical, in the 1990s.[26] The prevalence and popularity of the concept is reflected in the UNDP's own 'Gender Empowerment Measure' (GEM) which attempts a statistical approach (see Chapter 1). Even some SFs make claims to the empowerment potential of participatory and demand-led projects. In the 1980s, Staudt (1987) assessed the process of empowerment among women engaged in a project in northern Mexico. She found that while individual empowerment was relatively easy to attain, it was very difficult for women taking part in the courses to make the move from personal empowerment to establishing networks or organisations. Staudt concluded that, 'most are personally empowered but not politicised and involved in networks or organisations' (ibid., 1987:171). Kabeer (1999), looking at empowerment in a more global context, interrogates the 'power' aspect and links it to the ability to make choices. This changes according to the cultural context; for example, being able to choose a husband might say much about women's empowerment in a South Asian context but little in Latin America. Along with being able to make choices, it is also about being efficacious, that is, about being able to carry those choices through and to have an impact on policy, if that is the goal.

Whether people can be empowered by others through, for example, organised projects (of NGOs, SFs or governments), remains highly contentious and certainly there is no obvious path that guarantees empowerment. Given its personal nature, the process of women's empowerment is also a slow process. Nevertheless, the positive impact of collective action in terms of women's empowerment is clearly evident from the vast array of literature analysing women's participation in social movements in the region. The important interplay between collective action and individual experience is also evident in developing citizenship rights – rights generally being the result of *collective* struggle, although they are individual in practice.[27] State institutions and NGOs can facilitate the empowerment process by fostering collective solidarity and critical engagement with the political system, and states can pass laws that increase the potential for empowerment by creating the appropriate structures, including guaranteeing the vote or, as in Latin America, through establishing quotas. The full practice of citizenship benefits from empowerment since effective citizens are empowered ones.

For women, finding a 'voice' or learning to speak is often a central part of the empowerment process. Public arenas have been associated with male spaces (Craske, 1993:128) and women have often felt uncomfortable in speaking out. As one Chilean woman explains: 'When I talked to my husband I never looked at his eyes. I was afraid to speak in public. … In the Women's Centre I learned to speak, to look people in the eye' (María in Rodríguez, L. 1994:39). Developing a gender consciousness is another aspect of empowerment as women come to understand how multiple constraints, based on gender, class, ethnicity age and so on, limit their autonomy and ability to make choices. In Latin America there remains considerable nervousness among women about being identified as 'feminist'. Accordingly, many consumption-based social movements stress that they are working with men and identify themselves as poor people;[28] nevertheless, the organisations have provided women with a place to become more aware of the gender dimensions of their situation and some do come to identify with feminism (Craske, 1993, 1999; Schild, 1994; Stephen, 1997). It is likely that such sentiments remain with the women, but the more permanent impact of empowerment is unclear. We lack studies that take a long-term perspective to understand how people, who have been 'empowered', view the process five, ten or fifteen years later (cf. Lind, 1997:1210; Waylen, 1993). It is possible that the perception declines as the things won become more commonplace: younger women do not always appreciate the importance of their forebears' struggles. The lack of a new, younger generation to carry the flag is something that concerns many feminists in the region.[29]

Conclusion

Post-1980 economic conditions have had an impact on gender relations in various ways. Women and men have experienced and responded to these conditions differently and within these broad categories, the impacts have also varied by country, region, class and ethnicity. The problem of poverty has tested people's ingenuity to the limits. Governments have attempted to address this but not always in the fullest and most appropriate manner. Furthermore, the nature of macro-economic reform has had a particular impact on the reproductive arena by adding to women's workloads. At the same time, however, economic crisis has proven to be the catalyst for social movements where women have gained visibility in many ways. The impact of social movements has been both at the personal level of the participants and at a more general level of engendering 'public' life. As such, the crisis has provided both opportunity and constraint in terms of recasting gender relations, even if men do not seem to have matched the range of responses generated by women. Women's activities in crisis management, particularly in collective ways, has been understood as 'social capital' to be mobilised. While this can reinforce the importance of women's participation, there are concerns that it really means more exploitation (Molyneux, forthcoming). With women being regarded as a 'development panacea' (since helping women is seen as a more efficient way of improving standards for all through the effect it has on children), there is currently great emphasis on women's education in line with the view that better educated women are thought to have a wider impact on welfare. Some positive outcomes have occurred as a result of fundamental structural reorganisation in Latin America in the era of neoliberal reform, but caution must be exercised to ensure that women's successes do not translate into further burdens.

Gender and Population

SYLVIA CHANT

Introduction

Population behaviour interrelates with gender in a variety of ways, being both influenced by and impacting upon gender roles and identities. While Chapter 9 of this volume deals with spatial movements of population in Latin America, here the focus is on features of population composition and growth in the region. Following an overview of trends in fertility and mortality from the mid-twentieth century onwards, the bulk of the chapter deals with the role of gender in processes which have brought about demographic change, particularly in the sphere of population control and family planning. The chapter also discusses gendered dimensions of the progressive ageing of populations in Latin America, and the implications for women and men of declining birth rates and longer life expectancies.

Recent population trends in Latin America

Between the middle and end of the twentieth century, Latin America's population grew nearly three times over: from 164 million in 1950 to 481 million at the start of the new millennium (UN, 2000:9). Although Latin America is still one of the least densely settled regions of the world and is home to less than 8 per cent of the global population, in the period 1920–70 its population grew faster than in any other part of the world. Even into the 1970s, when population growth had dropped to less than 2 per cent per annum in the relatively wealthy countries of the Southern Cone, the annual growth rate in the region as a whole was surpassed only by Africa (UNCHS,1996:42). From 1980 onwards, however, the pace of growth slowed. By the early 1990s, the vast majority of countries in the region had growth rates under 2 per cent (see Table 4.1). The only notable exceptions, aside from Paraguay, were Nicaragua, Honduras and Guatemala. This was due in part to the repatriation of

Table 4.1 Population Growth Rates in Latin America, 1970–2000

	Population (millions, 1998)	Average annual population growth rate (%) 1970–80	1980–90	1990–94	1994–2000
Argentina	36.1	1.6	1.5	1.2	1.3
Bolivia	8.0	2.4	2.0	2.4	2.4
Brazil	165.9	2.4	2.0	1.7	1.3
Chile	14.8	1.6	1.7	1.5	1.4
Colombia	40.8	2.2	1.9	1.9	1.7
Costa Rica	3.8	2.8	2.8	2.1	2.1
Cuba	11.1	—	—	—	0.4
Dominican Republic	8.2	2.5	2.2	1.7	1.7
Ecuador	12.2	2.9	2.5	2.2	2.0
El Salvador	6.0	2.3	1.3	2.1	2.2
Guatemala	10.8	2.8	2.8	2.9	2.9
Honduras	6.1	3.2	3.3	3.0	2.8
Mexico	95.8	2.8	2.0	2.0	1.7
Nicaragua	4.8	3.1	2.7	3.1	2.7
Panama	2.8	2.6	2.1	1.9	1.7
Paraguay	5.2	2.9	3.1	2.8	2.6
Peru	24.8	2.7	2.2	1.9	1.8
Uruguay	3.3	0.4	0.6	0.6	0.6
Venezuela	23.2	3.4	2.6	2.3	2.1

Sources: UNDP (1997:Table 22), UNDP (2000:Table 19), World Bank (1995:Table 25), World Bank (1996:Table 4).
Note: — = no data.

refugees in the aftermath of civil war (see Dunkerley, 1993:48–9).

The general pattern of Latin American population growth in the last few decades has been broadly in line with the precepts of the so-called 'Demographic Transition Model', which, based on the historical experience of Europe and North America, posits an evolution from a situation of high mortality and fertility to low fertility and mortality, where population growth is close to zero, via two intermediate stages. In the first or 'early transition' phase, population expands significantly as death rates fall relative to birth rates on account of improvements in living standards, nutrition and public health (see Dickenson *et al.*, 1996:78; Potter *et al.*, 1999:114–6). In the second (or 'late transition') phase there is still a gap between birth and death rates, but of less magnitude because, *inter alia*, increased education, legislation on child employment and access to family planning encourage people to limit births. This means continued but lower rates of population growth, and is where the majority of Latin American countries are now.

Changing birth and death rates

In the last thirty years average national birth rates have shrunk by one-third to one-half in most parts of Latin America, the only exceptions being countries such as Argentina and Uruguay, where fertility levels had dipped well before 1970 (see Table 4.2). Much of the decline is attributable to family planning. Although figures for contraceptive use are not renowned for their comprehensive coverage or reliability (tending to refer only to married couples, for example), the data in Table 4.2 indicate a broadly inverted relationship between contraceptive prevalence and total fertility rates. In countries such as Colombia, Cuba, Costa Rica, Uruguay, Argentina and Brazil, where 70 per cent or more of the 'married' adult population use contraception, the average number of children born to women at a national level is less than three. Alternatively, in the majority of countries where 50 per cent or less

Table 4.2 Fertility and Contraception in Latin America, 1970–2000

	Total fertility rate*				Contraceptive prevalence
	1970	1980	1994	1995–2000	rate (%) 1990–99
Argentina	3.1	3.3	2.6	2.6	74
Bolivia	6.5	5.5	4.7	4.4	48
Brazil	4.9	3.9	2.8	2.3	77
Chile	4.0	2.8	2.5	2.4	43
Colombia	5.3	3.8	2.6	2.8	72
Costa Rica	4.9	3.7	2.9	2.8	75
Cuba	—	—	1.5	1.6	82
Dominican Republic	6.1	4.2	2.9	2.8	64
Ecuador	6.2	5.0	3.3	3.1	57
El Salvador	6.3	5.3	3.8	3.2	60
Guatemala	6.5	6.5	5.2	4.9	31
Honduras	7.2	6.5	4.7	4.3	50
Mexico	6.5	4.5	3.2	2.8	69
Nicaragua	6.9	6.2	4.9	4.4	60
Panama	5.2	3.7	2.7	2.6	58
Paraguay	5.9	4.8	4.5	4.2	59
Peru	6.2	4.5	3.1	3.0	64
Uruguay	2.9	2.7	2.2	2.4	84
Venezuela	5.3	4.1	3.2	3.0	49

Sources: UNDP (1997:Table 22), UNDP (2000:Table 19), World Bank (1995:Table 26), World Bank (1996:Table 6)

Notes:

* The total fertility rate refers to the average number of children likely to be born to a woman if she survives until the end of her childbearing years and gives birth at each age in accordance with prevailing age-specific fertility rates.

** Contraceptive prevalence refers to the proportion of women who are practising, or whose spouses are practising, any form of contraception. This is generally measured for married women aged between 15 and 49 years.

— = no data.

of the population use contraception, such as Guatemala, Honduras and Bolivia, the mean total fertility rate is four or more. By the same token, it is important to bear in mind that national averages often mask substantial variations along lines of class, locality and ethnicity. For example, although Mexico's total fertility rate at a national level dropped from 4.5 in 1980 to 3.2 by 1994, surveys in low-income urban neighbourhoods in the centre and west of the country during the 1980s indicated that women were continuing to give birth to at least six children (Chant, 1999c:230–1). Important reasons underlying high birth rates among poorer sections of Latin America's population include limited knowledge of, or access to, family planning, reluctance to resort to artificial birth control as a result of religious (and specifically Roman Catholic) *diktat*, the social importance attached to motherhood among women and virility among men, belief in the welfare gains of large families, and high rates of infant mortality (ibid.).

Although infant mortality rates declined significantly at national levels between 1970 and 1993 (see Table 4.3), mainly due to improvements in diet, living standards and the control of major killer diseases such as poliomyelitis and smallpox, in just over one-third of countries in the region there were slow downs in infant mortality reductions during the 'Lost Decade' of the 1980s (Stewart, 1995:187). Moreover, levels of infant mortality everywhere in the region are still far above the average for industrial market economies (7 per 1000). Disparities are again evident between groups of different socio-economic status. In Nicaragua, for example, although the national infant mortality rate in 1993 was 51 per 1000, the level among illiterate (a proxy for 'poor') mothers amounted to 138 per 1000 (CISAS, 1997:88). In the impoverished community of Alto do Cruzeiro in Northeast Brazil, women have an average of 9.5 pregnancies, 3.5 child deaths and 1.5 stillborn babies (Scheper-Hughes, 1997). With a total of 82 per cent of child deaths occurring in the first year of life, women often resist becoming attached to their children unless and/or until they are perceived to have a reasonable chance of survival. With 45 per cent of all deaths in the community made up of children under five years of age, the mean life expectancy in the region is only 40 years, which is less than two-thirds of the national average (ibid.; see Table 4.3).

Although fears of losing children play a part in maintaining higher-order births among some segments of the Latin American population, there is evidence from a number of countries to suggest that the vast majority of couples have continued to reduce their fertility during and after the crisis years. As Selby *et al.* (1990:169) argue in relation to Mexico:

> Children cost more and they are not able to earn as much as they did in the past. The economic basis for high fertility rates has been undermined, at least in the cities of Mexico, and ... fertility rates are declining rapidly.

Table 4.3 Life Expectancy and Mortality in Latin America, 1970–2000

	Life expectancy at birth (years)		Crude death rate (per 1000 population)		Infant mortality (per 1000 live births)		
	1970-1975	1995 2000	1970	1993	1970	1980	1998
Argentina	67*	73	9	8	52	26	25
Bolivia	47	61	20	10	153	118	60
Brazil	60	67	10	7	95	70	33
Chile	63	75	10	6	77	32	10
Colombia	62	70	9	6	77	41	23
Costa Rica	68	76	6	4	59	19	13
Cuba	71	76	—	—	—	—	—
Dominican Republic	60	71	11	6	98	76	40
Ecuador	59	70	12	6	100	74	32
El Salvador	58	60	12	7	103	84	31
Guatemala	54	64	14	8	100	84	42
Honduras	54	69	14	6	110	70	36
Mexico	62	72	10	5	72	51	30
Nicaragua	55	68	14	7	106	84	36
Panama	66	74	8	5	47	32	21
Paraguay	66	70	7	5	57	50	24
Peru	56	68	14	7	116	81	40
Uruguay	69	74	10	10	46	37	16
Venezuela	66	72	7	5	53	36	21

Sources: UNDP (2000: Table 9), World Bank (1995: Tables 26 & 27), World Bank (1996: Table 1), World Bank (2000b: Table 7).
Notes: * Figures rounded up to nearest whole number.
— = no data.

In demographic terms, fertility decline in the region has contributed to counteracting an upward pressure on population growth from two main sources: first, a rise in average life expectancy from 61 to 68 years between the 1970s and the 1990s (Roberts, B., 1995:92), and second, a halving of mortality rates in many countries during the same period, particularly those in which crude death rates exceeded 10 per 1000 in 1970 (see Table 4.3). The combination of falling birth rates and rising life expectancy in Latin America has begun to change the composition of dependency ratios in the continent, as discussed later in the chapter.

Family planning programmes, fertility and gender in global context

Reproductive behaviour is affected by a multiplicity of factors, such as culture, education, income and migration. Even so, higher levels of contraceptive prevalence in Latin American countries have clearly played an important role in the spectrum of processes leading to lower fertility (Table 4.2). Given that family planning has been actively promoted by the international population establishment, and that, along with Asia, Latin America was the first developing region targeted for lobbying and donor pressure by international agencies (Corrêa and Reichmann, 1994:15), it is important to consider family planning in Latin America within the context of global strategies for fertility reduction. This is all the more significant given that until the early 1970s, many Latin American countries had promoted pro-natalist policies as a means of addressing low population densities. Gender is a primary element in this discussion, as women have consistently been the main targets of family planning initiatives.

Population and development: conceptual and policy perspectives

Although there are numerous views on population, the Malthusian notion that unchecked fertility contributes to poverty, underdevelopment and environmental degradation has been a pervasive influence on international (Northern-dominated) population policy. Bearing in mind that this interpretation obscures 'the real causes of the current global crisis: the concentration of resources – economic, political, environmental – in the hands of an ever more tightly linked international elite' (Hartmann, 1997:84), fertility control programmes have been regarded as the answer to the world 'population problem'. It is not surprising, then, that such programmes have been more concerned with fertility reduction targets than with expanding women's and men's powers of determination over their reproductive behaviour. As Furedy (1997:65) summarises: 'Since population control programmes are designed to reduce fertility, their aim is not to provide free choice but to influence people towards a particular outcome.' Moreover, given that until recently the international population establishment tried to impose Malthusian logic selectively upon the poor majority in the Third World, Hartmann (1987:14) claims that this has effectively robbed people of choice and subordinated individual rights to the overriding imperative of population control (ibid.).[1]

This said, between the 1960s and the 1990s, there was a slow, and putative, shift in the underlying rationale for population regulation from a 'traditional economic development argument' to a case for 'environmental balance' and 'people-centred sustainable development' (Corrêa and Reichmann, 1994:13; Smyth,1994:3; UNIRDAP, 1995:8). In 1994, the third United Nations International Conference on

Population and Development in Cairo saw individual (and particularly women's) rights (in the guise of 'reproductive rights'), assume a more prominent place on the global agenda. This is evident in the Programme of Action 1994–2015 adopted at the conference, which made recommendations on six key issues (see Box 4.1)

BOX 4.1

International Conference on Population and Development, *Programme of Action* 1994–2015: Key Recommendations

1 Women's empowerment (including access to education to promote gender equality)

2 Reproductive and sexual health rights of men, women and adolescents

3 Elimination of unsustainable patterns of production and consumption

4 Population as an integral part of sustainable development and environment

5 Provision of universal access to reproductive health services

6 Family as the basic unit of society

Source: UNIRDAP (1995:8)

In an attempt to eliminate the coercive character of many previous interventions, the Cairo Programme of Action also recommended that family planning be guided by two central pillars of the 'quality of care' framework developed under Judith Bruce at the Population Council, namely 'appropriate patient–provider interaction' and 'informed choice' (see Box 4.2), as well as the greater incorporation of men.

While feminists had long criticised family planning programmes for sacrificing women's reproductive rights and general health to the demographic rationale of reducing population growth (see Smyth, 1994:11), the Cairo conference marked something of a victory for the women's movement. Corrêa and Reichmann (1994:4) went as far as to suggest that 'Official recognition of the reproductive rights and health approach to population may be one of the most significant achievements of contemporary feminism.' Yet it should also be recognised that as far back as the 1970s the population establishment had used the position of women in society as a means to pursue its objectives (Furedy, 1997:126), and although the 1990s saw much fuller adoption of the language of 'rights' and 'choice' for women, this could be regarded more cynically as a tactic to justify the continuation of anti-natalist agendas (ibid.).

BOX 4.2

Family Planning Programme Recommendations in the International Conference on Population and Development's *Programme of Action* 1994–2015

- Family planning programmes should ensure information and access to the widest possible range of safe and effective family planning methods (appropriate to the individual's age, reproductive history, family size preference and so on) to enable men and women to make free and informed choices.
- Information should be provided about the health risks and benefits of different methods, and on their side effects and effectiveness in preventing sexually transmitted diseases, including HIV/AIDS.
- Services should be safe, affordable and convenient for users.
- Services should ensure privacy and confidentiality.
- A continuous supply of high-quality contraceptives should be ensured.
- Services should comprise expansion and improvement of formal and informal training in sexual and reproductive health care and family planning, including better training in interpersonal communication and counselling for family planning personnel.
- Family planning services should provide adequate follow-up care, including for the side effects of contraceptive use.

Source: Hardon (1997a:8).

Population policies, family planning and women's reproductive rights in Latin America

The history of birth control in Latin America is an embattled and controversial one in which women have often been caught in the crossfire between polarised institutional positions on family planning, allowing little space for their own needs, rights and interests. On one hand the interventions of North American and international development agencies have often come in the shape of direct population control (Cubitt, 1995:110). This is most graphically exemplified by the testing of unsafe contraceptives on poor Latin American women, or even enforced sterilisation, which led in the past to the expulsion of the US Peace Corps from Bolivia and Peru (ibid.). On the other hand, some institutions within the region, most notably the Roman Catholic Church, have strongly resisted women's access to contraception.

Although some progressive Catholic clergy have chosen to eschew Vatican teachings in favour of a more 'rational' approach which supports women's decisions to plan their families (see de Barbieri, 1999:111 on Mexico; Shallat, 1994:149-50 on Chile), in broad terms the Church has remained resolute in its position on contraception as a high-order sin (see Schifter and Madrigal, 1996). Through a combination of formal and informal means, the Roman Catholic Church has frequently delayed, modified and/or prevented national family planning programmes. It has also refused to relax its resistance to abortion.

Except in Cuba, abortion in Latin America is either illegal (for example in El Salvador and Chile), or permissible only on very limited grounds, such as where the mother's or infant's health is at serious risk, or where pregnancy results from rape or incest (CRLP, 1997; Cubitt, 1995:110; Hardon,1997a:18). The Church's influence on the law is such that penalties for transgression are often extremely serious for all parties involved.[2] In Mexico, for instance, practitioners found to be giving abortions to people for reasons other than health problems, rape or incest, can be imprisoned for up to eight years, and women who induce their own miscarriages may be detained for between six months and five years (Hardon, 1997b:16). Religious influence at the grassroots adds considerably to general opposition, despite evidence that in practice women often do resort to termination (see below). In Costa Rica, for example, a study conducted in Guanacaste province revealed that while both male and female adolescents are open in principle to the idea of abortion for reasons of health, rape or incest, terminations are generally regarded as an 'assassination' and/or 'grave moral transgression' (Loáiciga Guillén, 1996:227, my translation). In Mexico, research with adult women (most of whom had children) in the Federal District, Sonora and Oaxaca, found that although adverse economic circumstances constituted another legitimate justification to abort, this was not deemed to be acceptable if the pregnancy 'merely' interfered with women's personal plans or desires (Rivas *et al.*, 1999:338; see also Fachel Leal and Leal, 1998 on Brazil).

Yet lack of abortion on demand has given rise to a situation where an estimated 4 per cent of Latin American women of reproductive age (15–49 years) have an unauthorised termination each year. This average rate of unauthorised terminations is higher than in any other region of the world, and in some parts of the continent much higher still, even if the subjective (and objective) identification of abortion remains a grey area. In a study of 200 men and women aged 14-60 years in four low-income settlements in Porto Alegre, Brazil, for example, 34 per cent of the sample reported that they or their partners had undergone an abortion. In more than half these cases, however, this had not entailed an operation *per se* but the use of medicinal remedies such as teas (*chapueradas*) or combinations of drugs known to provoke termination. Such methods are seen as less of a transgression than surgical and/or hospital interventions because they are more ambiguous and there is not the explicit recognition that the woman is actually pregnant (Fachel Leal and Leal, 1998:316). Whatever method might be used, however, and acknowledging the immense unreliability of statistics, around 43 per cent of women inducing abortions in Brazil are reported to suffer problems during or after terminations (Corrêa and Reichmann, 1994:40). In Mexico, clandestine abortions are the third cause of maternal mortality (de Barbieri, 1999:135), and in Peru, the second, being responsible for 22 per cent all maternal deaths (CRLP, 1997:179).

Those most likely to fall victim to complications (and who are also most neglected by health services) are women who have had an incomplete abortion (Huntington, 1999). One way of avoiding this unnecessary suffering would be the more widespread use of emergency contraception such as the 'morning after pill' (*píldora poscoital*). This can be taken up to 72 hours after intercourse, is extremely effective, and is, in fact, readily available from most pharmacies in Latin America. Yet emergency contraception measures have not been widely advertised or promoted by family planning agencies thus far (Vernon,1999).

Complications associated with pregnancy and childbirth are among the five principal causes of death among women of reproductive age in around half the countries in Latin America. Maternal mortality rates range between 48 and 600 per 100,000 live births in the continent as a whole (CRLP, 1997:13), despite the fact that there is the knowledge and scientific expertise to prevent the great majority of fatalities (Mora and Yunes, 1993:62). In Mexico, the estimated preventability is 52 per cent, and in Colombia as much as 92 per cent (ibid.). Although in countries such as Uruguay the risk of dying from pregnancy or delivery is only 1 in 873, this rises to 1 in 210 in Guatemala and to 1 in 50 in Bolivia (ibid.:63). This latter rate is over 250 times greater than in industrialised economies such as Canada (ibid.). Disproportionately high levels of maternal mortality are not surprising when it is considered that in Central America, for example, only 70 per cent of mothers received prenatal attention by trained personnel in 1998, and only 64 per cent of births were attended by the same. As far as the latter is concerned, the proportion ranged from as much as 97 per cent in Costa Rica, to a mere 35 per cent in Guatemala (PER, 1999:165, Table 6.1)

Concern about maternal deaths, as well as rising numbers of illegal abortions, has been a key factor prompting various Latin American governments to take a stronger stand against Roman Catholic objections to contraception over time. In the 1970s the Bolivian state was under such pressure from the Church that a Presidential Decree was issued in 1977 to prevent public institutions from providing family planning services (Parras and Morales, 1997:77). By the mid-1980s, however, alarm about maternal, perinatal and infant mortality led the government to introduce a child-spacing policy aimed at providing family planning information and services to high-risk groups. This was extended in 1993 with *Plan Vida*, which aims to widen access to family planning and reproductive health care (ibid.:78). While birth control is not a goal in itself, the National Population Council of Bolivia is concerned to improve health standards, especially among women. Strong emphasis is placed on individual rights to use contraception, and on increasing basic education for women in society (Hardon,1997a:16). The absence of demographic objectives, together with an orientation towards meeting women's social and health needs, has effectively brought Bolivia's population policy extremely close to the recent Cairo recommendations (Box 4.1).

Where Latin American countries have pursued full-blown state-led population programmes from the outset, the neo-Malthusian spirit of fertility reduction is more in evidence (see Box 4.3). In Puerto Rico, for example, the inauguration of the large scale modernisation and industrialisation programme in the 1950s, 'Operation Bootstrap', was accompanied by a draconian national family planning programme. In the interests of achieving its ambitious demographic goals, the state placed major emphasis on female sterilisation, particularly among the poor and black population (Pérez Sarduy and Stubbs, 1995:7).[3] In Mexico, which instituted its population policy in 1973 and where the public sector has been responsible for as much as 98 per cent of contraceptive provision, there has been less coercion and less explicit targeting than in Puerto Rico, but tactics have been none the less persuasive. Operating under the banner of slogans such as '*la familia pequeña vive mejor*' ('the small family lives better'), and making explicit links between fertility reduction and improvements in people's quality of life, particularly women's (see Alba, 1989:13; Sayavedra, 1997:95), a halving of fertility rates was effected within two decades (see Table 4.2). New guidelines for population policy in Mexico published in 1994 further highlighted family planning as a means of exercising reproductive rights and preventing health risks for men, women and children, although there is continued preference for permanent and semi-permanent methods for women (Sayavedra, 1997:97–8). Indeed, despite women's rights to be given full information on sterilisation and alternatives, research has revealed that power relations between health providers and clients are such that one-quarter of sterilised women claim not to receive this information before they undergo the operation, and as many as 40 per cent of women do not even sign the necessary paperwork (Figueroa, 1999a:163).

Most other Latin American countries have pursued what the Southern Feminist Network DAWN categorises as 'combined policies', which refer to mild or non-explicit population programmes (Box 4.3). Prominent examples include Brazil and Colombia, where governments themselves have not actively promoted family planning (in both instances because of resistance from the Roman Catholic Church) but have instead permitted non-governmental and private sector organisations to do so. In Colombia, for example, 42.4 per cent of contraception is distributed by the private sector, with the rest being provided by the government and the local

BOX 4.3

Fertility Management Policies in Developing Countries: A Typology*

1 *Fully-established state-led policies*
Governments adopt principle of reducing population as a component of development policies (often following a Malthusian model, and under pressure from the North). State takes a strong lead in promoting and providing family planning.

Key examples: China, Indonesia, India, Bangladesh, Mexico, Puerto Rico.

2 *Semi-established or 'incomplete' policies*
Refers to policies which have only been partially implemented, due to reasons such as recency of introduction, state inefficiency, or political controversies.

Key examples: Various countries in the Middle East, Africa and the Pacific.

3 *Combined policies*
Refers to situations in which state-led policies do not fully account for fertility decline, either due to major involvement of the private sector in family planning, or because of the significant role played by other development factors.

Key examples: Republic of Korea, Brazil, Colombia.

4 *Pro-natalism*
Can refer to explicit population policies, but more usually to situations in which there is resistance on cultural grounds to formal policies favouring family planning and population control.

Key examples: Chile, Argentina, Nicaragua, Guyana.

5 *Double-standard policies*
Often linked to pro-natalism, but where certain groups of the population are targeted for fertility control.

Key examples: Malaysia, South Africa under Apartheid.

6 *The Basic Needs approach*
Fertility decline is associated with the expansion of education, health services and better economic opportunities for women.

Key examples: Sri Lanka, Cuba.

Source: Corrêa and Reichmann (1994: 24–5.)
* This typology was developed out of a series of discussions among members of the Southern network of women activists and researchers, DAWN (Development Alternatives with Women for a New Era). The examples given are those cited in Corrêa and Reichmann's text.

associate of the International Planned Parenthood Federation, Profamilia (Côrrea and Reichmann, 1994).[4] Similar trends have occurred in Brazil, where as much as 68.3 per cent of contraceptive provision is in private hands (ibid.). Regardless of who administers family planning services, however, women have been the main targets for a generally very limited range of options. This raises important questions as to the extent to which the language of 'rights' and 'gender equality' have translated into practice in Latin America. As de Barbieri (1999:130) notes for Mexico, national population policy has encompassed a whole range of objectives such as improvements in the quality of life, particularly for poor and marginal groups, the incorporation of women into development and education, but official attention to these matters has been minimal compared with the expansion of contraceptive coverage. Rivas *et al.* (1999:345) add that violence and coercion within the family, as well as on the part of government agencies, constitute enormous barriers to the construction of a female subject with rights.

Gender dimensions of contraceptive use

Considering patterns of contraceptive use throughout Latin America, the burden of fertility regulation falls overwhelmingly on women. In Brazil, for example, only two per cent of couples practising 'modern' birth control use male condoms (hereafter referred to as condoms), and only one per cent have opted for vasectomy (Corrêa and Reichmann, 1994:39). Despite the fact that recent state family planning initiatives in Bolivia have been regarded as 'woman-friendly', there is no indication of male sterilisation, and condoms are used by only one per cent of couples (Hardon,1997b:25). In Colombia, a similar pattern obtains. Despite the fact that Profamilia started offering male sterilisation in the country back in 1971 (Viveros, 1999), vasectomy applies to only one per cent of couples, and condoms to 3 per cent (Corrêa and Reichmann, 1994:39). Indeed, in some countries of the region there is a 300:1 ratio of female to male sterilisation despite the fact that vasectomy is simpler, cheaper and reversible (Gómez Gómez, 1993a:xii). This compares with a ratio of approximately 3.5:1 in the world as a whole (see Chant and Gutmann, 2000:32).

As for the methods used by women, the pill, Intra-uterine Device (IUD), injectable contraceptives and sterilisation seem to have been the ones promoted most widely by agencies. In Mexico, for example, female sterilisation currently accounts for around 45 per cent of contraceptive use, followed by the IUD (20.8 per cent) and the pill (10.2 per cent) (CONAPO, 1999b:203–12).[5] Even if female sterilisation remains officially unrecognised as a form of family planning in Brazil and is not covered by the national insurance plan, doctors often perform the operation clandestinely when women give birth by Caesarean section (Gomes,

1994:71). The extent of the practice is such that in 1991 an estimated 27 per cent of married women in Brazil aged between 15 and 44 years had been sterilised (ibid.:71–2). As revealed by a study of domestic workers in Rio de Janeiro, sterilisation is preferred by women who have given birth to their ideal number of children (normally between one and three), because of negative experiences with the pill (the other main form of contraception in the country), limited knowledge of alternatives, and male reluctance to use condoms (Pitanguy and Mello E. Souza, 1997:91).

The continued skew towards women and limited use of barrier methods has serious impacts upon women's health, with high dosage oestrogen pills and IUDs associated with serious health problems such as cancer, thrombosis and pelvic inflammatory disease (Coe and Hanft, 1993). Lack of barrier methods also has implications for the spread of HIV/AIDS and other sexually transmitted diseases. For these reasons, it is not surprising that one of the major recommendations of the Cairo conference was that men should be more involved in reproductive health programmes (Engle, 1997:31).

Men and family planning

Reproduction is one of the few areas of gender and development policy in which emergent interest in men has taken its first steps (see Chant and Gutmann, 2000). Yet, one of the problems in exploring the actual and potential role of men in family planning is that so few studies have been carried out on this topic compared with those on women (Lerner, 1998). This bias possibly reflects the fact that women are the ones most directly affected by pregnancy and childbirth. Yet beyond this basic physiological difference, parenting, as a socially constructed process, does not need to be an exclusively or predominantly female task. The fact that it remains so among the vast majority of the population of Latin America has implications for the entire sequence of reproductive events. Bruce (1994:70), for example, argues that part of the reason why men have traditionally not been interested in limiting fertility, let alone in actually adopting family planning measures themselves, is because there are few incentives to do so. Not only are men spared the task of looking after children on a daily basis, but increases in women's labour force participation and rising levels of female household headship mean that men do not have as much responsibility as they might for financial provision. These patterns undoubtedly help to explain why in Costa Rica, for example, as many as one in four children born in the country in 1998 had a '*padre desconocido*' ('unknown father') (INAMU, 1998). This seemed to be particularly marked among younger age groups, with as many as 91 per cent of children born to women under 15 years of age not recognised by their fathers (CMF, 1997:12). Moreover, the overall rate of children with unregistered fathers rose to nearly one in three in 1999 (INAMU, 2001:9). The fact that recent programmes addressing adolescent pregnancy in Costa Rica, as well as in other countries such as Chile, are primarily, if not exclusively oriented to women, may well, as Olavarría and Parrini (1999) have argued, reinforce stereotypes of negligent fathers and generate institutional obstacles to their assumption of responsibilities for offspring (see also Chant, 2000). This said, 2001 saw the passing of the *Ley de Paternidad Responsable* (Responsible Paternity Law) in Costa Rica, which requires men who do not voluntarily register themselves as fathers in out-of-wedlock births to submit to a DNA test at the government Social Security Institute (CCSS/*Caja Costarricense de Seguro Social*). If the result is positive, the father is legally obliged not only to pay alimony from the time that the child is registered at the Civil Registry (*Registro Civil*), but to contribute part of the mother's pregnancy and maternity expenses and to pay the child's food bill for the first twelve months of life (INAMU, 2001). In the short term, it is envisaged that the law will assure financial support for children from both parents, and in the longer term lead to a 'heightened sense of responsibility in men and society regarding paternity', and to the notion that 'the care and education of children is a task to be shared by men and women' (ibid.:11).

Accepting that Costa Rica's Responsible Paternity Law is an historical first in the region, another reason for men's limited responsibility in family planning in Latin America to date is that women have been the main, if not only, target of reproductive interventions. Focus group discussions held with low-income men aged between 20 and 38 years in Chimbote, Peru, revealed that men did not use family planning services themselves because they felt these had been designed with women only in mind. The fact that health personnel were predominantly female made men feel embarrassed about attending family planning clinics, besides which the opening hours were inconvenient for male workers (Cobián and Reyes, 1998). In a broader consideration of reproductive health and rights, Figueroa (1998a:91) has argued that:

> It is not too much to say that the medicalisation of fertility regulation, supported by sexist processes in analytical interpretation, standard-setting and the pursuit of greater demographic impact, has discouraged male involvement in the processes of reproduction [my translation].

Another important reason for men's limited use of family planning is that so little research has gone into developing the array of alternatives that have been designed for women. As in most other world regions, the male condom and vasectomy have been the only two methods available, and neither has proved particularly popular. Although among some middle- and upper-income young men, carrying condoms has become something of a symbol of masculinity (see Chávez, 1999:61 on Mexico), this is by no means a guarantee they will be used. Resistance to condoms is often explained by the reduction of sensitivity and sexual pleasure for men. This is anathema where men see sexual gratification as a right. Moreover, among middle-class men in Mexico, using condoms is argued to go against the grain of masculinity insofar as 'being a man' is about taking risks and not wasting sexual opportunities (Arias and Rodríguez, 1998:337; see also Chapter 6). In turn, high fertility is also taken as emblematic of being a 'real man'. As observed by McCallum (1999:282) in the context of Salvador, Brazil:

> Men who father many children by different women show their skill in seduction and their procreative strength. An amusing insult in Salvador is to throw an accusation at a man that he has *gala rala* (thin semen). In other words, he is unable to impregnate a woman.

Sterilisation too has traditionally been linked with fear among men of 'emasculation' or reduction of their sexual potency, even if freedom from anxiety about unwanted pregnancies can offer greater sexual pleasure. Notwithstanding the reversibility of the operation, men may also be less inclined to undergo it in contexts where they are likely to have more than one partner over the life course. This said, although levels of male sterilisation remain low throughout the region, the establishment of specialist male clinics can have positive effects. In Colombia, for instance, the opening of '*Clínicas para el Hombre*' ('Men's Clinics') in Bogotá, Medellín and Calí in 1985 led to three times as many vasectomies being performed between 1985 and 1993 as the total carried out between 1970 and 1984 (Viveros,1999:158).

There are also signs that condoms are becoming more acceptable among younger age groups. In Costa Rica, for example, the use of condoms in first sexual encounters by 15–24 year olds rose from 39 per cent in 1986 to 66 per cent in 1993, even if young men's motivations for so doing were more to protect themselves from disease, than to prevent pregnancy, which is the prime concern for their female counterparts (Krauskopf, 1998:106). Similar considerations apply in Mexico, where 15–19 year old males are much more likely to use condoms than older age groups. Nearly half (44 per cent) of 15–19 year olds report that they use condoms at least occasionally with the purpose of protecting themselves from disease. This is a substantial change from the previous generation where men tended not to use condoms until their mid-twenties (around ten years after becoming sexually active), and then in the interests of avoiding pregnancy within the context of stable relationships (Chávez, 1999:61; see also Arias and Rodríguez, 1998).

Involving men in reproductive measures is not just about getting men themselves to take contraception, but, as Heise (1997:420) points out, is also about permitting their partners to do so. In Mexico and Peru, for example, even bringing up the subject of contraception is feared by some women because they think it will meet with violence, desertion or accusations of infidelity on the part of their husbands (ibid.). Only in places such as Cuba do men in general appear to have accommodated to women's increased desires and decisions for lower-order births (Fraga and Alvarez Suárez, 1998:383). This is possibly because women have been given the resources and legal support to determine their own fertility over a longer period of time than in most other Latin American countries, and Cuban men have also been encouraged to learn more about paternal responsibility (ibid.).

Whatever the range of scenarios in Latin America, the need to include men is felt to be increasingly paramount at a world scale by population agencies (see Chant and Gutmann, 2000). In 1992, for example, the International Planned Parenthood Federation (IPPF) approved as one of its key objectives:

> To increase men's commitment and joint responsibility in all areas of sexual and reproductive health and sensitise men to gender issues, as an essential element in ensuring women's equality and an enriched couple relationship for both men and women (IPPF, 1993:17).

This is also new policy on the part of the Population Council which deems that the participation of men in decisions on family planning is desirable provided explicit consent is given by their female partners (Solo, 1999).

As for strategies to increase men's participation in birth control, encouraging men to take a more active interest in fatherhood may be a good way of getting men into reproductive health, as well as into health matters more generally (de Keijzer, 1998). Although this may involve the daunting challenge of a wider overhaul of masculinity and gender power relations, there may be few other options. As Heise (1997:426) concludes on the basis of her several years of experience in work on violence and sexuality, the only way to work through problems such as male control of women's fertility is 'redefine what it means to be male'.

Fertility, education and female labour force participation

While falling fertility is clearly facilitated by increased availability of modern contraception, and this fact is no guarantee that men or even women will use it, applies as much to young as older age groups. Even in Cuba, for example, where contraception and abortion are widely available, a survey of female workers showed that nearly half had their first child before the age of 20 (Safa, 1995b:43). Although this figure for Costa Rica is lower (at 18 per cent), the proportion of women in the 15–19 year age group who have their first child at this time has remained virtually unchanged, despite a stepping-up of campaigns oriented to safe sex among youth (see Krauskopf, 1998:108). None the less, a broad relationship is also noted in Latin America between the take-up of family planning, increased educational opportunities for women, and rising female labour force participation (Safa,

1995b:39). Despite cutbacks in educational spending resulting from structural adjustment programmes, women's rising enrolment in educational establishments has persisted into the 1980s and 1990s, with particularly marked increases occurring in secondary education (see Table 4.4). The latter is important since there is often a significant gap in fertility between those who have not completed primary school and those who have at least one year of secondary education (UN, 1995:92). For example, among 15–19 year old women in Costa Rica, those with five years of primary education or less are twice as likely to have children as those with completed primary education, and six times as likely as those with secondary education or more (Muñoz, 1997:43). Partly as a result of increased education between 1971 and 1995, the number of children born to women aged 15–19 years in Mexico overall, dropped from 130 per 1000 to 75 per 1000. Yet the rate of adolescent fecundity remains lower in urban than in rural areas (61.7 births per 1000 women compared with 94.6 per 1000), and while there are only 21.7 births per 1000 female adolescents educated to secondary level or above, this figure is as high as 213.6 per 1000 among those who have not studied (see Stern, 2000).

Although the relationships between access to education and fertility are extremely complex, it would appear that education is associated with improvements in infant and maternal health, awareness of the advantages of limiting family size, and greater receptivity to modern contraceptive techniques (Buvinic, 1995:5–6). Detailed survey research in Mexico, for example, suggests that younger and more educated women are strongly aware of the costs of raising children and putting them through school, and therefore limit their fertility (García and de Oliveira, 1997). This is borne out by official figures: while 75 per cent of Mexican women with secondary education use contraception, this applies to only 48 per cent with no schooling. The average number of children among this latter group is 4.7, compared with 2.2 among those with up to one year of secondary education (CONAPO, 1999b). Differential rates of infant mortality may also be a factor, with research on Nicaragua indicating that the level of mortality is six times higher among infants born to women with incomplete primary education compared with more educated sectors of the population (CISAS, 1997:88). Similar patterns are found in Honduras: women without any education experience infant mortality rates of 67 per 1000 whereas this is only 27 per 1000 for women with seven or more years of education (López de Mazier, 1997:227).

As for links between fertility and women's work, female labour force participation in Latin America appears to have been encouraged by increased use of contraception and declining birth rates (see de los Ríos, 1993:10; Roberts, B., 1995:93 & 128). Yet the relationship between the two variables may be occluded by the nature of available data. As García and de Oliveira (1997) point out in their study of low-income and middle-class women in the Mexican cities of Tijuana, Mérida

Table 4.4 Women's Education and Economic Activity Rates in Latin America

	Female enrolment in primary education (% of age group)		Female enrolment in secondary education (% of age group)		Female economic activity rate age 15+	
	1980	**1993**	**1980**	**1993**	**1970**	**1998**
Argentina	106*	107	60	75	33**	34
Bolivia	81	—	32	—	25	48
Brazil	97	—	36	—	27	44
Chile	108	98	56	70	27	39
Colombia	126	120	41	68	26	47
Costa Rica	104	105	51	49	22	36
Cuba	—	—	—	—	24	49
Dominican Republic	—	99	—	43	13	39
Ecuador	116	122	53	56	19	32
El Salvador	75	80	23	30	26	45
Guatemala	65	78	17	23	15	35
Honduras	99	112	31	37	17	39
Mexico	121	110	46	58	21	37
Nicaragua	102	105	45	44	25	46
Panama	105	—	65	—	35	43
Paraguay	101	110	24	38	26	36
Peru	111	—	54	—	25	34
Uruguay	107	108	62	—	35	47
Venezuela	104	97	25	41	26	42

Sources: UNDP (1995: Table A2.6), UNDP (2000: Table 29), World Bank (1996: Table 7).

Notes:
* Enrolment rates in primary schools may exceed 100% because some pupils fall outside the standard age range for primary education.
** Rounded up to nearest whole number.
— = no data.

and Mexico City, fertility histories are usually well documented in macro-statistics, whereas data on employment may only be collected at one point in time. This has led to a situation where – possibly inappropriately – greater weight has been given to the effects of fertility on paid work than *vice versa*. Moreover, García and de Oliveira stress the importance of taking into account the mediating effects of women's socio-economic status on interactions between fertility and employment. For example, while women with smaller numbers of children are in some cases more likely to engage in extra-domestic income-generating activities, the relevance of fertility levels to working-class women seems less applicable, especially during periods of economic adversity (ibid.:368). Just as much as there are likely to be two-way interrelationships between fertility and female employment, fertility also appears to intersect strongly with women's age at marriage and household structure, both of which have undergone significant changes in the last twenty years, as discussed further in Chapter 7.

Gender dimensions of ageing

Although considerable attention has been given to gender in issues relating to birth and family planning, gender also matters as a population issue at the other end of the age spectrum. This is likely to become more significant still in the twenty-first century as Latin America proceeds to undergo a process of 'demographic ageing' in line with the precepts of the Demographic Transition model (see earlier; also Lloyd-Sherlock, 1997; Sen, 1994). In the context of Mexico, for example, demographic policies have succeeded in reducing birth rates, but, as de Barbieri (1999:140) points out, little consideration has been given to potential longer term outcomes:

> Who is worrying about the elderly population, who in 25 years will begin to be statistically significant, but who will have no more than two or three children? Who can provide for them and help them with survival, material and emotional needs? And let's not forget: in this elderly population, women will predominate [my translation].

Although 'demographic ageing' is commonly assumed to be a product of increasing life expectancy, Warnes (1994:157) stresses that this refers not only to the progressive increase in the *average age* of the population, but to the *share* of the population defined as 'elderly'. This is frequently regarded as people of 65 years or more in industrialised economies, and 60 in less developed economies (Berthel y Jiménez, 1995:7). Given the dominance of Eurocentric norms in international data sources, however, the 65 year cut-off point is more commonly used. On this basis, most Latin American countries in 1998 had an average of less than one-third the proportion of elderly people as high-income economies (14.5 per cent) (UNDP, 2000:226). The proportion is not greater because many countries in the region only began to experience declining mortality relatively recently, and have not yet achieved the final stage of low stable fertility (Lloyd-Sherlock, 1997:2; see also earlier). By the year 2015, however, when it is estimated that mean for the advanced economies will be in the order of 18.5 per cent, the majority of countries in the region will have at least one-third of this figure (see Table 4.5). In Peru, for example, the number of people aged 65 years or over has grown by 76 per cent since 1980, against an increase of 43 per cent for the population as a whole (Clark and Laurie, 2000:81).

Table 4.5 Actual and Estimated Dependency Ratios and Share of Elderly in Population in Latin America

	Dependency ratio* (percentage)		Population aged 65 years and above (percentage of total)	
	1998	**2015**	**1998**	**2015**
Argentina	60.6	54.5	9.6	10.7
Bolivia	78.5	62.7	3.9	4.9
Brazil	53.7	46.0	4.9	7.2
Chile	56.0	50.0	6.9	9.7
Colombia	61.4	50.1	4.6	6.4
Costa Rica	61.8	52.0	4.9	7.1
Cuba	45.2	44.0	9.3	14.1
Dominican Republic	61.9	49.0	4.3	6.6
Ecuador	65.0	50.0	4.6	6.2
El Salvador	69.6	55.3	4.8	6.1
Guatemala	91.2	69.9	3.5	3.8
Honduras	84.8	60.2	3.3	4.3
Mexico	62.8	49.4	4.5	6.8
Nicaragua	87.6	64.3	3.1	3.8
Panama	60.2	48.6	5.4	7.8
Paraguay	78.3	62.1	3.5	4.3
Peru	64.1	49.7	4.6	6.5
Uruguay	60.2	56.3	12.7	13.4
Venezuela	64.6	51.7	4.3	6.5

Source: UNDP (2000: Table 19).
Note:
* Dependency ratio is the ratio of the population defined as dependent (those aged under 15 years and over 64 years) to the working age population (15–64 years).

Women are likely to figure prominently among this growing cohort of elderly people given the differential in male–female life expectancies. Data for Central America for the period 1995–2000 show women's life expectancy as 74 years compared with only 69 years among men, and for South America, 73 and 67 years respectively (UN, 2000:54). These averages clearly mask variations, but translate in Mexico, for example, to there being 112 women for every 100 men aged 60 years or more (Varley and Blasco, 2000a:48). In Bolivia, there are 121 women per 100 men aged 60 or more, in Chile, 132 per 100, and in Argentina, 135 per 100 (UN, 2000:18). Among people aged 80 or over, gender imbalances are even greater, at

153 women per 100 men in Bolivia, 188 per 100 in Chile, and 199 per 100 in Argentina (ibid.). Elderly women are also likely to be concentrated in urban areas in the light of women's long-standing movement in the region from countryside to town (Berthel y Jiménez, 1995:12; see also Chapters 7 and 9), as well as to live alone. For every 100 men living alone in Mexico, for example, there are 170 women, and the ratio is 224 women per 100 men in the largest urban centres (Varley and Blasco, 2000a:48).

Dependency and vulnerability

While dependency ratios are conventionally calculated on the basis of numbers of persons under 15 and over 64 years vis-à-vis the working age population (see Sen, 1994:8; also Table 4.5), it should be noted many elderly people are not dependent on others, or at least their dependence is not one-way (Lloyd-Sherlock, 1997; Warnes, 1994; Wilson, 2000). This is perhaps especially so in Latin America, where many elderly people have no choice but to work (or beg) for a living, especially where they are living in poverty, where relatives cannot support them and they do not receive pensions. In Central America, for example, pension coverage is extremely low, tending to be limited to salaried employees and not extending to informal sector or rural workers. Although in the period 1990–5, a total of 77.3 per cent of the economically active population in Costa Rica, and 64 per cent in Panama were paying into pension schemes, this was only 29 per cent in Guatemala, 22.6 per cent in El Salvador and a mere 14.3 per cent in Nicaragua (PER, 1999:168). While in countries outside the Isthmus, such as Chile, 60 per cent of the population are covered by private pensions (partly as a result of World Bank promotion), these have made a cumulative loss over the years (Wilson, 2000:97). Pension funds in Peru and Argentina have also been severely strained by economic conditions in the 1990s (Clark and Laurie, 2000; Lloyd-Sherlock, 1997). In Mexico, state pensions awarded through the Mexican Social Security Institute (IMSS/*Instituto Mexicano de Seguro Social*) rarely amount to more than 1.7 times the minimum wage, and, in the majority of cases are equivalent to only 80 per cent of the minimum wage (Berthel y Jiménez, 1995:25). In the Dominican Republic, there is no social security provision for older people except for those employed formerly as civil servants (Cheetham and Alba, 2000:66). In the light of this, it is no surprise that ILO figures for 1990 estimated that a much higher proportion of men in Latin America would be working in the 55 plus age group (56 per cent), than in North America (41 per cent) or Europe (37 per cent). For women, however, rates of labour force participation were estimated to be lower, at 12 per cent in Latin America compared with 19 per cent in North America and 13 per cent in Europe (Wilson, 2000:88, Table 7.1). Figures for Mexico (1997) corroborate this general picture: men aged 55–59 years have a labour force participation rate of 87.5 per cent, those aged 60–64 years, 79.2 per cent and those aged 65 or more, 52.3 per cent, whereas the corresponding figures for women are 32.2 per cent, 27.9 per cent and 14.8 per cent respectively (Garduno-Rivera, 2000:11).

Lack of pensions (and other benefits such as health care entitlements) tend to hit women more than men, given lower earnings and less continuity in their working lives. Women are also less likely to have had formal and/or full-time employment where employers' contributions to social security complement those of workers (Bertranou, 2001; Cheetham and Alba, 2000; Sennott-Miller, 1993; see also Chapter 8). In Peru, for example, women's periodic unemployment and fluctuating incomes make it hard for them to fulfil the minimum requirement of 20 years' contributions for a pension. Women's only option in these cases is to rely on their husbands' pensions, notwithstanding that these drop to only 35 to 40 per cent of their value on their spouses' death (Clark and Laurie, 2000:82). In the Dominican Republic, only 5.7 per cent of women in a study conducted in 11 low-income communities in the eastern part of the capital, Santo Domingo, received a monthly state pension, and even then this was not enough to live on for a week (Cheetham and Alba, 2000:69). In Chile, a woman with incomplete primary education and an average length of time in the labour market, on the statutory retirement age of 60 years, receives only 29 per cent of the pension of a similarly qualified male retiring at his statutory retirement age of 65. The Chilean social security reforms of the 1980s which replaced the old public system with a mandatory privately managed one, in which benefits are determined on the basis of individual characteristics and contributions, disadvantages women because it requires continuity and because the average lifespan of women is longer than men's, both in general and in post-retirement (Arenas de Mesa and Montecinos, 1999). Fortunately some compensation for women is achievable through Chile's mixed pension system, whereby in addition to the contributory fund, there is a 'social assistance' scheme for poor elderly people excluded from the former. Since the social assistance scheme is means-tested as opposed to employment-based, women tend to benefit more from these funds (ibid.; World Bank, 2000b:154). Even then, there are men as well as women who do not receive pensions in Latin America and who cannot work. Beales (2000:12), for example, discusses a report of organisations working with HelpAge International (HAI) in Bolivia, which points up that men who cannot provide an income for the household in which they live are often marginalised and maltreated. On the basis of a detailed study of the elderly in Guadalajara, Mexico, Varley and Blasco (2000b) found that although numbers are relatively small, elderly widowers seem to have greater difficulty in finding or keeping accommodation than their female counterparts, mainly because they lose the role that hegemonic masculinity defines as their principal contribution to family life, notably breadwinning. Women, on the other hand, can feel useful and appreciated by continuing to fulfil traditional 'female' tasks such as childcare and housework.

Care of the elderly

Although the continued growth of the working-age population in Latin America means that it will probably be some time before the economic burden of a growing elderly cohort is felt (Chant, 1999c:232), the fact that almost 75 per cent of the population aged 65 or more in Mexico are economically inactive indicates that there are few options other than to depend on relatives (López and Izazola, 1995:53). This is compounded by the fact that only 10 per cent of the population aged 60 or more is covered by social security, and there have been no specific government programmes to date directed to elderly women (Berthel y Jiménez, 1995). A paucity of institutional care relates to the fact that 'idealisation of the caring family provides hard-pressed governments with a pretext for them to pass the buck to relatives, expecting them to care for the elderly with minimal support from health or welfare services' (Varley and Blasco, 2000a:48). Although a National Institute for Old Age *(Instituto Nacional de la Senectud)* was set up in Mexico in 1979 as a decentralised government organisation to assist, protect and orient elderly people, it has only managed to establish a handful of hostels and old age clubs to date (ibid.:17). In turn, the DIF (*Desarrollo Integral Familiar*/Integrated Family Development) is the main provider of shelter (*asilos*) to the vulnerable elderly, but only has spaces for a few hundred clients in Mexico's major cities (ibid.:48).

Lack of public provision usually impacts most on other women, given that caring for the elderly seems to be part and parcel of women's domestic and familial roles (see Figure 4.1). In Puerto Rico, Sánchez-Ayéndez's (1993) review of research on the elderly shows that 'the family' is the principal institution for assisting older age groups, and that the latter prefer to seek support from relatives and other members of their social networks than to rely on services provided by the state. In one study of Santo Domingo in the Dominican Republic, for instance, 47 per cent of elderly women reported living wholly or partially on remittances from children (Cheetham and Alba, 2000:70). The functions provided by the family for elderly people in Puerto Rico range from the purchase and preparation of food, to the provision of accommodation and transport, to assistance with housework, and addressing needs for company, emotional support and so on (ibid.). This work is usually performed by daughters for two main reasons: first, parents expect their daughters to take on more of the 'burden' than sons, and second, within the context of prevailing gender norms, daughters tend to see this as part of their filial obligations. At the same time, increases in labour force participation among women of reproductive age mean that elderly women are increasingly assuming responsibility for the care

Figure 4.1 Caring for the old: daughter and elderly mother, Liberia, Costa Rica (Photograph by Sylvia Chant)

of grandchildren, as well as assisting with domestic labour (Berthel y Jiménez, 1995:24; Cheetham and Alba, 2000:70). Although there is little research on the impacts of this 'gender skew' in caring in Latin America at present, it is highly likely that this compromises women's attachment to the workplace, and, in turn, their pension rights and independence in later life. As summed up by Joseph and Martin Matthews (1994:181).

> As long as elder care remains primarily a women's issue, its implications for economic performance and social productivity will be intimately bound up with the unfolding role of women in the workforce.

Other issues which need attention relate to limited coverage of geriatric medicine, the fact that many elderly people do not have access to hospital care due to their isolated locations, and the virtual absence of *Tercer Edad* ('Third Age') women from muncipal and national politics (Berthel y Jiménez, 1995).

Initiatives by and for older people in Latin America

The neglect of elderly people is in many senses surprising, given the variety of international initiatives to safeguard their rights and protection over the last two decades. As far back as 1982 the Vienna Plan of Action on Ageing established specific targets for the inclusion of older people in social and economic development (Beales, 2000:15). More recently, the Beijing Declaration of 1995 stressed approaches to development that were explicitly inclusive of women of all ages, and the Copenhagen Declaration of the same year called for generations to 'invest in one another and recognise diversity and generational interdependence guided by the twin principles of reciprocity and equity' (ibid.). The year 1999 was designated by the United Nations as the International Year for the Older Person (Clark and Laurie, 2000:80), with the protection of health of older people being one of its key tenets (Cheetham and Alba, 2000:67). More generally, the policy and programming framework associated with the United Nations Principles for Older Persons emphasises independence, dignity, self-fulfilment, care and participation, and international NGO networks such as HelpAge International, which has 7,000 member and partner organisations, is trying to get these principles adopted as a legally binding charter of rights which all governments would have to observe (Scobie, 2000:8).

Given that much of this rhetoric has not yet translated into practice, it is no surprise that older people have, in various instances, been forced to act for themselves. In Bolivia, for example, male beggars[6] have organised themselves into a Council of Venerable Old Persons (which now includes women), to demand legal documentation (Beales, 2000:17). This has spawned other groups such as 'New Dawn' which campaigns for pensions and free health care for elderly Bolivians (Scobie, 2000:6). In Peru too, social movements have established *Clubes de Tercer Edad* (Elderly People's Clubs) (Clark and Laurie, 2000:85). Following work with the NGO Aquelarre, women in 12 communities in eastern Santo Domingo in the Dominican Republic formed their own organisation – Fundompromued – in 1997. Among its first tasks was to conduct a survey to identify the needs and priorities of older women. Subsequently, 20 women have been selected as representatives from a total of 15 communities and are being trained by workers from Aquelarre's project 'Gender and the Third Age' as *multiplicadoras* (community educators, trainers and facilitators) who then pass on what they have learned to their communities. Among their many activities, Fundompromued have also joined a lobbying coalition of local government and NGOs, the *Red por Una Vejez Digna* (Network for a Dignified Old Age). In 1998, this network succeeded in pressurising the government to pass a Law for the Protection of Older People which promises various rights and services, including social security. Their main task now is to ensure that these principles are followed through into practice (Cheetham and Alba, 2000:73).

Conclusion

The 1980s and 1990s witnessed a slowdown in population growth in Latin America, mainly due to increased women's access to, and use of, contraception. This in turn has been influenced directly and indirectly by global initiatives for fertility reduction. Regrettably, falling fertility does not seem to have been accompanied by substantial improvements in maternal and child health, as examined further in the next chapter. If the spirit of the Cairo consensus is to be carried forward, it would seem imperative for governments to implement the full range of services itemised in the Plan of Action. Here, international funding could play a major role in integrating basic medical entitlements and sanitary infrastructure within reproductive healthcare. It should also seek to support initiatives to redress the massive gender bias in reproductive responsibilities, and ensure greater guarantees of women's reproductive rights.

Attention and forward planning also need to be given to women and gender at the other end of the age spectrum. As noted by Beales (2000:9), 'for many, old age is a period of chronic poverty and powerlessness', even if a large-scale crisis is still some way off. In Mexico, for example, the working-age population, which was 52.3 per cent of the total in 1980, is estimated to increase to 68.5 per cent in 2010 (Alba, 1989:15). Technically speaking, therefore, there will be more workers to dependents. This, however, is clearly contingent upon the job market, where prospects do not encourage optimism (Chapter 8), as well upon as the structure and composition of families, where there are various signs of shrinkage and/or atomisation (Chapter 7). Moreover, too many assumptions are conceivably made about the family as a fount of care. As Varley and Blasco (2000a:47) have argued:

> In Mexico, strong family ties are often thought to be a distinguishing feature of the national soul, and the family is popularly seen as an unfailing source of support to its members The possibility that families might refuse to care for elderly relatives is seemingly too remote to be worth considering.

The health needs of growing numbers of elderly men, and especially women, in Latin America also need serious consideration as rising life expectancies present more complex morbidity patterns and the requirement to attend, not only to the biggest causes of mortality, but to conditions which severely undermine the quality of life.

5 Gender and Health

SYLVIA CHANT

Introduction

The health status of populations is governed by a complex spectrum of factors in which gender figures significantly, be this in respect of morbidity (disease) patterns, health-seeking behaviour, or access to health services. In regions of the South such as Latin America, these complexities are cross-cut by differing levels of development within as well as between countries, variations in health systems, and the mediation of gender differences by 'race' and ethnicity, class, age, occupation, region of origin and/or residence, and migrant status. While a full analysis of these variations is beyond the scope of the present chapter, an attempt is made to provide an overview of key gender differences in morbidity in Latin America, gender differences in access to healthcare, and the role of gender in the provision of preventative and curative healthcare at domestic, community and institutional levels. Discussion of these topics is preceded by a review of recent health trends in the region, and the nature of current healthcare systems.

Health and healthcare in Latin America: background and overview

Defining health

Health is defined constitutionally by the World Health Organisation as 'a state of complete physical, mental and social well-being and not merely the absence of disease or infirmity' (Gómez Gómez, 1993a:xiv). While the legal implications of such a broad definition are that states should remove barriers to, and promote services for, the fulfilment of these objectives (Cook,1993:244), health (and ill-health) are notoriously difficult concepts to pin down. While Western constructions of these concepts tend to dominate official and/or macro-level accounts (see

Foucault, 1973; also Coates, 2001), ill-health (and how it should be treated) is open to highly diverse and subjective identification. Yet even within the confines of Western scientific discourse, there is difficulty assessing health status when so many diseases seriously undermine the quality of life but do not readily translate into 'objective indicators'. Although many non-fatal illnesses may be severe or prolonged (mental conditions, osteoarthritis and so on), the fact that mortality is a much less ambiguous entity than morbidity means that the health status of populations is conventionally evaluated by the prevalence of diseases that result in death. While causes of death may not always be known or registered, there is approximately 90 per cent coverage of mortality data for 72 per cent of Latin America's population (Arrossi, 1996:45). Accepting the problems attached not only to the representation but to the partiality of statistical data, in order to provide a profile of health in Latin America as a whole, the bulk of this chapter draws more on information that pertains to formal dimensions of health and healthcare than to 'alternative' and/or 'traditional' health systems.

The 'epidemiological transition' in Latin America

Bearing in mind the need for caution with figures, until around 50 years ago, communicable or infectious diseases such as intestinal and respiratory illnesses were the leading causes of death in most parts of Latin America and other regions of the South. Deaths from these diseases were technically preventable in the majority of cases. Indeed, in Europe and North America, where the resources and know-how existed to control them as far back as the nineteenth century, neoplasms (cancer), degenerative diseases and cardiovascular conditions had long surpassed them as the major cause of fatality. This shift from communicable to non-communicable disease as the principal cause of death is often referred to as the 'epidemiological transition', although the term 'health transition' is sometimes preferred for its implied concern with health and survival (as opposed to mortality), and because of its emphasis on the importance of social factors in morbidity (Phillips and Verhasselt, 1994:13).

While the epidemiological transition has traditionally been regarded as a unidirectional three-stage process – from epidemics of infections and famine, through diminishing pandemics, to the predominance of degenerative and/or 'human-made' illnesses – a 'fourth stage' of chronic but non-fatal morbidity (including mental disorders) is evident in an increasing number of advanced economies as people's life expectancy approaches eight decades (ibid.). Moreover, Phillips and Verhasselt are at pains to point out that the idea of a straightforward, unilinear evolution of health is difficult to sustain given the immense diversity in living conditions and lifestyles within developing countries. This diversity results in the latter being characterised by:

> epidemiological profiles that reflect all types of medical and social needs: infectious and parasitic conditions; chronic and degenerative diseases; psychological and psychiatric morbidity; and the social care needs of very young and very old people (Phillips and Verhasselt, 1994:12; see also Wilson, 2000:100).

Latin America provides graphic illustration of epidemiological diversity at a variety of national and intra-national scales, although almost everywhere the death rate from communicable diseases has diminished over time in the wake of new medical interventions. In some countries, such as Mexico, this dates back to the 1940s and 1950s, when the use of vaccinations and antibiotics, and control of disease vectors became widespread. For the region more generally, the 1970s stands out as the decade which saw greatest expansion of internationally supported programmes of infant immunisation against major diseases such as diptheria, measles, tetanus and tuberculosis (Curto de Casas, 1994:235). These have now become routine health sector interventions in most of Latin America with the result that over half, and more usually three-quarters or more infants are nominally protected (see Table 5.1).

Yet medical interventions alone are not enough, with strong historical and contemporary evidence indicating that clean water, sanitation and improved diet are also critical in driving down mortality rates (see Larkin, 1998:92; van Naerssen and Barten, 1999:230). Given inequalities in nutrition and urban infrastructure in Latin America, major disparities in patterns of disease and death are found both between and within countries (Abel and Lloyd-Sherlock, 2000:3). In richer nations in the region, such as Argentina for example, the epidemiological profile is very similar to advanced economies, with cardiovascular diseases, tumours and trauma being the major causes of mortality (Arrossi, 1996:44). This is also true in Mexico, where between 1950 and 1997 heart disease moved from fifth to first place in the rank of killer diseases, the next most important being tumours, diabetes, accidents and cerebrovascular diseases (CONAPO, 1999a:17). In poorer countries such as Guatemala, on the other hand, despite a relatively high rate of immunisation against measles (Table 5.1), this is one of the three leading causes of death in the country, the others being influenza and pneumonia (Cubitt, 1995:93). It is no coincidence that one-quarter of the population of Central America does not have access to sewerage, and 29 per cent lack running water, with levels reaching 70 per cent or more in some rural areas of El Salvador and Nicaragua (PER, 1999:165-6). As for intra-national disparities, the under-five mortality rate is three times higher among the poorest 20 per cent of the population in Southeast and Northeast Brazil, than among the wealthiest quintile (World Bank, 2000b:27).

Other infectious but eminently preventable and curable diseases such as gastroenteritic illness and diarrhoea are also common in Latin America, and continue killing enough people to rank among the ten leading causes of death in the

Table 5.1 Latin America: Selected Health Indicators

	Percentage of one-year-olds fully immunised against: Tuberculosis 1995–8	Measles 1995–8	Percentage of pregnant women with anaemia 1975–91	Cases of tuberculosis per 100,000 people (0–49 years) 1997	People living with HIV/AIDS Total number 1997	Adult rate (% 15–49 years) 1997
Argentina	99	99	26	34.6	120,000	0.69
Bolivia	85	51	54	126.7	2,600	0.07
Brazil	99	96	33	51.1	580,000	0.63
Chile	96	93	13	26.5	16,000	0.20
Colombia	82	75	24	21.7	72,000	0.36
Costa Rica	87	86	27	17.7	10,000	0.55
Cuba	99	99	47	13.0	1,400	0.02
Dominican Republic	85	95	—	69.2	83,000	1.89
Ecuador	98	88	17	79.8	18,000	0.28
El Salvador	99	98	14	28.0	18,000	0.58
Guatemala	88	81	45	28.2	27,000	0.52
Honduras	96	99	14	67.4	43,000	1.46
Mexico	93	89	41	25.0	180,000	0.35
Nicaragua	96	71	36	64.5	4,100	0.19
Panama	99	96	—	39.2	9,000	0.61
Paraguay	83	—	44	39.2	3,200	0.13
Peru	96	90	53	172.6	72,000	0.56
Uruguay	99	92	20	22.2	5,200	0.33
Venezuela	80	94	29	26.3	82,000	0.69

Sources: UNDP (1995: Table A2.6), UNDP (2000: Table 29), World Bank (1996: Table 7).
Note: — = no data.

continent (Curto de Casas, 1994:237). Frequently termed 'diseases of poverty', these find fertile terrain not only in rural areas, but in the peri-urban settlements of Latin American cities, where housing is often overcrowded and there is limited or no provision of clean, piped domestic water, sewerage systems, and rubbish collection. In Metropolitan Buenos Aires, for example, the post neo-natal mortality rate is 80 per cent higher on the periphery of the city, where there are the worst housing conditions (and lowest levels of health insurance), than in the centrally located, and far wealthier, Federal District (Arrossi, 1996:56).[1] In Porto Alegre, Brazil, pneumonia is the leading cause of infant death in irregular low-income settlements, with the incidence being six times higher than in better-off areas of the city (Satterthwaite, 1993:91). Coupled with the polarisation of incomes, service and infrastructure deficiencies in poor neighbourhoods are largely responsible for the fact that the poor are disproportionately likely to suffer infectious diseases and malnutrition as well as, or instead of, more 'modern' disorders (Phillips and Verhasselt, 1994:15).

Mental health problems also seem to be skewed towards low-income populations and environments. While mental conditions can clearly occur as a result of individual heredity, genetic malfunction and so on, the contexts in which people live and work also have a significant role to play (Larkin,1998:98; Paltiel, 1993). This is especially so in the context of 'common mental disorders' (CMD), which describe 'non-psychotic mental disorders or neurotic disorders, manifest with a mixture of somatic, anxiety and depressive symptoms' (Patel *et al.*, 1999:1462).

Aside from the fact that physical ill-health undermines people's mental well-being, the anxieties attached to inadequate or insecure jobs and housing also constitute serious sources of stress, especially where people have migrated to cities and lack the support networks that may have been provided by kin in their areas of origin (Blue, 1996:96; Satterthwaite, 1993:108). As Ekblad (1993:127) sums up, mental disease can be a long-term outcome of stress arising in situations where individuals are prevented from satisfying their needs, whether in respect of quality of life and health, self-esteem, a sense of belonging, or self-realisation (see also Paltiel, 1993:139–41). Mapping the incidence of mental disorders in Latin America would certainly seem to indicate that poverty is not an inconsequential factor (Patel *et al.*, 1999; see also Box 5.1). A study of São Paulo carried out in the early 1990s, for example, showed that the incidence of mental disorders was highest in the poorest socio-economic sub-district in the survey (at 21 per cent), and lowest (12 per cent) in the highest income area (Blue, 1996:95). There is also evidence that mental infirmity is on the increase, with Latin America's rate of neuropsychiatric disorders now being 10.2 per 100,000 persons, which is 56 per cent higher than the world average of 6.5 (Londoño and Frenk, 2000:24). At one level this is arguably due to increased visibility of psychological and psychiatric illnesses in health statistics. At another level, it may be attributable to contemporary social, demographic and economic factors, many associated with neoliberal restructuring, such as temporary and permanent migration (national and international), employment insecurity and lay-offs, the erosion of family and community support systems, and high levels of violence and civil unrest (Larkin, 1998:98; Paltiel, 1993).[2] Indeed, worldwide, common mental disorders are now the third most important cause of morbidity in adults (Patel *et al.*, 1999:1462). Yet despite these problems, and calls on the part of the World Health Organisation to redress the situation, mental health is rarely given the same attention as physical well-being (Blue, 1996:92).

Aside from health differences on grounds of income and residential environment, ethnicity is a significant factor in differentiated mortality risks, mainly because

BOX 5.1

Patel *et al.*'s Model of the Relationship Between Poverty and Common Mental Disorders

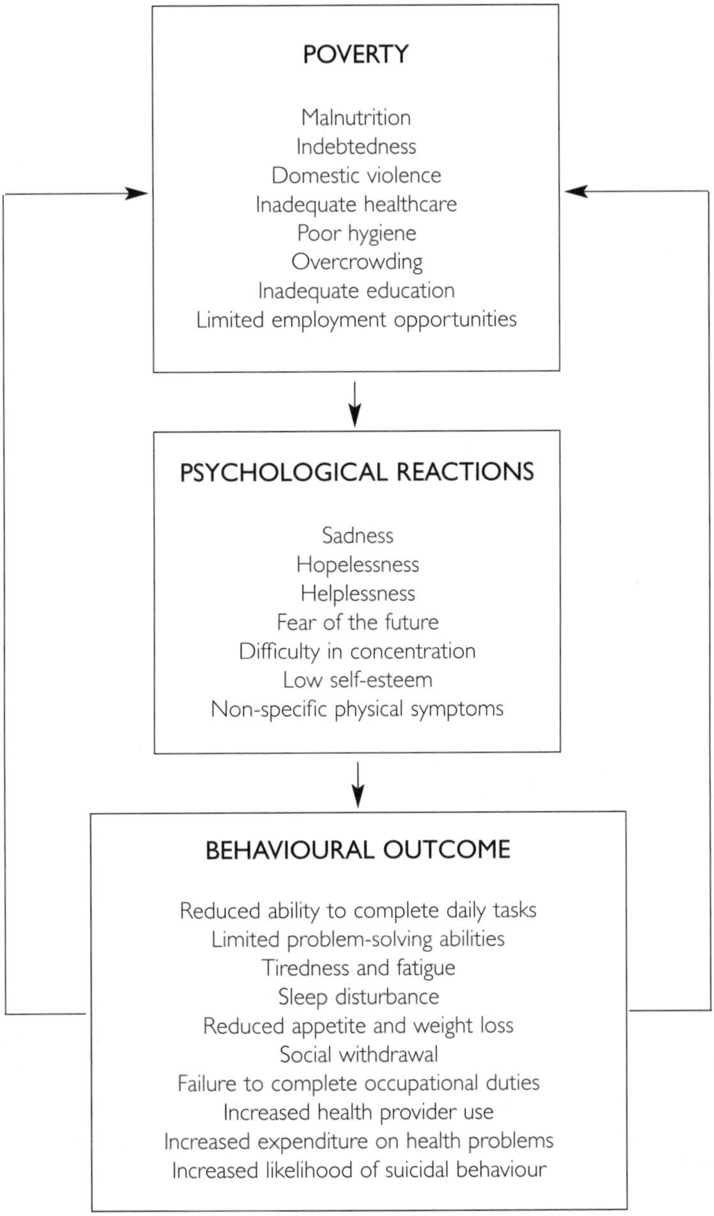

POVERTY

Malnutrition
Indebtedness
Domestic violence
Inadequate healthcare
Poor hygiene
Overcrowding
Inadequate education
Limited employment opportunities

↓

PSYCHOLOGICAL REACTIONS

Sadness
Hopelessness
Helplessness
Fear of the future
Difficulty in concentration
Low self-esteem
Non-specific physical symptoms

↓

BEHAVIOURAL OUTCOME

Reduced ability to complete daily tasks
Limited problem-solving abilities
Tiredness and fatigue
Sleep disturbance
Reduced appetite and weight loss
Social withdrawal
Failure to complete occupational duties
Increased health provider use
Increased expenditure on health problems
Increased likelihood of suicidal behaviour

Source: Patel *et al.* (1999: Fig 1).

of social and economic disadvantage among indigenous groups. In the province of Bocas de Toro in Panama, for example, which is home to the Ngobe Buglé, Teribes and Bokotas, the mortality rate from measles is 34.4 per 100,000. This is five times higher than the national average of 6.4 per 100,000 (PER, 1999:166). In Guatemala, too, 78 per cent of Garífuna children under 12 years of age had malnutrition in 1993 (ibid.) Beyond this, many indigenous populations suffer lower life expectancies. In Honduras, the life expectancy for men at a national level is 65.4 years, and for women, 70.1 years, but among the Lenca population, these figures are only 47 and 57 years respectively, and among the Pech, as low as 39 and 42 years (ibid.). In Mexico, such are the disparities in health needs between rich and poor, between urban and rural areas, and between northern and southern states of the country (the latter in each pair corresponding to the majority of the country's indigenous population) that the term 'epidemiological polarisation' has been used to describe the situation (Gómez-Dantes, 2000:129).

Contemporary health problems in Latin America

Despite pockets of 'protracted transition' (Gómez-Dantes, 2000:129), the overall shift in deaths resulting from communicable to non-communicable disease over time is not just the product of improvements in the control and prevention of the former. Although in part related, ageing is a major factor, with life expectancy in Mexico, for example, having grown from 41.9 to 75 years between 1942 and 1999 (CONAPO, 1999a). This, as noted in Chapter 4, has given rise to an increased prevalence of non-communicable diseases such as cancer, which is discussed further later in this chapter. Another set of variables relates to lifestyle changes, as in Costa Rica, where the primacy of cardiovascular diseases in mortality since 1975 has been attributed to people's increasingly sedentary lifestyles, new patterns of consumption, including smoking, and growing obesity. A study carried out by one of Costa Rica's decentralised health units (EBAIS – *Equipos Básicos de Atención Integral en Salud*/Basic Comprehensive Healthcare Teams) found that the diets among the majority of the sample were high in fats and sugars and low in fibre, and 70 per cent of people did not take regular physical exercise (Brenes, 1999). The latter is in part a function of changing work patterns, with a range of occupational health conditions also on the increase in various Latin American countries. For example, in multinational export-processing manufacturing plants on the northern Mexican border (see Chapter 8), automated technologies, intensive and oppressive work regimes involving long hours of standing and few toilet breaks, and the use of noxious chemicals, are associated with a range of health problems among women workers, such as headaches, nausea, dizziness and menstrual disorders (see Hernández Espinosa, 2000; also Pearson, 1995).

Other significant contemporary health problems facing Latin Americans include increasing dependency on drugs and alcohol (Henriques-Mueller and Yunes, 1993:57), which in many respects may be linked with the growth in mental disorders discussed earlier. In Costa Rica, despite numerous campaigns on the part of IAFA (*Instituto Sobre el Alcoholismo y Farmacodependencia*/Institute for Alcohol and Drug Dependency), an estimated 15–17 per cent of the population aged 12–70 years have a drinking problem (MEP, 1994:12). Even if distinctions are not generally made between 'hard' and 'soft drugs', there is also evidence to suggest that the average age of drug users is getting lower. Recent data from the Pan American Health Organisation suggest that, aside from alcohol, use of tobacco and illegal drugs is mounting to the extent that 3–4 per cent of secondary school students in Chile and Mexico engage in glue-sniffing, while somewhere between 4 and 16.8 per cent of their peers consume cocaine (Curto de Casas, 1994:237). Alcohol and drug use, which are frequently associated with conditions such as lung cancer, heart disease and cirrhosis of the liver, have numerous physical and mental health implications not only for users, but for their offspring and other family members (Henriques-Mueller and Yunes, 1993:57).

HIV/AIDS and other sexually transmitted diseases (STDs) are also on the rise and seem to be strongly related to the mounting incidence of casual sexual contact associated with large-scale migration and urbanisation (Larkin, 1998:97–8). Another important issue is conflict, with guerilla activity and militarisation tending to exacerbate the incidence of STDs and AIDs: first, through increases in prostitution, and second, through the withdrawal or running down of government health services (see Coates, 2001: Chapter 3). In Central America, for example, the rate of HIV/AIDS infection grew from 32.1 per million inhabitants in 1991 to 80.5 per million in 1996 and is disproportionately concentrated in the most densely settled areas (PER, 1999:167). This said, high-incidence pockets are also noted among certain groups of the population, such as the Garífuna on the north coast of Honduras.

The increase in HIV/AIDS has led to programmes of prevention in many parts of the continent. In Brazil, for example, which has one the highest rates of HIV infection in the world, the state government of São Paulo has been distributing 100,000 condoms a month to its state prisons since 1997. Rates of HIV infection are particularly high among men in detention (averaging 10 per cent as against the national rate of 0.63 per cent), and spread is more pronounced as a result of high levels of injecting drug use and sexual contact between prisoners (Scheffer and Marthe, 1999).

In Mexico, too, where around 4 in every 1000 adults are now HIV-positive (see Table 5.1), a programme for the Prevention and Control of Sexually Transmitted Diseases and HIV/AIDS was launched as part of the Programme for Reproductive

Health and Family Planning (1995–2000). This encompassed a permanent programme of education, awareness and promotion of responsible sexual behaviour, information on reproductive health and sexually-transmitted diseases, and the design of preventive measures, diagnosis, referral and notification of new cases of HIV/AIDS (see CRLP, 1997:19). Yet Chávez (1999:52) notes that conservative attitudes towards sexuality have often obstructed these interventions. For example, in Tlaquepaque on the outskirts of Guadalajara in 1995, the police stopped the public distribution of free condoms, and in Ciudad Juárez in 1997, women putting up AIDS posters were charged with 'offences against public morality and good custom'.

At another extreme, more draconian measures for containing the spread of AIDS have been implemented in Cuba where AIDS is primarily a heterosexual disease first introduced into the country by soldiers returning from Africa (Leiner, 1994:13). Being the only country to have contravened World Health Organisation guidelines by introducing mass testing and the quarantining of seropositive individuals, Cuba's strategy has often met with severe criticism. As Lumsden (1996) contends, however, aside from the fact that similar public health measures have been used by the Cuban authorities to control other epidemics such as dengue and African swine fever, quarantined individuals have been well treated in respect of continuing to be paid a full salary, receiving high quality treatment and so on. Moreover, although the measures used have often been linked with Cuba's traditionally antipathetic attitude towards gay men, these have arguably been less homophobic than in other countries such as Costa Rica where early reaction to the disease involved posters which blatantly identified 'risk groups' such as homosexuals, drug addicts and prostitutes (ibid.:165; see also Chapter 6).

Accidents and violence are also on the increase in Latin America, as discussed later in the context of gender differences in morbidity and mortality.

Health and health care provision

Accepting that various, mainly indigenous, populations in Latin America have recourse to their own forms of healthcare, in respect of official systems, 60 per cent of health expenditure in Latin America in 1990 was by the public sector, with average spending across the continent being 4 per cent of GNP, amounting to $105 US per person. While less than one-tenth of average public expenditure on health in advanced economies, this figure outstripped all other regions of the South, with the average for developing countries at the time being US$41 per capita (World Bank, 1993:52, Table 3.1). Yet there is by no means uniformity in levels and types of health financing in the region. Cubitt (1995:94) identifies four main health systems in Latin America, all of which are accompanied by some degree of private practice:[3]

1) Countries with state national health systems in which the Ministry of Health is wholly or mainly responsible for the provision of services, and there is minimal participation by the private sector. Examples of this type include Cuba and Nicaragua.
2) Countries with private, state or joint insurance-supported systems, where health services are owned and administered by the Ministry of Health, the social security system or the private sector. Examples include Argentina, Brazil, Costa Rica, Mexico, Panama and Venezuela.
3) Countries where care is provided mainly by the Ministry of Health, but with some participation by the social security system. Examples include Belize, Bolivia, Colombia, Dominican Republic, Ecuador, El Salvador, Guatemala, Honduras, Paraguay and Peru.
4) Countries where the provision of health services are provided by the Ministry of Health and the social security system in equal parts. The only example of this is Uruguay.

Although, theoretically, most of these systems provide care for all members of society, Cubitt (1995:94–5) notes a number of features which discriminate against poorer sectors of the population. One is a long-term concentration of health services in urban areas such that more isolated rural groups lose out. In Costa Rica, for example, the Health Ministry (*Ministerio de Salud*), which is the leading provider of healthcare, effectively only covers around 80 per cent of the population given the large numbers of people living in dispersed rural communities (Oficina de la Primera Dama *et al*, 1999:71). In Guatemala, the nearest health post to one-third of the rural population is 12 kilometres away, often entailing a two-hour walk. Even then, 60 per cent of these health posts are described as having 'unsatisfactory equipment' (PNUD, 1998:52–3). In Chiapas, Mexico, Coates (2001: Chapter 3) notes that public provision of healthcare is so limited that non-governmental and church-affiliated organisations often have to step in to fill the breach.

Another problem has been the traditional skew towards bio-medically based curative systems usually characterised by expenditure on hospitals, high-tech equipment and medical specialisms such as surgery which are arguably irrelevant when the bulk of the population suffers from preventable, infectious diseases, and the rich can afford to pay for private treatment (Cubitt, 1995:95; see also Abel and Lloyd-Sherlock, 2000:2; Larkin, 1998:95). Other problems include the fact that public systems are often underfunded and lose the best practitioners to the private sector (or overseas). This leaves the poor with an inferior service to those protected by social security or who have the resources to go privately. It also means that the poor spend a disproportionately high amount of their income on health needs. In 1992, for example, the poorest decile of the Colombian population spent 12 per cent of their household income on health, and in Ecuador this was as much as 17 per cent (Londoño and Frenk, 2000:25). In many respects inequalities between rich and poor have been exacerbated by recent developments in primary healthcare, and by neoliberal economic restructuring. Another factor noted as dissuading indigenous groups in particular from using public health services is the fact that Spanish is usually the only language used in formal institutions (Coates, 2001: Chapter 3).

From primary health care to selective primary health care

While developments in healthcare for most of the twentieth century in Latin America followed a centralised, technological model, in the aftermath of a joint World Health Organisation and UNICEF conference in Alma Ata in 1978, primary healthcare (PHC) became the new prescription for developing regions. Founded in experiences from socialist countries such as China, Cuba and Tanzania, the primary healthcare approach was based on a holistic conceptualisation of health as dependent on a wide range of social, economic and environmental influences. In turn, PHC called for intersectoral strategies to reduce poverty and inequality, to galvanise efforts in preventive and promotional as well as curative activities, and to decentralise healthcare across national territories and populations (Asthana, 1994b:182; see also Harrison, 1991; Larkin, 1998:95; van Naerssen and Barten, 1999:236). Part and parcel of the primary healthcare approach, evolving as it did in the wake of global tendencies towards decentralisation and democratisation in the 1980s, was the encouragement of greater community participation in preventative health and the delivery of services. In Latin America this took the form of 'SILOS' (*sistemas locales de salud*/ local healthcare systems) (Curto de Casas, 1994:239). In Costa Rica, for example, where PHC was formally adopted in 1983 and oriented to the most vulnerable sectors of the population, each of the country's 800 'health zones' is assigned a comprehensive healthcare team (EBAIS – see earlier) responsible for first-level healthcare and referrals to higher order facilities. Each team, in turn, is supported by a local community-based health committee (see Rivas, 1999:70; World Bank, 2000b:153).

Despite the hypothetical, and in some cases proven, benefits of primary healthcare, PHC has never attracted sufficient support to supplant the 'top-down' model. Instead, it has usually existed as part of a common 'two-tier' system of welfare services more generally in Latin America, where the rich use the private sector, leaving poorer groups in society to 'secondary' and frequently underfunded state services (see Gywnne and Kay, 2000:150; Harrison, 1991:256). Moreover, partly as a result of the encroaching burdens of recession and adjustment from the 1980s onwards, comprehensive forms of primary care have been seen by many donors as 'too ambitious, expensive and uncertain in outcome' (Larkin, 1998:105; see also Portugal and Matamala, 1993:271). In practice, this has usually meant that PHC has been 'downsized' to a targeted approach known as selective primary healthcare (SPHC).

SPHC isolates particular conditions on the basis of prevalence, morbidity, mortality and feasibility of control (including cost effectiveness), where 'quantifiable and measurable outcomes' constitute a primary criterion (Larkin, 1998:101; van Naerssen and Barten, 1999:236). SPHC packages favour low-cost interventions such as immunisation for a restricted range of mainly childhood diseases such as measles and whooping cough, or oral rehydration therapy for diarrhoeal conditions (Asthana, 1994b:183). While this selective approach may be in some senses more efficient and save lives in the short term, the disregard for underlying problems of poverty, malnutrition, inadequate sanitary infrastructure and related services does not bode well for the longer term (Larkin, 1998:105–6). Moreover, the participatory element tends to be limited to an implementing rather than decision-making or policy input on the part of local populations which does very little to empower the poor or to change fundamental social and economic inequalities as originally envisioned by PHC proponents (Asthana, 1994b:195; see also Beall, 1995:216). As noted by van Naerssen and Barten (1999:235), 'Decentralisation ... is often a hidden form of saving, whereby the local level is supposed to organise its own income, including, among other things, charging fees for health services.' In Mexico, for instance, the PHC system administered by the Health Ministry (SSA/*Secretaría de Salubridad y Asistencia*) from 1982, has been described as extremely top-down, leaving little scope for meaningful citizen input (Harrison, 1991:243–4). Moreover, the targeting of women in participatory health strategies on the basis of their identities as mothers, and as instruments to reach children, leaves a lot to be desired in terms of gender, as discussed later in the chapter.

Neoliberal economic restructuring: the impacts on health and healthcare in Latin America

As for the evolving shape of the health sector in general, numerous Latin American countries undergoing structural adjustment programmes (SAPs) in the 1980s and 1990s saw declining public budget allocations to health compounded by sharp falls in GNP (see Stewart, 1995:182–4). In Bolivia, for instance, central government health spending per capita plummeted by two-thirds between 1980 and 1984 (Asthana, 1994a:59). In Mexico, the real value of health expenditure per capita in 1987 was only 41 per cent of its 1981 level (Stewart, 1995:203). Alongside general cuts in health expenditure, it is also significant that figures for the 1980s show that many adjusting countries (including Argentina, Bolivia, Brazil and Venezuela) attached lower priority to environmental health, primary healthcare, preventative medicine, and programmes for the poor (as opposed to hospitals and hospital equipment for example) (ibid.:186). This also occurred in Nicaragua where, on top of the destruction of primary medical infrastructure wrought by the Contra War, economic adjustment in the late 1980s and early 1990s resulted in the erosion of several basic health programmes. Immunisation against major preventable diseases such as diphtheria dropped by 23 per cent between 1988 and 1994, tetanus immunisations by 44 per cent, and measles by 61 per cent (CISAS, 1997:88). In this light, it is no surprise that Nicaragua has suffered rising rates of infant, child and maternal morbidity and mortality in the aftermath of adjustment, not to mention increased numbers of deaths from respiratory and gastro-intestinal illnesses (ibid.:87).

In turn, declining funds for urban environmental improvements so integral to disease prevention have had serious effects, with epidemics of dengue, cholera, hepatitis, typhoid and tuberculosis resurfacing during the 1980s and 1990s (Asthana, 1994a:59; Ferguson and Maurer, 1986). In Peru for example, cholera was responsible for morbidity and mortality on a wide scale in the early 1990s (Phillips and Verhasselt, 1994:14), ultimately spreading as far as Mexico (Cubitt, 1995:93). When it hit Central America in 1991 it took as long as six years to bring it under control in two of the poorest countries in the Isthmus: Guatemala and Honduras (PER, 1999:167).

Besides shrinking levels of public expenditure for disease prevention and control, declining household incomes and rising food prices (often triggered by the lifting of government subsidies on basic staples), have posed additional threats to people's health and well-being. In Mexico, for example, annual per capita consumption of staples such as milk dropped from 112 to 101 litres per person between 1980 and 1987, beans from around 18 to 14 kilogrammes, and corn from more than 200 kilogrammes to only 142 (Cordera Campos and González Tiburcio, 1991:32–3). In Nicaragua, the per capita consumption of food staples in general also fell by 25 per cent between 1989 and 1992 (CISAS, 1997:87). Elsewhere in Latin America, such as in Peru and Uruguay, increased poverty reduced the availability of calories per capita in the early 1990s to levels below those of 1965 (Curto de Casas, 1994:236).

Although between 1970 and 1997 malnutrition in Latin America as a whole decreased from 21 per cent to 7.2 per cent (UNICEF, 1998:21), between 1979 and 1986 numbers of low birthweight babies increased in parts of Brazil, Colombia, the Dominican Republic, El Salvador, and Mexico (Stewart, 1995:189). In Mexico, three diseases that became more important causes of death among children during the 1980s – dysentery, malnutrition and anaemia – are strongly linked with socio-economic deterioration, in the first case due to poor hygiene, and in the latter two to dietary insufficiency (Langer *et al.*, 1991:211). Indeed, infant deaths from anaemia in Mexico carried on rising, from 6.3 to 7.9 per 100,000 live births, between 1993 and 1995 (World Bank, 2000b:164). Although by the late 1990s many countries in the region had seen an increase in resources spent on health care (see Table 5.2), and despite a rhetoric of equity and efficiency accompanying the growing participation of the private sector (Abel and Lloyd-Sherlock, 2000:12), the prospect of growing disparities between the quality of state provision and other health service providers means that fundamental inequalities in healthcare coverage are unlikely to be redressed in the immediate future. These problems may well be exacerbated by the on-going liberalisation of labour markets in which progressively fewer workers are likely to be protected by social security (see Chapter 8). Added to this, the progressive dismantling of subsidies on basic foodstuffs, the rising privatisation of services and infrastructure in general, and the mounting proportion of elderly

Table 5.2 Latin America: Selected Healthcare Indicators

	Doctors per 100,000 people 1992–5	Nurses per 100,000 people 1992–5	Public expenditure on health (as percentage of GDP)	
			1990	1996–8
Argentina	268	54	4.2	4.7
Bolivia	51	25	0.9	1.1
Brazil	134	41	3.0	3.4
Chile	108	42	2.0	2.4
Colombia	105	49	1.0	1.5
Costa Rica	126	95	6.6	6.7
Cuba	518	752	4.9	8.2
Dominican Republic	77	20	1.6	1.6
Ecuador	111	34	1.5	2.5
El Salvador	91	38	1.4	2.6
Guatemala	—	130	0.9	1.5
Honduras	22	17	2.9	2.7
Mexico	85	241	2.1	2.8
Nicaragua	82	56	1.0	4.4
Panama	119	98	4.6	5.8
Paraguay	67	10	0.4	2.6
Peru	73	49	1.0	2.2
Uruguay	309	61	1.2	1.9
Venezuela	194	77	2.0	1.0

Source: UNDP (2000: Tables 10 & 16).
Note: — = no data.

people in populations (Chapters 3 & 4), is likely to severely undermine the capacity (not to mention the will) of Latin American governments to ensure more adequate healthcare. Homedes *et al.* (2000:76) note of health reform in El Salvador in the 1990s, for example, that this has merely 'contributed to an increase in social tensions and a return to a violent past by failing to increase equity, by neglecting to satisfy public health needs and by failing to increase the quality of medical care' (see also Butler, 1999 on Nicaragua). This also has important implications for gender, as noted by Pearson (2000b:231) in relation to Cuba which, relatively speaking, has had a model health service:

> the increasing cost of services results in an increase in the threshold of sickness at which the poor seek medical assistance from whichever source, implying an absorption into the household of care and management of such individuals. There has also been an increase in self-diagnosis and treatment where there are significant cost barriers to access. While it is certainly true that men as well as women face these constraints in reduction in access to health care, it also appears to be true that the implications for the re-domestication of health activities tends to fall on women in line with traditional sexual divisions of labour in the private sphere.

Gender, health and healthcare: conceptual perspectives

Leading on from the above, and as identified at the beginning of this chapter, gender is a significant factor in health throughout the world, not only in respect of access and provision of healthcare, but also in terms of gender-differentiated patterns of morbidity and mortality. These issues are not only interrelated, but are also influenced by a wide range of economic, social and institutional structures which embody difference and inequality between men and women. One attempt to carve a route through some of the complexities in gendered patterns of health and healthcare is the framework developed by Sundari Ravindran (1997) which divides the factors affecting women's health status into four main categories:

1) 'background factors', which range from international factors such as North–South power relations and the transnational pharmaceutical and medical supplies industry to grassroots phenomena such as community structures and resource distribution;
2) 'health service' factors extending from the financing and organisation of health-care at a national level, to local-level issues such as access to services and local priorities;
3) issues relating to women's 'status' such as autonomy and access to resources;
4) women's illness burdens and health-seeking behaviour.

Sundari Ravindran's model highlights the ways in which physiological, psychological, material, social and political factors are so closely intertwined that it is difficult to deal with any aspect of gender, health and healthcare in isolation. These notions are echoed by Gómez Gómez (1993:x) in her introduction to the book on *Gender, Women and Health in the Americas* published by the Pan-American Health Organisation (PAHO).

> There are two basic mechanisms through which the gender construct influences the health of individuals and the role they play in health development: socialisation and institutional control. Society, through an internalisation of the expectations that govern the paradigms of maleness and femaleness, conditions men and women in different ways, motivating them to make different choices from among alternative behaviours that have varying implications for their own health and that of others. Then, reinforcing individual mechanisms of motivation, institutions ensure that those expectations are fulfilled by rewarding adherence to male and female stereotypes and penalising deviation from them, by facilitating or hindering – depending on the sex of the individual in question – access to certain activities or positions that command different levels of compensation, and, finally, by paying men and women differently for the same work.

Adding weight to the relevance of these analytical perspectives is the evolution of the women's health movement in Latin America and the Caribbean. From the 1980s onwards, regional approaches to women's health care at the grassroots became increasingly guided by feminist principles wherein socio-political and cultural factors were regarded as inseparable from women's health needs and existing systems (Portugal and Matamala, 1993:269). A gender approach to health accordingly needed to focus on the dialectical relationship between biology and the social environment (de los Ríos, 1993; Gómez Gómez, 1993a). The extent to which this call for holism has translated significantly into practice in the formal echelons of health services thus far is in doubt, however, as detailed later in the chapter.

Gender, morbidity and health in Latin America

Gender-differentiated morbidity patterns

As in other parts of the world, men and women in Latin America often have different experiences of morbidity. Some of these differences stem from what might be regarded as physiological differences between women and men, although, as suggested above, a narrow bio-medical view of health is inadequate to grasp the vast range of social and economic factors responsible for mediating the extent and nature of vulnerability among women and men to different types of disease. In short, 'inherent' biological attributes rarely operate in a gender-neutral environment. This said, there are three main types of health issue in which men's and women's different physiologies are crucial in exposing them to different kinds of health risk.

The first of these is that women have a genetic disposition to better survival rates than men, as evidenced in longer life expectancy. Latin America is no exception in this regard. While the world average life expectancy is 69.1 years for women, and 64.9 years for men, the figures are 73.2 years and 66.7 years respectively for Latin America and the Caribbean as a whole (UNDP, 2000:164, Table 2; see also Table 4.3). At the same time, Latin American life expectancies continue to trail behind high-income regions where women and men can expect to live for 81 and 74.6 years respectively (ibid.). Moreover, there is considerable intra-regional diversity in Latin America, with female and male life expectancies being as high as 79.1 and 74.4 years in Costa Rica, but as low as 67.6 and 61.7 years in Guatemala (ibid.). There are also significant intra-national differences, as discussed earlier in relation to the generally lower life expectancies among indigenous populations in the region.

While higher life expectancies for women represent, in one sense, a positive indication of their health status, it is important to recognise that women suffer more frequently from ill-health during their lifetimes, and their comparative longevity places them at greater risk of age-related degenerative diseases (de los Ríos, 1993; Gómez Gómez, 1993). Added to the fact that women's longer life expectancy means greater vulnerability to illnesses such as Parkinson's disease and neoplasms than men, is a second physiologically-based gender difference in health, that of organ-specific conditions. While men suffer testicular and prostate cancer, women fall victim to the risk of cervical, uterine, ovarian and breast cancer. Notwithstanding differential severity and spread patterns of these conditions, some cancers are related to contraception taken by women, and female deaths from cancer in Latin America are often unduly high due to limited access to preventive and curative technology (see Restrepo, 1993).

A third major physiological reason for differences in health between men and women, which also helps to account for the fact that the latter are prone to more health problems over the life course, relates to pregnancy and child-bearing. Again, however, it is difficult to treat this as solely physiological when the numbers of children women have, and with what frequency, is heavily affected by social factors such as gendered norms of motherhood, decisions over fertility, family planning services, and the attention accorded to women's health during their reproductive years by health services and society at large. Evidence that care for women's reproductive health needs is wanting in Latin America is found in high rates of maternal mortality, as discussed in Chapter 4. Moreover, iron-deficiency-induced anaemia, which is particularly common during pregnancy, is often much higher than in developed regions. As many as 17 per cent of women in Latin America aged 15–49 years are estimated to be anaemic compared with 8 per cent of their counterparts in North America (Gueri *et al.*, 1993).

Gender roles and health

Beyond women's and men's relative exposure to health risks on account of their different physiological make-up, most other gendered patterns of morbidity and mortality in Latin America reflect social and economic disparities between male and female populations. Some socially conditioned differences begin to have an impact in early life. Although excess female mortality during the first five years of childhood is often regarded as a primarily Asiatic and African phenomenon, this is also found in a number of Latin American countries, particularly those which are poorer and/or have lower life expectancies. In Peru, Guatemala, El Salvador and Paraguay, for example, female children bear a disproportionate risk of dying from common childhood diseases. This is attributable to the under-nutrition of young girls relative to their male counterparts, and to the greater attention given to immunising boys, and/or using health services when they fall ill (Gómez Gómez, 1993b).

In adult life, women's social roles as mothers encompass numerous responsibilities which place them at above-average risk of contracting disease and/or weakening their defences to combat infection. One major set of obligations is women's position as primary carers within households and families. Because it is women who tend to care most closely for sick children and relatives, handling body wastes and so on, it also follows that women are more likely to contract diseases from others. These problems are compounded where households have low incomes and live in poorly serviced, overcrowded dwelling conditions. Over and above caring for the sick, conducting daily domestic labour under conditions where water, electricity and fuel supplies are wanting, and where there is no connection to public sewerage networks and/or no rubbish collection, poses a number of risks to women, including exhaustion and infection through environmental contamination. Health hazards also arise from tasks such as cooking in enclosed spaces over open fires, or collecting and transporting water from rivers or public standpipes (see Browner, 1989; Chant, 1984; Fritz and Wagner, 1993; Moser, 1982; Satterthwaite, 1993; also Figure 5.1).

Many of these health risks have intensified with structural adjustment programmes in Latin American countries. The effects of reduced subsidies on basic goods, clampdowns on wage rises, and cutbacks in social spending are widely shown to be gender-differentiated, and to affect women and women's health in a variety of ways (see also Chapter 3). It is usually women who are forced into seeking greater amounts of work in the wage economy in order to make ends meet. This is

Figure 5.1 The struggle for hygiene: outdoor 'kitchen' in low-income settlement, Querétaro, Mexico (Photograph by Sylvia Chant)

compounded by having to work harder in the home as well to compensate for reduced services from the social sector and the need to stretch lower incomes further still. The result is massively increased labour burdens which make women more likely than ever to experience fatigue and susceptibility to ill-health (Moser, 1992; Potter, 2000:88). In turn, the stress attached to these processes is likely to exacerbate the situation whereby women are more prone than men to suffer common mental disorders such as anxiety, depression, inability to concentrate, and sleeplessness (Blue, 1996:92–3; Patel *et al.*, 1999).

Gender relations, masculinities and health

HIV/AIDS

If one major set of health risks can be ascribed to adult women's gender roles, then others are more directly attributable to gender relations, with sexually transmitted diseases and HIV/AIDS constituting prime examples. Although men have traditionally been more affected by HIV/AIDS than women, mainly because of the prevalence of homosexual transmission, the gender balance is beginning to shift in various parts of Latin America. In Mexico, for example, although the dominant route for HIV transmission is still through homosexual and bisexual males, increasing numbers of women are being infected by their husbands and it is predicted that heterosexual transmission will become the primary route in the near future (Rivas *et al.*, 1999:274; see also Sufía, 1992). In Central America, heterosexual transmission is already responsible for 62.6 per cent of cases of HIV (PER, 1999: 167), and elsewhere in the region, the biggest rises are now registered among women. In Brazil, the male–female ratio of HIV infection dropped from 28:1 to 5:1 between 1985 and 1991 due to the increase in heterosexual transmission (CRLP, 1997:60). In Argentina, the ratio fell from 12.6:1 to 3.6:1 between 1998 and 1996 (ibid.:25). Given on-going male dominance in the majority of heterosexual partnerships, and the low-incidence of condom use among men (see Chapter 4), women may have limited scope to protect themselves from infection, which is serious given women's greater physiological vulnerability. While there is a 1 in 500 chance of men passing the HIV virus to women in a single act of vaginal intercourse, there is only a 1000 to 1 chance of women passing it on to men. The fact that women's risk of contracting HIV is two to four times greater than men's in unprotected vaginal intercourse owes to higher concentrations of the virus in men's secretions and because of the larger surface area in women which is exposed to these secretions (UN, 2000:68). Besides this, women tend to have far fewer sexual partners than men, especially once married or in a stable relationship, which reduces the relative risk to their menfolk (Foreman, 1999:6). One observation offered in relation to the increase in heterosexual transmission is that men are often reluctant to admit to engaging in homosexual relationships, thereby concealing information that in other circumstances might encourage their female partners to exert stronger pressure in favour of protected sex (see Bliss, 2001 for discussion and references; also Chapter 6). Moreover, the fact that health programmes often misguidedly focus on educating women on promiscuity and condom use is likely to have a part to play (see Coates, 2001).

VIOLENCE

In a similar vein, although violence is a serious health problem for women and men throughout Latin America, and there are different types of violence, women are the main victims (Bolis, 1993). The Guatemalan Lesbian Collective, Colectivo Mujer-Es Somos (1997:62) describes violence as 'the force exerted over one or more persons to oblige them to do things they do not wish to do' (my translation). Women's primary experiences of this fall under the aegis of 'domestic violence' which encompasses four main forms: physical, psychological or emotional, economic and sexual (Venguer *et al.*, 1998). Despite elaborate typologies of domestic violence, accurate information is extremely hard to obtain because denunciation of violent acts is much less frequent than their incidence, there is no system of compulsory notification of domestic violence, and, for many authorities, domestic violence is invisible (Claramunt, 1997:91). These caveats aside, a national survey on demography and health in Colombia carried out by the family planning organisation Profamilia (see Chapter 4), revealed that 33 per cent of a sample of 5,390 women reported suffering psychological violence, 20 per cent, physical violence, and 10 per cent sexual violence (Venguer *et al.*, 1998:12; see also Chapter 6). Some of the more specific health consequences of gender-based violence are given in Box 5.2.

BOX 5.2

Health Consequences of Gender-based Violence

Fatal outcomes
Suicide
Homicide

Non-fatal outcomes

a) Physical health consequences
- STDs
- Injury
- Pelvic inflammation
- Chronic pelvic pain
- Miscarriage
- Gynaecological problems
- Headaches
- Asthma
- Alcohol or drug abuse
- Irritable bowel syndrome
- Harmful health behaviours (e.g. smoking, unprotected sex)
- Partial or permanent disability

b) Mental health consequences
- Post-traumatic stress disorder
- Depression
- Anxiety
- Sexual dysfunction
- Multiple personality disorder
- Obsessive–compulsive disorder

Source: Heise *et al.* (1994: Box 3).

Most domestic violence is directed by men towards women and children, especially when it is economic, physical or sexual in nature. Around 90 per cent of sexual attacks, for example, are committed by men against women and children (Claramunt, 1997:64; see also Henthorne, 2000; Moser and McIlwaine, 2000).

Claramunt (1997:46) argues in relation to Costa Rica that this gender bias results from the fact that violent behaviour (or behaviour that can lead to violent acts, such as heavy drinking), is endorsed through men's socialisation. For example, men are often encouraged to use violence rather than conciliation to solve conflicts, to play war games in which violence is valued, to subscribe to the idea that caring functions are a female rather than male domain, and that they have power over their wives and children. The latter is exacerbated by the fact that men often marry women younger than themselves. Men may also be unconcerned about social and family legislation regarding violence because of scant public intervention in 'private matters'. On top of this, women's own internalisation of gender stereotypes adds to the syndrome, notably the idea that being a 'good wife' entails obedience and submission. This is often exacerbated by pressure from wider family networks for women to keep quiet, women's economic dependence on their menfolk, and victims' beliefs that their complaints will not be taken seriously by the authorities (ibid.:125; Salas, 1998; see also Moser and McIlwaine, 2000 on Colombia). Indeed, Claramunt (1997:60) points out that many instances of domestic violence in Costa Rica have conventionally been regarded as contraventions rather than crimes. Even where women and children might be incapacitated by violence for up to ten days, husbands and fathers usually get away with modest fines or short prison sentences of between 3 and 30 days.

Leading on from this, de los Ríos (1993:11) observes that 'in most countries violence against women continues to be sanctioned by custom, and even by law, because it is considered a "private crime" and is therefore not penalised' (see also Dobles Oropeza, 1998). In some instances, for example, certain forms of violence against women are not contemplated in the legal codes which clearly makes it difficult to correct them (Bolis, 1993:237). Rape within marriage, which is not legally defined as a crime in many countries in Latin America, is one of the clearest expressions of this (ibid.:242). Moreover, even when laws do exist with regard to male violence towards women, they are often far from adequate or effective. In Honduras, for example, 'domestic' violence is not considered a crime unless, paradoxically, it occurs *outside* the home.[4] In Paraguay, the Penal Code exempts from punishment men who wound, abuse or even kill their wives, when the latter are found committing adultery (Bolis, 1993:241). Quite apart from the fact that the adultery rule does not apply when wives kill husbands, in several cases female adultery is considered a sufficiently extenuating circumstance to absolve men who resort to murder (ibid.).

The women's movement has been critically important in drawing attention to domestic violence and in forcing changes in legislation and institutional practice to curb its incidence. Domestic violence has been recognised as a public health problem in Costa Rica since 1994, for example, and in Mexico in 1997 the government finally made it illegal for men to beat or rape their wives (Chávez, 1999:58). One significant aspect of the new Mexican legislation is that husbands now face the same jail sentences (of between 8 and 14 years), as other men who commit acts of (sexual) violence on their spouses (ibid.:59). Individual country initiatives (on which there is further discussion in Chapter 7), have been buttressed by regional programmes against domestic violence, such as that organised by the Latin American Institute of the United Nations for the Prevention and Treatment of Delinquency (ILANUD/*Instituto Latinoamericano de Naciones Unidas para la Prevención y Tratamiento del Delincuente*) for Central America. Operating out of its headquarters in San José, Costa Rica, the aim of the programme is to sensitise and train civil servants in the judiciary, police and educational establishments in matters of domestic violence as a means of prevention and control (see ILANUD, 1999). These kinds of initiatives would seem to be paramount given that in Colombia, murder is now the main cause of death among women of child-bearing age, and this is not happening in the street, but in women's own homes at the hands of husbands or boyfriends (de los Ríos, 1993:11).

As far as violence against men is concerned, this is much less likely to be domestic in nature, and is more commonly meted out by other men, notwithstanding that reliable statistical data on male-on-male violence, often motivated by homophobia, is also difficult to obtain (Schifter, 1998). Accepting inevitable inaccuracies, in Calí, Colombia, violence is adjudged to have affected everyone's life expectancy, but to have disproportionately affected men who are currently estimated to lose 4.8 years of life through violence compared with only 0.4 years among women (Pineda, 2000:75). In Mexico in 1999, homicides were the second leading cause of death among men aged 15–29 years (accounting for 22 per cent of the total), compared with the fourth cause of death among their female peers, taking the lives of only 5.8 per cent of women in this age group (CONAPO, 1999a). In Latin America as a whole, three out of four young persons who die from violence are male (Figueroa, 1998a).

The role of violence as a major health risk for men fits into a more general pattern whereby male morbidity and mortality is more likely than women's to occur as a result of behavioural factors such as risk-taking, self abuse, or attempts to abuse others, including drinking, smoking, car accidents and fighting (Henriques Mueller and Yunes, 1993; Reyes Zapata *et al.*, 1999:8). Notwithstanding that military conscription and guerilla warfare have an important part to play here, especially in the light of historically high rates of conflict in various parts of Latin America, Jiménez (1996:45) points out that men have to prove their masculinity all their lives, and often at high personal cost. This, he claims, is obvious in the high rate of accidents (through work and traffic), affective deficiencies, imprisonment for aggression, and isolation through lack of communication (ibid.).

Gender, health-seeking behaviour and access to healthcare

On top of differences in men's and women's health problems, there are also gender differences in patterns of health-seeking behaviour. A common observation about men, for example, is that they typically delay their visits to medical personnel until their conditions are quite advanced. This is not to say, however, that they do not make their conditions known at home, and in the process rely on informal care and additional labour from wives or mothers. Moreover, while women often make greater use of formal health services, this is not necessarily for themselves, but on behalf of other household and family members, particularly children. Despite the fact that women's needs to use health services are often greater, whether on their own or their children's account, access to state healthcare in their own right is often limited by the fact that entitlements to public healthcare and social security are frequently determined by the 'formality' of employment (see Chapter 8). Given that women are disproportionately concentrated in the informal sector, or work in the home, they are less protected than men, at least on an independent basis (Gómez Gómez, 1993a:xii). Additional factors noted as discouraging women from using health services include offputting and time-consuming bureaucracy, limited confidence in dealing with health officials because of women's frequent lack of experience with formal institutions, and the often authoritarian and patronising attitudes of doctors, the bulk of whom have traditionally been male (see Coates, 2001).

In order to get around some of these problems, the Primary Healthcare initiative launched by the World Health Organisation back in 1978 has tried to to get more medicine into communities rather than making people seek help outside, often by involving local women in preventive and curative work (see Beall, 1995:216). In Chiapas, for example, where women have long been caretakers of community health in their roles as *curanderas* (healers) and/or *parteras* (midwives), female health promoters (*promotoras*) have been trained by local clinics to advise their neighbours on aspects of preventive healthcare such as cooking and sanitation (Coates, 2001).

Participatory approaches to healthcare provision have proven to be successful in many cases, as exemplified by a recent programme to improve maternal and neonatal health in Bolivia (see Box 5.3). By the same token, participatory approaches can also act to reinforce gender inequalities. For example, the Chilean initiative *Salud con la Gente* (Health with the People), set up in 1995, was nominally interested in recognising and supporting social organisations in health. However, another agenda was to place greater responsibility for health in the hands of individuals and communities, and to capitalise on unpaid female labour at the grassroots (Gideon, 2000). Apart from the fact that this added to women's responsibilities in the productive and reproductive economy, meaning that willingness and ability to

BOX 5.3

Women's Participation in a Health Project in Bolivia

The USAID-funded Warmi Project was set up in the remote rural province of Inquisivi in Bolivia between the late 1980s and early 1990s and was implemented by the Save the Children/USA Bolivia field office. 'Warmi' means 'woman' in Aymara, which is spoken in this part of Bolivia, and reflects the fact that the project was not only oriented to women, but was also about involving them in its execution.

The Warmi project used a community-based approach to improve maternal and neonatal health in an area traditionally lacking access to formal heath services. In three areas of the province, the project worked with various groups of women, sometimes based on existing ones, in other cases representing new formations, in a wide range of aspects of maternal and neonatal health. The methodology was highly participatory, and based to a very large degree on women determining the most pressing needs within their communities. Other activities included training and demonstration sessions, literacy programmes, the establishment of emergency funds and the selection of women within the community to learn midwifery locally and in La Paz. Within a short space of time (1998–90 to 1991–3), perinatal and neonatal mortality decreased by almost two-thirds, and there was a substantial impovement in health practices, including hygienic births, immediate breastfeeding and care of the newborn, and tetanus toxoid vaccination.

Source: Howard-Grabman (1996).

participate tended to diminish over time, the use of women as instruments of service delivery resulted in next to no 'female empowerment' (ibid.; see also Gideon, 1998:316 for other examples)

Other alternatives to conventional formal healthcare which have addressed gender as a mainstream rather than peripheral concern have increasingly been provided by civil society organisations and NGOs. In many cases these have facilitated access to healthcare that benefits women and men in ways that are more appropriate to their needs, which have increased their basic medical knowledge, and which seem to have presented an attractive alternative to top-down bureaucratic modes of provision.

For example, the Health and Female Sexuality Collective in São Paulo began with a small group of women in 1981 whose main concerns were to find alternatives to the formal health system in which women were often intimidated by male medical personnel and left ignorant of their own bodies. In 1986, the Collective opened a female-run clinic serving mainly poor women from the western zone of São Paulo. Aside from clinical services, they now have programmes on education, training, protection and research (see Díaz and Rogow, 1995). A similar initiative in Mexico,

SIPAM *(Salud Integral Para la Mujer/*Whole Health for Women) was created in 1987 with financial assistance from the Ford and MacArthur foundations in the USA. This organisation seeks to improve women's health, especially in relation to reproduction, sexuality and mental health, alongside defence of the 'free and full expression of women' (Reyes Zapata *et al.*, 1999; my translation). Amongst other things, SIPAM's future plans include strengthening women's self-esteem, confidence and participation in health consultations, sensitising women to their reproductive rights and how to exercise them, and getting women to know, care about and look after their bodies. It is also deemed necessary for men to be brought on board with a view to helping them overcome the negative consequences of their masculine roles such as exposure to risk (accidents, AIDS and so on), and the tendency for men not to seek help when they fall ill. Through workshops and talks, it is also hoped to increase men's awareness of women's reproductive rights, to encourage them to share domestic labour and childcare with their wives, and to reduce the incidence of domestic violence (ibid.: 9–10).

Another Mexican initiative with a similar brief is that of Salud y Género (Health and Gender) founded in 1992 by health workers under the leadership of Benno de Keijzer. Salud y Género is a health promotion outfit with offices in two cities: Xalapa and Guanajuato. Originally the organisation started working with women, but women soon called for men to be involved. Much of the work with men includes group discussions on masculinity and how this impacts on men's own health and that of others (for example, through domestic violence). At a wider scale, Salud y Género has also worked with the media to raise awareness about gender equity, and gender and parenting (Chant and Gutmann, 2000:33). In Nicaragua, an

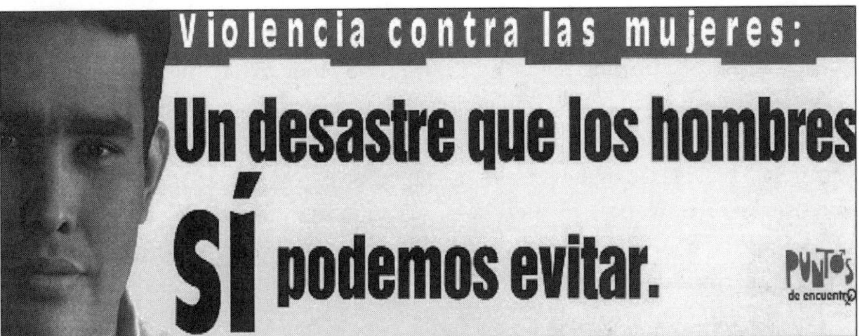

Figure 5.2 Men's anti-violence campaign, Nicaragua. The slogan, which appeared in posters, on car windscreens stickers and in television advertisements, reads 'Violence against women: a disaster which YES, we men can avoid'

(Reproduced with kind permission from Puntos de Encuentro, Nicaragua)

NGO called Puntos de Encuentro is an example where men themselves have started to mobilise against violence, with the organisation of workshops with men, and TV, radio, press and public information campaigns, to eliminate domestic violence (Montoya, 1998; also Henthorne, 2000; Sternberg, 2000; Chapter 7). A preliminary evaluation of this programme suggests a range of positive impacts. Several men in Nicaragua are aware of the campaign and familiar with its slogans (see Figure 5.2), and have also engaged in more interpersonal communication with other men. By the same token, finding more effective means of reaching men who are unable to read and write remains a challenge (Solórzano *et al*, 2000).

The above initiatives play an important role in enhancing health and access to healthcare among male and female populations, and, in the longer term, could go some way to addressing the problems inherent in systems that undervalue or underpay women participants.

Gender and healthcare provision

We have already noted that health is women's rather than men's domain in the Latin American region on account of their socialisation in caring and nurturing functions and because of prevailing gender divisions of labour (see earlier). In considering women's roles in healthcare provision it is important to bear in mind that this falls into preventative and curative branches, into paid and unpaid sectors, and also takes place at a variety of levels, ranging from individual efforts, to collective action, to formal health institutions.

Unpaid initiatives

As regards individual inputs, women's primary responsibilities for maintaining household health, treating illness and caring for other family members, including elderly relatives as well as children and husbands (see Chapter 4), can be extremely onerous given that in many parts of Latin America 'sickness is a fact of daily life' (Browner, 1989:465). In Puerto Rico, for instance, Sánchez-Ayéndez (1993:264) notes that although some men do take care of sick and disabled wives, daughters play a big role in helping out, especially in matters of patient hygiene and housework. Indeed, while not conventionally recognised as 'healthcare', it was mentioned earlier that women's routine domestic labour in low-income settlements plays an enormous part in preventing or reducing the incidence of environmental and/or infectious diseases. Attempts to remove rubbish and faecal material away from dwelling plots, for example, are crucial when rotting refuse is frequently subject to infestations of lice and fleas, and can lead to other health risks such as dermatitis and impetigo. In turn, the disposal of refuse away from areas of food preparation, especially in hot climates, and where insects and animals can act as disease vectors, are fundamental in preventing potentially fatal gastro-enteritic infections such as amoebic dysentery, poliomyelitis and Hepatitis 'A' (Chant, 1984). The fact that deaths from these kinds of illness are not higher in Latin America is in large part due to women's labour. As summed up by Grau *et al.* (1991:9):

> The daily reproduction of the labour force requires an enormous amount of health care (nutrition, shelter, prevention, health education, personal and domestic hygiene, rubbish disposal, attention to the sick and disabled etc.), which are incorporated within that invisible and undervalued world of domestic labour [my translation].

The effort individual women have to expend in their own homes is often such that they join forces with other women in order to make life easier and/or better achieve their aims. This has included mobilisation in neighbourhood struggles for health services such as clinics and infant feeding support. These localised movements have often flourished, in turn, into wider urban struggles geared to curative and preventive health, such as the now famous Health Movement in São Paulo, Brazil (see Corcoran-Nantes, 1990; Machado, 1988). Such initiatives are not only often enduring, but may become formalised over time. Grassroots groups may form alliances with NGOs and other activitists, and eventually bring pressure to bear on national governments (Portugal and Matamala, 1993; see also Chapter 3).

Yet despite the fact that women provide the vast bulk of informal and unpaid healthcare services in Latin America (including in the context of participatory PHC programmes), and have such an important influence on the health status and health-seeking behaviour of others, their efforts in preventative and curative health care have frequently been ignored, undervalued and/or used in narrowly instrumentalist ways by healthcare institutions (Gideon, 2000; Gómez Gómez, 1993a:xiii).[5]

The formal healthcare sector

In many respects this undervaluation is also apparent within formal healthcare institutions, with Gómez Gómez (1993a:ix) pointing out the major paradox whereby although women outnumber men in the healthcare sector, they seldom hold the positions of highest power, status and remuneration. Women make up 45 per cent of the health workforce in the Americas as a whole, and in some countries such as Chile up to 70 per cent (Grau *et al.*, 1991:11), but have only scant representation in decision-making and authority. While men are 'the doctors, the hospital chiefs, the service managers, the professors and the ministers' (ibid.), women are concentrated in the lowest-paid, least prestigious occupations (Gómez Gómez, 1993:xiii). A study of physicians conducted in Mexico in 1990, for example, revealed that only ten women held management positions compared with 108 men. Moreover, women were often absent from 'male specialisms' such as surgery, pediatric surgery, neurology and traumatology (Machado, 1993:259). Although there have been progressive increases in women's participation in the highest echelons of the medical profession, as recently as 1990 women were still only 34 per cent of medical students in Peru, 40 per cent in Uruguay, and 47 per cent in Panama. Although by the 1990s 50 per cent of medical students in Brazil were female, in 1980 women were only 20.6 per cent of doctors and 37.7 per cent of pharmacists, but 94 per cent of nurses (ibid.). Similar patterns are found in Bolivia where, in 1988, women were only 22.3 per cent of doctors but 81.5 per cent of nurses. In Paraguay in 1985 the corresponding figures were 27 per cent and 98 per cent (ibid.:259–60).

Such divisions are very clearly reflected in salary differentials. In 1985, for example, women in the medical profession in Brazil earned incomes that were on average 17 per cent lower than their male counterparts, and even in heavily female-dominated fields, women earned 20 per cent less than men (Machado, 1993:260). The issue of low wages has become particularly stressful in the context of economic restructuring, given the pressure on women to do more work not only in their homes, but in the health sector as well. In Chile, for example, cuts in public expenditure on health have vastly increased the workloads of medical and auxiliary staff. Coupled with the exigencies of shift work, and progressively poorer infrastructure and resources, this has created an immensely demoralising environment where workers' time to eat properly and/or to attend to their own health needs is minimal. Evidence suggests that these trends have had particularly deleterious effects on the physical and psychological health and well-being of women health workers (see Grau *et al.*, 1991; Ministerio de Salud, 1996).

It could be argued that, as long as women's position in the health field in general is primarily as un- or under-paid workers, women's health concerns are unlikely to be a priority on formal agendas (except in respect of obstetrics and gynaecology). Yet as Portugal and Matamala (1993:279) point out with reference to the women's health movement in Latin America and the Caribbean:

> In short, the health movement launched by the Region's women – whether it be a health movement as such or actions in the broader context of the feminist movement or of women as a whole – has increasingly affected society through the alternative agendas it has proposed … the implementation of health services *for* women which are staffed *by* women has made it possible to expand the scope of coverage, establish new standards regarding the quality and care of services, and invent new forms of human relationship that exclude competitiveness and violence and are strongly rooted in solidarity and respect for women's dignity as human beings [emphasis in original].

Conclusion

We have seen in this chapter that the health of populations in Latin America is affected by numerous factors, many of which have to do with inequalities in people's dwelling environments, incomes and quality of life, and a substantial number of which relate to the uneven coverage of healthcare services. In several cases, efforts at the grassroots and in civil society, many of them spawned and executed by women, have gone some way to compensate for the threats to health and inadequacies in healthcare provision that affect more vulnerable segments of society. Yet the fact that gender continues to be a crucial axis of difference in health and healthcare constitutes a clear sign that more can and should be done to redress existing inequalities.

One of the most pressing issues for the future is to find ways of resolving the major contradiction of women bearing greater burdens of personal ill-health, yet at the same time shouldering bigger but largely unrecognised responsibilities for the health of others, whether in the home, in grassroots movements, or as low-paid workers in the health industry. While there are several steps that can be taken within the formal healthcare sector itself, such as policies of affirmative action to ensure that women have equal chances for promotion as men, and more effective outreach to women in communities, these are unlikely to have much impact so long as caring and nurturing continue to be seen as the exclusive domain of women, and women's control over their own bodies is compromised by lack of power. In turn, priority needs to be given not just to women's reproductive health, which at some level reinforces the notion that women's health only matters when it is in the service of others, but to women's health in general. With the progressive ageing and increase in life expectancy of Latin American populations, for example, which affects women more than men, it is vital to remember that 'Underlying diseases or degenerative diseases may be more important in terms of human suffering and needs for health services than the actual diseases that ultimately cause death' (Phillips and Verhasselt, 1994:21).

By the same token, men's health should not take a back seat, especially given that potentially considerable work could be done to reduce the incidence of behaviourally induced morbidity and mortality among male populations. Initiatives have already been taken by grassroots and civil society organisations to work towards the practical and ideological renegotiation of male identities, with important implications for preventing premature deaths from violence, drug abuse and unsafe sex. These initiatives, in turn, hold longer-term prospects not only for corresponding improvements in women's and children's health and quality of life, but also for greater sharing of responsibility for preventative healthcare. While we detailed moves in this direction in the context of reproductive health and rights in Chapter 4, Chapter 6 turns to sexuality, which forms another crucial part of the picture.

6 Gender and Sexuality

SYLVIA CHANT
with NIKKI CRASKE

Introduction

Sexuality is difficult to define, but in broad terms describes a spectrum of behaviour that extends from the procreative to the erotic, and encompasses ideals, desires, practices, preferences and identities. The aim of this chapter is to explore the interrelations between gender and sexuality in Latin American societies, concentrating on the ways in which gender is negotiated through sexual behaviour, and how sexuality contributes to defining gender. This entails discussions of expressions, representations and stereotypes of male and female sexuality, of heterosexuality and homosexuality, and of societal attitudes towards different forms of sexuality over time.[1] In order to establish background to these themes, the chapter commences with a brief review of conceptual perspectives on sexuality and their particular relevance to Latin American contexts past and present.

Conceptual perspectives on gender, sexuality and the body

While writing on sex and sexual morality goes back several hundred years, the term 'sexuality' did not appear until the nineteenth century (Foucault, 1978; Giddens, 1992:23). In turn, the history of sexuality has emerged as a dedicated field of academic study only in the last few decades. In Latin America itself, this evolution been even more recent, since as little as ten years ago sexuality lurked in the shadows of largely quantitative studies of population growth and reproductive health (see Bliss, 2001). Growing interest in the increasingly international, interdisciplinary field of sexuality has been attributed largely to the expansion of Gender Studies, and to 'the important work of a generation of philosophers and of feminist, gay and lesbian theorists who have found it useful to explain social relationships – including norms governing sex and reproduction – as cultural products amenable to change' (Nye, 1999:5).

One major debate in the field of sexuality has revolved around the extent to which sexual nature is 'essential' and unchanging vis-à-vis a more constructionist approach which posits that sexuality is determined by the institutions, customs and social practices developed by men and women in particular times and places (Nye, 1999:5–6). As Giddens (1992:23), amongst others, has argued: 'Sexuality is a social construct, operating within the fields of power, not merely a set of biological promptings', or as Weeks (2000:129) puts it: 'Sexuality is not a given. It is the product of negotiation, struggle and human agency'.

Social constructionism has opened up possibilities for imagining sexuality and gender in ways that depart from narrow, essentialist norms in which stable heterosexual relations have been regarded as natural and normal, and in turn privileged with social recognition denied to 'deviant' forms of sexual expression (see Rubin, 1984). Such approaches have exploded the myth that female sexuality is 'inherently dangerous' and in need of restraint by patriarchal institutions to effect transition from a 'primitive' to a 'modern', regulated, social order (see Pateman, 1988). Feminism has distinguished between sex and gender in an effort to 'denaturalise asymmetry' (Morris, R., 1995:567), but it is important to acknowledge that the diversity of feminist viewpoints on sexuality precludes the unproblematical and categorical displacement of biological by social determinism (see Scott and Jackson, 1996:6). The detail of constructionist/essentialist debates lies beyond the scope of the present chapter, but suffice it to say that recent work has begun to make significant inroads into exploring what Nye (1999:7) calls the 'middle ground' between these epistemological traditions. This has mainly taken the shape of attempts to

> amalgamate a 'nominalist' and constructionist analysis that emphasises language with the 'realist' assessment of lived bodily experience.... The question is, are bodies and their pleasures independent of the ways that language characterises them, or do we require linguistic and cultural representations to prompt and interpret bodily experience? Can the experience or identity of homosexuality exist, for instance, if the concept 'homosexuality' has not yet appeared or the word has not yet been coined?

These questions are of major significance in the domain of sexualities in Latin America, as we shall see later.

A related and critically important debate arising from studies of sexuality devolves upon the conceptualisation of the body and its relationship to 'sex' and 'gender'. Here, the work of Michel Foucault (1978) has been central in destabilising the notion that bodies, on which the social construction of gender differences are purportedly inscribed, are an anatomical and biological 'given'. Instead, he proposes, 'sex' is not an origin, but an *outcome* of specific discursive practices. As Moore (1994b:12–13) sums up, Foucault's main argument is that:

> the notion of 'sex' does not exist prior to its determination within a discourse in which its constellations of meanings are specified, and that therefore bodies have no 'sex' outside discourses in which they are designated as sexed. Consequently, the construction of fixed binary sexes, with fixed categorical differences, is the effect of a specific discourse. What is more, if binary sex is an effect of discourse, then it cannot be considered as a unitary essentialism and, more importantly, it cannot be recognised as invariant and natural.

Moore (1994b:13) notes that Foucault's work has given rise to two very important developments in respect of gender. One is associated with the radical constructivist work of Judith Butler, which disrupts one of the major foundations of Feminist Anthropology in presenting the case that no distinction should be made between sex and gender. Butler argues that the body is not fixed, but a site of multiple, contested meanings, and in constant, mutual and simultaneous motion with configurations of sex and gender. In short, 'if gender is the cultural meanings that a sexed body assumes, then a gender cannot be said to follow from a sex in any one way' (Butler, 1990:6). Rather than concentrating on how gender is constituted as, and through, specific interpretations of sex, the concern lies with examining the regulatory norms through which sex itself is 'materialised' (Butler, 1993). While sex is not the only norm by which bodies are materialised, it also becomes important to consider how the materialisation of 'bodies that matter' through regulatory norms produces a realm of excluded and delegitimated 'sex' that serves to further heterosexual hegemony (ibid.; see also Jolly, 2000:84–5). Butler's concepts of performance (where gender is effectively embodied through everyday practice), and latterly, performativity (where greater emphasis is given to language and discourse in producing gendered bodies), have been taken up, debated, modified and elaborated upon by numerous feminist theorists (see Busby, 2000:11–12; also Battersby, 1998; Grosz, 1994; Morris, R.1995).

The second development noted by Moore (1994b:13) as arising out of Foucault's work on sexuality is the notion elaborated on by Sylvia Yanagisako and Jane Collier (1987), that it cannot necessarily be assumed that 'binary biological sex everywhere provides the universal basis for the categories "male" and "female"'. Categories of sexual difference are likely to be equally variable across time and place as constructs of gender. This in turn, has led to awareness of the need to consider cultural variations in different parts of the world. As Balderston and Guy (1997:3) argue in their introduction to the first major text on sex and sexuality in Latin America: 'biases inherent in much of Anglo-American gender and sexuality studies have meant that some culture-bound characteristics have been taken to be universal', and cross-cultural work introduces a 'useful corrective to this tendency'.[2]

Images and representations of gender and sexuality in Latin America

Although there is a broad and growing spectrum of images and representations of sexuality in Latin America, two stereotypical extremes have tended to stand out. One is that of sexual repression, associated with religion, and particularly, Roman Catholicism, in which notions of guilt, sin, and restraint preponderate. The other is that of exoticism and sensuality, especially in relation to Brazil and the Hispanic Caribbean, and is reflected most vividly and visually in the tradition of the carnival (see Parker, 1997). While these themes are discussed below, it is important to point out that no consideration of either can be made without some reference to pre-Columbian and indigenous sexualities and to the period of conquest and colonisation of the New World, in which power relations assumed markedly sexualised and racialised forms.

Pre-Columbian sexualities

Although most of our knowledge of sexuality in the diverse pre-Hispanic cultures of Latin America is fragmented and circumscribed by the filtering effects of colonial reportage, some consonances between indigenous and colonial religious beliefs and practices may be discerned. One area of correspondence evident among some groups in the region was the avoidance of sexual excess. With reference to Aztec society, for example, Mirandé (1997:51) talks about the belief that 'those who gave themselves excessively to the carnal act endangered themselves'. Sexual excess could bring about physical ruin, provoke rotting genitalia in young women who lost their virginity prior to marriage, and, at its logical extreme, the 'diseases of sin' could threaten entire villages (Ruz, 1998:194). Moreover, those falling outside 'natural law' by engaging in same-sex relations, especially women, were deplored and sometimes subject to enslavement (see Clendinnen, 1995: 165 & 169). Although some degree of polygyny was tolerated among the Aztec nobility *(pipiltin)* who could afford the luxury of more than one woman, for the masses (*macehualtin*), fidelity in marriage was expected of both husbands and wives (Mirandé, 1997:52). The practice of temperance is echoed by Dávalos (1998:98) who observes that pre-Columbian Mexican peoples 'combated sexual transgression in order to maintain cosmic and social equilibrium'. Among the Maya, for example, who occupied most of what is now southeast Mexico down through Guatemala, insistence on monogamy was felt necessary to maintain the best possible basis for healthy reproduction given the risks of death to men in battle, and to women in childbirth (Ruz, 1998:202). This in turn, rested on the belief that pregnancy only arose after repeated sexual relations over a length of time with the same partner (ibid.:209).

The exercise of restraint in the interests of personal and community stability also extended to other realms of life such as the consumption of food and drink (Mirandé, 1997:58). Prudence did not necessarily equate with prudishness, however. Pre-Columbian ceramics from the Andes indicate that indigenous populations were much more overt in public expressions of sexuality than the Spanish (Hocquenghem, 1987). In Mayan society, it was not sex, or sensuality, or the pleasure to be derived from these that met with censure, but lasciviousness (Ruz, 1998:197). Among some indigenous communities in Brazil, such as the Tupi, it was also the case that rules of incest, which did not apply, for example, to uncles marrying nieces, were deeply offensive to the religious and moral norms of the colonisers.

Conquest, 'race' and gender

Despite discourses of sexual restraint among the Catholic clergy, in diverting their attention from the 'rapacious sexuality of the Spanish soldiery' (Stavans, 1998:229), they effectively became silent accomplices in the savage brutality of New World conquest. Echoing a more general point made by Moore (1994b:63) that: 'Gender and race idioms are … frequently used to order differences in power and prestige', the powerful iconography of 'sexual relations between conquering white soldiers and dominated Indian women' (Cubitt, 1995:111) resonates not only with the exertion of dominance, control, and aggression of individual Spanish men over individual indigenous women, but serves as a wider metaphor for penetration of the colonised body. As Lancaster (1997b:195) has noted: 'In popular discourses across Latin America, images of sexuality are mobilised to support the reign of conquering masculinities as well as wounded nationhoods'.

As summed up yet more graphically by Stavans (1998:228–9):

> A violent eroticism was a fundamental element in the colonisation of the Hispanic world, from Macchu Picchu to Chichén Iztá and Uxmal. The primal scene of the clash with the Spaniards is a still-unhealed rape: the phallus, as well as gunpowder, was a crucial weapon used to subdue. *Machismo* as a cultural style endlessly rehearses this humiliating episode in the history of the Americas, imitating the violent swagger of the Spanish conquerers. (This, despite the Indian legends that Cortés was the owner of a tiny, ridiculous penis.)[3]

Concern to maintain racial purity and hierarchy during the colonisation of the New World was such that Luso-Hispanic women were subject to the strict edicts that had contained their sexuality in the Iberian peninsula. Their sexuality was strongly tied to reproduction, both of the family and of colonial social relations, and they became the embodiment of chastity, virtue, morality and respectability (Bieber, 1998; Lomnitz Adler, 1992; Wilson, 1995). Those women without families fell to the protection of the Church and/or became nuns (Wilson, 1995). Since there were relatively few Luso-Hispanic women who accompanied their menfolk to Latin

America in the early years of the conquest, indigenous women, and later, imported black slave women, were placed under even greater pressure to satiate the sexual appetites of the *conquistadores*. Sexual abuse and violence is widely noted in these relationships, with women's predicament further exacerbated by the fact that their *mestizo* and *mulato* offspring were not uncommonly held in fear and disdain and/or abandoned by their fathers, because they threatened the racial order (see Stolcke, 1995). Indigenous and black women, despite their powerlessness to resist sexual contact with white men, were denigrated and despised (Wilson, 1995). The link between female sexuality and the colonial order is reflected most markedly perhaps in the myths around Hernán Cortés's indigenous consort, Doña Marina ('La Malinche'/Malintzin), whose union with the enemy purportedly led to the betrayal of her fellow Mexicans: '*los hijos de la chingada*' ('the sons of the violated mother') (Almaguer, 1998:540; Mirandé, 1997:36; Paz, 1959; cf Martin, 1990:472–3).

The overlapping hierarchies of class, 'race' and gender forged during the colonial period have remained strikingly persistent through time. Citing the work of Borja (1993) on seventeenth- and eighteenth-century Colombia, Viveros (1998b) points out that the sexual proclivities attributed to black people were not only perceived as a major threat to the institution of the family, but also acted as an integral element in the dualism between body and spirit characterising the Catholic Christian tradition. In turn, linking black with 'bad' and white with 'good', Catholic iconography portrayed the devil as dark, and the virgins and angels as blond and fair-skinned. In order to attract people of African descent into Catholicism the Church in Brazil also created cults of black saints, such as São Benedict, Sant' Elesbão, and Santa Efigenia,[4] in the late nineteenth century. Here, as in many other parts of the region, there was concern to regulate prostitutes, although women of Northern European descent in Brazil (most notably 'French'), and *mulatas* (of joint African and European descent), were allowed much greater freedoms than *pretas* (black) women (Caulfield, 1997, 2000). In present-day Argentina, Stølen (1996) notes that among many ideological, moral and material differences, attributed female sexuality plays a central role in distinguishing between higher-ranking farmers of northern Italian origin (known locally *as los gringos*), and the subordinate group of indigenous and Spanish descent (*los criollos*), who for the most part are seasonal labourers. Whereas *gringas* are nominally '*casera*' (housebound/home-loving), staunchly Catholic, and 'decent' unless proved otherwise, *criollas* are deemed to be '*fáciles*' ('easy'). This is deemed to derive from their '*sangre caliente*' ('hot blood'), and an upbringing devoid of censure on their sexual urges (ibid.:171). A common fear, stemming from the fact that many *criollo* children are forced to share bedrooms with parents, is that they will have early and improper exposure to sexual relations.

Another contemporary case where notions of gender have been documented as central to meanings of class and 'race' is in Cartagena, Colombia. Research carried out by Striecker (1995) in the neighbourhood of Santa Ana indicates that while there is little blatant 'race' discrimination in the locality, *santaneros* use the terms '*champetudo*' ('disrespectful', 'vulgar'), and '*clase baja*' ('lower class'), as euphemisms for '*negro*' ('black'). In turn, 'an important means of establishing an individual's class and "race" identity is to measure that person's actions against standards of gender conduct' (ibid.:57). Women who are stigmatised as '*champetada*' are those who 'flout feminine ideals', for example by being unchaste, unfaithful or spending time in the street rather than in their homes.

Projections of the 'dangerous' sexuality of subordinated ethnic groups have also been integral to stereotypical portrayals of exotic sensualities in Latin American societies.

Religion and sexuality

CATHOLICISM

Although the influence of Roman Catholicism was by no means uniform across the New World, there is little doubt that religious conquest played a significant role in determining what sexual behaviour was, or was not, permissible, with attempts evident on the part of the clergy to combat, both in public and in private, practices such as polygyny and homosexuality (Ruz, 1998:198). In Brazil for example, legislation was already in place by the time the Inquisition arrived in 1591 that penalised 'deviant' activities such as sodomy and mutual masturbation (see Cornwall, 1994:122).

As far as the sixteenth century Catholic Church was concerned, the only legitimate arena for sex was monogamous, heterosexual marriage. All other carnal contact was forbidden, whether in the form of men's relationships with 'loose women' (Nye, 1999:13), or with other men (see below). These proscriptions have been remarkably persistent, and have played a major part in influencing hegemonic sexual discourses not only in Latin America, but elsewhere, both past and present (see Horrocks, 1997). In the schema developed of sexual models in the context of Spain by Marqués (1980), for example, this can be seen as falling into what he terms the 'repressive clerical' model.

Sinning is induced by the devil, has the power to make human beings 'lose themselves', and leads to decadence and debacle (Schifter and Madrigal, 1996:62). The primary purpose of sex is procreation. That masturbation is oriented to the pleasuring of self, makes this a sin, alongside the ranks of more obvious transgressions such as 'fornication' (out-of-wedlock sexual relations) (ibid.: 64–5). 'Good' or 'bad sex' is defined not in terms of pleasure, but morality (Craske, forthcoming). Moreover, the penalties for women's transgression have always been greater than for men, with a link drawn by some between negative Catholic views of sex and misogyny (see Stavans, 1998:229).

Although the influence of religion on the normative contours of sexual behaviour in Western societies has waned in the wake of secularisation, medicalisation and the rise of the modern state (see Espada Calpe, 2001; Foucault, 1978), in the particular context of contemporary Latin America, the Catholic Church's legacy can arguably be seen in a variety of spheres, including dualisms between male and female sexuality, and the repression of homosexuality.

Although discussed in more detail later, it is important to note here that the Church's idealisation of woman as mother – expressed in references to '*madrecita santa*' ('holy [little] mother'), '*el sagrado deber de ser madre*' ('the sacred duty to be a mother'), and '*la mujer sufrida y sacrificada*' ('the suffering and self-sacrificing mother') – makes it difficult for women not to see motherhood as their destiny (Ehrenfeld Lenkiewicz, 1989:392). In turn, and in accordance with ideals of *marianismo*, sex is only endorsed when linked with marriage and reproduction, and 'concealed and forbidden in words' (Jelin, 1997:76). Yet it is also important to recognise that contradictory ideals are established by Catholicism's iconography of the Virgin Mary, and its insistence on the Immaculate Conception.

> As the Catholic symbol of the perfect woman, the Virgin Mary presents a definition that is, in the end, damaging to women. The twin ideal of mother and virgin is impossible for a woman to achieve. The destiny and purpose that this myth establishes for women (i.e. motherhood) is then also devalued – since sex is necessary for a woman to fulfill her destiny. A symbol of renunciation, the Virgin puts the female believer in a position of acknowledged inferiority and so underlines the dangers of sex, the fear of corruption and her sense of sin (Deighton *et al.*, 1983:146).

These observations relate to the widely noted dichotomy of 'virgin/madonna' and 'whore' in *mestizo* Latin America, which is associated with considerable ambivalence towards women on the part of men.[5] Men's relationships with their mothers are often prioritised over those they have with their sexual partners. In turn, men have been observed to divide their sexual relationships into two main types: those with wives, which tend to be emotional but sexually conservative, and those with casual partners or prostitutes, which are sexually carnal but lacking in sentiment. As argued by Ennew (1986:58) 'The reproductive object is a wife/mother and the recreational object is a prostitute'. The power of these images is such that one of the biggest insults in Latin America is to refer to a man's mother as a 'whore' (Sandoval García, 1997:190).

While extramarital sex continues to be frowned upon by the Catholic Church, views on homosexuality are perhaps even more negative. Homosexuality is deemed to be unnatural and intrinsically bad, with the story of Sodom and Gomorrah illustrating the force of divine punishment for sexual depravity and corruption (Schifter and Madrigal, 1996:62). As echoed by Lumsden (1996:45):

> Condemnation of sodomy, and subsequently homosexuality, have long been at the core of Spanish Catholic dogmas regarding sexuality. In the Middle Ages, sodomy was regarded as the ultimate crime, uniting sin, physical degradation, and unmasculine behaviour.

The idea of homosexuality as abomination shows no sign of abating in most quarters of the Catholic Church in Latin America today. In Costa Rica, for example, the Easter address to the nation in 1998 by the Archbishop of San José, Monseñor Román Arrieta, described the capital as an '*antro de putrefacción*' ('den of iniquity', literally 'putrefaction'), rivalling major global cities for 'anti-social' vices such as 'the prostitution of minors, alcoholism, drug addiction, homosexuality and lesbianism'.[6] This, in turn, accords with the continued conservatism of the Vatican, which in 1995 mounted a major attack on the term 'gender' at the Fourth World Conference for Women in Beijing. One of the underlying fears was that, as a social construction, 'gender' opens up room for alternative behaviours and sexualities. As Franco (1998:280) summarises the case:

> The Vatican quite correctly deduced that the use of the word 'gender' might have practical consequences ranging from legalised abortion to the acceptance of homosexuality, the recognition of irregular families, and the collapse of family values.

In June 2000 Pope John Paul II himself also bitterly denounced Guatemala City's first Lesbian and Gay Pride March as an 'offence against Christian values … in a city so loved by Catholics the world over'. Yet while the Vatican stands firm in its position that homosexual acts are 'against the laws of nature', and that homosexuals should remain celibate, it claims to be against discrimination against gays, instead urging that they should be treated with 'respect, compassion and delicacy' on account of their condition.[7] Failure to win anything approaching approval from the religious hierarchy has been a source of anguish to many gays and lesbians in the region. This is revealed in discussions on websites and in journals where people make reference to segments of the Bible in which tolerance for sexual minorities is indicated, and/or debate whether it is possible to indulge their sexual preferences and be a 'true Christian' at the same time.[8]

NON-CATHOLIC POPULAR FAITHS

Although Catholicism has undoubtedly been the single most powerful faith in post-colonial Latin America, at a regional level, it is important to recognise the steadily mounting influence of Protestant sects. In the latter half of the twentieth century in particular, there has been considerable growth in Pentecostal-Charismatic Christianity which possesses its own take on sin and sexuality (see below). Presently Pentecostal-Charismatics (also known as *evangélicos*/evangelicals), make up two-thirds of Latin America's Protestants, who, in turn, represent around 10 per cent of the population (Freston, 1997:187). Brazil has the largest Protestant community in terms of numbers, although Guatemala, El Salvador and Chile have higher percentages (ibid.). While Charismaticism has more of a middle-class following, Pentecostalism has taken deepest root among the poor, where it is now a major rival to Catholicism in the 'struggle for the spirit' (Lehmann, 1996).

Self-control, self-discipline and 'liberation from temptation' are abiding tenets of Pentecostalism, with the conversion experience strongly linked with the abrupt and total renunciation of the 'pleasures of the flesh'. Although women feature more prominently among Pentecostal converts, accounts of conversion often draw attention to the more obvious life changes wrought for men who, in turning to the faith, abandon their 'past ways' of smoking, drinking to excess, and womanising (Lehmann, 1996:196).

As far as women are concerned, Pentecostalism might be construed as being equally oppressive and constraining as Catholicism, with its emphases on asceticism, conservative gender relations, sex within the confines of monogamous marriage, home and motherhood for women, and the (re)assertion of the stable nuclear family unit. However, Drogus (1997) draws attention to elements which make for greater equality between women and men. One of the most important is that Pentecostalism calls on men to comply with the moral norms of restraint and fidelity which have historically tended to apply much more in practice (if not in principle) to women in Latin America.

> By reinforcing women's moral code and extending it to men, Pentecostal churches may open the way for attitudinal and behavioural changes that empower women, truly equalising domestic roles. (Drogus, 1997:63)

While Marianist ideologies espoused by the Catholic Church (see Chapter 1) have discouraged divorce and emphasised how women's suffering at the hands of recalcitrant husbands proves their spiritual superiority, Pentecostal women are not expected to persist in unions with 'ungodly men', and seem to have more support from their religion that enables them to 'bring their husbands to heel'. There is also evidence that women may join Pentecostal churches in the first place as a means of finding a 'decent' husband (Drogus, 1997:62).

One of the most graphic illustrations of Pentecostal men's and women's compliance with sobriety and sexual restraint is that many abandon the annual carnival in Rio de Janiero, Brazil (Freston, 1997:188). Moreover, even where they do participate, as is more the case among Charismatics, their floats are marked by the absence of the states of undress and 'excessive sensuality' which characterise the majority in the festival (ibid.). The only major sources of religious endorsement for the obvious celebration of sensuality and sexuality in the Brazilian carnival more generally, and particularly in Salvador, are Afro-Brazilian cults such as Candomblé, which does not subscribe to the Christian notion of sex as sin, and is marked by its high proportion of female devotees and tolerance of homosexuality among the priesthood as much as among its followers (see below).

Sensuality and exoticism

In contrast to the narrow and forbidding nature of sexual stereotypes associated with its mainstream religions, Latin America has also been a terrain for exoticised representations of sensuality revolving around the power of the *macho* and his member, and 'flamboyant women' portrayed as 'provocative, well-built, sensual, lascivious, with indomitable, even bestial, nerve and intensity' (Stavans, 1998:230). This is hardly surprising given Kulick's (1995:3) more general observation that 'the sex of "the Other" has always constituted one of the gawdiest exhibits in the anthropological sideshow'. By the same token, the 'exoticising gaze' which provides 'endless fodder for reflection, speculation and flourish' (ibid.), is not solely the domain of projections from outside the countries concerned. In the context of Cuba, for example, Lumsden (1996:43) maintains that the subjugation complex attached to *marianismo* (see Chapter 1), is challenged by *hembrismo*, which encompasses the celebration of women's sensual attributes. Noting that the term *hembrismo* is derived from '*hembra*' (which refers to the female of any animal species), Lumsden claims that this complex approximates a female equivalent of *machismo*, with a popular *hembrista* saying being '*Soy tan hembra como tú macho*' ('I'm as much a woman as you are a man') (ibid.:220–1; see also McCallum, 1999 on the cult of the sensual female in Brazil).

One reason why the Hispanic Caribbean, Brazil, and areas such as the Chocó region of Colombia stand out as places in which 'exotic stereotypes' have held greatest sway is because they embody a strong racial dimension and are often associated with groups of African or Afro-Caribbean origin (see Wade, 1993). Yet as Viveros (1998b) points out, while the arts of music, dance, seduction and eroticism were historically acknowledged as those in which blacks excelled, these domains were undervalued on three counts: morally, because the body and carnality were considered territories of sin; materially, because these skills did not raise people's economic status, and symbolically, because on the scale of dominant values the physical was inferior to the spiritual. Notwithstanding these qualifications, the historical record is replete with dubious celebrations of black eroticism. In nineteenth-century Brazil, for example, where prostitutes 'had figured prominently in both negative and positive images of Rio's tropical sensuality' (Caulfield, 1997:88), the term *mulata* evoked sexual desirability (ibid.:89). In early twentieth-century Costa

Rica, Foote (2001) recounts the view of a Costa Rican 'gentleman' conveyed to the author of the 1930s book *Banana Gold* (Carleton Beals), that Africans:

> should be kept naked with loin cloths only. They are good animals with too beautiful bodies for clothes. And the women – now their firm ample flesh seems ready to burst through the satin skin – like ripe fruit! But when they are clothed – a travesty! (cited in Foote, 2001:3; see also Beals, 1932).

As Foote (2001:3) observes more generally for Latin America and the Caribbean:

> the dominant discourse used black women's bodies as a vehicle for the presentation of Africans as primitive, animal-like and savage: black women's sexuality has thus been presented as primal and available.

As for the effects on those subjected to these stereotypes, a common response, especially among better-off segments of the Afro-Caribbean community in Costa Rica, was for women to imitate the 'virtuous' and 'moral' behaviour of their white counterparts (Foote, 2001:3). In so doing, they not only aimed to shake-off racist and sexist labels *per se*, but also to assimilate into white culture in order to advance the general cause of black people in the country (ibid.). It is also the case, therefore, that the oppression embodied in monolithic stereotypes may provide a catalyst for resistance and subversion (see Pérez-Sarduy and Stubbs, 1995; Wade, 1993).

The latter is to some extent apparent in Cuba, where, since the growth of international tourism in the post-Soviet 'Special Period', there has been a substantial rebirth of prostitution catering to foreign clientèle.[9] Forrest (1999) argues that many individuals involved in *jineterismo* (derived from '*jinetero*', which means jockey, but which can loosely be interpreted as 'hustling'/'gold-digging'/'commandeering') actively play on notions of 'otherness', and make blatant claims about their high levels of passion and erotic sexuality. While *jineterismo* might be used generically to describe 'prostitution', and female sex workers usually refer to themselves as '*jineteras*' rather than prostitutes, Hodge (2001:22) argues that men who engage in commercial sex have coined their own separate term – *pinguero*– to highlight the fact that, unlike women, they do not allow themselves to be penetrated by male tourists.[10] The term derives from '*pinga*', the Cuban slang for penis, and makes it clear that *pingueros* play the 'active' (penetrating) role in anal intercourse (see later discussion on homosexuality). According to Hodge (2001:23), *pingueros* 'represent the strength of the powerful Cuban phallus conquering the bodies of foreigners … in a *pinguero*–tourist sex act, the Cuban has invaded the tourist, "screwed" him as it were' (ibid.:23).

In a slightly different vein, contemporary Brazil provides another showcase, *par excellence*, for exoticisation, with the *mulata* playing a special role in the symbolic universe of the *carnaval* not only as a representation of Brazil 'formed from the mixture of three races and three cultures', but as 'the perfect embodiment of the heat and sensuality of the tropics' (Parker, 1997:370–1). While based on the early Christian Lenten festivals, the Brazilian carnival takes place each year in most cities throughout the country, and in the major ones attracts numerous foreign visitors. Parker (1997:368) argues that the carnival has become thoroughly 'Brazilianised', creates an important space for indigenous and African traditions, and permits an unbridled range of sexual expression and performance in which transvestism occupies centre stage (ibid.: 366). As summed up in his own words:

> Linking notions about the sensuality of *sol* (sun), *suar* (sweat), *praia* (beach), and *verão* (summer) to the practice of *sacanagem* (transgressive sexual interaction), … the *carnaval* embodies a 'tropical' vision of the world. Like the carnivals of the northern hemisphere, this *carnaval*, too, offers a vision of the future: a utopian vision of the possibilities of life in a tropical paradise, somewhere south of the equator, where the struggles, suffering, and sadness of normal human existence have been destroyed by pleasure and passion. In the *carnaval*, everything is permitted, as it would be in the best of all possible worlds. The polymorphous pleasures of erotic ideology become the norm, rather than the transgression of the established order, and the fullest possibilities of sexual life take concrete form in the play of human bodies (Parker,1997:367).

The *carnaval* not only symbolises a world in which pleasures of sexual desire are, albeit temporarily, granted licence to 'escape the restrictions imposed by an oppressive social order' (Parker, 1997:363), but is also a realm for the inversion of a wide range of other stereotypes. As noted by Lancaster for Nicaragua (1997a:20):

> If Carnival lends itself to ritual rehearsals in the performance of *gender and sexuality*, it no less takes up questions of *race, class and ethnicity*. The famous peach-complexioned masks of Monimbó, with their rosy cheeks and pencil moustaches, recall the Spanish gentry and reveal the colonial dimension of Carnival's history: Indians take on the colour, wear the face, mimic the dances – and thereby mime the powers – of white Spaniard rulers. More modern Carnival images likewise traffic in depictions of class, administrative or neocolonial power [emphasis in original].

Clearly, carnival can play out the socially proscribed and also re-inscribe normative constructions.[11] It might also be argued that ideas of 'transgressive native sexualities' emanating from the views of New World outsiders may be appropriated by their 'objects', transformed and deployed in defiance of the norms of both colonisation and neocolonialism.

Men, women and heterosexuality

On the matter of 'everyday' practices, heterosexuality has long been a social ideal in the majority of *mestizo* Latin America. This has predominated in a form based on a strong hierarchical delineation between male and female sexual behaviours, as discussed below in relation first, to adults, and second, to youth.

Men's and women's sexuality in Latin America: a question of difference?

Preponderant stereotypical constructions of male and female sexuality in Latin America have long been characterised in a binary fashion, mapped unproblematically onto male and female bodies so as to confer on men a sexuality which is active and dominant, and on women a sexuality which is passive and submissive. While stereotypes about men as dominant and predatory form a crucial part of the hegemonic concept of *machismo* (see Nencel, 1996:57; also Chapter 1), the more general precept of difference is common to many Western cultures in which, Moore (1994c:138) argues, male sexuality and persons of the male gender are portrayed as 'active, aggressive, thrusting and powerful', compared with counterpart female categories of passivity, powerlessness, submissiveness and receptivity. Moore further observes that: 'The interesting fact about such constructions is that they have only the most tangential relation to the behaviours, qualities, attributes and self-images of individual women and men' (ibid.).

Accepting the importance of recognising hiatuses between norms and practice, assumptions underlying male–female divisions in sexuality in Latin America are grounded in part in essentialised notions of gendered bodies. Whereas, at one level, men might ideally exercise restraint in their positions as husbands and fathers, they are presented as having natural sexual urges governed by 'explosive' and 'uncontainable' instincts (Amuchástegui Herrera, 1998; Barker and Lowenstein, 1997; Sternberg, 2001). As observed in relation to recent surveys of sexuality in Mexico, for example, 'men consider that their sexual desire is based on strong biological impulses which require immediate relief' (Szasz, 1998:156; our translation). In Peru, Nencel (1996:61) points out that one of the most salient aspects of the discourse on male sexuality is the 'relational construction of gender which positions men and women oppositionally, and the singular, essentialist concept of sexuality in which sexual desire is imagined to be virtually instinctual, and therefore, uncontrollable.'

At the grassroots, such constructions are often as deeply felt by women as by men. In low-income urban communities in north-west Costa Rica, for example, women complain that regardless of whether men are married or not, they cannot help '*buscando la carne*' (literally 'hunting for flesh/game'), or '*brincando de mujer a mujer como conejitos*' ('jumping from woman to woman like rabbits') (Chant,1997a:218). In this light female sexual restraint is construed as imperative since men cannot effectively be blamed if they are seduced into 'sinning' by 'unchaste women' (see also Craske, forthcoming). This, in turn, fuels the 'sexual double standard', whereby women's restricted access to sex before and during marriage, is counterposed by the

toleration and/or endorsement of men's engagement in multiple sexual liaisons (see also Chapter 7). As summed up by Ennew (1986:59):

> Because they are the repository of male honour, women must be controlled as if they were children, men on the other hands, *are* like children, whose lack of control must be excused and from whose excesses women must be protected (emphasis in original; see also Stevens, 1973:95).

Men's 'congenitally driven' urges are deemed partly to do with the fact that the male phallus is overt and 'on show' (see Stavans, 1998 on the adulation of the phallus in Latin American culture). Infused with the symbolism of courage, pride, power, and strength, the phallus is subject to being conceived as separate from the body, and as possessing its own will (Szasz, 1998:151). In turn, erection and penetration – whether vaginal or anal – are argued to be regarded by most men as the only genuine form of sexual expression (ibid.; see also Sternberg, 2001:63). By contrast, the sexual organs of women are hidden and unknown, and women, unlike men, are not deemed to be 'unfaithful' by nature (Sternberg, 2001:63). This feeds into ideas of the innate moral superiority of women, and their strong link with reproduction, which not only regulates desire in itself, but also by association with the institutions of marriage and the family (see Stevens, 1973; and below).

Normative female sexuality is defined not only in relation to men, but is policed by its own dualisms, which we have explored in part in relation to 'race' and class, and in respect of religious iconography. As summed-up by Nencel (1996:62), even if in practice, there are more than two 'categories': 'The oppositional, bounded discursive categories of femininity divide women into two groups: the good woman (the mother), and the bad woman (whore)'. As Szasz (1998:153) elaborates, 'decent women' are tender, tranquil, understanding, serious, and resist male advances, whereas 'eroticised women' are promiscuous, untrustworthy, provocative, express desires and impulses, and take the initiative in sexual relations.

Given predominant constructions of male and female sexualities in Latin America, it is perhaps no surprise that heterosexual relations are often marked by assertions of power and violence on the part of men. Focus groups conducted with women in Mexico, for example, revealed that among women's main concerns about their sexual relationships with husbands was coercion into sex either by the use of physical force, or the threat of being abandoned. In turn, many women reported humiliation and physical dissatisfaction in the sexual act (Folch-Lyon *et al.*, 1981). Sexual infidelity seems to provide particularly fertile grounds for violence. While women's suspected adultery is the most common catalyst on the part of husbands or boyfriends, Stolcke (1991:96) notes for Brazil that men may also resort to violence in the wake of potential or actual reprimands for their own infidelities (see also Chapter 5).

LANGUAGE, SEXUALITY AND GENDER

Language both reflects and reinforces the powerful gender messages encoded in sexuality. In Lima, Peru, for example, Nencel (1996:63) notes that men's descriptions of their sexual encounters with women have 'connotations of conquest, possession and sexual assertiveness'. The verb '*agarrar*' (to seize or grab), for example, is often used to describe the act of touching a women, and another verb for the same, '*meter*' (to put), has connotations of pushing or shoving. Men's sexual desire is often equated to a 'functioning machine', such that they can feel 'sexually loaded' (*cargado sexualmente*), and need to 'unload' ('*descargar*') (ibid.:64). Revealingly, the language men use to depict their female sexual partners is of a much 'softer' and 'subordinate' nature, with women, helped on by men's sexual skills, 'falling easily' (*caer facilmente*), 'loosening up' (*aflojar*), or 'letting go' (*soltar*).

Similar binaries are found in Costa Rica, where Schifter and Madrigal (1996:34) note that the penis is often depicted as a violent and powerful weapon, such as a '*pistola*' (pistol), '*rifle*' (rifle) or '*ametralladora*' (machine gun), whereas women's sexual organs are presented as 'inferior and passive', such as '*hueco*' or '*hoyo*' ('hole'), or '*raja*' ('cut'). Sandoval García (1997:180–2) also observes the generally greater use of genitally oriented language among men in their discussions of women than *vice versa.*

With language being an important signifier and component of gendered power, it is no surprise to find the use of 'masculine' and 'feminine' terms in sexual language pertaining to same-sex relationships among men. In Nicaragua, Lancaster (1992:242) observes that 'to take by force', 'to seize', to 'grab hold of' ('*coger*', or sometimes '*tomar*') is to be masculine, whereas 'to surrender', 'yield' or 'give-up' ('*rendirse*', sometimes '*dar*') is to be feminine (see later). This is echoed for Brazil by Cornwall (1994:119) who argues that:

> Representations of gender difference in mainstream discourse do not only draw on appearance and anatomy. They present *homens* ('men') and *mulheres* ('women') in terms of agency and its apparent absence.

Cornwall continues that being '*ativo*' ('active') in bed, and a '*comedor*' (literally 'eater', inserter) defines the behaviour of a 'real man', regardless of whether his partner is male or female (ibid.). Just as much as women often define their own identities in relation to other women (albeit within confines of patriarchally imposed categories), men too assert their masculinity in front of other men. For most men it is vitally important that they define their own sexuality and not be labelled (as well as having the power to define and label others) (Craske, forthcoming).

Socialisation and sexuality: perspectives on youth

The forging of asymmetrical sexualities in men and women starts early in Latin America. Long before puberty, girls in many parts of the region are controlled, kept within or close to the home in their play, encouraged to be demure and deferential, and to build up a solid repertoire of domestic skills. Boys, on the other hand, are allowed greater spatial and social freedoms, and receive positive endorsement of aggressive or ostentatious behaviour (loud or boisterous play, for example), that would meet with serious disapproval among their female counterparts. As puberty approaches, these patterns are either extended or reinforced, as argued by Krauskopf (1999:103) for Costa Rica, where: 'From a cultural perspective, sexual development tends to be addressed differently by adults depending on the young person's gender: control and monitoring for young women and encouragement and freedom for young men.' This is echoed for Nicaragua by Lancaster (1992:41) where boys are repeatedly exhorted to 'show aggressiveness, dominate women, or be deprived of your masculinity'. Whereas male children are often taunted by their older siblings into expressions of rage, learn profane language, and are allowed a certain amount of rule breaking by parents, disobedience among girls is much more likely to be penalised, including with the use of physical force (ibid.:42). This seems to represent strong continuity with the past, not only for *mestizo* society, but among other ethnic groups. In early twentieth century Costa Rica, for example, Foote (2001:3) reports that among the black population of the Caribbean coast, girls from better-off families who were tutored in the arts of sewing, cooking and music recalled beatings from their mothers 'for fishing in creeks with boys, riding with them on horseback, and scrumping mangoes'.

For many women, the social acceptance of sex only when linked to marriage and reproduction, and widespread valorisation of the 'fertile mother' (Ehrenfeld Lenkiewicz, 1991:392), makes conformism with heterosexist norms immensely compelling. Female sexuality is not so much an expression of sexual desires as an expression of women's 'nature' as women, which binds them to determined roles. In recent surveys of Mexican youth, for example, it is clear that little distinction is made by girls between sex, procreation and conjugal union, and that girls often conceal their expression of sexual pleasure (see Szasz, 1998:149). This seems to be particularly marked among less educated, rural women (Figueroa and Rivera, 1993:147). In Chile, Willmott (2002) reveals that when women participants in a workshop were asked to identify pictures representing their sexuality, most pointed to images of brides or babies.

Sexual conservatism among girls is fomented not only by parents and wider family, but by schooling and the mass media. Sternberg (2001:60) notes for Nicaragua, for example, that sex education in schools is taught within a 'framework of "family values" which views sex as a necessary evil for perpetuating the species'. In respect of mass media, a study of US and Brazilian teen magazines by Osterman and Keller-Cohen (1998) found that these not only reinforced heterosexuality, but also encouraged girls to conform to particular modes of behaviour within heterosexual partnerships, such as not being too pushy or assertive (feminist).

Across the region, females enter marriage or consensual unions younger than their male counterparts and are more likely to identify themselves as involved in such relationships than are men (Valdés and Gomáriz, 1995:54–7). One-third of women become mothers in Latin America in their teenage years, and even in Cuba, where contraception and abortion have long been widely available, a survey of female workers showed that nearly half had their first child before their twentieth birthday (Safa, 1995b:43; see also Chapter 4). When this is within marriage it is accepted by society, but outside it, much less so. According to a national survey carried out in Costa Rica, people are three times more likely to disapprove of young women having sexual relations as young men (Krauskopf, 1999:103). As Muñoz (1997:44) echoes, in a culture which exalts the links between marriage and motherhood, it is no surprise to find strong censure of unmarried mothers in general, and young single mothers in particular (see also Villareal, 1996:91 on Mexico).

While virginity is possibly less important as a female credential for marriage than in the past, sexual promiscuity is still less acceptable for women, and men in many parts of the region would not consider marrying an obviously promiscuous woman. In rural Argentina, for example, Stølen (1996:171) notes that a woman who sleeps around before marriage is likely to attract an indelible *mancha* (stain or mark), which affects her own reputation, that of her family, and her conjugal prospects. Szasz (1998:154) reports similar patterns for Mexico, where young men are only likely to marry 'decent girls' who allow them to express positive aspects of their evolving masculine identities such as protection, respect and responsibility (see also Amuchástegui Herrera, 1998:118; Melhuus, 1996:245).

That young women, in practice, may be involved in sexual relations, and/or get pregnant at an early age, is often beyond their control. In Nicaragua, for example, a conference organised in 1991 by CISAS (see Chapter 5), an NGO which runs a training programme to help 8–15 year olds provide better childcare for their siblings, suggested that sexual abuse was the foremost health priority among young people in the country (Heise, 1997:415; see also Szasz, 1998:156 on Mexico). Sexual abuse through incest or rape (by boyfriends and stepfathers more commonly than strangers – see Ennew, 1986:61 on Peru) is by no means a new phenomenon in Latin America, but has possibly become more visible over time. As noted by Rodríguez, E. (1994:30) for nineteenth-century Costa Rica, many families did not permit denunciations by their daughters because it was scandalous and put them in the unwelcome gaze of the public eye.

Whereas women in many parts of the region are still told they should save themselves for marriage, boys are encouraged to gain premarital sexual experience in order to 'instruct their women'. This often produces a serious dilemma when the boys ask their girlfriends for a '*prueba de amor*' (proof of love), which usually consists of penetrative sex (Schifter and Madrigal, 1996:53). When this is unduly difficult, or where men wish to 'cut their teeth' without compromising their reputation, they may turn to practices which appear to have been traditionally quite common among wealthier groups, notably having their first sexual experience with prostitutes or with live-in maids (see Ennew, 1986:58; Foote, 2001; Gutmann, 1996:132–3; Nencel, 1996; Stavans, 1998). Another alternative for young heterosexual couples is anal sex (see Parker, 1999:259).

Young men accept their sexual activities as natural, and frequently construe engaging in intercourse as a 'conquest' rather than as a display of affection (Barker and Lowenstein, 1997:187). In Mexico, Amuchástegui Herrera (1998:116) notes that male adolescents in rural areas are keen to have sex with women as a 'proof against the threat of homosexuality'. Indeed, as in many other Western societies, fear of being feminine lies at the heart of male sexuality, with Franco (2001) highlighting the scandal when Independence hero, Simón Bolívar was depicted with breasts and rounded hips by the artist Juan Dávila (see also Craske, forthcoming). In contemporary Nicaragua, workshops with men have revealed varying degrees of homophobia, comprising ideas about homosexuality being 'against nature' or 'against God's will', and/or being a pathological condition triggered by sexually transmitted diseases, by non-communicable illnesses such as cancer, physical causes such as a small penis, or a more general malaise linked with society's loss of values (Sternberg, 2001:63). To some extent, these antipathy-ridden views are contradicted by reports of homoerotic wordplay and discreet physical experimentation among male youth (as well as older men) (see Archetti, 1996; Barker and Lowenstein, 1997; Carrier, 1995; Gutmann, 1996; Lancaster, 1997b; Parker, 1999; Szasz, 1998). Sexual encounters are often limited, however, by the restricted space for young people in Latin America to explore intimacy or alternative sexual behaviours: they usually live at home until they are married, which controls and shapes their sexual practice (see Lancaster, 1998:98). In turn, as summed up by Almaguer (1998:541) in relation to Mexico, the family 'remains a crucial institution that defines both gender and sexual relations between men and women'.

Despite the constraints imposed by parents, recent studies suggest that young people in Latin America are becoming more open about sexual relations. Rivas Zivy (1998), for example, argues that younger women are breaking some of the myths surrounding passive female sexuality (see also Krauskopf, 1999; Schifter and Madrigal, 1996). Reasons for current inter-generational change are numerous, if often hard to pin down categorically, although one major one is the increased availability of contraception which has reduced the risks of pregnancy (something of particular concern for young unmarried women), and thereby helped to separate sex from reproduction (Gutmann, 1997:199; also Chapter 4). Another influence stems from the growth of feminist movements in the region wherein an increasing amount of information, support and identification is provided for young women that has not traditionally been available within the family (see Krauskopf, 1999). Other factors include higher levels of education (which have been linked with later age at marriage – see Chapter 4), and related forms of female validation such as labour force participation which have tended to increase women's autonomy and self-esteem (Ennew, 1986:59). As summed up by Lumsden (1996:115):

> The hegemony of *machista* values – and by extension homophobia – is weakened to the extent that male privilege in social relations is challenged by women at work and in the home. It is also undermined by cultural changes which question traditional stereotypes of masculinity and legitimate alternative forms of sexual expression (Lumsden, 1996:115).

Leading on from the above, there are signs of gradually increasing tolerance of 'alternative sexualities' in Latin America, as discussed below.

Men, women and homosexuality

Acknowledging the difficulties of fixing bodies, sex and gender (Battersby, 1998; Butler, 1993), an analysis of homosexuality in Latin America allows us to see, in crude terms, a wide range of 'masculine' and 'feminine' behaviours crossing male and female 'anatomies' in the region.

Representations of male homosexuality in Latin America

One of the primary themes in work on homosexuality in Latin America has been the notion of a distinctive Latin/circum-Mediterranean view of homosexuality which distinguishes it from popular interpretations in North American and North European contexts. In the latter areas, homosexuality is usually regarded as an 'oral phenomenon' and characterised by same-sex preference. In Latin America, the central defining feature of homosexuality is argued to hinge upon being 'active' or 'passive' in anal intercourse (Lancaster, 1992: 238 *et seq*.; see also Carrier, 1995; Salessi, 1995). With the latter offering fewer possibilities than the former for reciprocal sexual practice, this has also been construed in relation to the Latino diaspora as a difference between object choice and the distribution of power (Almaguer, 1998). In more general terms, these constructions display considerable consonance with an emerging body of Queer theory, which:

> emphasises the performativity of gender and views sexual identities as products of social disciplinary practices. Insofar as behaviour is theatrical, it need not be attributed to any underlying trait or 'essence' of the actor. Seen in this way, masculinity, femininity, queerness, straightness are not so much what one is but what one does (Greenberg, 1997:191; see also Jolly, 2000; Probyn, 1995).

It is also important to take into consideration here that both sexual preference and sexual 'role' may be contingent and shifting (see Cornwall, 1994; Jolly, 2000).

HOMOSEXUALITIES AND MASCULINITIES

The idea of a distinctive Latino homosexuality has been challenged by the argument that not all Latino 'men who have sex with men' in the active role will necessarily deny homosexuality (Mirandé, 1997:138–9; see also Forrest, 1999). None the less, various studies conducted within Latin America indicate that the label 'homosexual' is applied only to men who allow themselves to be anally penetrated and/or that only those men will define themselves as gay. In turn, men who play the active role are less likely to identifty themselves as gay, and importantly do not impugn their masculinity or heterosexual persona in so doing. In Mexico, for example, Prieur (1996:90) notes that men who penetrate men are not stigmatised (see also Szasz, 1998:154). This also applies in Nicaragua, with Lancaster (1992:241) noting that 'While there is clearly a stigma in Nicaraguan homosexual practice … it is not a stigma which clings equally to both parties'. Boasting of having penetrated a gay man frequently features in male talk, and indeed, can even enhance men's manliness, helping them attain the status of *machista* or *hombre-hombre* (very manly) (ibid.:239). In Honduras, too, one saying goes that in order to become a man, one should have sex with a *culero* (passive male) and two women (ibid.:241). As Sandoval García (1997:203) notes of Costa Rica, to conquer men, as well as women, expresses virility and manliness, reaffirming male identity in front of other men. In contrast, effeminate men are not 'real men', but abject, degraded, and the object of 'derision and social contempt' (Almaguer, 1998:541; see also Salessi, 1995).

Beyond this, it is also important to note that men who would consider themselves gay under this model, have their own, often elaborate lexicon to describe different types of same-sex relationship. For example, in the low-income district of Ciudad Nezahuacoyotl in Mexico City, Prieur (1996:85–7) observes that homosexuals who adopt the 'woman's role' in sex with a man refer to themselves as *jotos* or *jotas*, a term which possibly derives from a Spanish dance where men move in a feminine way, or from a Mexican prison where homosexual inmates were lodged in block 'J'. The catch-all *joto/a* also covers transvestites, although a more specific term for the latter is *vestidas* (literally 'dressed-up', and denoted in the feminine). As for masculine-looking men who have sex with effeminate men, *jotos* refer to these as *mayates* ('may-bugs' – flying beetles which come out in the month of May, and are often tied to the end of sticks by children, one possible connotation here being that of 'play'). More graphically, men who like to be both active and passive in anal intercourse are referred to as *tortillas* ('pancakes' which, in their making, are tossed from one hand to another). Other words used self-referentially by homosexuals are *gay* or *homosexual*, and occasionally *puto* (literally, male whore, or more colloquially 'faggot').

The word '*puto*' has conventionally been quite pejorative, but now seems to have been appropriated by some gays themselves. One word that *jotos* decline to use, however is '*maricón*', which derives from the common girl's name María. Interestingly, too, Prieur's conversation with her informant Fidel/Fifi revealed that although *jotos* have traditionally described *bugas* as men who only like to have sex with women, pure *bugas* are now deemed to be so rare in Mexico that the term has effectively been emptied of its original meaning (ibid.:86).

Transvestism

Tranvestism is an important sub-culture within the Latin American homosexual scene, and is also endorsed by wider society, albeit fleetingly, within the framework of the carnival (Cornwall, 1994; Green, 1999; Lancaster, 1997a; Parker, 1997). In Brazil, where, as we have seen, the carnival tradition reaches its most elaborate expression in Latin America, McCallum (1999:277) asserts that *travestis* see themselves as the 'perfect embodiment of the "whore"'. Desiring to be 'feminine', rather than 'female' (Kulick, 1998:309), *travestis* can exercise a 'feminine capacity to attract and to give sexually, without the burdens (as they see it) of motherhood and descendant kin' (McCallum, 1999:277). This said, as Cornwall (1994:112) points out in relation to western European discourse,

> To call someone a 'transvestite' involves making a series of prior assumptions about them. These cluster around the notion that there is some original 'sex' or 'gender' to which they 'really' belong: transvestites *cross*-dress, they do not just dress. Transvestites transgress, moving across the boundaries marking gendered difference. In so doing they pose a challenge to the taken-for-granted association of 'men' with 'male' and 'masculinity', and 'women' with 'female' and 'femininity' [emphasis in original].

Taking on board the importance of this contribution in conceptualising transvestism, it should be noted that in practice some transvestites revel in representing feminine sexuality in an exaggerated form, with some considering themselves better women than their biological namesakes because they always 'dress-up' and 'look after their men' (Lancaster, 1998:265). In Brazil and Mexico, transvestites manipulate various physical attributes (hair, breasts, buttocks) through surgical, hormonal and other interventions to emphasise their 'femininity' (see Cornwall, 1994:113; Kulick, 1998:301; Prieur, 1996:85). For Nicaragua, Lancaster (1997a:14) observes that

> Transvestism lends itself to performances of gender and sexuality, race and class, desire and repulsion, ego and alter – not to mention the physical body, its carnal practices, and its ideal representations.

Many transvestites work as prostitutes, which partly reflects the paucity of spaces available to 'transgressive individuals' within mainstream society and economy (see

Jolly 2000 for a wider discussion of the economic consequences of sexual marginalisation). Although it is not clear whether the clients of *travestis* are looking for male or female companions, it is often argued, particularly in relation to Mexico, that *travestis* appear to want to be sought out and penetrated by men they consider to be heterosexual. In turn, the attraction between *travestis* and heterosexual men is 'related to hidden sexuality, to transgression, and to diverse expressions of manliness in contexts in which sexual access to women is difficult, scarce or expensive' (Szasz, 1998:155; our translation). Prieur (1996:91) also observes that when a man engages in relations with a highly feminine *vestida* whom he may not definitively know to be male from the outset, he often deludes himself in the act of penetration with the help of his partner's willingness to give him 'the excuses and pretexts he needs'. In some circumstances, however, 'feminine' behaviour can readily convert to a more 'masculine' mode. In Salvador, Brazil, for example, when clients refuse to pay or offend in other ways, *travestis* are frequently known to '*virar machão*' (turn *macho*) or act like a '*homem machão*' ('he-man') (Cornwall, 1994:121).

Yet for the most part *travestis* frequently position themselves as more 'authentic' women than women, and this, it is argued, has undermined attempts to find a common struggle for gay and lesbian rights in Latin America. This is further complicated by the often misogynistic attitudes of *travestis* towards women, whether lesbian or heterosexual (see Sifuentes Jáuregui, 1997). One reason for the latter, as Kulick (1998) argues in the case of Brazil, is that lesbians unsettle and/or offend *travestis*' notions of femininity. Lesbians 'disturb because they blur the normative binary modes of gender … that *travestis* draw upon to make sense of their own lives' (ibid.:309). This effectively mocks the *travestis*' efforts at perfecting the art of being 'feminine', and, in turn, gives *travestis* reason to put their own gender subjectivities under the spotlight.

Lesbianism

In comparison with gay men, lesbians are even less visible in Latin America. The conspicuous absence of public proclamations about lesbianism past and present are variously linked to assumptions surrounding female sexual passivity, to *machista* beliefs that only men really matter, and to the fact that female criminality (with which same-sex relations have often been forcefully linked) has been regarded as posing little threat (see for example, Buffington, 1997:127; Leiner, 1994:37; also Green, 1999). Moreover, in a context in which sexuality is centred around penile penetration, lesbians do not have a meaningful sexuality, and are thus invisible and anomalous.[12] As far as lesbians themselves are concerned, the invisibility of lesbianism is a form not only of discrimination, but of violence against them (CMS, 1997: 62). Notwithstanding the plethora of literature on and by Chicana/Latina lesbians in the USA (see for example, Anzaldúa, 1991; Haggerty, 2000),[13] the academic literature on lesbianism in Latin America *per se* remains scant. While not to deny the existence of a growing number of organisations (sometimes linked to international movements) which promote lesbian rights, and an increasing amount of information targeted at lesbian audiences through campaign material, websites and so on, this invisibility highlights the spaces of secrecy, discretion and ambiguity which even publicly identified lesbians have often been forced to inhabit. Although the legendary lesbian singer Chavela Vargas,[14] for example, adopted an uncompromisingly 'butch' image throughout most of her performance and recording musical career in Mexico, she was often less direct when it came to her songs. Although these usually eroticised women as the object of desire, they frequently left the voice of the song 'either unmarked or identified as male' (Yarbro-Bejerano, 1997:38). This gave the songs sufficient ambiguity to be open to male heterosexual as well as lesbian readings.

The movement of openly lesbian women like Chavela into positions in the public eye can clearly send positive messages to lesbians in general. While this has traditionally been rare in politics, and lesbians in Mexico who have taken on important party roles have often kept their sexuality out of the headlines, 1997 saw Patria Jiménez become the first 'openly gay legislator in Latin America' when she was elected to the Mexican congress for the PRD (*Partido de la Revolución Democrática*/ Party of the Democratic Revolution).[15]

Lesbian organising is another important vehicle in this regard. Following in the footsteps of their counterparts in the USA, who founded organisations such as 'Gay and Lesbian Latinos Unidos' (GLLU) in 1981, and its sub-group 'Lesbianas Unidas' (LU) three years later, in the 1980s and early 1990s 'fledgling lesbian movements' sprouted in various parts of the region, including Chile (1983), Argentina (1985), Costa Rica (1987), Honduras (1987), Nicaragua (1991), and El Salvador (1992) (Thayer, 1997:386). These movements have by no means been similar, however: Thayer, comparing Costa Rica and Nicaragua, suggested that the lesbian movement in the former (originating with a small middle-class group who called themselves '*Las Entendidas*'/'The Understood') tended to have an 'inward orientation', characterised by 'creation of a community, and assertion of autonomy as a sexual minority' (ibid.:389). Lesbian organising in Costa Rica emerged out of a long-standing feminist movement comprising strong liberal and academic feminist strands, and had no obvious alignment with the country's small and effectively 'silenced' left (ibid.:390). *Las Entendidas* primarily involved the provision of a supportive space for lesbians to share their personal feelings and experiences (see also Madden Arias, 1996).

In the Nicaraguan case, by contrast, lesbians (and gays) joined forces to work for full social integration and 'to project to the society at large its vision of a free sexuality for all' (Thayer, 1997:390). In the early phase of lesbian organising in the country, there were two groups, *Nosotras*, which worked directly with lesbians, and *Xoxchiquezta1*, which worked on behalf of lesbians and gays. Both organisations, however, collaborated with a range of other civil society groups including feminists. In contrast to Costa Rica, in Nicaragua, 'the feminist and lesbian movements were born simultaneously, led by women whose worldview and sense of politics were shaped by a once-strong class-based movement' (ibid.).

Thayer attributes these differences to a wide variety of phenomena relating to the broader social, political and economic contexts of the two countries, and, *inter alia*, draws attention to the Sandinista legacy of mobilising in defence of 'commitment to social justice for the majority, and to collective, rather than individual, solutions' (ibid.:401). This is seen as having provided the basis for a much stronger, outward-oriented lesbian movement in Nicaragua, galvanised by the homophobic campaigns of President Violeta Chamorro and the then Mayor of Managua Arnoldo Alemán (later president) in the early 1990s, to reinvigorate 'family values', to clean the capital's streets of homosexual activity, and to pass what has been described as 'the most repressive anti-sodomy law in the hemisphere' (ibid.:400).[16] By contrast, in Costa Rica, lesbians' weaker profile conceivably reflected the fact that there were fewer obvious social, economic and political problems to address, that 'participation in a semi-autonomous community was a viable possibility for a certain group of women' (ibid.:395), and that the 'Costa Rican state, with its largely invisible moral foundation and stable integration with civil society, offered a slippery target for transformatory challenges and discouraged a focus on politics *per se*' (ibid.:397). While feminism was important to *Las Entendidas*, the latter did not have a particularly comfortable relationship with other women's organisations in Costa Rica. For example, feminists failed to rally to the defence of the organisers of the Second Latin American and Caribbean Lesbian Feminist Encounter in San José in 1990 when they were faced with attacks from the Church, state and media. One group also backed out of offering the lesbians a meeting place at the university (ibid.:398; see also Madden Arias, 1996). In Chile, too, Rivera Fuentes (1996b:143) argues that despite the common discourse between lesbian and heterosexual feminists about gender oppression in the 1980s, the primacy attached to overthrowing the Pinochet dictatorship prevented a deeper analysis of different sexual options. In addition, women's movements, which at the time experienced enough problems being identified as 'feminist', feared that matters would be worse still if they had 'out' lesbians on their files (ibid.).

While lesbians in other contexts have often been marginalised within women's movements (see for example, Scott and Jackson, 1996:13–15; also Anzaldúa, 1991 on 'lesbians-of-colour' in relation to white lesbians in the USA), it is also significant that demands for lesbian rights were not linked with those of gay men, as they were in Nicaragua and in the US Latino diaspora. This has also been the case in

Argentina, where although lesbians have often fought alongside other women as part of feminist and human rights movements (see Fúskova-Kornreich and Argor, 1993), the 'deep misogyny' of gay men is claimed to have made it difficult for lesbians to participate in mixed groups (Csörnyei and Palumbo, 1996:154). Another context where this is noted is Cuba, where Lumsden (1996:151) argues that:

> As a rule, lesbians who challenge and refuse to conform with … oppressive stereotypes (conventional feminine and *machista* norms) are no more part of an integrated homosexual scene than they are anywhere else in Latin America.

Notwithstanding the apparent difficulties of achieving consensus *within*, as well as *between*, groups with different identities and agendas, a major point of interest is the extent to which collaboration in different contexts can provide greater visibility to marginalised groups, and, in so doing, give rise to more effective ways of advancing an agenda for inclusive citizenship and human rights (see also Chapters 2 and 3). On a wider, global scale Tielman and Hammelburg (1993:251) assert that:

> Generally speaking, the success of gay and lesbian movements is closely related to the capacity for pragmatic cooperation within and outside the movement, and the support of key figures and allies in the general public.

Gay and lesbian rights in Latin America

Although Mirandé (1997) maintains that, over time, gay male culture in Mexico has emerged from blanket negativity and a 'shroud of silence', and is beginning to become more visible in big cities (partly as a result of HIV/AIDS), traditionally it has been closeted and concealed. This is also true of most other countries in the region, especially in rural areas. For example, in pre-revolutionary Cuba, discreet gays, referred to as '*entendidos*', as in '*entendido pero no dicho*' ('understood but not declared'), were much less likely to invite social opprobrium than gays who engaged in obvious displays of same-sex passion (Lumdsen, 1996:30).[17] In both Argentina and Mexico, Almaguer (1998:543) asserts that more masculine homosexuals (referred to as *macho maricas* ['butch queens'] in Argentina) are more likely to be able to engage in 'gay lifestyles' insofar as they can gain legitimacy through their gender conformity. Yet although more effeminate homosexuals who have never identified themselves as heterosexual are decidely more stigmatised by society at large, in personal terms they tend to report fewer problems in 'coming out' (ibid.). The literature that exists on lesbianism, however, documents that constraints on free sexual expression and 'visibility' are perhaps even more deeply felt (see, for example, CMS, 1997).

The situation whereby the majority of gays and lesbians in Latin America have had to keep their lifestyles and practices under wraps is in large part a reflection of the dominance of heterosexism in the region, which has often equated homosexuality with crime, deviance and other forms of social pathology, and viewed 'sexual transgression' as a serious threat to the gender order. Antipathy to homosexuality has been expressed in a variety of ways, ranging from the killing of homosexuals under military regimes in Argentina, Chile and Guatemala, to less draconian, but still powerful, attempts at elimination in revolutionary Cuba, where the puritanism and social rigidity of Marxism–Leninism marked homosexuality as a remnant of diseased capitalism, and as antithetical to the socialist project (Leiner, 1994:25; see also Forrest, 1999; Hodge, 2001). As Lumsden (1996:65) notes, these Stalinist dogmas

> found fertile ground in Cuba, given its own traditional prejudices and the universal belief of Cuban doctors, psychiatrists and lawyers that homosexuality entailed crime and social delinquency as much as gender inversion and medical disease.

Concern to protect the goals of the Cuban revolution led to organised repression in the mid-1960s in the form of camps dedicated to work and 'rehabilitation' (UMAP camps – Military Units to Aid Protection). Many homosexuals, whose behaviour was deemed to fall outside the public definition of 'good citizenship' found themselves interned, while beyond the camp enclosures, 'Yellow Brigades' of children were set to the task of 'toughening up' effeminate boys (Leiner, 1994:34). In 1970, the *Ley de Peligrosidad* (Law of Dangerousness) made homosexuals subject to preventive detention (Lumsden, 1996:82), and in 1974 homosexuals were legally banned from the teaching of children in the interests of arresting the spread of 'socially pathological homosexual deviations' (Leiner, 1994:35). Although the Penal Code of 1979 decriminalised homosexuality, it still provided for the fining of 'scandalous' and 'ostentatious' acts of homosexuality (ibid.:43; see also Lumsden, 1996:81–2).

The language used by 'outsiders' to describe gays is often demeaning and pejorative. For example, whereas gays in Cuba prefer to call themselves *locas* (literally 'mad', but more appropriately translated as 'queens'), the outsider label '*maricón*' (see earlier), embodies connotations of cowardice. The latter is also used to goad men who fail to live up to heterosexual expectations (Lumsden, 1996:29; see also Prieur, 1996:99 on Mexico). In Nicaragua, too, if a man does not 'come out on top', he literally, or effectively, becomes a *cochón* (queer), the term deriving from '*colchón*', meaning mattress and symbolising the passive partner lying under his active counterpart in anal intercourse (Lancaster, 1992:237–9). According to research conducted under the auspices of the Central American Programme for Sustainability, Costa Rica's long-standing reputation for 'democratic values' sits in glaring contrast with the fact that its citizens are much less tolerant of minority groups than other Central Americans, with homosexuals ranking top of the list of 'most disliked groups', Nicaraguans second, and atheists third.[18] As noted earlier in the chapter, Church pronouncements have also targeted gays and lesbians, along with single parents, as responsible for the deteriorating state of the country's values and morality and for the breakdown of family traditions (see Chant, 2002b; also Chapter 7). In Brazil, it is estimated that at least one homosexual is murdered every four days as a result of societal homophobia (Green, 1999:3). Yet as Lancaster (1992:269) notes in relation to Nicaragua:

> It is not that homophobia is more intense in a culture of *machismo*, but that it is a different sort of thing altogether. Indeed the word homophobia, meaning a fear of homosexuals or homosexual intercourse, is quite inappropriate in a milieu where unlabelled men desire and actively seek intercourse with labelled men.

Aside from overt curtailments of homosexual freedoms discussed in relation to Cuba above, and to killings in military dictatorships, Latin American states have resorted to other modes of homosexual repression, even if homosexuality is not technically a criminal offence (see Box 6.1).[19] In post-dictatorship Argentina, for example, lesbians have been sacked from jobs on grounds of their sexuality (Csörnyei and Palumbo, 1996:153), as has also been the case for over 100 allegedly homosexual civil servants in Peru (Box 6.1). In turn, lesbians and gays have often been excluded from more prominent public positions. In Mexico, for example, it is rumoured that when naming his cabinet as newly incumbent president, Vicente Fox of the National Action Party (PAN) overlooked an eminently suitable candidate for Culture Minister on grounds of her sexuality (Craske, forthcoming). Such rumours are unlikely to be unfounded given the party's unconcealed hostility to the fact that the 250 feminist groups making up the Mexican delegation to Beijing in 1995 'gave their support to the "concept of the Lesbian family as a legal option in juridical and economic terms"' (Franco, 1998:280, citing an article in the Mexican political magazine, *Proceso*, of January 1995). In Argentina, campaigners have sought urgent attention to the rights of lesbian mothers to the custody of children (Csörnyei and Palumbo,1996:153). Beyond the more obvious forms of condemnatory treatment, it is also important to recognise that:

> Homosexual oppression exists almost by definition so long as a society is *machista* and the state accords privileges to certain forms of gender and sexual relations – physical expressions among heterosexuals in public, conventional definitions of what constitutes a family, and heterosexual parenting and custody of children … and reinforces their superior status though the educational system and especially in the mass media (Lumsden, 1996:146; see also CMS, 1997:70).

In countries such as Guatemala, where assertions of identity and human rights have been all but decimated by years of repression and violence, these discriminations are even more deeply experienced and result in scores of people leading isolated and silenced lives (see for example, Acevedo, 2000 on lesbians in Guatemala). In Argentina too, any effective activism, let alone that of gays and lesbians, is

BOX 6.1

Attitudes Towards Homosexuality in Selected Latin American Countries

ARGENTINA

Official Attitudes and the Law
Neither the Constitution nor the Penal Code specifically condemns homosexuality among adults. Moreover, in 1992, the country's main gay rights organisation, the *Comunidad Homosexual Argentina* (CHA/Argentinian Homosexual Community), was granted legal standing. Nevertheless, in the capital, Buenos Aires, as well as in many of the provinces, *edictos policiales* (police edicts) continue to exist. Under these edicts, individuals can be detained for up to thirty days under the charge of being 'morally offensive'. They can also be detained for up to forty-eight hours for so-called 'preliminary investigation'. The application of these rules falls especially on gay men and renders them subject to registration.

Society
There is limited open discussion or public visibility of homosexuality, and little social support for gay and lesbian rights. Society is guided by the concept of *machismo* and heavily influenced by a conservative, anti-homosexual Catholic church.

BRAZIL

Official Attitudes and the Law
The age of consent for both homosexuals and heterosexuals is eighteen years. Homosexual behaviour between consenting adults is not mentioned in the law as being a criminal offence, except for Article 235 of the military Penal Code which criminalises 'indecent acts, homosexual or not', between soldiers. Although homosexuality is not illegal, the police use the pretext of 'safeguarding morality and public decency' and 'preventing outrageous behaviour' to apprehend, arrest and bring homosexuals to trial where they would be unlikely to proceed against heterosexuals in similar situations. None the less, 77 municipalities in the country forbid discrimination on grounds of sexual orientation, and in June 2000 the federal government decreed that same-sex partners should have equal rights as married heterosexual couples in respect of taxes, social security benefits, and inheritance.

Society
Despite the centrality of gays in Carnival celebrations, and the fact that over 50 per cent of the population declare themselves in favour of same-sex unions, Brazil has one of the highest rates of violence against homosexuals. An estimated total of 130 gays were murdered in the year 2000 alone.

CHILE

Official Attitudes and the Law
In 1989, the Reform Act of the Constitution deleted Article 8 of the old Constitution,

which gave legal provision for the persecution of gays and lesbians. None the less, male homosexual acts remain illegal. Article 365 of the Penal Code defines consenting male homosexual activity as a sodomy delict, with a penalty of between one-and-a-half and three years' imprisonment. The length of the sentence depends upon the complaints of the 'victim'. Lesbian sexual contact is not mentioned in the law. Homosexuals are often subjected to official and police harassment and violence. A policy also exists of compulsory HIV testing of all known gay men.

Society
Homosexuality is taboo. There is no visible support for gay and lesbian rights. Gay and lesbian groups exist, but are illegal. Following the organisation of the first lesbian and gay meeting in Chile in 1987, the lesbian group *Colectivo Ayuquelén* received written death threats from right-wing factions.

DOMINICAN REPUBLIC

Official Attitudes and the Law
Homosexual behaviour between consenting adults is not mentioned in the law as being a criminal offence. However, gay men are disproportionately affected by laws regarding 'offences against morality' and 'corruption of minors'. Homosexuals are often subjected to police harassment and violence.

Society
Although a minority of the population is in favour of gay and lesbian rights, society is generally hostile to homosexuality. Homosexuals in prison are treated badly.

HONDURAS

Official Attitudes and the Law
Homosexual behaviour between consenting adults is not mentioned in the law or in the Penal Code as being a criminal offence. According to Section 60 of the Honduran Constitution, every citizen has equal rights, and acts of discrimination violating human dignity are punishable. In March 1987, the Honduran Embassy in The Hague stated that 'no legal protection of homosexuals is necessary'.

Society
There is no visible support for gay and lesbian rights.

MEXICO

Official Attitudes and the Law
Homosexual behaviour between consenting adults is not mentioned in the law as a criminal offence, yet there is a difference between heterosexual 'abuse of minors' (which carries a maximum penalty of five years), and homosexual 'abuse of minors' (which carries a penalty of up to ten years). In 1991, the local authorities in the city of Guadalajara prohibited the annual conference of the International Lesbian and Gay

Association (ILGA) from taking place, forcing the organisers to move the venue to Acapulco. In 1992, there were killings of many gay activists by death squads, and the police raided gay bars in Tijuana.

Society
Although only a minority of the population is in favour of gay and lesbian rights, same-sex partnerships were granted legal status as *sociedades de convivencia* (civil unions) in 2001.

PERU

Official Attitudes and the Law
Homosexual behaviour between consenting adults is not mentioned in the law as being a criminal offence. Although homosexual acts, in private and among consenting adults, are not illegal, an exception is made for the military and police forces. Under the provisions of Section 269 of the Military Penal Code of 1980, the performance of 'dishonourable acts of carnal knowledge against the order of nature' with a person of the same sex carries a penalty of between two months' and twenty years' imprisonment. Sometimes punishment extends to dismissal from the forces as well. The Civil Code also allows for the annulment of marriage where one spouse has been ignorant of the other's homosexuality, and homosexuality is a ground for separation or divorce. Laws referring to 'public morality' are often used against gays and lesbians, and in 1993 President Fujimori fired 117 top civil servants on the basis of their alleged homosexuality.

Society
Only a minority of the population are in support of lesbian and gay rights. In general, society is hostile. The Maoist terrorist group *Sendero Luminoso* (Shining Path) has killed many gay men for 'corrupting youth'.

VENEZUELA

Official Attitudes and the Law
Homosexual behaviour between consenting adults is not mentioned as a criminal offence in the law. However, gay men and lesbians are not admitted into the armed forces. Moreover. homosexuals are often subjected to police harassment and violence.

Society
A minority of the population are in favour of gay and lesbian rights. Although social attitudes in general are quite hostile, however, they are relatively tolerant compared with other Latin American countries.

Sources: Tielman and Hammelburg (1993); www.divamag.co.uk; www.indiana.edu/~arenal/

reported to have been completely paralysed during the period of dictatorship between 1976 and 1983 (Fuskóva-Kornreich and Argov, 1993:81).

Despite the weight of societal prejudices, Gutmann (1996:128–9) notes for Mexico that attitudes towards homosexuality are gradually changing, and in turn influencing the ways in which people identify themselves sexually. Class and education play important roles in sexual identity, with evidence to suggest that more middle-class professional men identify themselves as gay on the basis of their orientation rather than the acts in which they engage, which reflects a more Anglo-American perspective (Green, 1999). In addition, same-sex partnerships, as in Brazil, have recently been granted legal recognition (see Box 6.1).

In Nicaragua, where, as noted earlier, lesbian organising has been strong and has involved active collaboration with straight feminists and gay men alike, lesbian groups have had an increasing presence in International Women's Day celebrations since the early 1990s, and June 1991 saw the first open Gay Pride celebration (Thayer, 1997:401). Lumsden (1996:26) asserts, for Cuba, that the progressive erosion of *machismo* has created space for a more overt, if not by any means ostentatious, homosexuality, and that the government seems to tolerate the semi-public gay parties (despite their illegal cover charges and sale of black market alcohol), which have become an important feature of weekend life in the capital (ibid.:141). In addition, the first public meeting of lesbians and gays in Cuba took place in Havana on 28 July 1994, with that day thereafter being named as the annual 'Gay Pride Day of Cuba'. Such obvious displays of homosexual identity would have been inconceivable at the height of the Soviet period. In Guatemala, too, the first Lesbian and Gay Pride March was held in June 2000, following on the heels of the formation of a Central American Regional Lesbian Network (*Red Regional Lésbica*) in April of that year. Under the banner of slogans such as 'we are part of a society of equal rights' and 'respect for sexual diversity', around 100 gays and lesbians turned out to join the rally, although fear of being recognised meant that several came in disguise.[20] Some indigenous groups in Guatemala, with their own agendas for battling discrimination on grounds of ethnicity, have also stressed their support for a wider remit which extends to abolishing discrimination on grounds of sexual orientation (Congreso de la República, 1999:13).

Another, less auspicious, reason for greater visibility of homosexuality, is the spread of HIV/AIDS in Latin America. While Cuba is the only country which has gone to the lengths of physically confining seropositive individuals (see Chapter 5), and Chile has a policy of compulsory testing of known gay men (see Box 6.1), other countries in the region have often drawn direct links between the spread of the disease and 'risk *groups*', rather than 'risk *activity*'. Indeed, Lumsden (1996:165) asserts that, compared with the initial homophobic pronouncements made by public health officials in Mexico and Costa Rica, the Cuban quarantining policy (which had also been used for other epidemics in the country such as dengue and African swine fever), looks less draconian. Moreover, regardless of whether or not Latin American governments themselves consciously resist fomenting the notion that HIV/AIDS is a 'gay scourge', as has occurred in other regions of the world, these may have little impact on popular bigotries and hostilities among the population at large. By the same token, for homosexual people themselves, concern about AIDS and protecting the rights of sexual minorities has been a galvanising force in forging lesbian and gay solidarity, as in the Guatemalan organisation OASIS (*Organización de Apoyo a una Sexualidad Integral Frente al SIDA*/Organisation for Support of an Integrated Sexuality in the Face of AIDS), founded in 1993.

Conclusion

While this discussion of sexualities in Latin America has necessarily been limited and schematic, it has demonstrated that hierarchical heterosexist norms have circumscribed and constrained the behaviours and identities of all people in the region in one form or another, whether male or female, gay, straight, transvestite, or undecided/determined, and/or black, *mestizo, mulato* or indigenous. While in many respects, these norms show striking levels of persistence, at some levels and in some quarters it is possible to discern greater tolerance towards departures from past beliefs and practices over time. This is unambiguously due to the efforts of people whose 'marginalised' or 'inferior' sexualities have confined them to a situation where they have not been able to enjoy their full sexual rights in any open manner. This is especially so among lesbians and gay men who, in contexts where they have found ways of confident and expressive organising, have drawn strength from their own, collectively self-generated frames of reference. This has helped them to resist oppressive modes of family, state and religious socialisation, and to gain spaces of legitimacy.

This is not to say that the battle for sexual pluralism is anywhere near being won. There are many obstacles to be overcome, and whether these will diminish or not in a time of AIDS is a question that is likely to be fraught with tension. Another potential conflict, as noted in the work of Lancaster (1992) and Lumsden (1996) in particular, is how the relations between homophobia and *machismo* will be negotiated in future, especially as 'traditional masculine identities' continue to come under threat from changes in the family and in the labour market.

While we consider labour market changes in Chapter 8, the following chapter deals with 'the family'. This is the arena where arguably the most marked tensions between male and female sexualities are played out, with consequences, in turn, for almost all aspects of public, private and personal life.

7 Gender, Families and Households

SYLVIA CHANT

Introduction

This chapter concentrates on gender, families and households in Latin America, focusing particularly on the changing shape of household arrangements over the last few decades, shifts in family norms and legislation, and the interrelations of these changes with transformations in gender.

The chapter begins with a brief review of conceptual perspectives on households and families, and a summary of issues which are dominating this field of enquiry globally at the start of the twenty-first century. It then moves on to discuss 'the Latin American family', drawing attention not only to the significance of familial norms for the construction of gender roles, relations and identities in the region, but also to the immense diversity of household organisation in practice. The second part of the chapter traces broad trends in family and household life in the late twentieth century, and identifies the principal factors contributing to a decline in the 'patriarchal family' which seems to have prevailed as an ideal, if not a reality, throughout most of Latin America until the relatively recent past. It also looks at state and civil society responses to changes in household organisation and intra-household relations and responsibilities. The chapter concludes with a discussion of the prospective shape of family life and household organisation in Latin America in the twenty-first century.

Conceptual perspectives on families and households

Although 'families' and 'households' have become increasingly contested concepts in recent years, both have occupied a central position in the analysis of gender, not only in Latin America, but globally. With 'family' generally taken to be a set of normative (and frequently patriarchal) relations centred on blood and marriage, and 'household' a unit of co-residence (Roberts, 1994:10), the fact that most households worldwide consist of people related affinally or consanguineally means that the latter are not only viewed as a conduit for gendered familial ideologies (Kuznesof, 1989:169), but as 'a primary site of women's subordination' (Kabeer and Joekes, 1991:1).

So close is the association between 'families' and 'households' that the two are often deployed interchangeably. However, Moore (1994a:2) reminds us that overlap does not imply synonymity, and the 'degree of congruence between them will always require empirical specification' (ibid.:3). Families, which have traditionally and symbolically been defined through the functions of reproduction and the regulation of sexuality (Arriagada, 1998:86), are usually wider and more abstract than households, and, depending on household composition and the links maintained among kin, may or may not affect significantly daily aspects of household organisation and survival. Moreover, some indigenous groups in Latin America, such as the Zinacantecos of Mexico, do not have a term for 'household', but instead define the basic social unit as a 'house' and draw no boundaries between family units (Collier *et al.*,1997:73).

Theorising the relationship between households and families is complicated not only by competing interpretations and cultural-linguistic specificities, but by the fact that both entities themselves are open to seemingly infinite variations on the ground. With regard to 'the family', for example, Moore (1994a:2) points up that 'there is no such thing as *the* family, only families' (emphasis in original), which vary within and between regions, and over time, due to myriad constellations of structural factors (local economies and cultures, patterns of landholding, class, ethnicity and so on), juxtaposed with features instrinsic to family units such as stage in the life course. In turn, there has been long-standing debate, dating from the work of the anthropologist Bronislaw Malinowski in the early 1900s, as to the universalism of 'the family' as an essentially 'natural' institution for the nurturance of young children, *vis-à-vis* the idea of family as an 'ideological construct associated with the modern state' (see Collier *et al.*, 1997:72 *et seq.*; also Moore, 1988:23–7).

Debates over 'the household' have followed similar trajectories. Aside from on-going attempts to reject pervasive notions of naturalism and universalism (Harris, 1981; Roberts, 1991), the range of meanings ascribed to 'household' in different languages and cultures, coupled with immense diversity in patterns of daily social organisation, leads also to the observation that we cannot treat households as singular entities. This strikes right to the core of defining criteria. Although census bureaux, social scientists and policy-makers are wont to define households as residentially based 'housekeeping' units comprising people who share a domestic space and basic reproductive activities, they may just as readily be be understood as kinship units or economic units (Chant, 1997a:5–7; Guyer and Peters, 1987;

Thorner and Ranadive, 1992). The concept of 'household head' has also been subject to debate. Mirroring the geographical spread of Eurocentric ideas of 'family' and 'household' from the colonial period onwards, the notion that households have one member who is nominally responsible for others and who occupies a position of authority at the apex of the household unit (which translates into questions about who is defined as the head by family members themselves or on the basis of imposed categories such as breadwinning or decision-making power), has been heralded by feminist writers as a construct of patriarchal thought and practice (Folbre, 1991:90; Harris, 1981).

The importance of households and families in gender analysis

Accepting the difficulties of generalising about households and families, their importance for gender lies in the role of domestic units as a (if not *the*) major arena for socialisation, in which messages and meanings concerning gender are transmitted inter-generationally through norms and practices of parenting, conjugality and filial obligation. This, in turn, intermeshes with wider societal corollaries such as divisions of labour, the distribution of resources, entitlements and capabilities, and divisions of power (see Scott, 1994:77). Somewhat ironically perhaps, although women are often the most stable members of household units, and the 'notion of "family" is often strongly identified with female gender and focal female members' (McCallum, 1999:278),[1] since historically households and families in most parts of the world have been embedded within patriarchal, if not necessarily patrilineal, kinship systems, they are often conceived as playing a primary role in gender difference and inequality, not to mention women's subordination. As summed up by Castells (1997:134):

> Patriarchalism is a founding structure of all contemporary societies. It is characterised by the institutionally enforced authority of males over females and children in the family unit. For this authority to be exercised, patriarchalism must permeate the entire organisation of society, from production to consumption to politics, law and culture.... Yet is is analytically, and politically, essential not to forget the rooting of patriarchalism in the family structure, and in the socio-biological reproduction of the species, as historically and culturally framed.

While subjection to male authority has also, in many cases, won protection and security for women – encapsulated in Deniz Kandiyoti's (1991) concept of the 'patriarchal bargain' – for the most part feminist analyses have highlighted families and households as sources of gender oppression. In turn, feminists have sought to disrupt precepts about the 'natural' rule of husbands and fathers and its benefits for women and children. In economic analyses, for example, collective bargaining models associated with New Institutional Economics (NIE) which see households as loci of 'competing interests, rights, obligations and resources' (Moore, 1994b: 87; see also Bruce and Lloyd, 1992; Feijoó, 1999; Schmink, 1984) have gradually replaced approaches which either treated households as unproblematised 'black boxes', or which subscribed to a unitary household model. The latter is most commonly associated with the 'New Household Economics' (NHE) approach of Gary Becker (1976, 1981) who proposed that in the interests of 'joint household utility', women would altruistically sacrifice personal consumption and cede decision-making and income-generating roles to husbands who were likely to secure the greatest returns from employment. This division of labour would best maximise family welfare (see Kabeer, 1994: Chapter 5 for a fuller discussion; also Hart, 1997).

Among the bargaining models, that of 'Cooperative Conflict' developed by Amartya Sen (1991) has aroused particular interest among feminists in its concern with intra-household disparities in gender and power. By the same token, the model does not completely dismiss altruism, which in turn feeds into the situation where, among policy-makers and among more conservative sectors of society in particular, 'gender is represented as an inherent part of the human condition rather than a social product' (Scott, 1994:77).

Current issues in gender and family/household analysis

HOUSEHOLDS AS ARENAS OF GENDER INEQUALITY

Leading on from the above, one of the primary issues in the contemporary study of households and families is that of gender inequality and the need to focus on internal household dynamics and power relations in order to understand men's and women's personal experiences, as well as wider social disparities between them. Intra-household gender inequality has received particular attention in the South in the wake of post-1980 neoliberal economic restructuring. Women's rising labour force participation during the last two decades has been compounded by intensified work in their homes and communities in the wake of cutbacks in state services and increased reliance on subsistence strategies with rising costs of basic goods (see for example Arriagada, 1998; Chant, 1996b; González de la Rocha, 1988; Kanji, 1991; Moser, 1992; also Chapter 3). This has brought the unequal gendered costs and benefits of household membership into especially stark relief.

HOUSEHOLDS AS SPACES OF RESISTANCE AND NEGOTIATION

Women have not necessarily accepted these additional burdens without struggle, however. This has led to the view that while households are often a setting for the emergence of gender divisions and inequalities, they can also be regarded as spaces for agency, resistance and negotiation. Recent labour market changes, for example, which have contributed to increasing women's access to employment, have been accompanied by some significant challenges to male power and privilege in households. Men who fail to fulfil their obligations to household survival, for instance, are under greater threat of losing wives who are now better placed to fend for themselves economically (Benería, 1991; Safa, 1995a,1999). Similarly, men can no longer necessarily dictate that their wives should not work, notwithstanding that not all men have resisted women's employment but made personal adaptations to accommodate patterns which benefit the household collectively (see Bastos, 1999 on Guatemala).

MEN AND MASCULINITIES IN FAMILIES

An offshoot of this has been the concerted attempt to redress the 'female bias' in studies of household change by considering the role of men in families and households (see for example, Chant, 2000; Fuller, 2000; Gutmann, 1996; Pineda, 2000; Westwood, 1996; Willott and Griffin, 1996). Many of these studies have concluded that market-driven economic changes which have undermined men's ability to fulfil their normative duties as 'family providers' have spawned a perceptible crisis of 'masculine identity' in many parts of the world, not least in Latin America (Chant, 2000; Escobar Latapí, 1998; Kaztman, 1992). As noted by Fuller (2000:111) in the context of Peru: 'work is … represented as a masculine space *par excellence* because it is where the male accumulates the social, symbolic and productive capitals that are their contribution to their families'. Yet, as the same author continues, work is precisely the sphere of gender relations that has 'undergone the most dramatic changes during the decades' (ibid.). This has been linked in many cases with a rising incidence of domestic and community violence, and increased male desertion of spouses and offspring (de Barbieri and de Oliveira, 1989; Gutmann, 1996, 1997; Moser and McIlwaine, 2000; Selby *et al.*, 1990:176). By the same token, research has revealed the profound significance of family life and membership for men (see Chant, 2000; Engle and Alatorre Rico, 1994; also later). It has also drawn attention to the fact that many men feel disadvantaged and vulnerable in their later years when they lose their connection to the world of work and effectively become 'de-gendered' (Varley and Blasco, 2000b).

CONTINUITY OR CHANGE IN FAMILY PATTERNS?

In some senses work on masculinities in families has plugged into a fourth key issue in contemporary household and family studies, that of continuity or change in family patterns. While some maintain that family forms have always been diverse, others argue that current plurality symptomises the 'breakdown' of the 'traditional' family, which is commonly taken to be a patriarchal nuclear unit (see Moore, 1994a:4). As Castells (1997:138) sums up, this encompasses:

> the weakening of a model of family based on the stable exercise of authority/domination over the whole family by the adult male head of the family. It is possible, in the 1990s, to find indicators of such a crisis in most societies… .

Part of the fall-out from concern about the demise of the patriarchal family unit is the stigmatisation of female-headed households, which contemporary feminist studies have made concerted efforts to 'unpack' (see Baylies, 1996; Chant, 1997a, 1999a; Feijoó, 1999).

THE IMPORTANCE OF FAMILIES AND HOUSEHOLDS IN SOCIAL POLICY

Last but not least, a fifth issue dominating current research on families and households is their role in social policy. The place of the family in social policy has perhaps received most attention in the North in the context of declining state welfare provision (see Moore, 1994a). Yet while historically families and households in most parts of the South have borne greater responsibility for their own survival and reproduction than in places where governments have been able to devote more resources to social spending, neoliberal cutbacks in state services and subsidies have placed a larger share of this burden on people's shoulders (see Chapter 3). At the same time, growing economic polarisation and poverty have exerted fragmentary influences on a range of family relationships. As in Europe and North America, the dissolution of the 'traditional' family in various parts of the South has provoked alarm in various quarters. While the Catholic Church has deplored the decline of the marriage-based family mainly on moral grounds, state concern about 'family disintegration' devolves upon cuts in social expenditure and the reduced potential for assisting low-income groups (Bruce and Lloyd, 1992; Engle and Breaux, 1994). In the interests of bolstering self-reliance among the population, 'the family' has increasingly been emphasised as a means of strengthening grassroots 'social capital' and maintaining survival in conditions of economic insecurity (Chant, 2002b; Molyneux, forthcoming). As in other regions of the world, official appeals to fortify family cohesion can be seen as embedded within a wider imperative of redrawing the boundaries between citizens, the market and the state (see Molyneux, 1998; Moore, 1996:73; Muncie and Wetherell, 1995:74). In Latin America, as Arriagada (1998:86) concludes:

> the family is increasingly considered as the main space for the action of public policies and the area in which they can have the biggest impact.… There is a debate from various angles on the role of the family in building solid, integrated societies, but paradoxically no consideration is given to the fact that it is assigned functions and faced with demands which are increasingly difficult to fulfil, both because of the great changes which have taken place in its formation, size and functions, the new roles that its members have to play in society and the scanty internal resources available to families today, and because of the changes in the State's role in providing certain services.

'The Latin American family' and gender

In the light of preceding discussions, it is clear that we cannot in any way talk about a typical 'Latin American family'. Yet despite differentiation on grounds of place, time, class, ethnicity and so on, common threads are not completely elusive. While acknowledging inter-class differences in the case of eighteenth- and nineteenth-century Peru, for example, Scott (1994:75–6) draws attention to a range of shared features. These include: the importance of the state and the Roman Catholic Church in influencing and legitimating family roles; a bias towards patrilineal inheritance; a tendency for people to reside in nuclear households but also to value extended kin relations; differences in men's and women's roles; an authoritarian character to intra-family relations, and some regulation of female sexuality (see also Rodríguez, 1998, 2000 on Costa Rica). While some have argued that the authoritarian patriarchal nature of the family has diminished over time, others have asserted that this still holds as a norm in many parts of Latin America today (see for example, Cubitt, 1995:107; Sánchez-Ayéndez, 1993:265; Varley, 2000). In part this is attributable to legislation. In Brazil, for example, despite the principle of equality established by the Federal Constitution, men are civilly defined as heads of conjugal units, and have power to act as legal representatives of their families and to manage family assets. Men also have the right to dissolve their marriages if, within the first ten days, they discover their wives are not virgins (CRLP, 1997:62; see also Chapter 2). An equally, if not more important factor, is the social and cultural legacy of historical familial norms as popularly interpreted. As far as one men's group in Chile is concerned, for example, the traditional family reproduces male violence and authoritarianism, and is also responsible for the 'emotional castration' of male children (Falabella, 1997:63; see also Henthorne, 2000; Quesada, 1996). In turn, until quite recently marriage and/or motherhood constituted a virtually inescapable destiny for women. Those failing to fulfil these roles stood the risk of being cast as 'bad women' or even 'whores' (Nencel, 1996: 62; Stølen, 1996:171; see also Chapters 1, 4 & 6). Within the household, men's and women's roles were also highly polarised. As little as twenty years ago, for example, depictions of 'traditional' familial gender patterns in many parts of Latin America revolved around men as primary (if not sole) breadwinners and decision-makers within household units, and as possessors of considerably greater power and freedoms than their female counterparts. While husbands might spend considerable amounts of time out of the home with male friends and colleagues, women's main relationships with men were forged with their sons (Lomnitz, 1977; see also Fonseca, 1991; McCallum, 1999; Moreno, 1997). Women tended to be portrayed as mothers and housewives, dependent on men financially, and with few powers of determination over their own lives. Moreover, basic divisions between men and women with regard to labour, power and resources within the home were (and in many cases still are) seen as accompanied by, and embedded in, polarisations in morality, sexuality and social behaviour, with the boundaries of female activity drawn tightly around the domestic domain, and not uncommonly associated with suffering and self-denial (Melhuus, 1996:232; Townsend *et al.*, 1999:29; Villareal, 1996:191; see also Chapter 6). While in terms of dominant imagery, women's sphere was the secluded, private world of the house (*casa*), men's domain was that of the public realm of the street (*calle*) (Melhuus and Stølen, 1996:5; see also Drogus, 1997; Fisher, 1993; Fuller, 2000; McCallum, 1999; Streicker, 1995).

Undoubtedly men did (and still do) have considerably more licence for extra-domestic pursuits than women, and for some men, in some contexts, such as Salvador, Brazil, 'Male freedom of movement and independence from their spouses is valued above the institution of marriage' (McCallum, 1999:282). By the same token, in most places this is juxtaposed with a strong family orientation. As noted by Escobar Latapí *et al.* (1987:60), for Mexico:

> the family is vital to a man's self-respect, as well as to enjoying a lifestyle that includes frequent visiting amongst kin and going to sporting events or drinking with their friends, kinsmen or sons. The man also knows that the family based network is essential to his well-being when he is older, or in times of emergency (see also Melhuus, 1996:242–3).

Competing modes of male behaviour falling under the rubric of masculinity are also noted in the Dominican Republic, where Krohn-Hansen (1996) argues that at one level, being a 'real man' entails womanising, whereas at another level, being a 'good father' is also emphasised to such an extent that men often go on providing for children even after their marriages terminate. As such: 'A good deal of men's constructions of male identity can be understood as continuous attempts to strike a balance between these two sets of moral ideals' (Krohn-Hansen, 1996:116; see also Chant, 2000 on Costa Rica; Viveros, 1998a; Wade, 1994:117–21 on Colombia). Beyond this, it is equally important to note that spending time outside the home, and socialising with male peers, can be vital to men's success in the labour market, which in turn impacts upon their role as family providers. As summed up by Fuller (2000:111) for Peru:

> Masculine identity is intersected by contradictions due to the fact that it is installed in spheres which imply different rationalities and demands.

While it has increasingly been shown that masculinities and femininities are made and negotiated rather than given, as discussed in Chapter 1, there has been corresponding recognition of gender's variegation by class, 'race', age and locality over time. As for age, for example, Fuller (2000) argues that different aspects of 'manliness' are important at different stages of the lifecycle. Among young Peruvian males, virility is the main route to affirmation of masculinity, but as men enter adulthood, work becomes more important as they aspire to be family providers. As for 'race', among black populations in the Pacific and Atlantic regions of Colombia, Wade (1994:116) shows there is much more fluidity in family relations, and much less in the way of formal marriage, monogamy and so on than in the Andean interior where there is a bigger white/*mestizo* population, and stronger observance of Roman Catholicism (see also Friedemann and Arocha, 1995:63). Studies of indigenous groups have demonstrated strong continuity in gender patterns, despite economic modernisation and migration, as well as noting that divisions of labour and power between women and men are less prounounced than among *mestizo* populations (see Wolf, 1959). For example, Hamilton's (1998) work on Chanchaló, an indigenous highland farming community in Ecuador, indicates rejection by local people of national bureaucratic dictates of a singular head of household. Chanchaleños stress categorically that their households have '*dos cabezas*' (two heads), with adult couples bearing joint responsibility for household welfare. Similarly, among Mayan migrants in Guatemala City, Bastos (1999) argues that so-called 'traditional' gender divisions of labour hold little water, with both men and women recognising the value of complementarity in gender roles. Thus while women's income-generating work has been noted as threat to male authority in many parts of *mestizo* Latin America, among the indigenous groups discussed, as well as others such as the Otavaleños of highland Ecuador, it has long been accepted as a vital component of household survival. More generally, the changes in household livelihood strategies driven by structural adjustment programmes in the region have also played an important part in forcing household members to renegotiate their responsibilities. As Radcliffe (1999:199) has noted: 'Latin American research highlights the microscale household-gender negotiations which have been – in various places and recent times – so crucial in changing women's social position and sense of themselves'. Another critical factor in considering variations in gender roles and relations is the immense diversity of households in the region.

Household diversity in Latin America

Household diversity is a long-standing feature of Latin America. Indigenous, Hispanic and Afro-Caribbean cultural influences have intermeshed with differing economic, demographic and political circumstances to produce a vast array of household forms, not to mention varied and often elaborate networks of exchange with kin (see Dore, 1997; Fonseca, 1991; González de la Rocha, 1994; Minority Rights Group [ed], 1995; Safa, 1999; Scott, 1994; Willis,1993, 2000; also Boxes 7.1 and 7.2).

Beyond recognising diversity in household form, and the fact that households are not bounded entities (Chant, 1998), we should note that the contractual arrangements on which they are based may also vary. Although legal marriage is usually

BOX 7.1

Commonly Occurring Household Structures in Contemporary Latin America

Household structure	*Brief description*
Nuclear household	Couple and their biological children
Blended/step-family household*	Household in which one or both partners in a couple is not the biological parent of one or more co-resident children
Female-headed household	Generic term for a household where the senior woman or household head lacks a co-resident male partner. Often, although not always, household head is a lone mother (see also Box 7.2)
Extended household	Household which, in addition to one or both parents and children, comprises other blood relatives or in-laws (*de facto* or *de jure*). May be male- or female-headed, laterally or vertically extended, and/or multi-generational
Nuclear-compound household	Arrangement where two or more related households share the same living space (e.g. dwelling or land plot), but operate separate household budgets and daily reproduction (e.g. cooking, eating etc.)
Grandmother-headed household	Grandmother and her grandchildren, but without intermediate generation
Lone/single person household	Woman or man living alone

Sources: Brydon and Chant (1989), Chant (1991, 1992).
Note: * Also referred to in some sources as 'reconstituted household'.

regarded as a social ideal (and in many countries in Latin America is the norm in practice), in parts of Central America, the Hispanic Caribbean and pockets of Afro-Latin America, partnerships between men and women have often taken the form of consensual unions (McIlwaine, 1993; Minority Rights Group [ed], 1995). In Cuba, for example, fewer than three in five couples legally marry (Lumsden 1996:44). In Nicaragua, 33 per cent of women aged 15–49 years were in consensual unions in the period 1992–8, and 35 per cent in the Dominican Republic (UN, 2000:27). Informal unions tend to be more common among low-income groups which also applies elsewhere in the continent. In rural Argentina it tends only to be economically

BOX 7.2

Typology of Female-headed Households

Type	Brief description	Frequency among female-headed households in Latin America
Lone mother household	Mother with co-resident children	High
Female-headed extended household	Household comprising lone mother, children and other relatives	High
Lone female household	Woman living alone (usually elderly)	Low but increasing
Single sex/female-only household	Woman living with other women (female relatives or friends)	Low
Lesbian household	Woman living with female sexual partner	Low
Female-dominant/ predominant household	Household headed by woman, where although males may be present, they are only junior males with less power and authority than adult females	Low
Grandmother-headed household	Grandmother and her grandchildren, but without intermediate generation	Low
'Embedded' female-headed unit	Unit comprising a young mother and her children contained within larger household (usually that of parents). Sometimes referred to as 'female-headed sub-family'	Moderate to high

Source: Chant (1997a:10–26)

superior groups who marry, whereas lower-income people in consensual unions openly refer to themselves as *juntados* (together, but not legally) (Stølen, 1996:172).

Factors contributing to the lack of formal marriage include indigenous antecedents, such as the non-practice of marriage among the Chorotegas of north-west Costa Rica and southern Nicaragua (Chant 1997a:170). This is also found among the former black slave population of Colombia (Wade, 1994). Another role is played by the financial costs of marriage proceedings, especially in isolated rural communities lacking permanent clerical personnel or infrastructure (Rudolf, 1999). An additional factor is the perceived irrelevance of life-long contracts in situations where people's economic status is precarious on account, *inter alia*, of the seasonality of tropical agricultural production (Jayawardena, 1960), or where men's mobility is an integral part of economic strategies (Wade, 1994). For example, aside from the practices of their Chorotegan forebears, one reason for unwillingness to formalise conjugal relationships in Guanacaste, Costa Rica, is that the province has traditionally offered little in the way of regular employment. One of the least urbanised areas in the country, Guanacaste's only major agricultural activity is sugar cultivation, which is labour-intensive, and then only on a seasonal basis, with significant recruitment of workers generally restricted to the harvest period between January and April. For low-income men, who are the vast bulk of workers in agriculture, and on whom the responsibility for household 'breadwinning' has conventionally fallen, this has implied migration to other parts of the country for spells of varying duration to support their families. Yet finding work away from home is not always easy, leading to frustration and hardship for migrants and their families alike. The situation is aggravated by the fact that prolonged periods of separation place a variety of stresses on couples. It is not uncommon for men to cease sending remittances after time has elapsed, and sometimes not to return home at all. Although this is occasionally because men feel they cannot go back to their families with nothing to show for their efforts, more usually it is because they have set up homes with other women (Chant, 2000).

In Nicaragua, too, where Lancaster (1992:xiv) describes the traditional family structure as 'both patriarchal and brittle', it is often the case that men initiate conjugal breakdown, frequently moving on to the households of women with whom they have already begun sexual relationships:

> Men in Nicaragua often maintain more than one household, and informal polygamy is a sanctioned aspect of the culture of *machismo*. When life gets harder, however, men often abandon wives, *compañeras*, and families, burdening them with all the economic and social disadvantages that await households headed by women (ibid.).

Yet, according to Vance (1987:141–2), the instability of the Nicaraguan household is 'not merely a question of the irresponsibility of men or attributable to cultural attitudes', but is linked to the expansion of plantation agriculture during the Somoza regime, the mechanisation of farming production, the proletarianisation of the rural labour force, and the enforced migration of men in search of wages. Moreover, consensual unions are not always linked with adversity, nor are they necessarily determined by men. In Nicaragua, men often prefer to marry to deter women from leaving. Women, on the other hand, may resist marriage because it erodes their bargaining power with spouses (Lancaster, 1992:46).

While consensual unions can be as, if not more, enduring than marriages, the absence of legal impediment to separation, especially in circumstances of material privation, means that they are more likely to be temporary, even where children are involved (Chant, 1992). In turn, because serial conjugal partnerships give rise to people's homes being shared with a number of partners over the life course, large numbers of households contain step-children and half-siblings (Lumsden, 1996:121; Wade, 1994:116). These are sometimes referred to as 'blended' or 'reconstituted' households. Although it is difficult to get data on these, one non-random study of single 15–18 year olds in the Metropolitan Area of Buenos Aires, Argentina, found that 10 per cent were living in reconstituted units (Geldstein, 1994:56). One-fifth of children with unregistered paternity in Costa Rica are likely to spend some of their childhood living with a step-father (Budowski and Rosero Bixby, forthcoming). In Brazil, too, men's frequent involvement in multiple sexual partnerships leads to weak ties with a number of households in which they have children (McCallum, 1999:286). Whereas blended households also existed in the past, their contemporary formation is due increasingly less to the death of one partner, and move to separation or divorce (ibid.). They may also form part of larger multi-generational extended units (Gomáriz, 1997:50–1; see also Box 7.1).

Extended households can be laterally as well as vertically extended, and comprise a complex range of close and more distantly related individuals. A recent survey of *ejidatarias* (female members of agrarian cooperatives) in Mexico, for example, showed that among 487 households, as many as 131 were extended. This latter group, in turn, comprised over 30 different types of extended units, even if the majority were formed around a nexus of daughters or sons-in-law and grandchildren (Robles Berlanga *et al.*, 2000:51, Cuadro 14). Citing data from a 1995 survey of Latin American countries by Valdés and Gomáriz, Wiest (1998:66) reports a total of 27 per cent extended family households in Venezuela, and 30 per cent in Colombia. Although extended households (along with other non-nuclear units such as female-headed households), are often viewed as being more common among low-income groups, Lomnitz and Pérez-Lizaur's (1991) study of Mexico indicates that the 'grand-family' or three-generation descent group is a distinctive feature of middle-income and elite sectors as well.

Female-headed households are another important household sub-group in Latin America, and are not just a late-twentieth-century phenomenon (see Cicerchia, 1997; Dore, 1997; Gudmundson, 1996; Rodríguez, 2000). Their growth has been fairly ubiquitous throughout the region in recent decades, with estimates based on data pertaining to the period 1985–97 showing the average for Latin America as a whole as 22 per cent (UN, 2000:42). The growth in female-headed households is arguably one of the most prominent trends in households in recent times, as discussed in greater detail later.[2]

Where the extent of Latin American household diversity reaches something of an impasse is when it comes to homosexual households. This is arguably partly due to the fact that writings on homosexuality have tended to focus on issues of identity and sexuality, rather than household arrangements (Buffington, 1997; Lancaster 1997; Mirandé, 1997; Quiroga, 1997). The lack of attention in research notwithstanding, it would appear that both male and female homosexual households are rare in practice in Latin America. As noted in Chapter 6, for example, in Cuba, homophobia along with pressure on gay men to be discreet means that very few live openly with one another (Lumsden, 1996). This also applies to Costa Rica and is again undoubtedly due to anti-gay sentiment on the part of the Church, and in wider society. As also noted in the previous chapter, same sex cohabitation in Nicaragua was classified as an act of sodomy by law in 1992, carrying with it serious penalties. Although most gay people are accordingly forced to remain in conventional family households and to conduct their sexual relationships on a non-coresidential basis (see Jolly, 2000:86), recent legislation permitting the registration of same-sex unions in Brazil and Mexico may help to tip attitudes in favour of a more inclusive stance to household diversity.

Recent trends in household organisation

Whether greater space for 'alternative' households may emerge over time is difficult to evaluate with any confidence, mainly because many contemporary as well as historical records are superficial and sketchy, and they are not consistent between countries (Chant, 1997a:149). Another factor is that the baselines for change – where they can be established – are themselves often highly complex and differentiated. In addition, as Radcliffe (1999:200) observes, 'Household forms have not changed in any easily discernible or unitary direction. In some areas family size has shrunk, and, in others, family members are joined by relatives, friends and other *allegados* (coresidents)'. Diverse trends can often be seen at the micro-level of individual towns and cities on account of the cross-cutting influences of class, ethnicity, gender, age and migrant status.

For example, although crisis and economic restructuring in the 1980s and 1990s saw increases in extended households in low-income communities in Mexican cities such as Guadalajara (González de la Rocha, 1988) and Querétaro (Chant, 1996b), and smaller rural towns such as San Cosme Mazatecocho (Rothstein, 1995), the proportion of extended households nationally dropped from 9.3 to 8 per cent between 1960 and 1990. This has been attributed partly to unfavourable conditions for multi-generational households in cities, and partly to improving health among older age groups which may have encouraged elderly citizens to adopt more independent lifestyles. Indeed, whereas 9 per cent of the population in the 65 year plus age group in Mexico live alone, this is only one per cent across the population as a whole (López and Izazola, 1995: 56). The increase in lone person households looks set to increase with demographic ageing and, if gender differences in life expectancy persist, then it is also likely that more women will live alone than men (see Chapter 4). At present, for instance, as many as 27.5 per cent of female household heads in Costa Rica reside independently, compared with only 10.9 per cent of male heads (PEN, 1998: 44).

Alongside the role of lone person households in reducing household size in Latin America, another important factor is falling fertility. This is strongly associated with increased rates of contraceptive use (see Chapter 4), and women's rising age at marriage. Although data on this are rather patchy (see Table 7.1), and wedlock is not necessarily a prelude to having children, later age at marriage, often thought to have been stimulated by women's rising education and labour force participation, may clearly exert downward pressure on birth rates. In Mexico, for example, the median age at marriage for the population as a whole increased from 20.8 to 22 years between 1970 and 1990, largely due to a decline in early marriages (López and Izazola, 1995:12). In turn, the mean size of family-based households (male- and female-headed) fell from 5.4 to 5 between 1960 and 1990 (ibid.:15).

Another influence identified as important in reducing household size is the growth in number of single-parent families, most of which are headed by women (UN/ECLAC 1994:76; see also Box 7.2). Yet although this may conceivably have some effect, it is important to recognise that lone parenthood does not necessarily entail mothers living alone with their children; indeed, often lone mothers head households (or form part of other female-headed households) which have a much greater likelihood of being extended than male-headed units (Arriagada, 1998; Chant, 1997a; Wartenburg, 1999). Moreover, despite gradual improvements in the gender sensitivity of data collection, establishing numbers of lone parent and/or female-headed households remains difficult. Data on female household headship are often inaccurate and underestimated, not to mention occluded by vague definitions which vary across countries (Chant 1997a). When it comes to establishing trends in household headship over time, complexities are further

Table 7.1 Women's Average Age at Marriage and Household Headship in Latin America

	Women's average age at marriage (years)		Proportion of households headed by women (%)	
	1970*	1990–2	1980	1990–2
Argentina	22.9	23.3	19.2	22.3
Bolivia	—	22.7	—	24.5
Brazil	23.0	—	14.4	20.1
Chile	23.3	23.4	21.6	21.0
Colombia	22.4	22.6	—	22.7
Costa Rica	21.7	—	17.6	20.0
Cuba	19.5	—	28.2	—
Dominican Republic	19.7	—	21.7	25.0
Ecuador	21.1	22.0	—	—
El Salvador	19.4	22.3	—	26.6
Guatemala	19.7	21.3	—	16.9
Honduras	20.0	—	—	20.4
Mexico	21.2	—	15.2	17.3
Nicaragua	20.2	—	—	24.3
Panama	20.4	21.9	21.5	22.3
Paraguay	21.7	21.5	18.1	17.0
Peru	21.6	—	—	17.3
Uruguay	—	22.9	21.0	23.0
Venezuela	20.4	—	21.8	21.3

Sources: González de la Rocha (1999b:153, Anexo 1), UN (1995: Table 33), UN (1997: Table 26), UNDP (1995: Table A2.5).

Notes: * Data for these years or nearest available year.
— = no data.

compounded by the fact that census bureaux in most Latin American countries have only recently begun to register gender breakdowns of household headship. While purported increases may also be due as much to perceptions about the growing autonomy of women as real changes in household arrangements, official data for the latter decades of the twentieth century point to increases in most parts of the region, even if these vary quite considerably between countries. Whereas in Guyana women-headed households grew from 22.4 per cent to 35 per cent of the population between 1970 and 1987 (Patterson, 1994:122), in other countries, such as Colombia, the increase between 1978 and 1995 was more modest – from 20.4 per cent to 22.5 per cent (Wartenburg, 1999:80). During the 1980s, however, the majority of countries in the region experienced an upward trend (see Table 7.1) that was most pronounced in large cities and metropolitan areas (Geldstein, 1994:55).

These tendencies, which, as noted earlier, are not confined to Latin America, have fed into a general consensus that the 'patriarchal family model' is on the wane. The growing incidence of lone motherhood and female household headship has been accompanied by, and embedded in, falling levels of legal marriage, rising numbers of out-of-wedlock births, greater rates of divorce and separation, and mounting involvement of women in the historically male preserve of family 'breadwinning' (Arriagada,1998; Benería, 1991; CEPAL, 2001; Cerrutti and Zenteno, 1999; Fauné, 1997; Folbre, 1991; González de la Rocha, 1995; Jelin, 1991; Kaztman, 1992).[3] Even if these phenomena were also present in earlier historical periods, and are possibly just more visible now due to their greater registration and documentation (Rico de Alonso and López Tellez, 1998:196), shifts in some countries have been substantial. In Costa Rica, for example, official figures indicate that the proportion of births outside marriage had increased to 44 per cent by 1994, from a level of 37 per cent in 1980 (MIDEPLAN, 1995:5–6). Over the same period, marriage rates fell from 30.8 to 23.5 per 100 (ibid.), and between 1980 and 1996, the number of divorces rose from 9.9 to 21.2 per 100 (PEN, 1998:210). More recently, a report by the *Instituto Nacional de las Mujeres* (National Institute for Women) (INAMU, 1998) revealed not only that one in four Costa Rican children had a *padre desconocido* (unknown father), but that teenage motherhood was on the rise, with 60 per cent of single parents in the country being under 25 years of age, and 16 per cent under 18 years (see also Chapter 4).

Factors contributing to the decline of patriarchal households in contemporary Latin America

Latin America's highly variegated patchwork of household types derives in part from historical legacies. However, the ascendancy of households which depart from the normative patriarchal ideal stems from a variety of factors. Some, such as declining fertility, have already been discussed. Other important influences on contemporary household dynamics, and particularly the undermining of patriarchal household organisation, include migration, social and legal changes around marriage and divorce, and neoliberal economic restructuring.

MIGRATION AND HOUSEHOLDS

Migration's role in eroding patriarchal household organisation derives primarily from its gender selectivity, and more specifically the fact that since the mid-twentieth century, women have tended to dominate rural–urban migration flows in Latin America. As discussed in more detail in Chapters 8 and 9, this is partly a function of the juxtaposition of declining productive possibilities for women in the countryside, and relatively greater income-earning opportunities in towns. Many studies have also shown that female-selective migration is both a cause and consequence of female household headship. On one hand, the female bias in migration flows is responsible for a 'surplus' of women in towns (normally referred to as a 'feminisation' of sex ratios) (see Table 7.2), which makes the establishment of female-headed households more likely. On the other hand, female household heads are an important sub-group of women migrants from rural areas, especially where lack of land, labour supply or employment opportunities renders them unable to support their dependants (see Bradshaw, 1995a on Honduras; Chant, 1997a: Chapter 5 on Mexico and Costa Rica; Yudelman, 1989 on Central America in general).

Table 7.2 Urban Sex Ratios, Selected Latin American Countries

	Men per 100 women	Percentage of all men in urban areas	Percentage of all women in urban areas
Bolivia (1992)*	94**	56.6	58.5
Brazil (1991)	94	74.3	76.9
Chile (1995)	95	83.1	85.8
Costa Rica (1994)	96	42.9	45.2
Cuba (1993)	97	73.0	75.8
Dominican Republic (1995)	98	59.9	63.5
Ecuador (1993)	97	57.9	60.4
El Salvador (1992)	90	49.1	51.7
Honduras (1988)	84	37.6	41.2
Nicaragua (1989)	95	58.1	61.4
Panama (1995)	95	52.9	56.9
Paraguay (1992)	93	48.3	52.4
Peru (1993)	97	69.4	70.8
Uruguay (1995)	91	88.1	92.0
Venezuela (1990)	99	83.0	85.0

Source: UN (1997: Table 6).
Notes: * Data for latest available year.
** Figures rounded up to nearest whole number.
NB. Argentina, Colombia, Guatemala and Mexico have been omitted due to lack of data and/or their non-inclusion in the UN table.

Gender selective international as well as rural–urban migration is also critical in the establishment of *de facto* as well as *de jure* female-headed households (Acosta-Belén and Bose 1995:25), as is temporary and seasonal migration (see Chapter 9).

SOCIAL AND LEGAL CHANGES RELATING TO MARRIAGE AND DIVORCE

Another set of factors associated with the erosion of patriarchal household structures in Latin America lies in the sphere of legislative changes, particularly those which have strengthened women's position as individual citizens, or as family members, through interventions in family law, reproductive rights, sexual abuse, domestic violence, and labour market discrimination (see Chapter 2). Many of these changes have been driven by women's and feminist movements in Latin America (see for example, Craske, 1999, 2000a; Ewig, 1999; Jaquette [ed], 1994; Jelin [ed], 1990; Molyneux, 2001). In most countries, for example, access to divorce on the part of women is now easier than in the past. This is a function not only of widened grounds for divorce, but of measures to protect women's interests in the aftermath of conjugal breakdown. For example, the amendment of Article 138 of the Costa Rican Family Code in the 1990s removed men's right to decide on the custody of children unless otherwise decreed by the courts (Vincenzi, 1991). Having said this, although the number of divorces per 100 marriages in Costa Rica increased sevenfold between 1975 and 1991 (from 2 per 100 to 15.3 per 100), it is only one-third of the rate of Cuba, where there is now only a one-in-two chance that marriages will survive. Part of the reason for the increase in Costa Rica is that, according to opinion polls, divorce is still not socially acceptable to the majority of people (Fernández, 1992). Another element is that divorce proceedings are costly and long drawn-out (Chant, 1997a: 137). The disparity between Cuba and Mexico is even greater, with Mexico having only one-twelfth of the Cuban level (Lumsden, 1996:120). LeVine (1993:95) observes for Mexico that: 'though nowadays there may be a good deal of talk about divorce, women who remain in seemingly untenable relationships still greatly outnumber those who get out'. Thus although there is arguably increased social acceptance of divorce in Latin America in general (Durham, 1991:61), one must be wary of taking legislative shifts in isolation.

In order to avoid the expense, trauma and social stigma attached to the breakdown of a formalised, and particularly a religious, union, cohabitation is often seen as a more realistic alternative (see earlier). Although consensual unions have traditionally been less protected than formal marriages or have had no legal protection whatsoever (CRLP 1997:12), the boundaries between marriage and cohabitation have diminished in a variety of Latin American countries in recent years. In Nicaragua, for example, the Sandinista regime introduced new laws which recognised stable, permanent unions as having the status of *acompañado* or common-law marriage (Lancaster, 1992:18). This has also occurred in Guatemala, and in Colombia in 1990 a law was passed which gave legal status to free unions, and permitted common law husbands and wives (defined as *compañeros permanentes/* 'permanent companions') to have access to each other's old age or invalidity pensions in cases where the union had endured more than two years (CRLP, 1997:82). In Costa Rica, the Social Equality Law passed in 1990 also made explicit recognition of free unions and gave rise to legislation which required compulsory registration of property in women's names in the event of separation (Molina,

1993). Subsequent to this, a series of reforms and additions to the Costa Rican Family Code have, *inter alia*, established the legal validity of consensual unions and recognised children born outside marriage (see CMF, 1996:22; Colaboración Area Legal, 1997). Along with other initiatives which have followed in their wake, such as the National Plan for Equality of Opportunity Between Men and Women, a Programme for Female Heads of Household and the National Plan for the Prevention of Intra-Family Violence, women's choices about whether or not to stay with partners have been enlarged, and this has conceivably made female household headship more viable (Chant, 1997a, 2002b; also below).

NEOLIBERAL ECONOMIC RESTRUCTURING

The profound economic transformations that have occurred in Latin America in the 'Lost Decade' of the 1980s and beyond have also played a significant role in changing household structures. As noted by Radcliffe (1999:197): 'the advocation of neoliberal development policies by most governments has significantly influenced the ways in which the nexus of labour–household–economy is organised, with consequences in turn for the nature of gender relations'. As discussed in further detail in Chapter 8, for example, recession and structural adjustment in Latin America have given rise to greater open unemployment and informalisation of labour markets, but although there has been a downward trend in demand for male labour, especially in the formal sector, traditionally feminised occupations such as multinational export manufacturing and low-skilled service activities have been left relatively unscathed. On top of this, given rising pressures on household incomes from the relaxation of price controls, removal of subsidies and so on (see Chapter 3), more women have had to enter the workforce over time (see Benería, 1991; Chant, 1996b; González de la Rocha, 1988). The crisis has effectively increased the 'importance and visibility of women's contribution to the household economy as additional women enter the labour force to meet the rising cost of living and the decreased wage-earning capacity of men' (Safa, 1995b:33). Not only has there been a general rise in women's employment, but an increased proportion of older and/or married women workers too. In Costa Rica there was only one female worker for every three men in the 20–39 year age cohort in 1980, but by 1990 the gap had narrowed to one in two (Dierckxsens, 1992:22). In Mexico, over one-quarter of married women were recorded as working in 1991, compared with only 10 per cent in 1970, and the highest levels of economic activity are now in the 35–39 year age cohort (50.8 per cent as of 1997) (CEPAL, 1994: 15; Garduno-Rivera, 2000:11).

Although women's entry into the labour force has helped to compensate in part for men's deteriorating incomes, the rising precariousness of employment and loss of fringe benefits which subsidised healthcare, or which provided cover for illness and accident, have conspired to exacerbate pressure on low-income families. A now seemingly long-term situation of financial scarcity and employment insecurity is observed to have weakened solidarity among household members as a result of stress, frustration and despair, even when they are not forced physically apart through migration (see González de la Rocha, 1997, 2000). In addition, although women's income-generating work may have gone some way to cushioning the impact of crisis and restructuring in economic terms, ideologically and psychologically men's loss of employment and the mounting dependence of households on women's earnings has threatened masculine identities (Gutmann, 1996). In the light of popular expressions such as the Mexican saying *'Pobre el hogar en que canta la gallina'* (basically, 'Poor is the household where women rule the roost'), it is perhaps no surprise to find reports of an intensification of domestic strife during the crisis period (Benería, 1991; Geldstein, 1994:57; Gledhill, 1995:137; González de la Rocha *et al.*, 1990; Safa, 1999; Salas, 1998). As Selby *et al.* (1990:176) argue:

> Male dignity has been so assaulted by unemployment and the necessity of relying on women for the subsistence that men formerly provided, that men have taken it out on their wives and domestic violence has increased … the families which have been riven by fighting and brutality can easily be said to be the true victims of economic crisis….

In some cases conflict has led to household break-up. This has arguably been exacerbated by the fact that women's new financial independence is often seen as having strengthened their ability to terminate relationships, with the rise in women's labour force participation frequently linked with the 'feminisation' of household headship in Latin America (see, for example, Bradshaw,1995a; Chant, 1997a; Safa, 1995a,1999).[4] Although poorer women are still more likely to be abandoned than better-off women (who are more likely to take the initiative themselves), there has still been some change.

Gender implications of recent trends in household organisation

Female household headship

Female-headed households in Latin America are often, although not always headed by lone mothers (Box 7.2). While many are widows, the majority are unmarried, divorced or separated women. In this light, female household headship is frequently regarded as symptomatic of the 'breakdown' of the patriarchal family. While we have already noted that the growth of female-headed households in Latin America is commonly associated with the expansion of economic opportunities for women, continued male–female earnings differentials mean that they are also routinely linked with poverty and vulnerability (see Buvinic and Gupta, 1997; Rico de Alonso and López Tellez, 1998). Another major factor is the lack of child support from absent fathers. In Costa Rica, for example, one national survey showed that only 24 per cent of lone mothers received officially determined child maintenance, a further 42 per cent received voluntary payments, and the remainder received no support whatsoever (Budowski and Rosero Bixby, forthcoming). While there is convincing evidence to show that female heads face many obstacles to survival, however, the analysis of poverty is fraught and imprecise, especially when one begins to look beyond aggregate household incomes to intra-household resource distribution (see Chapter 3). Whatever the case, an increasing body of empirical evidence from the region suggests that women-headed households are not necessarily the 'poorest of the poor', including in Costa Rica (Chant, 1997b, 1999a), Mexico (ibid., González de la Rocha, 1999a), Panama (Fuwa, 2000), Guyana (Gafar, 1998:605), Colombia (Wartenburg, 1999), and Argentina (Geldstein, 1997). In turn, despite a tendency for women-headed households to be linked with an 'inter-generational transmission of disadvantage' to children, evidence suggests that levels of nutrition, healthcare and education are often comparable, if not better, particularly when comparing daughters in male- and female-headed units (Blumberg, 1995:215 *et seq.*; Chant, 1999a; Engle, 1995). Aside from ignoring evidence of the often fairer distribution of resources within female-headed households, blanket poverty projections have frequently glossed over the fact that women-headed households are a highly heterogeneous group, differentiated, amongst other things, by their route into female headship, stage in the life course, household composition, class and educational status (see Feijoó, 1999; Geldstein, 1997; Wartenburg, 1999). Moreover, an important role in underpinning subsistence in female-headed households is often played by networks of kin, even though these are usually smaller for female- than male-headed units (Fonseca, 1991; González de la Rocha, 1994; Rico de Alonso and López Tellez, 1998; Safa, 1999; Willis, 1993). Following on from the idea that the rise in female headship in Latin America may reflect increased consciousness of gender subordination (Harris, 1981), some have viewed female household headship as having had positive outcomes for women's autonomy and 'empowerment', primarily through creating a space for women free of direct male control (Bradshaw, 1995a; Chant,1985, 1997a; Feijoó, 1999:162; Safa, 1995a).

Potentially empancipatory dimensions of female household headship can be regarded as a positive outcome of recent household and family transitions. However it would be wrong to assume that the formation of female-headed households is necessarily advantageous for all women (or, by implication, that all male-headed households are bad) (Chant 1999a:112–3; Gutmann, 1996:256; Feijoó, 1999:162). As Stacey (1997:464) notes:

> Portraying nuclear families primarily as sites of patriarchal violence, as some feminists have done, is inaccurate and impolitic. It reinforces a stereotypical association of feminism with antifamilism, which does not even accurately represent feminist perspectives on this subject. Certainly, protecting women's rights to resist and exit unequal, hostile, dangerous marriages remains a crucial project, but one we cannot advance by denying that many women, many of them feminists, sustain desires for successful and legally protected relationships with men and children. We must steer a tenuous course between cultural warriors who blame public violence on (patriarchal) family decline, and those who blame family decline on (patriarchal) domestic violence.

The impacts of female labour force participation on gender in households

Aside from its association with rising levels of female household headship, women's increased labour force participation is often linked with gains for women within male-headed units. In the case of Mexico, for example, Cerrutti and Zenteno (1999:71) assert that rising female labour force participation 'has had profound repercussions in the breaking of the traditional model of male head as the sole economic breadwinner in the household' (my translation; see also Martin, 1996:197; also Box 7.3). With reference to Puerto Rico, Cuba and the Dominican Republic, Safa (1995a:58) also notes that although the cultural norm of the male breadwinner remains decidedly embedded in the workplace and the state, women's massive incorporation into the labour force has increased their bargaining power in households. Safa (1995b:33) further observes that women's declining dependence on male incomes and growing economic participation in their own right have presented a major challenge to the 'myth of the male breadwinner' at the grassroots.

Despite the transformative potential of these changes, however, especially in questioning the legitimacy of masculine dominance: 'current changes in gender relations ... have not meant a revision (as was the case for women) of the foundations of masculinity which rest upon the identification of maleness with economic responsibility and authority' (Fuller, 2000:103; see also Escobar Latapí, 1998). Moreover, while women may have increased their workforce participation, they are far from entering the labour market on an equal footing with men. Women are hampered not only by lower levels of education and vocational training, but by domestic and childrearing responsibilities (González de la Rocha 1994:141–2). In some parts of the region, women's choice of employment is also subject to approval from husbands, and, as noted for Mexico by Townsend *et al.* (1999:38), women may need their husbands' permission to work at all. Sometimes such prescriptions are enshrined in civil law. For example, as flagged up in Chapter 2, the Guatemalan Civil Code states that a woman has a 'special right and duty to nurture and care for her children' and can only be employed outside the home if this does not go against the

BOX 7.3

Work, Marriage and Gender Relations in Puerto Vallarta, Mexico: Fidelina's Story

Fidelina was 38 when I last visited her in April 1997. She was working five-and-a-half days a week, combining two domestic service jobs with occasional home-based hairdressing. One of Fidelina's domestic jobs is in the house of a wealthy Californian woman who lives in Puerto Vallarta, and she is well paid by local standards.

Fidelina lives with her husband, David, and her two sons, aged 18 and 12, in the neighbourhood of El Caloso. Caloso began as a collection of untitled shacks back in 1968, but is now a regularised settlement, complete with roads, services and basic amenities. Fidelina and David's house in 1997 bears no resemblance to the one-roomed *lámina de cartón* hut that they were living in when I first interviewed Fidelina in 1986. Their newly consolidated brick house comprises four brightly painted rooms and is stocked with numerous pieces of furniture, many of which Fidelina has obtained as gifts from her employers. Without Fidelina's work it is unlikely that the family would be living so well, and the dramatic changes in their domestic environment in many senses mirror those which have taken place at a personal level between Fidelina and her husband over the last decade. Although many issues come into this transformation, the couple's employment and financial arrangements figure prominently, initially as a source of conflict and inequality, and latterly as an avenue to greater harmony and unity.

Fidelina and David had moved into Caloso in 1984 towards the end of their fourth year of marriage. The catalyst for their moving to the settlement was David's desire to prevent Fidelina working in a doctor's surgery situated close to their former downtown rental accommodation. Although David, a maintenance man at a four-star hotel, earned a reasonable wage and had never wanted Fidelina to work, after three years of marriage he started withholding more of his earnings and not coming home until late at night. Part of this time (and money) was spent seeing other women, which Fidelina learned to her cost when she contracted a sexually transmitted disease from her husband. In desperation at the situation in which the cash David gave her for housekeeping was not stretching to cover basic needs, and in which her economic dependence rendered her feeling powerless to do anything other than accept David's behaviour, Fidelina started working behind his back. In order that he would not find out, she took a part-time cleaning job in a nearby doctor's surgery, where she was able to take her infant son and from which she could be home by the time David finished work. Unfortunately, a neighbour informed on her, and in his rage David arranged for them to move home immediately.

Their new abode at the top of the hill in Caloso, as yet without roads and many other services, was extremely isolated. Although this presented difficulties, and Fidelina had been forbidden outright to work, she still managed to make a little extra here and there by haircutting and taking in the odd bundle of washing from a neighbour whom she swore to secrecy. Fidelina was so unhappy during this time that she spent several hours in Church praying for her husband to change, and obtaining tranquillisers from the family doctor to calm her nerves. Both her priest and doctor advised her that she should stay with David.

By the late 1980s, however, when economic crisis began to hit Puerto Vallarta hard with a fall-off in international tourism, matters came to something of a head. Fidelina begged her husband to let her work, but he persisted in his refusal to negotiate. While this was considerable cause for conflict in its own right, when Fidelina then discovered that David was about to make a trip to the United States with a lover, she went against her beliefs and the teachings of the Church, and threatened him with a divorce on grounds of adultery. According to Fidelina, David's fear of losing his wife (and the even greater fear that she might meet someone else), forced a dramatic about-turn in his behaviour. Within hours of the showdown he pleaded with her to forgive him and professed he would do anything to make her stay. Since Fidelina was in an unprecedented position to make conditions, she not only requested assurance of his fidelity, but licence to take a job. She won both these battles, and little by little, David began to appreciate how helpful it was to have two incomes coming in. They started planning things together much more than in the past, and made the building of a brick-and-mortar house their joint goal. Now that their home is a much more agreeable place, David goes out less and spends more time with Fidelina and the children. The shift has benefited the entire family, and there is no desire for a return to past ways.

Source: Interviews by Sylvia Chant in Puerto Vallarta, Mexico, 1986, 1992, 1994 & 1997.

children's interests or undermine the needs of the household (Steiner and Alston, 1996:890). Moreover, husbands have the right to prohibit the work of wives if they themselves provide sufficient income, however that might be determined (CRLP, 1997:120).

Questions of how men and women view their own and each other's identities are also critical here. McClenaghan (1997: 29) notes for the Dominican Republic, for example, that even where women are the primary providers, men are usually still acknowledged as *el jefe* (head of household). This is partly because men's ownership of land and property places them in a position of authority regardless of whether they are actually employed (see also Safa, 1999:6 on Alta Gracia in the Dominican Republic). Debate remains, therefore, as to how far women's rising involvement in income-generating activity has translated into major shifts in identity or personal power. On one hand, Cerrutti and Zenteno (1999:71) claim in the Mexican context that:

> the increase and diversification of women's labour experience has implied an erosion of prescriptive norms and their roles, particularly in relation to the ideology of reproduction [my translation].

Yet García's and de Oliveira's (1997) comparative research on low-income and middle-class groups in three Mexican cities (Tijuana, Mérida and Mexico City) finds that for low-income women in particular, motherhood remains their primary source of identity, with employment viewed mainly as a means by which they can better fulfil their mothering roles (García and de Oliveira, 1997:368; see also Tiano, 2001:202). Only among middle-class mothers, who are able to afford paid childcare and who have sufficient education to enter non-manual occupations, is work more likely to be a significant aspect of their personal identity (ibid:381). One plausible reason is that educated middle class women are more likely to have sustained rather than intermittent involvement in the workforce (Cerrutti, 2000a); another is that they may be more reluctant to give up professions and the fulfilment they derive from them (Willis, 2000). Another reason is that most middle-class women are able to pass on basic reproductive tasks to domestic servants. For low-income women, however, housework and childcare remain firmly in their domain (González de la Rocha, 2000). Although employment often has positive outcomes in respect of empowering women and making them less dependent on their spouses, pragmatically this means heavy double burdens of labour, less time for leisure and friendships, and little scope for reflecting on how their critical efforts in household survival might be a route to more egalitarian gender relations (Arce and Escamilla, 1996:22; Chant,1996b:298; Sandoval García, 1997:170; see also Chapter 8).

Gender and labour loads in the home

Growth in employment among women also seems to have impacted directly and indirectly on their overall workloads. As noted by Nash (1995:162): 'rising rates of marital instability, often caused by unemployment or the forced migration of men to find new sources of work, put even greater responsibility on women for the care and welfare of dependants'. Women may have to ensure that domestic labour continues to be performed as before as a condition for obtaining permission to work (Bee and Vogel, 1997:93). In turn, women's continued obligation to meet childcare and domestic responsibilities is highlighted by González de la Rocha (1994:141–2) as a major reason for rising demands on women's time and the absence of significant changes in domestic power relations in Guadalajara, Mexico. Additional factors include the gender gap in wages, and women's lack of ability to control their own earnings. Indeed, given that there has been such little movement by men into reproductive tasks, it is not surprising that women's labour burdens have grown in the last fifteen to twenty years (Chant, 1996b:298; Langer *et al.*, 1991:197; Moser, 1997; UNICEF, 1997:19). Although Gutmann (1999:167) claims for Mexico that young husbands and fathers are doing more childcare than their elders, and in some instances, as in Santiago, Chile, men whose wives earn more than they do tend to assume a bigger share of reproductive work (Alméras, 2000:149), in

Panama, Rudolf (1999) argues that there was more gender complementarity in reproductive as well as productive labour in the past, at least in rural areas. For the Dominican Republic, Safa (1999:16) reports that even where men are unemployed, they tend not to switch their 'surplus' time to housework and childcare. This is also the case in Cuba, regardless of the fact that the Family Code of 1975 prescribed that men should assume an equal share of work in the home.[5] As Pearson (1997:677) asserts: 'In spite of official desires to dissolve the social division of work by gender, the redistribution of reproductive work between men and women was in fact limited'. Pearson goes on to observe that during the economic crisis of the 1990s: 'the pressures to maintain household consumption levels in increasingly difficult circumstances tended to reinforce the traditional gender division of labour rather than resolve it' (ibid.:700). This is mainly because of the additional work involved in reproductive labour arising from cutbacks in state services, and the time and care required to secure the fulfilment of household members' basic needs (see Chapter 3). In short, women may be reluctant to let their spouses waste precious resources through lack of skill or experience. Women may also resist men participating in housework or childcare because it suggests that they do not have a 'real man' for a partner, an issue which also reflects on them. In communities such as Ocongate in the Peruvian Andes, for example, Harvey (1994:74) maintains that women gain respect from working hard in the home, and men are not generally expected to show 'aptitude or interest' in day-to-day household chores. The nurturance of 'traditional' gender stereotypes continues in many cases to be perpetuated by both sexes amongst their peers, as well as through the socialisation of children (see Gomáriz, 1997; Lancaster 1992:44; also Chapter 6).

Men in crisis?

Part of men's apparent unwillingness to participate in reproductive labour conceivably owes to desires to protect the remaining vestiges of 'masculine identity' in a world in which women's activities are widening, not to mention encroaching upon 'male territory' (Chant, 1994:227). This is perhaps especially so in contexts such as Argentina, where a man who does housework is referred to by a variety of pejorative terms – *dominado* ('dominated'), *pollerón* (someone who 'hangs on to their wife's skirts'), *máquina de lavar* ('washing machine'), and for a man who is seen to *enjoy* doing housework *putonesco* ('gayish') (Stølen, 1996:170; see also Gutmann, 1996 on Mexico). Refusal to assist women could therefore be interpreted as passive resistance to a situation which threatens the gender *status quo,* and/or provokes ridicule. As Townsend *et al.* (1999:29) observe for Mexico:

> In the 1980s, many men lost the possibility of being a good provider, and lost much of their power and status outside the home. The patriarchal bargain came

> under threat. Women could still go on suffering (not a virtue in a man): men could no longer be real men, but women were still real women. In both urban and rural areas, many men took out their frustrations and loss of power outside the home within it, with appalling consequences for women and children....

Aside from non-participation in reproductive labour, resistance to change has been noted in other forms. For example, a common male 'backlash' to women's enhanced income-earning opportunities is for men to withdraw their own financial support from the household (Chant, 1997a; Safilios-Rothschild, 1990). Similarly, inability to provide can drive men away from 'paternal responsibilities' (Engle, 1997:37). At a more extreme level, men's frustrations can also take the form of violence (see UNICEF, 1997).

Although men in Latin American countries have retained a larger share of employment and earnings, their mounting fragility as primary breadwinners seems to be the central issue in the increasingly widely noted 'crisis of masculinity' in the region (Chant, 2000; Escobar Latapí, 1998; Gomáriz, 1997; Kaztman, 1992), not to mention elsewhere in the world (Pearson, 2000b:222). Within the context of conjugal households, this has tended to undermine men's security about their position and privileges, about dependency and allegiance on the part of wives and children, and ultimately about their own power to determine the course of family unity and/or disunity (Chant, 2000). As Safa (1999:8) observes for the Dominican Republic: 'Marital life still consists of a succession of consensual unions, but now the initiative for break-up rests as much with women as with men'. Indeed, while men have often been rather peripatetic figures in many Latin American households, this was not really a source of concern so long as men themselves could rely on the family being there when they needed it. Now that more women are earning and have greater bargaining power and independence, these guarantees have been undermined. Indeed, in a recent study on 'family crisis' with male and female youth and adults in Costa Rica, it was men who voiced most concern about the demise of the 'traditional' family, and a large share of the blame was placed on women's increased absence from the home through employment (Chant, 1999b, 2002b). Somewhat ironically, perhaps, although men are usually those whose involvement with their households is limited through migration or abandonment, it is women's short-term daily absence that is held responsible for 'family breakdown', even if women's work hours are often deliberately scaled down to dovetail with school shifts. Indeed, another interesting point which emerged from a national study of men in Costa Rica is that although women apparently value their households more, it is actually men who look more quickly to reconstitute one following family breakdown (Gomáriz, 1997:53; see also Pearson, 2000b:224; Varley and Blasco, 2000b:122). This can either involve setting up home with another partner, or returning to the homes of natal kin (usually mothers). The latter ensures men the receipt of masculine privileges such as domestic attentions without necessarily having to actively negotiate for them (Chant, 2000). Another reason for men going back to the maternal fold, noted for Salvador, Brazil by McCallum (1999:286), is that this provides space for men's sexuality insofar as it allows them to 'assert a virile freedom on the street' (see also Chapter 6).

Trends towards men's increasingly precarious position within conjugal households are widely perceived to have been exacerbated by legislative and policy initiatives in women's interests. Although in principle most men in Guanacaste, Costa Rica claim to be in favour of gender equality, and express distaste for what they feel are outmoded *machista* attitudes, considerable concern is voiced over the potential 'abuse' by women of new entitlements accorded through recent laws and government programmes (see earlier; also Dobles Oropeza, 1998). As one twenty-five year-old construction worker interviewed in 1997, put it, the Law for Social Equality '*no funciona*' ('doesn't work') because it encourages women to think they are superior to men, and many women '*quisieran ser más del hombre*' ('want to be more than men') (see Chant, 2000). This was echoed by a respondent in his sixties who said that although he thought it was good that there was more equality between women and men nowadays: '*a veces, sobrepasa la cosa y la mujer regaña al hombre!*' ('at times this goes too far, and women tell men off!'). He felt that new laws had made it difficult for men to '*volar haches*' ('wield the axe'), meaning to exert control, but with overtones of domestic violence, which has recently become more likely to meet with imprisonment than in the past (ibid.).

State and civil society responses to household change

Having documented some of the major changes in gender and household organisation at the grassroots in Latin America, it remains to examine how state and civil society organisations have reacted to shifting household realities. Clearly, these reactions have been variable across groups as well as over time. In the space of a single decade, for example, the Catholic Church voiced resistance to a programme for lone mothers in Honduras (Grosh, 1994:84–5), but was actively involved in selecting candidates for a similar programme in Costa Rica a few years later (Chant, 1999a). By the same token, it is possible to see that despite the fact that in many Latin American constitutions 'the family' is regarded as the basic unit of society (see Chapter 2), in general terms, resistance to accepting family transitions seems to be diminishing in various parts of the region. In the early 1980s, for example, the Nicaraguan women's organisation AMNLAE was charged by its political opponents with 'mounting a communistic attack on the sanctity of the family', in the wake of its calls for legislation to reformulate the family as an 'institution not of *machismo* and patriarchy but of equality and responsibility', and to promote recognition and acceptance of household diversity (including high numbers of female-headed households) (Lancaster, 1992:17–18). In the 1990s, however, a different mood prevails, with the case of ex-President Daniel Ortega's alleged sexual abuse of his step-daughter, Zoliamérica Narvaez, having brought condemnation from men and women in all sectors of Nicaraguan society, and having galvanised ground-breaking efforts to address the issue of gender-based intra-family violence (see also below).

While in general terms there is clearly on-going anxiety about the 'breakdown' of the patriarchal nuclear family, it seems equally apparent that some change within conjugal households is deemed necessary to prevent further disintegration, and, for those households, predominantly low-income ones, who have already 'broken out' of the conventional mould, to provide assistance that better ensures their security and stability (see Guëndel and González, 1998:28). These imperatives are especially pertinent in an era of state cutbacks and the aggressive marketisation of national economies in which family cohesion is increasingly turned to as a repository of resourcefulness against growing poverty.

In the case of Costa Rica, interviews conducted with a range of government officials and NGO representatives in 1999 (Chant, 2002a, b) indicated some willingness to disregard traditional moral objections to declining rates of marriage and rises in divorce and separation, and to take steps towards adjusting to greater diversity in family patterns over time. This is reflected both in rhetoric and in practice. For example, Costa Rica's 1998 *State of the Nation* report professed that the form a household takes is no predictor of the quality of life for its members, and that in circumstances where domestic violence obtains it is better for households to disband (PEN, 1998:210). In turn, from the late 1990s, there has been increased targeting of social assistance to 'vulnerable groups' such as lone parents and adolescent mothers, alongside attempts to strengthen the protection and rights of children. For example, the 'Solidarity Plan' of Costa Rica's current Social Democratic government (1998–2002), which aims primarily to reduce poverty, has geared three of its six main strategic areas to family support, one being to strengthen family cohesion, one to assist women in conditions of poverty (see later), and one to provide assistance for children and young people. This initiative is accompanied by new legislation for low-income women and youth, and the extension of the activities and responsibilities of specialist organisations such as the National Child Welfare Institute. Beyond this, the work of the Catholic Church and international agencies such as UNICEF and the United Nations Institute for the Prevention of Crime and the Treatment of Delinquency (ILANUD) are complementing the programmes of the Costa Rican state with interventions to strengthen family unity, promote the human rights of women and children, and effect reductions in child abuse and domestic violence. These initiatives are not confined to Costa Rica, as illustrated in relation to two specific examples of these recent types of intervention below.

Public intervention to reduce domestic violence

Although domestic violence has existed in most societies throughout history, from the 1980s onwards the rise of groups demanding women's rights in Latin America has shone a more intense spotlight on the problem (Claramunt, 1997:96). While, as noted in Chapter 5, data remain scarce and unreliable, a report by the Panamerican Health Organisation from the early 1990s suggested that around 50 per cent of Guatemalan women suffered from domestic violence (ibid.). In Nicaragua, where some of the most systematic efforts have been made to record and respond to domestic violence, research carried out in 1996, in León, Nicaragua's second largest city, showed that among 488 women of 15 years or more, 52 per cent had been victim to some kind of conjugal violence in their lives. Among these, 27 per cent had experienced physical assult by their partners in the year leading up to the study, and in 70 per cent of cases, these were catalogued as severe (ibid.). Frequently, coercive intercourse is part and parcel of domestic violence, with Heise (1997:418–9) stating that in Colombia, 48 per cent of battered wives report being sexually assaulted by their partners, a figure which rises to 56 per cent in Bolivia and Puerto Rico. In turn, children also suffer from domestic violence, forcing many of them onto the street (McIlwaine, 2001).

Reflecting the seriousness of the problem, most countries in Latin America now have some form of legislation and intervention against domestic violence in place. In Chile and Argentina, for example, laws against intra-family violence were passed in 1994, and have given rise to shelters, special police units, information centres and 24-hour telephone helplines (Arriagada, 1998:94). In Honduras, the Law for the prevention, punishment and elimination of violence against women was passed in 1997, and in addition to legal aid for women, workshops have been organised to increase awareness of the problem (ibid.). Nicaragua, whose law against intra-family violence was passed in 1996, stands out as one country in the region where men have organised to eliminate domestic violence, and in order to do so, are attempting to 'unlearn' their *machista* socialisation (Montoya Tellería, 1998; see also Chapter 5). Aside from men's own efforts to put a brake on violence, Gutmann (1997) adds that some men who have reacted violently towards women can and do change, as a result of women's instigation at a personal level.

Female-headed households and social policy

As noted earlier, another feature of social policy in recent years has been the increased attention accorded to female-headed households. Although this has not been quite as widespread in the region as initiatives to reduce domestic violence, it is conceivable that a general shift from universal to targeted social programmes will lead to more programmes for female-headed households in the future, especially given growing emphasis on child rights, protection and welfare.

In Costa Rica, the Social Welfare Ministry established its first programme for female household heads in 1997 during the regime of President José María Figueres (1994–1998) of the more left-wing of Costa Rica's two main political parties. This offered a temporary stipend for women to enable them to take courses in self-esteem, assertiveness and skills training. While arguably limited in its coverage and impacts (see Budowksi and Guzmán, 1998; Marenco *et al.*, 1998), this at least gave a substantial number of women access to new resources, as well as stressing women's empowerment (Budowski, 2000; Fauné, 1997:79). The programme has been extended into the current administration of Miguel Angel Rodríguez (1998–2002) under the auspices of the programme '*Creciendo Juntas*' ('Growing Together') (IMAS, 2001), and has been accompanied by two further programmes aimed at the young. The first of these *Amor Joven* ('Young Love), launched in 1999 by the First Lady Lorena Clare de Rodríguez, is concerned with preventing adolescent pregnancy; the second is entitled *Construyendo Oportunidades* ('Building Opportunities'), which seeks to (re)integrate young mothers into education and to provide special programmes of state support for their children (ibid.; see also Chant 1999a, 2000).

Other countries in Latin America which have launched programmes specifically targeted at women-headed households include Colombia, Chile, Honduras and Puerto Rico (see Badia, 1999; Grosh 1994, Safa, 1995a). As in Costa Rica, these have not always been unqualified successes. In Colombia, for example, Rico de Alonso and López Tellez (1998:197) point out that the relationship of female heads to the state remains weak, with only one-third of this group having any affiliation to social security or using public services targeted specifically for them or otherwise. In Chile too, which piloted a Programme for Female Heads of Household in 1992–3 that was later extended nationally, the objective of increasing women's access to employment through labour training, access to childcare and so on, was tempered by the government's failure to address the social and cultural structures underlying gender segregation in the labour market and the perpetuation of poverty among women (Badia,1999). Moreover, children born out of wedlock in Chile still do not have the same rights as their counterparts with married parents, with no recognition of the responsibilities of their own parents and extended kin (Arriagada, 1998:97). Even if elsewhere in the region governments are more hesitant about promoting schemes that may increase numbers of female-headed households (Buvinic and Gupta, 1997), other forms of support for women can actually have greater effects. In Cuba, for example, no special welfare benefits are given to female heads, but policies favouring greater gender equality, higher levels of female labour force participation, and the provision of daycare have all made it easier for women to raise children alone (Safa, 1995a).

Conclusion

While a number of trajectories in gender and 'the family' in Latin America seem possible, the most likely is that kin relationships will continue to form the core of social organisation, but in a greater variety of forms, and with more flexible positioning of the members of household units with regard to rights and responsibilities. Yet whether households which depart from traditional normative ideals of structure and internal divisions of labour will receive the same ideological and institutional legitimacy as others is less certain. As Datta and McIlwaine (2000) point out for Guatemala, continued social stigmatisation of female-headed households indicates the difficulty of changing embedded norms. Even in Costa Rica, where there have been important shifts in accepting 'new' household types, the common use in public and policy circles of terms such as 'family disintegration', and continued popular allegiance to marriage and conventional divisions of conjugal responsibilities, suggest on-going idealisation of the 'traditional' two-parent patriarchal family unit (Chant, 2002b). For this reason, the Costa Rican feminist lobby has found it necessary to maintain pressure on the state to adopt a wider vision of the family, to acknowledge that members of the same household do not necessarily share the same interests, and to recognise that the figure of the *hombre jefe de familia* (male head of family unit) can reproduce inequality and perpetuate the violation of women's and children's rights (Grupo Agenda Política de Mujeres Costarricenses, 1997:42). This is echoed in other countries such as Mexico, whose background paper on families for the Fourth World Conference on Women in Beijing included calls to legally redefine 'the family' as a more heterogeneous institution (de Oliveira *et al.*, 1995:27). But, as Feijoó (1999:161) writes:

> The battle for legitimising female headship is not yet assured.... Now that research has broken ground in respect of showing that these households are not necessarily living in the deepest penury in society, and that we can begin to recognise the potential of this form of domestic organisation, the battle is all the more pressing (my translation).

Another pressing issue for the future is that of how to enable and encourage men to participate in a broader range of activities relating to family life than is conventionally expected by hegemonic masculinity. This is especially pertinent in the light of men's increasing difficulties in the labour market, as explored further in the next chapter.

8 Gender and Employment

SYLVIA CHANT

Introduction

In the previous chapter we showed that one of the most notable changes in gender in Latin America over the last fifty years has been the rising labour force participation of women. The present chapter explores this trend in more detail and in relation to patterns of male employment. It also examines the reasons for, and consequences of, gender differentiation in urban labour markets.

The discussion begins with a brief introduction to theoretical approaches to female labour force participation, and proceeds to outline the changing shape of employment in Latin America between the mid-twentieth century and the present day, particularly in relation to post-war urbanisation and to post-1980 neoliberal economic restructuring. This includes analyses of sectoral shifts in employment, and the progressive 'informalisation' of labour markets in the region. The core of the chapter examines trends in male and female labour force participation in recent decades, the positioning of men and women in the workforce, the implications for wages, benefits and occupational mobility, and the prospects for eradication or entrenchment of gender divisions in the twenty-first century.

Theoretical perspectives on gender and employment

Theoretical work on gender and employment is wide-ranging. It varies not only in terms of issues – for example, why men and women are found in different segments of the labour market, what the outcomes are of gender differentiation in employment – but also in respect of the angle from which such questions are tackled, whether that of the micro-determinants of labour supply or the macro-level of labour demand. It should also be noted that while considerable attention has been given to the question of female labour force participation, few analyses have concentrated on accounting for persistently higher rates of male economic activity across space and through time. Although there are good reasons why women should have been singled out for attention, not least because of the traditional invisibilisation of their work, the charge might be levelled that continued female bias neglects the problems faced by an increasing number of men in labour markets. The implied acceptance of men's economic activity as a given also reinforces the idea that employment and breadwinning constitute fixed and universal components of male behaviour and identities.

Family determinants of female labour force participation

While long overdue attention is now being paid to men's employment from a gender perspective, most theoretical models concerned with women's more limited and discontinuous involvement in the workforce, and their relegation to less skilled and less remunerated jobs, have given considerable weight to family roles. More specifically, they have focused on how women's greater involvement in childcare and domestic labour impinges pragmatically and ideologically on their ability to enter the labour force on the same basis as men (Scott, 1990; Walby, 1985). At one end of the spectrum, neoclassical approaches such as the 'status attainment' model have sought to explain gender disparities in employment type and intensity (hours worked and so on), through male–female differentials in human capital and women's primary identification with the domestic sphere (see Beuchler, 1986). At the other end of the spectrum, Marxist-Feminist approaches have stressed how the influences of capitalism and patriarchy combine to position women in the interstices of home and workplace. This is not only deemed to contribute to upholding male privileges, but to create a 'reserve army' of cheap, 'floating' labour which can be drawn upon in times of boom, and discarded during slumps (ibid.). Threads of the latter formulation have been taken up in notions of women as 'secondary earners' in 'secondary labour markets', and that of a 'reproduction tax' on women (Palmer, 1992).

The focus on family factors in shaping female labour supply has not escaped criticisms. One is that the 'family' can sometimes be treated as a fixed and unitary entity, when in reality families are diverse and their effects on female labour force participation, historically and spatially contingent (see Chapter 7). A second criticism of the family focus is that it can divert attention from the fact that familial and gender ideologies are embedded within the 'public sphere' of labour markets and institutions as much as they are in the 'private' domestic domain (Scott, 1990; see also Chant, 1991; Elson, 1999). In response to calls for more nuanced analyses of family–labour market relations that move way from monolithic and stereotypical concepts of patriarchy and pay attention to the 'particular mechanisms' through which women enter paid work (Scott, 1990:213), there has been less exclusive emphasis accorded to 'the family' over time. In turn, greater attention has been paid to the dynamic interactions among a range of variables operating in the sphere of the home, the labour market, state organisations, the global economy and so on, that create the conditions under which women take up remunerated work, and which generate, modify and/or perpetuate gendered labour (see Pearson, 1998:180; see also Elson *et al.*, 1997).

Female labour force participation and industrial evolution

Another important strand within theory on gender and employment is how women's labour force participation interacts with different types and phases of economic development. Pearson's (1998) discussion of this topic identifies a shift in emphasis from 'marginality, to 'inclusion', to 'exploitation' in conjunction with industrial changes in the South in the final decades of the twentieth century.

In the early 1970s, and in the wake of Ester Boserup's seminal review of the effects of post-war modernisation on women, the common consensus was that industrially oriented development strategies excluded women from production, or confined them to marginal niches of urban and rural economies. This analysis came into question, however, when, from the mid-1970s onwards, import substitution industrialisation (ISI) began to be rivalled by export-oriented industrialisation (EOI) in a range of Third World countries. In general terms, export manufacturing, particularly in multinational branch plants, was considerably more labour-intensive than in firms producing for the domestic market, and brought about a substantial increase of women among the ranks of semi- and unskilled factory operatives. This gave rise to the notion that export-led industrialisation equated with 'female-led' industrialisation (Joekes, 1987:81), or at least that the selective incorporation of women workers in new firms called for distinctions between different dimensions of marginalisation in labour markets, as well as between different dimensions of gender (Faulkner and Lawson, 1991; Scott, 1986c). As recession hit a host of developing countries in the 1980s and 1990s, women were not discarded from the labour force (as earlier formulations had predicted), but instead became central to strategies of deregulation, casualisation and flexibilisation demanded by neoliberal restructuring and an increasingly competitive economic environment. This saw the birth of the notion of a 'global feminisation of labour' (Standing, 1989, 1999), which held not only that women were more likely to be employed that at any previous stage in the post-war period, but that industrialisation, now more exploitative than ever, and encompassing subcontracting as well as plant-based hiring, depended on the 'conversion of all industrial employment to the (inferior) conditions endured by female labour' (Pearson, 1998:176; see also Moghadam, 1995, 2000).

Women's employment and empowerment

Against this rather bleak portrayal of women's evolving position in industrial labour forces in the South, there has been considerable debate around the interrelationships between women's employment and empowerment. Although Pearson (1998:178) argues that for many years there was: 'an implicit assumption of the direct correlation between women's waged employment and the diminution of oppression and subordination of women', this idea has now squarely been rejected as overblown and over-romanticised (McClenagahan, 1997). The conditions of women's employment often leave much to be desired and the terms of their participation continue to be set largely by patriarchal norms. The significance of employment for women cannot be studied in isolation, but only in relation to their personal identities, domestic circumstances, and wider social and economic aspects of gender inequality (see Faulkner and Lawson, 1991:40–1; Moghadam, 1994: 99–102; Safa, 1990). Blumberg (1989), among others, has asked whether women's employment gives them any greater control over their own lives, demonstrating that it is highly contingent upon whether they have the liberty (or 'inclination') to control the income they derive from it. In addition, Elson (1999:615) notes that women's labour force participation may itself involve costs which cut into earnings, whether through a reduction in income transfers from non-market sources, or declining support from male partners for children. The social costs of women adopting a 'breadwinning role', especially in the absence of men, may also be prejudicial.

Although it is undeniable that the interrelationship between female employment and empowerment remains a 'vexed one', it is also true that 'many women themselves feel there is a connection' (Moore, 1988:111). With a shift away from patronising notions of 'false consciousness' and the idea that only the 'public sphere' counts for gains in women's status (see Chapter 1), an increasing number of studies have felt more comfortable about questions of women's agency, and accepting women's own, and frequently contradictory, accounts about what employment signifies in their lives (see Bradshaw, 1995a; Chant, 1991; Chant and McIlwaine, 1995; Kabeer, 2000; Safa, 1992, 1995a, 1999). This has been accompanied by ever stronger exhortations to acknowledge and scrutinise the intermeshing of women's and men's roles and relations in the 'productive' and 'reproductive economies' (Elson *et al.*, 1997; also Elson, 1999).

Latin American labour markets and employment 1995–2000: an overview

In the space of only fifty years, Latin American employment has shifted from being predominantly rural to predominantly urban-based. On top of this rural–urban transition, employment in the region has been further transformed during the last two decades by economic globalisation. According to Ward and Pyle (1995:38), this is marked by three main trends: 1) a shift to export-oriented growth under the influence of IMF and World Bank lending conditionalities; 2) the globalisation of the production and marketing operations of transnational companies; and 3) debt crises and recessions. Additional factors include shifts in terms of trade and technological change, and lessening intervention of the state in economic and labour matters (Berry, 1997:3; Sheahan, 1997:8). In the light of the multiplicity of these trends, it is clearly difficult to evaluate overall changes in labour markets (Tokman, 1989:1071). Aside from the fact that the implementation and experience of neoliberal reforms has not been uniform across the region (see Chapter 3), another complicating factor is that some of the improvements in employment following initial downturns in wages and job availability are still too recent, and under-researched, to enable firm conclusions on whether these will be sustained in the longer term (Gwynne and Kay, 2000:149–59; also Escobar Latapí, 2000c).

The urbanisation of Latin American employment

One established trend, however, is the on-going urbanisation of Latin American economies, with the last decades of the twentieth century characterised not only by losses in agriculture's contributions to GDP and export earnings, but also by declining shares of national employment (see Table 8.1). Even if most Central American economies remain heavily dependent for foreign exchange on primary products such as sugar, bananas, coffee and cotton (Klak, 1999:115), some countries in the Isthmus experienced a virtual halving of agricultural employment between 1960 and 1990.

In most of Latin America, dwindling possibilities for low-income groups to make a rural livelihood began in the wake of early twentieth-century attempts to modernise agriculture. Despite periodic bouts of agrarian reform, especially during the 1960s and 1970s, tenancies and sharecropping agreements progressively gave way to wage labour, and un- and under-employment in agriculture in the region rose from 13 per cent in 1950 to 17 per cent in 1970, and to 19 per cent in 1980 (Curto de Casas, 1994:236). Neoliberal reforms in the 1980s and 1990s did little to help the poor, but instead tended to consolidate and extend gains for middle- and large-scale farmers and wealthier groups of the peasantry, particularly those producing for the export market (Kay, 1999). In terms of contemporary trends, there has been an on-going rise in wage labour, much of it of a temporary or seasonal nature, and involving workers who live in towns but commute or migrate out to rural jobs on a casual basis, as observed in Brazil (ibid.), and Costa Rica (Chant, 1992). At the same time, an increasing number of rural dwellers have become reliant on income from

Table 8.1 Employment in Latin America by Sector, 1960–90

	Percentage of labour force in								
	Agriculture			Industry			Services		
	1960	1980	1990	1960	1980	1990	1960	1980	1990
Argentina	21	13	12	34	34	32	45	53	55
Bolivia	55	53	47	24	18	18	21	29	36
Brazil	55	37	23	17	24	23	28	39	54
Chile	30	21	19	30	25	25	39	54	56
Colombia	52	40	27	19	21	23	29	39	50
Costa Rica	51	35	26	18	23	27	30	42	47
Cuba	36	—	18	24	—	30	41	—	51
Dominican Republic	64	32	25	13	24	29	24	44	46
Ecuador	59	40	33	18	20	19	23	40	48
El Salvador	62	43	36	17	19	21	21	38	43
Guatemala	66	54	52	13	19	17	21	27	30
Honduras	72	57	41	9	15	20	18	28	39
Mexico	55	36	28	19	29	23	29	35	50
Nicaragua	63	39	28	15	24	26	21	37	46
Panama	51	29	26	19	16	14	35	52	58
Paraguay	54	45	39	18	20	22	27	35	39
Peru	52	40	36	20	18	18	28	42	46
Uruguay	24	17	14	29	28	27	50	55	59
Venezuela	—	15	12	—	28	27	—	57	61

Sources: UNDP (1997: Table 16), World Bank (1996: Table 4).
Note: — = no data.

off-farm sources (see Rothstein, 1995). Part and parcel of the casualisation of rural labour and the rising production of agro-exports is the 'feminisation' of agricultural employment (Kay, 1999:287–90), as discussed in greater detail later.

Industrialisation is another critical factor in the changing sectoral balance of Latin American labour markets, even if services have more or less consistently out-ranked industry in respect of employment (see Table 8.1). One reason why industrial expansion has not generated more jobs in Latin America is the use of capital-intensive technology, particularly during the era of ISI between the 1940s and 1970s (Roberts, B., 1995:118). Although the shift from ISI to EOI – especially of non-traditional exports – has been marked by more labour-intensive production methods (see Clark, 1997), growing levels of labour-saving technology are now being introduced in the export sector as well (Acero, 1997:71; Pearson, 2000c). This is lowering the relative demand for unskilled versus skilled industrial workers, with, as we shall see later, important implications for gender.

Although governments have sometimes generated industrial jobs through infrastructural developments and direct investment in industry, the expansion of the police and the armed forces, together with the growth of bureaucracies in most Latin American nations, also helps to explain the bias towards service employment in the region (Roberts, B., 1995:114–15; Thomas, 1996:86). For example, between 1978 and 1985, employment in public administration in Brazil grew by 5.8 per cent a year, against an annual growth rate of only 0.9 per cent in formal employment as a whole (Medeiros, 1986, cited in Roberts, B., 1995:115). This made the state the most important source of formal jobs in the country, and resulted in public employment being the mainstay of 11.4 per cent of the workforce in 1980. Although the annual growth rate in public sector employment dipped to 4.6 per cent in the 1980s, it still maintained its edge relative to the labour force as a whole (Gilbert, 1994:72). Indeed, in 1990, the Brazilian state bureaucracy, along with that in six other Latin American countries (Argentina, Chile, Costa Rica, Colombia, Mexico and Venezuela) occupied as much as 16.8 per cent of the workforce in non-agricultural employment (Thomas, 1999:88–9). Despite the relative protection afforded to the public sector, however, recession and restructuring have taken their toll.

Economic crisis and neoliberal restructuring: the impacts on employment

Economic crisis and restructuring have not only led to shrinkage in public employment but have been linked more generally with rising levels of un- and underemployment, deteriorating wages and working conditions, increased numbers of people seeking work, and mounting informalisation of labour markets (Tironi and Lagos, 1991; Feijoó, 2001:28).

UN- AND UNDER-EMPLOYMENT

The debt crisis of the early 1980s is commonly considered to have brought dramatic contractions in Latin American employment. Between 1980 and 1985, for example, underemployment in the region is estimated to have grown by 48 per cent (Safa, 1995b:33), and open unemployment stood at 14 per cent in 1984, which was more than double its 1974 level (6 per cent) (Cubitt, 1995:164). The fact that rates of open unemployment declined in most parts of Latin America to between 4 and 7 per cent by the mid 1990s (ECLAC, 1994:28) might support the notion that these downturns were only transitory in nature. In Chile, for example, employment more than doubled between 1983 (after its second period of debt-related restructuring) and 1996 (Gwynne, 1999:90). Two qualifications are important here, however. One is that the quantity and quality of employment are unevenly distributed, with women and young workers in Chile continuing to face an above-average risk of unemployment and/or of entering precarious work (Tuman, 2000:183). The second qualification is that the Chilean experience cannot be extrapolated to other parts of the continent.

In countries such as Argentina, for example, which has been described as a 'late but committed convert' to adjustment (Gwynne and Kay, 2000:145), a particularly draconian set of economic reforms introduced in 1991 led both to an increase in underemployment (from 7.9 per cent in 1991 to 11.3 per cent in 1995), and open unemployment (from 5.2 to 20.2 per cent) (Cerrutti, 2000b:882). A total of 51 state and parastatal companies were privatised between 1989 and 1992, and the number of workers in public sector employment nosedived from 250,000 to only 60,000 (Arias, 2000:3). In Nicaragua unemployment jumped from 4.5 per cent in 1986 to 23.5 per cent in 1994 (Bulmer-Thomas, 1996:326) and, as in Argentina, part of this was due to the firing of 250,000 public sector employees in the first three years of Violeta Chamorro's UNO regime as the economy came under the grip of the global financial institutions (Green, 1995:56–7). Elsewhere in the region, losses in public sector employment have also been marked, with the overall share of the public sector in non-agricultural employment falling from 15.3 to 13.2 per cent between 1990 and 1995 (Thomas, 1999:279). Although an upturn in private waged employment in the early 1990s went some way to cushioning losses in public sector jobs, unemployment rates continue to be very high among the poor, and are also mounting among young people aged 15–24 with 6–12 years of schooling (ECLAC, 1994:31). While open unemployment stood at 18.6 per cent in Panama in 1991, for example, the level for 15–24 year olds was 35.1 per cent (ibid.:144). Although youth unemployment had declined to 29.5 per cent by 1999, this still ranks as one of the highest rates in the region along with Argentina (26.4 per cent), Venezuela (26.6 per cent), and Uruguay (27.1 per cent) (see ILO Lima, 2000: Table 3A).[1] There is also evidence to suggest that new unemployment in some contexts is affecting young men to a greater degree than young women, as we shall see later. More generally, the problem of unemployment is extremely serious for all age groups when it is considered that in relatively well-off countries, such as Argentina, less than one-tenth of the unemployed are covered by unemployment insurance (Cerrutti, 2000b:887).

WAGES AND WORKING CONDITIONS IN THE FORMAL SECTOR

In addition to formal sector job losses, the 1980s and 1990s saw considerable changes in working conditions, particularly in manufacturing. The main tendencies were a greater incidence of subcontracting and short-term contracts, the restriction of trade union activities, the introduction of measures to ease hiring and firing, and reduced obligations on the part of employers for social security and pensions (Thomas, 1999). Many of these changes have resulted from the pressure exerted by international financial institutions to reduce 'structural rigidities' in the workforce and to encourage greater labour flexibility (Green, 1995:109–10; Standing, 1999; Tironi and Lagos, 1991).

Labour law revisions have played an important part in these strategies. The New

Economic Policy in Bolivia of 1985, for example, reduced protection for workers and eliminated a wage index, so that wage levels had to be negotiated within individual firms (Jenkins, 1997:113). In Peru, legislation was introduced in 1991 which granted employers the right to hire people on 'probationary contracts' that gave only minimal entitlements to fringe benefits and no severance pay (Thomas, 1996: 91). The proportion of the Peruvian labour force on temporary contracts rose from 41 per cent to more than 50 per cent between the early and late 1990s (Thomas, 1999: 276). This said, it is important to note that such practices were by no means absent before the crisis. As Roberts, B. (1995:118–) maintains in relation to Mexico: '"implicit deregulation" … antedades by many years the policy of explicit deregulation'.[2]

Wage restraints have also been a critical element in the restructuring process, which, coupled with inflationary costs of living, led to negative growth rates in average real earnings in many countries in the 1980s (see Table 8.2). In Mexico, for example, the real minimum urban wage was only 42 per cent of its 1980 value in 1994, and in Paraguay a mere 11.5 per cent (Thomas, 1999:270n; see also García and de Oliveira, 2000 on salary controls in Mexico in the 1990s).

Table 8.2 Latin America: Labour Force and Earnings

	Size of labour force (millions)		Average annual growth rate of labour force		Annual growth rate in real earnings per employee	
	1980	1994	1980–90	1990–99	1970–80	1980–92
Argentina	11	13	1.3	1.9	−2.2	−2.1
Bolivia	2	3	2.6	2.6	1.7	−0.8
Brazil	48	71	3.2	2.2	5.0	−2.4
Chile	4	5	2.7	2.4	8.1	−0.3
Colombia	9	15	4.0	2.7	−0.2	—
Costa Rica	1	1	3.8	2.6	—	—
Cuba	—	—	—	—	—	—
Dominican Republic	2	3	3.1	2.9	−1.1	—
Ecuador	3	4	3.5	3.3	3.3	−0.7
El Salvador	2	2	2.1	3.5	2.4	—
Guatemala	2	4	2.9	3.2	−3.2	−1.6
Honduras	1	2	3.4	3.8	—	—
Mexico	22	35	3.5	2.9	—	—
Nicaragua	1	2	2.7	4.0	−2.0	—
Panama	1	1	3.1	2.6	0.2	2.0
Paraguay	1	2	3.1	3.3	—	—
Peru	5	8	3.2	2.7	—	—
Uruguay	1	1	1.6	1.2	—	−2.3
Venezuela	5	8	3.4	3.0	4.9	−5.4

Sources: UNDP (1997:Table 16), World Bank (1996:Table 4), World Bank (2000b:Table 3).
Note: — = no data.

Wages have often been held down with the agreement of trade unions, whose bargaining power has dwindled with the downturn of the formal sector (Epstein, 2000; Gwynne and Kay, 2000:145 & 148). As Koonings *et al.* (1995:123) observe: 'Informalisation and endemic poverty pose a major threat to the capacity of trade unions to organise and defend the working population'. Interestingly, however, against a relative decline in union activity in the formal sector, there have been greater signs of organisation among informal entrepreneurs (ibid.:119). Part of this has undoubtedly been motivated by the need to survive against greater odds in a disadvantaged, but expanding, sector of the regional labour market.

THE URBAN INFORMAL SECTOR

Alongside the 'informalisation' of labour occurring in large-scale industry and services, Latin America's 'informal sector' of employment has undergone considerable expansion during the period of crisis and neoliberal reforms. Although many criteria have been used to define the 'informal sector' (see Gilbert, 1998:65; Scott, 1994:16–24; Thomas, 1995a), one of the most generally accepted definitions is 'income-generating activities unregulated by the state in contexts where similar activities are so regulated' (Roberts, 1994:6). This said, it is clear that informal sector firms vary widely in degrees of regulation, and that 'complete regulation' rarely applies to more than a handful of large (mainly multinational) firms (see Tokman, 1992; Tokman and Klein, 1996).

Definitional difficulties and inconsistencies aside, the urban informal sector primarily employs low-income groups in a mixture of low-productivity, low-profit commercial, service and manufacturing activities (see Table 8.3). Although the informal sector was already growing in the wake of rural–urban migration in the 1960s and 1970s (see Portes and Schauffler, 1993; Tokman, 1989), in urban areas, the share of employment made up by the informal sector grew from a regional average of 25.6 per cent to 30 per cent between 1980 and 1990 (Gilbert, 1995b), and vastly outstripped growth in the formal sector. During this time, the growth in own-account workers and workers in small firms in seven countries in the region (Argentina, Chile, Colombia, Costa Rica, Brazil, Mexico and Venezuela) was approximately four times that of the combined numbers employed in large firms and in the public sector (Thomas, 1996:88). Even in Cuba where, prior to the post-Soviet 'Special Period', informal work was regarded with suspicion, the sector has undergone such a massive expansion on the island that it is now recognised and accepted by the state as an important part of Cuban people's survival (Molyneux, 1996:33).

Aside from cutbacks in public and private sector employment, post-1980 growth in informal employment has been fuelled by the fact that many family firms have been forced into informality through declining ability to pay registration, tax and labour overheads (Roberts, B., 1995:124). Another critically important factor has

Table 8.3 Percentage of Production which is Informal in Selected Latin American Countries

	Percentage of production which is informal			
	Manufacturing	Transport	Services	Total
Brazil (1990)	12	23	23	18
Costa Rica (1984)	14	9	16	15
Honduras (1990)	26	17	28	26
Mexico (1992)	9	20	20	16
Uruguay (1985)	16	10	16	16
Venezuela (1992)	16	46	22	23

Source: United Nations (1995: Table 9)

been rising numbers of entrants to the labour force as a result of demographic growth, reflecting the legacy of high fertility from the 1960s and 1970s (Chapter 4), as well as pressure on household incomes (Alba, 1989:18–21; Gilbert, 1995a:327; see Table 8.2). The latter has played a particularly important role in stimulating the labour force participation of women, although at the same time they have suffered on account of their disproportionate concentration in the sector and the fact that, as we shall see later, their limited resource base normally confines them to the lowest productivity ventures within it (Acero, 1999:72; Bromley, 1997:135; Moser, 1997; Scott, 1994). Indeed, greater numbers of people needing to work, on top of lower purchasing power among the population in general, has substantially constrained the profitability of informal sector employment (Roberts, 1991:135). Despite people's efforts to work longer hours and to be innovatory within the sector (see Escobar Latapí and González de la Rocha, 1995; Miraftab, 1994:468), competition is such that between 1980 and 1989 there was an estimated drop in informal incomes of 42 per cent (Moghadam, 1995:122–3).

Gender and employment in Latin America: recent and contemporary trends in female and male labour force participation

In addition to changes in the general contours of Latin American urban labour markets over the last few decades, the configuration of the labour force has also been marked by important shifts in gender composition, with an overall decline in men's share of employment before and during crisis and restructuring. Bearing in mind that women's economic activities are often under-recorded in official figures owing to their informal and/or part-time nature, between 1950 and 1980 the female share of total employment (including agriculture) in Latin America purportedly rose from 18 to 26 per cent (Safa, 1995b:32). By 1990 the regional average was 34 per cent (UN, 1995:109), and upward trends have continued in most countries since that time (see Table 8.4).[3] In respect of rises in women's economic activity rates (the proportion of women working among the female population of working age), South America experienced the largest increase in the world between 1980 and 1997: from 29 to 45 per cent, with the corresponding rise in Central America being from 31 to 39 per cent (UN, 2000:110).

Table 8.4 Women's Share of Labour Force and Occupational Categories

	Female share of labour force (%)			Women as percentage of:			
				Administrative and managerial	Professional, technical & related workers	Clerical & sales	Services
	1980	1994	1999	1990	1990	1990	1990
Argentina	28	30	33	—	—	—	—
Bolivia	33	37	38	16.8	41.9	64.7	72.5
Brazil	28	34	35	—	—	—	—
Chile	26	31	33	19.4	51.9	46.3	72.5
Colombia	25	35	38	27.2	41.8	45.5	69.6
Costa Rica	21	29	31	23.1	44.8	40.4	59.3
Cuba	—	—	—	—	—	—	—
Dominican Republic	25	29	30	—	—	—	—
Ecuador	20	26	28	26.0	44.2	40.9	63.5
El Salvador	27	33	36	17.7	43.3	59.7	72.3
Guatemala	22	25	28	32.4	45.2	39.3	51.7
Honduras	25	28	31	27.8	50.0	59.6	72.4
Mexico	27	32	33	19.4	43.2	41.7	45.0
Nicaragua	28	36	35	—	—	—	—
Panama	30	33	35	28.9	50.7	57.5	55.8
Paraguay	26	28	30	16.1	51.2	46.2	71.8
Peru	24	28	31	22.1	40.9	52.1	37.6
Uruguay	31	40	42	20.6	61.1	45.9	67.7
Venezuela	27	33	34	18.6	55.2	45.7	57.5

Sources: UNDP (1995: Table A2.7); World Bank (1996: Table 4); World Bank (2000b: Table 3).
Note: — = no data.

Factors accounting for the rise in female labour force participation

Factors accounting for general increases in female labour force participation in the post-war period are not easily generalised. Part of this relates to different starting points in female labour force participation in different parts of the region. Another reason is the differential interplay of a range of influences pertinent to both the supply and demand for labour. Remembering, as discussed earlier, that these are not only closely interrelated but often mutually constitutive (see Chant, 1991:12 *et seq.*; Ríos, 1995:125; Scott, 1994:215–7), a summary of the principal factors is given in Box 8.1, and discussed in more detail below.

INDIVIDUAL AND HOUSEHOLD FACTORS

At the level of labour supply, post-1950 increases in female labour force participation in Latin America have been linked with secular changes such as improvements in education, postponement of marriage, declining fertility, and the transfer of women to towns through rural–urban migration (Cerrutti, 2000b:888; Safa, 1995a:16).

Women's education in Latin America has increased dramatically in the post-war period. This is especially so at primary and secondary levels (see Table 4.4). but, relative to men, at tertiary level too. Bearing in mind that only around 15 per cent of Latin Americans of the relevant age group were enrolled in tertiary education establishments in 1993 (World Bank, 1996:201), and that in some countries such as Bolivia and Guatemala there are only half as many women as men in further and higher education, Panama, Argentina, Colombia and Brazil stand out as cases where the ratio is now female-biased (UN, 1995:51–3). This is also the case in Cuba, where women are not only the majority of students in traditionally 'female subjects', but also in geology, metallurgy and mining (see Lumsden, 1999:120). In Guadalajara, Mexico, the uptake of university courses such as accountancy, business administration, systems engineering and management is also increasing (Escobar, 2000b). Notwithstanding that in most other parts of Latin America women continue to be more heavily represented in non-vocational arts and humanities degrees than in subjects such as science and engineering (see UN, 2000:93; also Fauné, 1997:80), labour force participation is higher among women with tertiary qualifications in general. In Argentina, for example, women with further and higher education are nine times more likely to have jobs than women with primary education or less (Cerrutti, 2000b:884). On the basis of comparative work on Buenos Aires and Mexico City, Cerrutti (2000a:41) also argues that:

> More educated women are not only likely to work, but they are also likely to stay in the labour force for longer periods, and to express greater commitment to their jobs (partly because they have access to more rewarding jobs). Education is not only important for accessing better jobs, but also for its effects on women's values and perceptions. Women with higher educations [*sic*] are less likely to hold traditional beliefs regarding the role of women. Traditional beliefs may contain positive elements of caring and responsibility. However, in the context of poverty and economic crisis they tend, I claim, to act against the best interests of

BOX 8.1

Factors Accounting for Women's Rising Labour Force Participation in Latin America, 1950–2000

Domain	
Individual	• Rising literacy rates
	• Rising levels of education
	• Later age of marriage and/or first birth
	• Declining fertility
	• Rural–urban migration
Household	• Changes in household structure, especially rising proportions of female-headed households
	• Increases in household poverty and need for multiple household incomes
	• Changing ideologies of motherhood in which financial contributions to household are increasingly regarded as integral to maternal obligations
Labour market	• Declining share of agriculture in overall employment
	• Growth of tertiary sector
	• Expansion of feminised occupational niches, e.g. as operatives in multinational export manufacturing firms
	• Increased competition due to neoliberal restructuring
	• Deregulation and informalisation
Institutional/legal	• Increases in anti-discriminatory employment legislation
	• Introduction of employment and training programmes for female-headed households in some countries
	• Some increase in childcare provision for working mothers

women and their children. In these contexts, traditional beliefs support a harmful culture of male irresponsibility and state indifference.

The overlap between variables should not be forgotten here, with education often associated with lower fertility, and, in turn, higher class status which almost always connotes the possibility of hiring domestic help (Stichter, 1990:56). The individual characteristics and endowments of women are plainly mediated by their domestic circumstances and status, with increases in female household headship in Latin America having played a particularly crucial role in releasing new cohorts of women into the labour force (see Chapter 7). This is driven not only by financial need, but also by the greater freedom of female heads from the constraints which are often imposed by husbands in male-headed households on whether, and where, women can participate in the labour market. As such, women heads of household usually display higher rates of labour force participation than their partnered counterparts (see Cerrutti, 2000a:38; 2000b:884; also Chant, 1991; Willis, 1993).

POST-WAR ECONOMIC DEVELOPMENT AND NEOLIBERAL RESTRUCTURING

Another critical factor explaining long-term rises in female labour force participation is the urbanisation of Latin American labour markets. Women's share of employment in urban areas currently ranges between around 25 and 35 per cent, but in rural areas it has long been under 20 per cent, even if many have argued that statistics on the latter are especially prone to under-recording, given women's preponderance in subsistence farming (see Elson and Gideon, 1997a; Sacayón Manzo, 1997). Nonetheless, in Costa Rica, where women are registered as only 6 per cent of the rural labour force in government statistics, none of the principal agricultural activities (coffee, bananas, sugar and cattle), employ women in significant numbers. Even if the coffee harvest has generally recruited women and children alongside men (Chant, 1997a:131), it is only with the growth of industry and services in the Costa Rican economy that female employment opportunities have increased appreciably (Chant, 2000). This has also been the case in the Dominican Republic and Puerto Rico, where the rise in the female workforce over the last four decades is attributed to the disintegration of the sugar economy and a shift to urban-based labour intensive manufacturing (Safa, 1995b). In Puerto Rico, specifically, unemployment rates have been higher among men since the 1950s (Safa, 1999:2).

Having identified the progressive eclipse of rural by urban employment as important in accounting for women's rising share of employment, it should also be noted that since the 1980s the expansion of export production of fruits, flowers and vegetables has led to increasingly 'feminised' pockets of agricultural labour in Latin America. In Mexico, for example, around one-quarter of the economically active rural population are now involved in fruit and vegetable production, and around half this group are women (Kay, 1999:289). In Costa Rica, women's employment in non-traditional agriculture is also increasing, mainly in packing, but in some sub-sectors, such as ornamental plants, in the planting phase as well (Fauné, 1997:65–6). In Chile, up to 70 per cent of *temporeras* (temporary workers) in the export production of fruit are female, with the bulk of their employment concentrated in fertilising, pruning, harvesting and packing for around four to six months a year (Barrientos and Perrons, 1999:154; Barrientos *et al.*, 1999; Bee and Vogel, 1997). If the widely-alleged underestimation of women in agricultural labour is accepted, the rise in agro-export production between 1982 and 1992 purportedly led to a 296 per cent increase in female agricultural workers against an increase of only 69.8 per cent in the national labour force as a whole (Barrientos, 1997:73). Currently women make up around half of a total of 250,000–500,000 temporary workers in Chilean agriculture (ibid.).

More significant still in creating jobs for women, however, has been the proliferation of service employment in Latin American cities (see Chant, 1991:17; Cerrutti, 2000b:863; Stichter, 1990:18). In the period 1990–97 an estimated 73 per cent of women workers in Central America were engaged in sevices, and 81 per cent in South America, compared with 38 per cent and 56 per cent respectively among men (UN, 2000:14). Within the service sector, women feature prominently in shop work, petty commerce, nursing, teaching, tourism and clerical employment, although by far the biggest employer of unskilled Latin American women, particularly young migrants, is domestic service, which in many cases involves 'living in' with employers (Bullock, 1994:18; Chant, 1992; Radcliffe, 1990a; see also Chapter 9).

The accuracy of figures on domestic service is often questioned, but as of 1993 this sector occupied an estimated 25 per cent of women wage workers in Honduras (López de Mazier, 1997:237). In the same year this applied to 14.4 per cent of all women workers in El Salvador (Gutiérrez Castillo, 1997:149). Rates tend to be higher still among low-income groups. In a survey of low-income settlements in Querétaro, Mexico in the early 1980s, for example, domestic service was the largest single occupational category among working female household heads and spouses, employing 32 per cent of the total (Chant, 1991:122).

Domestic service is characterised by varying degrees of 'formality', with much of this contingent upon employers and the manner in which they pay their employees. In Buenos Aires, for example, Lloyd-Sherlock (1997:179) notes that workers who receive a monthly salary are more likely to benefit from statutory rights such as an annual bonus, than those paid on an hourly basis. Similarly, deductions for bed and board among live-in servants can pare down already meagre wages considerably. Hours of work may also be long and opportunities for social life and recreation severely restricted. In the context of Peru, this leads Radcliffe (1990a:390) to assert that domestic service is 'only slightly better an occupation than begging and

Figure 8.1 Construction workers, Tamarindo, Costa Rica (Photograph by Sylvia Chant)

prostitution'. Given that it is often young women who move into domestic service as a first step in urban environments, their prospects for socio-economic mobility are seriously curtailed. This said, the low costs of domestic service are undoubtedly one reason why, along with other unskilled tertiary occupations such as waitressing, this was less hard-hit by the outbreak of recession in Latin America in the 1980s than sectors such as heavy industry and construction in which men predominated (de Barbieri and de Oliveira, 1989:23; Ward and Pyle, 1995; see Figure 8.1).[4]

Another 'female niche' which has sustained itself during and after the crisis years is multinational export-oriented manufacturing in the *maquiladora* or assembly sector. Mainly concentrated in the labour-intensive industries of garments and electronics, and a frontrunner in the 'New International Division of Labour',[5] export manufacturing has been deemed to have led to a 'very unrevolutionary division of labour' based on inequalities between nations, classes, 'races', and gender (Hossfeld, 1991:13). Often employing workforces which are more than 70 per cent female, multinational export processing operations have been in existence in places such as Puerto Rico, the Dominican Republic and the northern border area of Mexico since the 1950s and 1960s. From the 1980s onwards, however, there has been a surge in this type of production as Latin American countries have placed greater emphasis on export promotion under the aegis of neoliberal reforms (de Barbieri and de Oliveira, 1989:23; Safa, 1995b:33; Tiano, 1990; Ward and Pyle,

1995). Between the beginning and end of the 1980s for example, *maquila* production in Mexico increased by 350 per cent as against a mere 10 per cent increase in other industries, and out of every 100 jobs created during this time, 45 were in *maquilas* (see Chant, 1994). By 1995, the *maquiladora* sector was Mexico's leading source of export revenue, displacing oil and tourism (Hernández Espinosa, 2000:214). The importance of labour-intensive manufacturing work for women in Puerto Rico is such that since the inauguration of Operation Bootstrap four decades ago (see Chapter 4, Note 3), women's share of manufacturing employment on the island has been consistently greater than their overall share of jobs (Ríos,1995:133). Even though manufacturing lost its position as a leading source of employment and fell to third place in 1990 behind public administration and services, women's share of the manufacturing workforce was still 46.7 per cent, as against 38.6 per cent of employment overall (ibid.).

Multinational industrial relocation to countries in Latin America, as in other parts of the South, is driven primarily by the low cost of hiring Third World workers. In Mexico, for instance, industrial wages in leading sectors in 1995 were only 9 per cent of their US equivalents (Gledhill, 2000). Relocation has been facilitated by technological innovations that have permitted the fragmentation of manufacturing activities into smaller and simpler tasks, and also by the creation of free trade zones in destination countries (Ríos, 1995). Women have long been a favoured workforce in this sector for a variety of reasons, many of which were identified originally in Elson and Pearsons's classic 1981 paper on 'Nimble Fingers': women are not only cheaper to employ than men, but they are putatively more 'docile' and less likely to engage in industrial action; they have the manual dexterity to perform small labour-intensive tasks at speed; and, supposedly, they have greater capacity than men to withstand the repetitive monotony of assembly line work – all of which add-up to lower 'efficiency wages' (see also Standing,1989). An additional factor is that women have a 'natural disposability' insofar as they are thought likely to leave this work voluntarily on marriage and/or childbirth. This enables employers to make substantial savings on redundancy and react more effectively to fluctuations in production (Elson and Pearson, 1981). While the composition and turnover of female workers vary in different plants and places (see Pearson, 1986), the spirit of feminisation is pervasive. As Ríos (1995:127) has argued: 'gender typing of tasks is an ideological construct that, once crystallised in a particular labour market, plays a central role in the reproduction of the social relations of production'. In this light, it is not surprising that there have been very mixed outcomes of export manufacturing for women, both within and beyond Latin America (see Chant and McIlwaine, 1995; Pearson, 1998; Safa, 1995a).

Other than the expansion of *maquila* production in traditional 'core' areas during the 1980s, on-going restructuring and globalisation have had two further effects.

First, there has been more widespread dispersal of *maquila* operations. Nationally, for example, the North American Free Trade Agreement (NAFTA) of 1994 in Mexico saw *maquilas* spreading out of the northern border region into other parts of the country (Hernández Espinosa, 2000:213–4). There has also been regional dispersal, with an increase in export processing zones in Central America. In Costa Rica, 5 per cent of the national workforce is now employed in this sector, and in El Salvador, 15 per cent (Elson and Gideon, 1997:314). In Costa Rica, where much of the foreign capital in the new free trade zones has come from Taiwan and Korea as well as the USA, and is dedicated to the assembly of garments, electronics, jewellery and fashion accessories, women make up 80 per cent of the workforce (Sandóval García, 1997:37). A second general outcome of restructuring has been the increased use of subcontracting arrangements, which helps to keep down production costs, saves on employers' social security contributions, fragments the workforce, and takes particular advantage of the low 'aspiration wages' of married women (see Benería and Roldan, 1987; Miraftab, 1994:469; Peña Saint Martin, 1996; also Figure 8.2). In short, globalisation has played a central role in the massive increase of female labour force participation, with Moghadam (1999:304) noting that:

> In both developed and developing regions, the stable, organised and mostly male labour force has become increasingly 'flexible' and 'feminised'. Keeping the cost of labour low has encouraged the growth of demand for female labour, while declining household budgets have led to an increase in the supply of job-seeking women.

While women's share of the labour force was already growing before the recession in Latin America (Gilbert, 1998:74), this accelerated during the crisis years. In Mexico, for example, there was a doubling of female labour force participation between 1980 and 1996, with the major take-off dovetailing with Mexico's financial collapse of 1982 (Escobar Latapí, 2000b). In Brazil, the 'lost decade' of the 1980s also saw women's share of employment in the São Paulo Metropolitan Area climb from 33 to 39 per cent (Humphrey, 1997:171). In Argentina, women's labour force participation in the Metropolitan Area of Buenos Aires rose from 38 per cent in 1991 to 46 per cent in 1995, making this the highest rate in the whole of the twentieth century, yet, paradoxically perhaps, this occurred at a time when there was 20 per cent unemployment (male *and* female) (Cerrutti, 2000b:879).

While we have seen that the maintenance of low-level service work and increases in export-related labour demand have played a part in these trends, surges in female labour force participation have also been driven at the point of supply (Benería, 1991; Chant, 1996; González de la Rocha, 1988, 2000; Moser, 1987). In many cases, this is because of the decline of the purchasing power of male breadwinners' wages; in others, it is because men have lost their jobs altogether, particularly manual

Figure 8.2 Female footwear outworkers, León, Mexico (Photograph by Sylvia Chant)

workers (Geldstein, 1994:55). Nash (1995:155), for instance, attributes the rise in women's participation in the Uruguayan workforce from 38.7 to 44.2 per cent between 1981 and 1984 to rising levels of male unemployment. In a low-income *barrio* in Guayaquil, Ecuador, detailed survey work by Moser (1997:36–7) argues that the increased labour force participation of female spouses in male-headed households, from 31.5 to 45.5 per cent between 1978 and 1993, was mainly due to declining incomes among men, and the casualisation of male jobs. In Metropolitan Buenos Aires, Argentina, women's likelihood of entering the labour force during the 1990s was also positively associated with the increased instability of male employment (Cerrutti, 2000b:889). The extent to which female labour force deployment has helped to cushion the impacts of recession on households can be seen in the case of a low-income community in Guadalajara, Mexico studied by González de la Rocha (1988) in the 1980s. While the earnings of male heads dropped by 35 per cent over the period 1982 to 1985, household incomes fell by only 11 per cent thanks to the increase in multiple earning strategies, in which women played a major role (ibid.).

As part and parcel of the upward trend in female labour force participation, there have been important changes in the composition of female workers. For much of the post-war period, women's labour force participation conformed to an 'early peak' pattern whereby young (and usually single) women had the highest rates of labour force involvement. Levels then tailed off, drifting upwards again only around the age of 40 when some women went back to work because their children were older, or because they had become separated or widowed (Stichter, 1990:24–6). While this 'early peak' is still observable in many parts of Latin America, it is much less pronounced than previously, as touched upon in Chapter 7. In Argentina, for example, the first peak has become lower over time, is staying at more of a plateau during women's 30s and 40s, and does not fall off significantly until after the 50–59 year age cohort. This is attributed to younger women staying longer in education, to rising labour force participation among women in general, and among older women, growing life expectancy and the difficulties of exiting the labour force without pensions (Cerrutti, 2000b:883; see also Escobar Latapí, 2000b and Box 8.2 on Guadalajara, Mexico).

BOX 8.2

Principal Changes in the Urban Labour Market of Guadalajara, Western Mexico, 1987–96

- Ageing of working population
- 1980s: increase of labour force participation of women aged 30 years or more
- 1990s: increase in economically active population of women aged 50 years or more, and young women
- Men's labour force participation in Guadalajara does not decline as it does at national level
- Women improve their chances of becoming business owners and/or entering professional and public service employment (rising from 16 to 26 per cent of the total)
- Plateauing of informalisation process
- 1987–93: increase in incomes, with an increase in disparities according to class and gender
- 1996: fall in incomes with maintenance of disparities, although recuperation of employment
- Less inequality in labour market between men and women in 35 plus age group, but more gender inequality among the young
- More inequality among young men in labour market on grounds of class

Source: Escobar Latapí (2000b)

While economic necessity is often stressed as a crucial factor in the labour force participation of low-income women, Willis (2000:35) argues that this is increasingly the case for middle-class women in Mexico too, albeit at a different level. While career fulfilment is one reason for an ever more tenacious attachment to work, the imperatives of maintaining status and lifestyle with regard to living standards, housing, holidays, domestic servants and private education are equally compelling.

Table 8.5 Maternity Leave Benefits in Latin America, 1998

	Length of maternity leave	Percentage of wages paid in covered period	Provider of coverage
Argentina	90 days	100	Social Security
Bolivia	60 days	100% of national min wage + 70% of wages above min wage	Social Security
Brazil	120 days	100	Social Security
Chile	18 weeks	100	Social Security
Colombia	12 weeks	100	Social Security
Costa Rica	4 months	100	50% employer/50% SS
Cuba	18 weeks	100	Social Security
Dominican Republic	12 weeks	100	50% employer/50% SS
Ecuador	12 weeks	100	25% employer/75% SS
El Salvador	12 weeks	75	Social Security
Guatemala	12 weeks	100	33% employer/67% SS
Honduras	10 weeks	100 for 84 days	33% employer/67% SS
Mexico	12 weeks	100	Social Security
Nicaragua	12 weeks	60	Social Security
Panama	14 weeks	100	Social Security
Paraguay	12 weeks	50 for 9 weeks	Social Security
Peru	90 days	100	Social Security
Uruguay	12 weeks	100	Social Security
Venezuela	18 weeks	100	Social Security

Source: UN (2000:Table 5C).
Note: SS = Social Security.

Labour legislation and women's employment

Adding to the power of market forces in stimulating both the supply and demand of women workers are institutional and legal changes affecting employment. Over the last few decades, many Latin American countries have introduced legislation to combat discrimination against women in the workplace, to protect women from losing their jobs on pregnancy, and/or to facilitate female labour force participation through skills training, greater provision of childcare and so on (see Chapter 7). While these initiatives have helped to promote a better climate for gender equality, however, evidence would also suggest that greater enforcement is necessary. As a case in point, Mexico's National Development Plan of 1995–2000 called for guarantees of equality of opportunity for women in education, training and employment (Brown *et al.*, 1999:124). Women in Mexico are also entitled by law to up to 12 weeks' paid maternity leave and breastfeeding breaks when they return to their jobs (see Table 8.5). Yet these provisions are often far from being observed in practice. One study of *maquiladora* firms, for example, indicated that women are still tested for pregnancy. Even if they are not dismissed directly, being made to stand for long periods or to do overtime often forces them to hand in their notice. They may also be asked for proof of menstruation. This leads Hernández Espinosa (2000:218) to the conclusion that: 'Companies claim that pregnancy screening protects women from dangerous jobs, in line with Mexican labour law, but keeping women out of factory jobs is a policy designed to minimise costs, not pre-natal complications'. Flouting of the law is such that when Rosario Robles, Mexico City's first female mayor, was elected to office in October 1999, one of her first official acts was to amend the city's penal code such that employers violating legal pregnancy provisions would be subject to fines, at least 100 days' community service, and up to three years in prison (ibid.:219).

Men's employment

Against the general rise in female labour force participation in Latin America, what has been happening to men? We have seen in this and other chapters that men seem to be having greater difficulties in maintaining their formerly privileged position in employment, and in many cases that their rates of labour force participation are declining (Escobar Latapí, 1998, 2000b; Kaztman, 1992; Standing, 1999). Although education has undoubtedly contributed to this insofar as it has delayed entry into the labour force among young men (Escobar Latapí, 2000b), the slow speed of net job creation is a another factor (Arias, 2000:22). Moreover, evidence from a range of countries suggests that male labour instability is on the increase. In metropolitan Buenos Aires, for example, the chances of men being employed continuously over a single year decreased from 66.3 per cent during 1991–2 to 58.8 per cent in 1993–4 (Cerrutti, 2000b:887). At a national level, unemployment among the economically active male population in Argentina moved from 5.4 to 13.4 per cent between 1988 and 1997 (Arias, 2000:Table 1). Similar trends are found in Brazil, where between 1989 and 1995 male unemployment rose from 4.7 to 7.6 per cent, and in Costa Rica, where the increase was from 4.5 to 5.8 per cent (ibid.). Arias's comparative study of these latter three countries found that male marginalisation in employment tends to be skewed towards less educated youth, although the sharpest increase in unemployment rates between the 1980s and 1990s was actually among older men with higher educational qualifications (Arias, 2000:11). As of the late 1990s, however, young males aged 15–24 years represented more than half the unemployed male population in all three countries, with rates of unemployment being around twice as high as the national male average, at 23.6 per cent in Argentina, 14.6 per cent in Brazil, and 12.4 per cent in Costa Rica (ibid.).

Yet Arias (2000:23–4) also argues that since less than one-fifth of men aged 15 to 24 years are heads of household (compared with half of middle-aged male workers, and the vast majority of older men), this is less problematic than it might be. If tendencies in male youth unemployment persist, however, then it may well impact upon their capacity to be self-sufficient, let alone occupy a provisioning role in later life. At the other end of the age spectrum, older workers who become unemployed, especially given that they are more educated, may have savings, credit and assets that enable them to ride out longer spells of unemployment (ibid.:24). This may be especially pertinent to countries such as Peru, where between 1984 and 1993 there was a fall in the proportion of the unemployed male population between the ages of 14 and 24, but a rise in the share of unemployment borne by men 45 years or over (Thomas, 1999:263). By 1993, 28.2 per cent of total unemployment was concentrated in the 45 year plus age group, with many of these men being more, rather than less, educated (ibid.:264).

While, relatively speaking, men's share of employment has fallen, it is important to stress that this is not because women have taken men's jobs. Given that women have moved into expanding yet specific gender-typed segments of the labour force not previously occupied by men, 'male and female workers remain relatively uncompetitive' (Ríos, 1995:143.; see also Pearson, 1998). Whether or not this is *perceived* to be the case is another matter, however. In Puerto Rico in the 1960s and 1970s, for example, there was considerable alarm about the way in which Operation Bootstrap seemed to have led to a demise of male employment alongside women's increased labour force involvement. This provoked a range of public bodies into demanding that men's jobs should be given top priority, with the Law of Industrial Incentives of 1963 providing incentives to manufacturing firms to recruit male operatives (Ríos, 1995:139–40). Yet it should also be borne in mind that despite the fact that unemployed women are more likely to be classified as economically inactive 'housewives', in the vast majority of Latin American countries (not to mention globally) female unemployment rates remain higher than those of their male counterparts (Mehra and Gammage, 1999:546; Moghadam, 1995:111; Monteón, 1995:51; Radcliffe, 1999:201). Despite the fact that in many countries women's rates of increase in unemployment fell relative to men's during the 1980s and 1990s (Standing, 1999:597), in Central America 11 per cent of women were unemployed in 1997 compared with 8 per cent of men, and in South America the respective figures were 12 and 8 per cent, much of this accounted for by unemployment among young women (UN, 2000:118–20). Indeed, among 15–24 year olds in Mexico, the female unemployment rate is 6.4 per cent as against only 4.7 per cent among males (UNDP, 2000:Table 29).

Gender divisions in urban labour markets

In addition to suffering higher levels of unemployment, it is important to remember that women's rising labour force participation has taken place at a time of general deterioration in working conditions (see Moghadam, 1995:115–6), and that this has overlain, and in some cases exacerbated, a variety of existing gender inequalities in labour markets.

Although we have already discussed participation rates in broad terms, it is vital to note that women's involvement in economic activity tends to be much more punctuated than men's, owing partly to household and family circumstances, and partly to the more precarious and part-time nature of 'female' jobs. This conjuncture of influences is particularly pertinent to low-income women who cannot afford the luxury of paid domestic help, and who are also most likely to be in jobs which are insecure and/or 'dead-end' (Chant, 1991; Humphrey, 1997). In turn, there are reverberations on other aspects of women's employment, with Cerrutti (2000a: 20) observing that:

> working intermittently in any kind of job has potentially negative effects on women's careers since it prevents the accumulation of work experience, undermines promotions (internal labour markets) and decreases the likelihood of obtaining other benefits acquired from a stable job (especially social security and health insurance).

These factors interrelate in large measure with women's disproportionate representation in the informal sector (see Table 8.6), which has also been growing. In Mexico, for example, informal employment came to occupy 42 per cent of the female labour force in 1995, compared with 38 per cent in 1991 (Secretaría de Gobernación, 1996:27–8). Remembering that the informal sector is by no means a

Table 8.6 Percentage of Male and Female Labour Force in the Informal Sector in Selected Latin American Countries

	Percentage of labour force which is informal							
	Manufacturing		Transport		Services		Total	
	Men	Women	Men	Women	Men	Women	Men	Women
Brazil (1990)	14	5	24	2	23	24	19	21
Costa Rica (1984)	14	13	11	0	7	22	8	19
Honduras (1990)	15	52	29	0	26	29	21	34
Mexico (1992)	8	11	21	2	30	16	22	15
Uruguay (1985)	15	20	12	0	19	14	17	15
Venezuela (1992)	13	30	50	10	25	20	23	21

Source: United Nations (1995: Table 9).

'female sector', since men outnumber women in all occupations except domestic service (Scott, 1995), women usually occupy the lowest rungs of informal activity. While men predominate as owners of small family businesses, for example, their wives often perform critical tasks on an unpaid basis, as in footwear workshops in the Mexican City of León (see Chant, 1991). Aside from engaging in a rather limited range of informal sector activities such as food production, petty commerce and personal services (see Blumberg, 1995:195), women's business ventures in their own right are generally smaller in scale than men's. This is attributable to their lack of assets and start-up capital, constrained time schedules due to their responsibilities for domestic work and childcare, and a restricted range of space which limits their access to markets (see Scott, 1990:213). In the province of Guanacaste, Costa Rica, for example, women make up 41 per cent of informal workers in low-income urban settlements, and have such meagre resources that the most they can aspire to is to sell small quantities of snacks such as home-made sweets, flavoured ices and pastries from their front porches, outside local schools or on the streets. Even then, since most of their neighbours are forced to do the same, some women feel it is not worth the effort, thereby contributing to the so-called 'discouraged worker' effect (Chant, 1999c: 257). This said, in order to get around the problems of making ends meet in such competitive economic environments, many low-income women, in Costa Rica and elsewhere, resort to working long hours in a variety of activities simultaneously, such as combining part-time domestic service with *tortilla*-making, laundrywork, sewing, dress-making or hairdressing in their own homes (see Figure 8.3).

In many respects, gender divisions in informal employment are mirrored in the formal sector. Aside from the horizontal segregation of women into services and labour-intensive manufacturing, vertical segregation is also in evidence. Even within the largely feminised domain of export manufacturing, for example, women are

Figure 8.3 Multi-tasking in the home, Puerto Vallarta, Mexico. This woman takes in sewing and embroidery, and also sells soft drinks and sweets from her front porch (Photograph by Sylvia Chant)

more likely than men to be employed as semi- or unskilled operatives, as opposed to trained or prestige workers. They are also more commonly found in manual jobs than in positions requiring the use of precision machinery. In turn, in white collar posts, women are more likely to be represented among clerical staff than among professionals and administrators (see Ríos, 1995 on Puerto Rico). In the emergent, and predominantly labour-intensive, software production industry in Brazil, women are disproportionately represented in data entry. Akin to clerical work, this is the lowest occupational tier in the industry and is associated with minimal educational and skill requirements (Gaio, 1997). And within large industrial firms in Mexico, Escobar Latapí (2000b) also finds that men tend to get paid fixed wages, whereas women are more likely to be remunerated on a piece rate basis. The reasons behind these differences are hard to fathom unless one takes into account discriminatory gender practices. Detailed research on the evolving urban labour market of San

Cosme Mazatecocho in Mexico, for example, indicates that men obtain factory jobs with less education than women, and have better opportunities than women with comparable levels of education (Rothstein, 1995:184). In Nicaragua, women were 29 per cent of workers in unskilled urban jobs in 1994, but only 9 per cent of the skilled workforce (Elson and Gideon, 1997a:274). Despite widespread increases in women's access to employment, therefore, Humphrey (1997:171) argues with reference to Brazilian industry that: 'The continuing entry of women into the labour force has not in any way undermined the gender division of labour. Gender segregation and gender inequalities remain as great as ever'. Part of this pattern is attributed not only to the way that labour market divisions mirror gender divisions in wider society, but to the fact that 'gendered occupations and work structures are constructed within the factory and then institutionalised and legitimated through segmented labour markets' (ibid.).

WAGE AND BENEFIT GAPS

Divisions in both formal and informal employment help to explain the persistent and, in some cases, growing wage gap betwen men and women in Latin America. In Mexico, for instance, the disparity between average male and female earnings climbed from 20.8 to 22 per cent between 1987 and 1993 (Brown *et al.*, 1999:123). Although there were signs of the gender gap in earnings declining quite significantly in the manufacturing sector in the 1990s in countries such as Costa Rica and Paraguay (see UN, 2000:132, Chart 5.23), in the Latin American and Caribbean region as a whole, women's average wages in 1994 were only 67 per cent of men's (CRLP, 1997:12), and in some of the richest, as well as the poorest countries, including Chile and Bolivia respectively, the differential is even greater (see Table 8.7). These differences are often less a function of gender-differentiated endowments, than of the rewarding of those endowments (see Brown *et al.*, 1999:123). Another factor, however, is women's clustering in the informal sector, with the gender earnings gap in informal employment averaging 25 per cent as against 10 per cent in formal occupations (Funkhouser, 1996:1746). Evidence from Colombia, for example, shows that women's average earnings are 86 per cent of men's in the formal sector, but only 74 per cent in the informal sector (Tokman, 1989:1071). In Honduras, the respective levels are 83 and 63 per cent (López de Mazier, 1997:236). In the Dominican Republic, 62 per cent of female informal workers earn below the poverty line compared with only 35 per cent of their male counterparts (Lozano, 1997: Table 6.4).

Another important corollary of gender divisions in employment relates to social security and pensions, which we touched upon briefly in the context of gender and ageing in Chapter 4. Given that the vast majority of pension schemes are contributory, the nature of most women's working lives means they lose out relative to men (see Bertranou, 2001). In El Salvador, for example, as many as 74.1 per cent of the economically active female urban population are not covered by social benefits (Gutiérrez Castillo, 1997:151). In Argentina, a survey of low-income settlements indicated that while 53 per cent of men had made sufficient contributions to qualify for pensions, this applied to only 15 per cent of women (Lloyd-Sherlock, 1997: 180).[6] Aside from the fact that the discontinuous nature of most women's jobs discourages regular commitments, low wages also leave little surplus for contributions, (ibid.: 181). Women's disadvantage is exacerbated by the fact that they tend to use more of their earnings for daily household expenditure than men. Another important factor, in the context of domestic service, is that women rarely trust their employers to contribute their share of social security payments (ibid.: 182).

Table 8.7 Women's Average Wage as Percentage of Men's in Non-agricultural Employment in Selected Latin American Countries

Country	Women's mean wage as percentage of men's
Argentina	64.5
Bolivia	62.3
Brazil	76.0
Chile	60.5
Colombia	84.7
Costa Rica	83.0
Ecuador	63.7
Mexico	75.0
Paraguay	76.0
Uruguay	74.5

Source: United Nations (1995: Table 2.5).
Note: Data for latest available year.

Gender divisions in employment: the prospects for eradication or entrenchment

Having outlined some of the major aspects of gender divisions in labour markets in Latin America, it remains to ask how likely these are to persist in the twenty-first century. At one level, there is evidence to suggest that women and men could enjoy more balanced experiences of employment in years to come, especially when considering the upward trend in female labour supply resulting from education, the diversification of family structures, the growing social acceptance of women's work, and the pattern of daughters following their mothers' examples (Chant, 1991; Cerrutti, 2000a; see also Chapter 7). Moreover, women's new roles in the workplace have also given rise to collective action among women in defence of their labour rights, which, in turn, can enhance their living and working conditions, and thereby make employment more feasible and desirable (see Hernández Espinosa, 2000; Moghadam, 2000; Pearson, 1998).

Beyond this, although women still tend to be restricted to a narrower range of jobs than men, research on Cuba, Puerto Rico and the Dominican Republic reveals some diminution of occupational segregation as women's participation increases in the professions, clerical work and the public sector (Safa, 1995b:39). This is also noted for Mexico: whereas in 1987 women were only half as likely as men to enter professions such as the civil service, university teaching or technical work, by 1996 the probability had risen to 81 per cent (Escobar Latapí, 2000b). Moreover, as observed for the Mexican city of Oaxaca by Willis (2000:35), while older and even middle-aged middle-class women had often given up their careers when they married and started families, this is less the case with their daughters. In part, these tendencies can be explained by increasingly higher levels (and a broader range) of education among women, although, as we saw earlier, this does not automatically guarantee women (or indeed men) access to the labour market. In addition, that women might be increasing their representation in the middle and at the upper end of the occupational spectrum does not mean there is remunerative parity. Indeed, this is one stratum of the Mexican labour market in which the gender wage gap is actually widening (Escobar Latapí, 2000b).

In other sectors of Latin American labour markets, there would also appear to be mixed trends. In traditionally 'male industries' such as automobile production, for example, there are tentative signs of 'de-masculinisation' as women are taken on in labour-intensive assembly operations (Cooper Tory, 1990:76). Yet the fact that men continue to predominate in more skilled and more prestigious segments of the industry means little change in respect of gender divisions. In a similar vein, the tendency to some 'de-feminisation' of export manufacturing, especially in companies producing higher-tech goods that require more skills or greater levels of mechanisation, cannot be regarded as equalising male and female labour since men are still channelled into the more skilled jobs (Acero, 1997; Mehra and Gammage, 1997, 1999; Pearson, 1998:177; Roberts, 1991:31). This also applies to traditional 'female' sectors. In Puerto Rico, for example, technological innovations in tobacco and textile production have produced a situation where women are no longer the majority of workers (Ríos, 1995:136). As observed more generally by Pearson (2000c:13), aside from the fact that globalisation makes new employment opportunities vulnerable to externally induced economic crisis, 'ongoing technological change may actually override the reasons why women have become the preferred labour force in many industries'.

This said, there would still appear to be scope for some segments of the labour market to offer more promising possibilities for gender equality. Although the fast-paced nature of technological developments set against women's more limited access to skills and training, may hinder 'their full participation in the new knowledge-based economy' (Pearson, 2000c:13),[7] recent changes in Brazilian software manufacturing have led to people with different specialisms working in teams around specific products, rather than alongside people of the same occupational rank. In this context, lower-level workers (predominantly female data entry personnel) stand more chance of learning new skills and moving upwards in the occupational hierarchy. Another factor which may help to dissolve gender divisions in the IT industry is the demise of centralised mainframe computers which in the past have been primarily associated with men (Gaio, 1997:225–6). Potential developments in teleworking may also transfer more work into people's homes, which, notwithstanding the pitfalls attached to homeworking such as lack of job security and social insurance, could increase employment opportunities for women (Mitter, 1997:34),

Yet another interesting development in recent years has been the increased use of the home as a site of informal sector work among men as well as women (see Miraftab, 1994 on Mexico; also Bastos, 1999 on Guatemala; Pineda, 2000 on Colombia). Among the actual and potential outcomes of this trend, is the fact that men are forced to be more transparent about their earnings to family members than has often been the case in the past (Miraftab, 1994:485).

There has also been an upward trend in unpaid work among men. Between 1987 and 1996, for example, the level of unpaid workers among the female economically active population in Mexico stayed relatively constant (at around 11 per cent), but among men, there was an increase from 2.9 to 5.6 per cent (Escobar Latapí, 2000b). This to some degree reflects the general informalisation of work, which has impacted on men as well as women. In Argentina, for example, the percentage of men in the informal sector increased from 12 to 15 between 1987 and 1997 (Arias, 2000:26, Table 1). More generally, Elson (1999:611) argues that reductions in gender differentials in earnings may be the result of 'harmonising down rather than up'.

On balance, however, it has to be remembered that women's representation in the informal sector is higher than men's, and that the precarious conditions under which most women have entered the labour market in recent years are not conducive to high wages, to the receipt of labour benefits such as pension rights and health insurance, or to the acquisition of skills (Cerrutti, 2000b:889). Moreover, as long as the gender wage gap remains (and/or widens), significant diminution of women's economic dependence on men seems unlikely (Chant, 1996b:309). What is perhaps even more worrying is that in countries such as Mexico women seemed to make fewer gains than men during the recent period of economic stability (1987– 1994) (Escobar Latapí, 2000b). It therefore seems that the prospects of substantial reduction in gender disparities in Latin American labour markets continue to be rather remote. In turn, as Ríos (1995:125) has argued: 'The persistence of a gendered labour market … constitutes a major obstacle to the abolition of social and economic inequalities.'

Conclusion

In considering the gender aspects of recent shifts in Latin American labour markets two broad interpretations can be drawn. On one hand, there are signs that women's increased access to earnings has had some personally 'empowering' implications at the micro-scale, whether in respect of allowing women to negotiate more decisively their relationships with men, or affording them greater scope to head their own households (see also Chapter 7). The weight of these changes is such that they have also raised the profile of households within the theorisation of labour markets. As Radcliffe (1999:199) notes in relation to recent research on gendered worker identities in Latin America:

> there has been increased focus on the household – and the kin and nonfamily relations contained in it – as a site in which labour relations are made and remade in the context of micro-struggles over resources, skills, needs and identities.

A second line of interpretation, viewed from the angle of women and men within the wider economy, is of a more negative nature. Successive debt crises, structural adjustment, long-term economic liberalisation and increased global competition have been strongly associated with lower incomes and more precarious employment for most people (García and de Oliveira, 2000; Pearson, 2000b, c; Rey de Marulanda, 1996; Tuman, 2000). Signs of greater convergence in women's and men's employment (and particularly in the conditions of their employment), appear to be more to do with the greater informalisation and casualisation of men's work, than with improvements in women's employment (Standing, 1999:600). The erosion of regulatory mechanisms and protective legislation not only affects men and women in the short term, but also raises serious questions about what happens when they eventually exit the workforce and find themselves unprotected by pensions (see Escobar Latapí, 2000b on Mexico). Research on men has also provoked concern, especially in relation to the difficulties they appear to be encountering in fulfilling the normative role of 'household breadwinner'.

While there is no easy answer as to how gender regimes might be renegotiated to allow for more fluidity in men's and women's productive and reproductive responsibilities within households, given the 'potential link to violence and criminality in the region', there is arguably a pressing need for policy interventions that help men to rethink masculinity in relation to both work and family (Arias, 2000:24–5). Something also needs to be done about protecting households from further economic deterioration and self-exploitation. In Mexico, for example, González de la Rocha (1997:2) cautions that persistent poverty over the last few decades has greatly weakened the survival mechanisms of urban households, with women in particular bearing such heavy burdens of labour that these are now close to unsustainable and seriously affecting their physical and psychological well-being.

Other crucial policy issues for the twenty-first century include more support for the informal sector which looks like being a permanent feature of Latin American economies, not to mention those elsewhere in the South (see Pearson, 2000c:16). Discussions about measures that could help the sector operate more efficiently and become a source of 'decent work' (see ILO, 2001) have stressed the desirability of reducing regulatory requirements and/or lowering the costs of formality by allowing informal sector firms to comply with regulatory obligations on a piecemeal basis. Supply-side policies such as education and training to promote diversification of informal sector activity have also been emphasised, alongside the provision of subsidies, investment and enhanced access to credit (see Chickering and Salahdine, 1991:6; Grabowski and Shields, 1996:172; Rodgers, 1989; Tokman, 1989:155). Support for women micro-entrepreneurs is likely to be particularly important given women's existing concentration in informal activity. As noted by Leach (1999:60): 'Training and back-up need to be directed systematically at the informal sector if women are to survive economically.' In addition where women-oriented credit schemes have operated, the results have generally been positive. Despite the common assumption that women's enterprises are subsistence- rather than profit-oriented, Blumberg's (1995) comparative review of micro-credit projects in the Dominican Republic, Ecuador and Guatemala suggests that they do as well as men, if not better, in respect of creating higher returns more quickly, and in generating more jobs.[8] As Blumberg (1995:220) concludes:

> the evidence indicates that when given a chance in an area in which they are already economically active, women microentrepreneurs spurred by their strong unmet needs for income (especially if they have provisioning responsibilities for their children) tend to do their utmost to succeed. They benefit (although this may increase their workday and self-exploitation), their children benefit, the credit project benefits, and the planet's equity account becomes a little less tilted toward power, privilege and patriarchy.

Skills training for informal activities might also be complemented by increased vocational education in expanding spheres such as information technology, with the need for increased technical and professional training recognised by various governments in the region (see for example MINDESP, 2001 on Bolivia). This could enhance indigenous economic activity insofar as the more skilled and educated the labour force, the greater its likely productivity, which in turn might provide an important market for goods and services and reduce the need for external orientation (Szirmai, 1997:90–1). At the very least, and in view of the likely powerlessness of Latin American countries to resist the forces of globalisation, greater investment in IT skills could bring more foreign investment into the region. As Mitter (1997:26–7) points out, the youthfulness of developing country populations, set against demands for new technological skills, is likely to motivate Northern companies to spread more information-intensive aspects of production to the South in the next few decades. Concerted attempts on the part of governments and employers to ensure that women benefit to the same degree as men from these and other possible developments are vital if gender imbalances in employment are to be redressed to any significant degree.

9 Gender and Migration

SYLVIA CHANT

Introduction

Latin America's highly mobile population is engaged in a vast and complex range of migration flows, most of which are characterised by gender selectivity. One of the main aims of this chapter is to detail the reasons for, and consequences of, the differential involvement of men and women in three of the most prominent migration patterns in the continent: rural–urban, temporary and international movements. The discussion also considers gender dimensions of linkages between migrant source and destination areas, and the extent to which different aspects of migration interrelate with and impact upon gender roles, relations and identities. Analysis of these issues is preceded by a brief review of theoretical approaches to migration.

Theorising migration

Partly reflecting the wide range of migratory movements in developing regions, there are numerous theoretical approaches to migration. In terms of overarching conceptual perspectives, the mainstream models have concentrated on what is widely taken to be the dominant type of migration, namely permanent labour migration from rural to urban areas. Three of the most significant models for analysing these movements include: 1) neo-classical/equilibrium approaches, which regard migration as a rational individual response to wage-rate differentials, 2) structuralist/Marxist approaches which focus on the moves impelled by the spatial redistribution of economic activity, and 3) structuration approaches, which attempt to unravel the interactions between macro-level structural constraints, on the one hand, and micro-social perspectives and individual agency on the other (see Chant and Radcliffe, 1992). Although there is value in both of the first two models in respect of explaining rural–urban mobility in Latin America, the importance of incorporating a blend of structural and behavioural factors in the analysis of migration has been increasingly borne out by empirical studies. With emerging interest in gender from the 1980s onwards, a new offshoot of structuration evolved in the guise of the 'household strategies' approach (ibid.).

The case for a 'household strategies' approach

Based on the notion of the domestic unit as 'an analytical instance where the macro-structural conditions facilitating migratory flows and family and individual determinants converge' (de Oliveira, 1991:111), the household strategies approach views the organisation of household livelihood and reproduction as crucial in shaping mobility. Given the tendency for households to be characterised by differences and divisions between members in respect of tasks, obligations, power, identity and so on, households are also critical to understanding who migrates, why, where, with whom, and for how long (see Radcliffe, 1991; also Hondagneu-Sotelo, 1992:395-6). A focus on the household, where ideologies of gender are often established (Gregorio Gil, 1998), is particularly enriching for the conceptualisation of women's migration for two reasons. The first is that women's behaviour is usually less autonomous than men's and more contingent on their roles within domestic environments at different stages of the life course. Second, viewing individuals in the context of their households highlights the ways in which gender is cross-cut by other dimensions of migrant selectivity such as age, marital status, fertility and education.

This said, operationalising the 'household' part of this theoretical framework is by no means an easy task, especially when some members of the domestic unit may make individual decisions that take little account of the wishes of others within it (see Escobar *et al*, 1987:57; Hondagneu-Sotelo, 1992:396). Moreover, since households are both diverse and dynamic (see Chapter 7), consideration must be made of how a heterogeneous household universe influences the mobility of individual members. Beyond this, households have a range of dimensions and functions each of which needs to be taken into account. At the very least these include what Boyd (1989:642) terms a 'sustenance' function which, in practical terms, conditions who might be released to migration (or not), a 'socialising' function, which has an important ideological effect on who migrates and why (ibid.:643), and a 'network' function which arises once migration is under way and relates to the manner in which dispersed members of family groups affect the moves of others (ibid.). Indeed, in respect of the latter, Hondagneu-Sotelo (1992: 395–6) cautions that 'an exclusive focus on the household risks ignoring the significance of broader kin and non-kin networks'.

The 'strategies' part of this theoretical approach is no less problematic. While household strategies may on the surface imply forethought and collectivity, as Escobar *et al.* (1987:57) have pointed out,

> Identifying strategies, especially household strategies, is difficult since migration decisions are often short-term reactions to circumstances rather than well-laid plans (see also Boyd, 1989:657; Rothstein, 1995:170).

Notwithstanding these problems, in adopting a more holistic view of mobility than other models, the household strategies approach has proved of greater use in capturing the multifaceted nature of migration, and in demonstrating that even if employment and economic imperatives are major factors, they are intimately interwoven with social, family and cultural considerations.

Migration patterns in Latin America: background and overview

As in other regions of the South, Latin America is characterised by a plethora of migrant flows. The fact that the region has undergone a notable rural–urban transition in the post-war period suggests that permanent movement of populations from rural areas to towns and cities has prevailed. Yet although this is broadly true, it is important to acknowledge that most Latin American censuses fail to capture short-term movements over small distances. In Mexico, for instance, the census only documents inter-state or international migration (López *et al.*, 1993:134). In Costa Rica, moves are registered at the level of the 'canton' (an intermediate administrative entity between provinces and districts), but people are only classified as migrants when living in a canton different to their place of birth or to that where they resided five years prior to the census enumeration (Chant, 1992:50). This does not, accordingly, pick up on temporary migrations in the intervening period, whether internally or overseas. As an international example, among migrants to the United States from the village of Acuitzio in the state of Michoacán, Mexico, only 25 per cent stay for more than a year at a time, with the bulk going for seven to twelve months (Wiest, 1983:169). As Escobar *et al.* (1987:43) note in relation to the neighbouring state of Jalisco, further complications arise from the fact that decisions on the duration of migration are not a 'one-off' process:

> The difference between 'permanent' and 'temporary' migration is ... difficult to establish in terms of individual intentions and life careers. A Mexican migrant may live in Los Angeles for twenty years and return to Mexico at the end of his or her working life. Conversely, the migrant who crosses the border temporarily to gain some needed cash may find a good job, marry and stay permanently.

Although longitudinal community-level case studies reveal more of the complexity of migratory patterns, the problem then becomes one of extrapolation (Durand and Massey, 1992; Radcliffe, 1991).

These caveats aside, as far as the factors influencing migration in general are concerned, a major part of Latin America's urban transition in the last fifty years reflects the progressive shift of employment and investment to urban areas. As noted in Chapter 8, this has occurred at the expense of opportunities for livelihood in the countryside. At first rural dwellers may hedge their bets by sending just one or two household members to towns on a temporary basis. This minimises risk insofar as it diminishes the vulnerability attached to dependence on work in one locality (Arzipe, 1982b; Roberts, 1985). It can also enhance income insofar as wages from higher-earning areas have greater purchasing power in low-wage areas (see Chant, 1992 on migration between Guanacaste province and San José in Costa Rica). None the less, in many cases temporary migration eventually converts to permanent settlement.

Even if urban economic growth fails to assure employment for migrants, urban areas have usually been able to offer higher wages. In the Mexican state of Querétaro in the early 1980s, minimum wage levels were 20 per cent higher in the state capital than in the surrounding countryside, and represented an important motive for people's move to the city (Chant, 1991:33). Beyond this, greater public investment in towns and cities means that urban areas are usually better equipped with education and health facilities, which constitute important incentives for people with young families (Chant, 1992; Moßrucker,1997). Another factor influencing migration, especially once movements are under way, is the role of kin-based networks. The presence of relatives is often a deciding factor in people's migration, since jobs and accommodation are best assured where migrants are able to tap into social networks. As Boyd (1989:647) observes, labour migration has strong potential for turning into family migration over time. This applies as much to international as national migration, although in the case of the former political factors and refugeeism figure alongside economic imperatives, again underlining the importance of holistic conceptual frameworks that recognise the variable and multidimensional nature of migration across space and through time (see below). There are also important gender dimensions to the factors underpinning different types of migratory movement in Latin America, as discussed below.

Rural–urban migration in Latin America

Trends and patterns in the post-war period

Between 1950 and 1980, 27 million people in Latin America left their farms and villages for the cities of the continent (Green, 1996:19). During this period the annual rate of urban population growth was 4.8 per cent, bringing the overall urban population from a level of 40.9 per cent to 63.3 per cent (Gilbert, 1990:44; Safa,1995b:32). Although rates of urban growth in the 1980s and 1990s continued to exceed those of national populations (compare Table 9.1 with Table 4.1), and the urban population of Latin America is now around 75 per cent, rural–urban migration has contributed less to urban expansion over time, particularly in metropolises such as Mexico City, São Paulo and Rio de Janeiro. In these contexts, urban growth since the 1970s has been more a product of natural increase of the population *in situ* (Roberts, B., 1995:90 & 93). This itself is a product of migratory legacies, since young people have long formed the bulk of rural–urban migrants (see below).

Table 9.1 Latin America: Trends in Urbanisation

	Urban population as % of total population		Average annual growth rate of urban population (%)		Population in urban agglomerations of 1 million or more in 1990 as % of urban population		Growth rate of largest city(%)
	1980	1999	1980–90	1990–94	1980	1994	1990–95
Argentina	83	90	1.9	1.6	31	35	0.7
Bolivia	46	62	4.2	3.2	14	17	3.6
Brazil	66	81	3.3	2.7	27	32	1.5
Chile	81	85	2.1	1.8	33	35	2.0
Colombia	64	73	2.8	2.7	22	28	2.9
Costa Rica	43	48	3.8	3.3	0	0	2.9
Cuba	—	—	—	—	—	—	1.1
Dominican Republic	50	64	4.1	3.1	25	33	3.2
Ecuador	47	64	4.2	3.4	14	26	2.8
El Salvador	42	46	1.9	2.7	0	0	—
Guatemala	37	39	3.4	4.0	0	0	2.3
Honduras	36	52	5.4	4.9	0	0	—
Mexico	66	74	2.9	2.8	27	28	0.7
Nicaragua	53	56	3.9	4.2	23	28	4.3
Panama	50	56	2.8	2.7	0	0	2.8
Paraguay	42	55	4.8	4.4	0	0	—
Peru	65	72	3.0	2.6	26	31	2.8
Uruguay	85	91	1.0	0.9	42	42	0.6
Venezuela	83	87	3.5	2.9	16	27	1.3

Sources: UNDP (1997: Table 21), World Bank (1996: Table 9), World Bank (2000b: Table 2).
Note: — = no data.

Set against this trend, it is also possible to discern a general decline in rural–urban migration, especially from the 1980s onwards. Three prominent reasons include, first, that the proportion of people living in rural areas is much reduced compared with the early post-war period; second, that growing amounts of movement are comprised by flows between urban areas; and third, that disparities between countryside and town have lessened over time. In the view of Bryan Roberts (1995:112), 'the legacy of past movements and the commercialisation of most rural areas mean that the distinction between rural and urban is often not a great one. Economic enterprise spans rural and urban locations. The pattern of consumption of the village may be different in scale to those of the town, but they are not different in kind'. This argument is echoed by Gilbert (1998:50) who further observes that as a result of improvements in transport and communications, 'the city has absorbed the country', with people in places up to 50 miles or more from towns now able to make their living by selling their produce to wholesalers who supply urban markets (see also Kay, 1999:302). Another factor reducing the pace of rural–urban migration in Latin America has been neoliberal economic restructuring (Becker and Morrison, 1997:98). Structural adjustment programmes have been observed to lead to a relative increase in poverty in urban versus rural areas because cutbacks in employment and food subsidies have hit cities hardest (see Chant, 1999c; Stewart, 1995:23–4). Indeed, the proportion of the poor living in cities was as high as 55–60 per cent in 1990, compared with 46 per cent in 1980 and only 37 per cent in 1970 (Koonings *et al.*, 1995:117). While this is partly a function of the fact that the majority of people now reside in cities and the relative incidence of poverty is still lower here than in the countryside, levels of urban poverty have risen more acutely in the last two decades (Boltvinik and Hernández Laos, 2000; González de la Rocha, 1997; Korzeniewicz and Smith, 2000).

Rural–urban migration remains important, however, in two main ways. First, in parts of the region such as Colombia, civil strife is often associated with rural exodus – in 1998 alone, 1.2 million Colombians fled their rural homes (Moser and McIlwaine, 2000:64). Second, along with intra-urban migration, rural–urban migration continues to feed the the rising growth of smaller and medium-sized cities (Portés, 1989; Roberts, B., 1995:90). The expansion of secondary urban settlement has long been part of government policies for economic decentralisation in the region, as in Peru, where successive administrations between 1958 and 1990 granted tax incentives to companies locating outside Lima (Becker and Morrison, 1997:96). Nonetheless, market-driven macro-economic policies and change have usually been more significant than government initiatives to (re)direct migration. Figuring prominently here is 'spontaneous' industrial relocation stemming from dis-economies of scale in metropolitan areas and/or the development and expansion of new economic activities associated with restructuring, such as international tourism and export manufacturing. In some cases, movement to smaller towns has also been prompted by crisis-induced job losses in principal cities. This has led Gilbert (1995a:

322) to argue that: 'The recession achieved in ten years what attempts at regional development had failed to do in thirty.' Besides economic reasons for the deflection of movement from primate cities, there is also evidence to suggest that middle-class metropolitan groups are transferring to secondary centres as a result of concerns about the environment and quality of life (Izazola, 2001; Izazola *et al.*, 1998).

Having noted that the contribution of migration to growth in large cities has gradually been overtaken by natural increase, the latter is in many ways a product of the former, in that younger and better-educated individuals have traditionally been prominent in rural–urban movements and thus led to a youthful age structure in cities (Gilbert, 1990:46). Moreover, although the depletion of migrant pools in the countryside and the progressive establishment of kin networks in cities have acted to depress this and other aspects of migrant selectivity over time, there are still quite pronounced differences in proportions of women and men in rural–urban movement.

Gender selectivity in rural–urban migration

Women have formed the bulk of rural–urban population flows in post-war Latin America (Butterworth and Chance, 1991; Clarke and Howard, 1999). In Mexico, for example, where intra-national rural out-migration was at its height between 1950 and 1970, there were 100 female to every 88 male inter-state migrants (Rivas *et al.*, 1999:272). Women have also tended to move primarily to large urban centres and metropolitan areas (see Bradshaw, 1995b on Honduras; Chant, 1992 on Costa Rica; de Oliveira, 1991 on Mexico; Radcliffe, 1992 on Peru). This has led to higher numbers of women among the population in major towns and cities (Gilbert, 1998:47). Despite declining levels of 'feminisation' over time, national averages in the late 1980s and 1990s continue to reflect the legacy of female bias in rural–urban migration flows (see Table 7.2, and compare with Chant and Radcliffe, 1992:6, Table 1.2).

Factors affecting female-selective migration to towns and cities

While many women move in 'family migration' streams as members of their parents' or spouses' households, it is nevertheless a primary explaination of individual female movement that labour opportunities for women are considerably greater in towns than in the countryside. Despite new opportunities for women in agro-export production (see Chapter 8), women have generally been more assured of employment by moving to urban areas. Towns specialising in tourism, where there is often a high demand for female service workers (see Chant, 1991; López *et al*, 1993), or multinational export-processing manufacturing – as in the *maquiladora* belt on the northern border of Mexico, in Puerto Rico and the Dominican Republic, and

BOX 9.1

Women's Migration Histories in Mexico and Costa Rica

Employment, public services and family networks are often cited as key factors influencing rural–urban migration in Latin America, but the finer details of these and their interactions are often neglected in macro-level analyses. Even brief accounts of individual women's migration, however, enhance our understanding of the complex underpinnings of gendered mobility.

Case 1: Migration as a means of avoiding family contact

Lupe is a 39-year-old single mother living in the international tourist resort of Puerto Vallarta, Jalisco, Mexico. Her decision to migrate to the town in her teens was spurred by conjugal breakdown. A native of Guadalajara, the capital of Jalisco state, around 140 miles to the west of Puerto Vallarta, Lupe had married at the age of 15 in order to escape the pressures of an unhappy home life dominated by a hostile and authoritarian stepfather. She termed this bid for freedom '*Salida número uno*' ('Exit no. 1'). Regrettably, married life proved equally disagreeable and claustrophobic, so, shortly after the birth of her first child, Lupe decided to leave her husband, thereby embarking on '*Salida número dos*' ('Exit no. 2'). Since Lupe's decision was strongly disapproved of by her mother and stepfather, she decided it would be best to leave Guadalajara in order to escape family pressure to return to the marital home. The reasons that Lupe chose the tourist town of Puerto Vallarta were material and psychosocial in nature. On a practical front, she recognised that, as a woman, she was more likely to find a job in a town which was dominated by services rather than industry. In personal terms, she felt she would fare better as a lone mother in Puerto Vallarta which, like other coastal resorts in Mexico, had a reputation for being less conservative than inland cities. Another factor influencing Lupe's decision was that since she knew no-one in Puerto Vallarta, her anonymity would provide greater protection from scrutiny and gossip than in a city where people knew her background, and might have a vested interest in encouraging her to patch things up with her husband.

Case 2: Migration as a means of conjugal separation

Martilina's migration to Liberia, the capital of Guanacaste province in northwest Costa Rica was stimulated by a similar catalyst – conjugal breakdown – although in this case the primary reason for moving to a town where no-one knew her was to avoid violent recriminations from her husband, Hernán. As a mother of five children living in the town of Nicoya, about 65 miles south of Liberia, Martilina had suffered for several years from Hernán's economic unreliability and his unpredictable and violent bouts of temper. She had thought about leaving home on several occasions, but could not bring herself to do so, partly for fear of reprisals and partly because, with few skills and only two years of primary education, she feared she would be unable to find a job to support her children. Beyond this, she had invested considerable effort in building their home in Nicoya and knew she stood to lose everything if she was to leave. None the less, when her eldest children reached an age when they could provide some economic assistance, Martilina grew more confident about making the break. After a few weeks of secret planning, Martilina and her children left home in the middle of the night carrying as many belongings as they could between them. They left no indication of where they had gone for fear that Hernán would track them down, and have had no contact with him since. The decision to move to Liberia was mainly because the family's lack of contacts in the town was a fair guarantee that information on their whereabouts would not trickle back to Hernán. By the same token, as the capital of the province, it offered more likelihood of finding employment, and schools for the younger children.

Source: Interviews by Sylvia Chant in Mexico and Costa Rica, 1980s and 1990s.

increasingly in Central America – have been particularly attractive to female migrants (see Fernández-Kelly, 1983; Klak, 1999; Safa, 1995a, 1999). In cities more generally, however, the bulk of low-income unskilled female migrants have traditionally been accommodated in domestic service and/or the informal sector (Clarke and Howard, 1999:305; see also Chapter 8).

Aside from employment for women in towns and cities, other factors which influence their migration include greater facilities in urban areas for education and healthcare. While these are important considerations for men as well, they are perhaps especially so for women given their greater involvement in the daily care of children. Other conjugal and family considerations are an important part of the picture. Female household heads who have been widowed or fallen victim to conjugal breakdown are particularly likely to move to urban areas given the social and economic difficulties of living as lone women or lone mothers in rural areas (Chapter 7). Socially, the prospects of anonymity afforded by urban environments in which they perhaps have no prior contacts may make their new status more viable. This is especially relevant for women who wish to escape from family or community disapproval in their areas of origin, not to mention partners or husbands (see Box 9.1).

Nothwithstanding that some women's decisions to migrate are taken 'autonomously', particularly as heads of household, many others may not be in a position to decide on their own migration, but instead are directed by parents and/or spouses. This again underlines the importance of households in women's mobility, and the need to consider the different roles women occupy in source areas.

THE SELECTIVITY OF FEMALE RURAL–URBAN MOVEMENT

It is important to recognise that, just as the constellation of factors governing women's movements may differ in various ways from men's, so women themselves are not a homogeneous group. Marital status, age and position in the household of origin are significant factors here. As noted by de Oliveira (1991:113) for Mexico:

> women's duties and obligations are different from men's; those of mothers distinct from those of daughters. Young daughters are more frequently faced with the opportunity or option to migrate, while their mothers take care of productive activities for family consumption, do the necessary housework, take care of small children, and perform the agricultural tasks assigned to them within the peasant group. The place of destination and the duration of the move will depend on the opportunities of incorporation of the female labourer either in rural or urban labour markets (see also Rivas *et al.*, 1999:272; Weist, 1983).

A similar pattern is observed for the village of Kallarayan in the southern Peruvian Andes by Radcliffe (1992). Here, it is young women, most of whom are single and in their teens or early twenties, who tend to move because they have no place in agriculture and/or are 'surplus' to household labour requirements in areas of origin.

This is echoed by research in small towns in northwest Costa Rica where traditionally women have had limited access to employment. Teenage daughters who are unencumbered by dependents commonly leave to work in domestic service in the capital, San José. Their movement, however, is anything but autonomous. Generally speaking this involves negotiation with, if not decisions by parents who, in turn, attempt to place their daughters in posts through personal and family contacts. Often the young women are expected to take jobs with bed and board provided, to spend their holidays, and sometimes weekends, back in Guanacaste, and to send home remittances for as long as they remain single, if not thereafter (Chant, 1992). Young women tend to comply with these demands, and are usually more reliable than their brothers in this regard. This is another persuasive reason for parents to encourage the migration of daughters, as is also observed in other regions of the South (see Chant, 1998).

An additional factor explaining the prevalence of younger women in rural–urban migration is that young people are generally more educated than their parents and migration tends to be positively associated with education. In Mexico, for example, a larger proportion of male migrants in 1990 (47 per cent) had upwards of six years of schooling than their non-migrant counterparts (33 per cent) (López *et al.*, 1993:143).[1] Although a slightly narrower differential applies to women, 42 per cent of female migrants in 1990 had six or more years of schooling, compared with 31 per cent of non-movers (ibid.). One possible reason for this lower differential is that female household heads (who tend as a group to be older and therefore to have had less education) are an important sub-group of women migrants from rural areas.

Gender implications of female-selective rural–urban migration

As noted in Chapter 7, the creation of a 'surplus' female population in towns and cities through gender-selective migration has contributed to a greater presence of households headed by women in urban areas. Whereas levels of female household headship in most parts of Latin America are under 10 per cent in the countryside, they are often 25 per cent in towns (Browner, 1989:467). By the same token, female-headed households are no more homogeneous than the female population in general, so whereas middle-aged and younger female heads with dependants may be more likely to establish themselves or emerge in towns, this may not apply to more elderly women, especially in source areas. This does not rule out an increase in female-headed households in rural areas, however, since some evolve through the migration of younger women. Rudolf's (1999) longitudinal study of the highland village of Loma Bonita in Coclé province, Panama provides a pertinent example here. In the wake of an upsurge of rural–urban movement in the 1960s and 1970s, two to three times as many women left Loma Bonita as men (Rudolf, 1999:107). Although the majority of female migrants were young, single and childless, lack of opportunities in the village meant that, increasingly, lone mothers also had to uproot and leave their children behind, thereby leading to the evolution of grandparent and/or grandmother-headed households. As reported by Rudolf (1999:119):

> In the past young women commonly raised a child in their parents' household without the father's presence, at least until they formed a stable union – but they had always stayed in the household to care for the child and help with the work. Now their families could no longer afford to support a daughter with her children in the highlands, nor could daughters afford to set up independent households with their children in the city. The only option, therefore, was for women to leave babies as young as a few months old with their parents in Loma Bonita so they could return to work in the city to help support them.

In turn, increases in female headship in rural areas are sometimes precipitated by the temporary out-migration of men, with short-term *de facto* female headship converting to permanent, *de jure* status where long spells of separation result in lapsed remittances, emotional stress, and/or conjugal infidelity (Chant, 1998; see also below).

Temporary migration

There are many forms of temporary migration which occur for differing lengths of time, and which may be national or international (Chant and Radcliffe, 1992:10–13). Notwithstanding the difficulties of establishing links between decisions on migration with actual behaviour, especially given that some 'temporary' migration involves a virtual lifetime away from home, 'temporary' movements are nominally distinguished from 'permanent' movements by migrants' intentions to return, eventually, to their source areas. Within Latin America, two types of temporary movement seem to prevail. One is that of 'cross-border' mobility. While this is dealt with in more detail in the following section on international migration, it is important to emphasise here that such movements are extremely important in certain areas. For example, cross-border labour migration between Mexico and the USA has declined in the last decade, but in 1995 alone involved an estimated total of 543 million crossings (see Avila and Tuirán, 2000:3). Daily or weekly crossings evade the problems attached to permanent emigration, although Durand *et al.* (2001:122) note that the granting of visas for permanent residence can actually increase circulation since it reduces the danger and costs of an illegal border crossing. The other main type of temporary migration in Latin America is seasonal migration, which has a long history in many parts of the region, including the Peruvian Andes, Colombia, Ecuador, Venezuela, Honduras, Belize, El Salvador and Costa Rica (see Bailey and Hane, 1995; Hattaya, 1992; Skeldon, 1990:49 *et seq.*; Wade, 1994). Although cross-border movements, and rural–urban movements may feature under the rubric of seasonal migration, the bulk of the latter comprises intra-national movements between rural areas (see Chant, 1991, 1992; Kratochwil, 1995). Seasonal migration proper generally lasts for just a few weeks or months at a time, but repeated spells mean that migrants may end up spending more time away from their families than they do at home. The increase in seasonally specific short-term contracts in agricultural employment, especially in the agro-export production of fruits and vegetables (Kay, 1999), may also spawn rises in seasonal migration.

Gender dimensions of temporary migration

While the feminisation of agro-export farming may give rise to larger numbers of female seasonal migrants in future – and women in some countries such as Peru have traditionally migrated seasonally, and alongside men, between highland and lowland areas for the harvest of coffee, tea, cacao, tropical fruits and coca leaves (Baca, 1985; Radcliffe, 1985) – women have generally preponderated in permanent and longer-term migration, leaving men in the majority among short-term and/or seasonal movers. For example, in rural areas of the municipality of Yuscarán in southeastern Honduras, women's higher rates of permanent migration to towns and cities are reflected in the fact that only 48.6 per cent of the population is female. However, of the 8.1 per cent of the population who migrate on a temporary basis (with two-thirds of these returning every two weeks), as many as 66 per cent are male (Paolisso and Gammage, 1996:25).

Seasonal migration, especially of the rural–rural variety, has historically been male-dominated on account of the preponderance of men in agricultural production in the continent. In small towns in Guanacaste in northwest Costa Rica, for example, where most low-income men work in agriculture, they can only be assured of finding local employment during the sugar harvest between January and April. At other points in the year, therefore, many have to migrate out of the province to find work such as clearing pasture in wetter provinces such as Puntarenas, working on banana plantations in the Osa Peninsula or the Atlantic Coast, and/or picking coffee during the harvest period in the Central Valley (Chant, 1992).

Seasonal migration to tourist resorts with pronounced difference in volumes of tourist traffic between seasons also occurs, and is again dominated by men, as in Puerto Vallarta, Mexico (see Chant, 1991).

Gender implications of temporary migration

As for the implications of gender-selective temporary migration, research suggests that this is often associated with instability and insecurity within families (see Jayawardena, 1960; Moreno, 1997; Vance, 1987). In Guanacaste, Costa Rica, for example, men's absences from home often lead to stress and mistrust among spouses, and not infrequently culminate in men abandoning their families and forming new relationships in destination areas (see Chant, 1992). The women left behind become even more solidly identified as the central figure in family units where membership can vary greatly over a very short span of time. By the same token, another set of implications of male-selective seasonal migration is that women tend to enjoy greater personal freedom and decision-making power. *De facto* female heads usually find themselves with an enlarged range of responsibilities, such as having to deal with short-term crises single-handedly (or in conjunction with their consanguineal kin), making immediate decisions if required, and acting as representatives of 'the family' with schoolteachers, community leaders, government officials and so on. Another major impact of male absence is the freeing-up of women's time. In Guanacaste, men tend to place heavy demands on the domestic services of women, such that when they are away from home this alleviates their wives' labour burdens (Chant, 1992). Indeed, some women are able to find time to take a temporary job or to engage in small-scale commercial ventures. Although this is also driven by the irregularity of remittances, women's own employment often gives them more scope to determine household expenditure. Other impacts include the fact that women are freer to socialise with other people in their spouses' absence, which tends to reduce their social isolation. Some women also find that periodic separation from their *compañeros* diffuses marital conflict (ibid.:63–6). While women's gains from male-selective seasonal migration are significant, however, they have traditionally been tempered by the fact that on the return of their menfolk former patterns of life and livelihood are commonly resumed.

International migration

Until early in the twentieth century, Latin America was a major destination for overseas migrants. Since then, most international movements have been *within* the continent or *from* the region to North America. Bearing in mind that undocumented international migration makes it extremely difficult to calculate the exact size of migratory flows (Diaz-Briquets, 1989:33), in 1990, an estimated ten million Latin Americans were living outside their countries of origin, mainly in the USA, which was equivalent to 4.2 per cent of the regional population at the time (Doria Bilac, 1999:10). As far as dominant international migration patterns today are concerned, a 'permanent northward flow of Latin Americans in transit', usually illegally to the USA, coexists with a 'slower continuous flow' to countries within the region such as Argentina, Brazil and Mexico (Kratochwil, 1995:14). Much intra-regional migration is in the form of frontier or 'cross-border' migration, as discussed below.

Trends and patterns of international migration

In respect of extra-regional movement, the USA stands out as the most important country of destination, mainly for migrants from Mexico and other parts of Middle America, with Mexico representing about half the population estimated to be of 'Hispanic' origin (Green, 1991:59). As of 1996 the number of Mexican-born migrants in the USA stood at between 7 and 7.3 millions (Escobar Latapí, 2000a:320). In 1997, these made up 18.4 per cent of the country's entire legal immigrant population (Frey, 2000:64), and approximately 3 per cent of the US population as a whole (Avila and Tuirán, 2000:2). While in the 1960s only 1.5 per cent of Mexicans lived in the USA, this figure is currently in the region of 8 per cent (ibid.; Escobar Latapí, 2000a:321). At present, around 230,000 people emigrate from Mexico each year (Escobar Latapí, 2000c:6), and official figures for the period 1987–92 indicate that the USA was the destination for as many as 98.5 per cent of male overseas migrants (Garduno-Rivera, 2000:24n).

These contemporary levels reflect an historical legacy of annexation of half of Mexico's territory in the mid-nineteenth century which, Gledhill (1997b:1) notes, 'turned mobile workers into international migrants'. This was revived by the Bracero Programme of 1942, which encouraged the migration of mainly male migrants from Mexico to ease US labour shortages during the Second World War. During the 22 years the programme operated, around 4.6 million migrants took up labour contracts in the USA (Durand and Massey, 1992:6). This is a conservative estimate, however, since in the 1950s there was an estimated ratio of four 'wetbacks' (undocumented migrants) to every legal migrant who crossed the border (Potts, 1990:150). Most of the legal *bracero* migrants were employed on farms, but the fact that there are large Mexican communities in Los Angeles, Chicago, and the cities of Texas suggests that many 'illegal' migrants ended up in cities (Escobar *et al.*, 1987:43). Recurrent problems in estimating the number of migrants (especially 'illegal' ones) stem from the seasonality of migratory movements, the lack of concrete knowledge and reliance on estimates, and the fact that two countries with very different 'interests, perceptions and histories' are involved (Durand and Massey, 1992:10). Since the conclusion of the Bracero Programme in 1965 the number of illegal migrants has increased, and they currently make up 40 per cent of people moving from Mexico (Escobar Latapí *et al.*, 1999:8; see also Durand *et al.*, 2001:111). The bulk of this migration is of low-skilled labour, and increasingly comprises people who are unemployed in Mexico (Escobar Latapí, 2000a:236).

Dominicans are another sizeable group in the USA, with Sørensen's (1985) study revealing that about 15–20 per cent of the population has been involved in migration in recent years, and that between 500,000 and one million, or around one-third of the island's population, currently reside abroad (mainly in New York City) (see also Ríos, 1995:130).

As for intra-regional flows of international migrants in Latin America, Argentina and Venezuela are important destinations, with around 5 per cent of their respective populations in 1990 being foreign-born (see Thomas, 1990:94). Whereas the origins of migrants to Argentina are quite diverse, including nationals from Bolivia and Paraguay (Green, 1991:59), in Venezuela this is mainly restricted to Colombians, of whom half a million (around 4 per cent of the population) have been displaced by land reform, civil violence centred on drugs and political factionalism, and/or the desire to escape military conscription (Morris, A. 1995:80-1). This has overlaid the seasonal frontier migration historically associated with cotton and coffee production in Venezuela (Mármora, 1999:95).

In the Andean region, migration from Peru has increased in recent years, and although the largest single group (34 per cent) ends up in the USA, substantial numbers also go to Chile (30 per cent) (Aquino Rodríguez, 2000:186, Table 2). Many cross-border migrations in the Andes consist of families, as opposed to longer-distance international migrants who tend in the first instance to be male (Mármora, 1999:101).

With regard to Central America, steep rises in international migration in the late 1970s were driven by war and conflict in Nicaragua, El Salvador and Guatemala. Noting that Salvadoreans have engaged in international migration throughout the twentieth century, Bailey and Hane (1995:179) argue that political crisis in the late 1970s merely 'amplified Salvadorean international mobility'. Between 1980 and 1990, El Salvador accounted for 40 per cent of regional emigration with nearly half a million people (PER, 1999:363). This, in turn, contributed to an estimated 4.5 per cent of the Central American population living in the USA, Mexico or Canada (OIM, 2000). Forced migration persisted through the 1980s when it was estimated that about 2 million people had to abandon their homes in the region, a process which started to diminish only with the conclusion of the peace processes in Nicaragua in 1990, El Salvador in 1992, and Guatemala in 1996, although the devastating effects of Hurricane Mitch on Honduras in 1998, and earthquakes in El Salvador in 2000, look set to give rise to a new exodus (OIM, 2000). In the past, Salvadorean refugees have tended to go to the United States, as did some of those from Guatemala, although many of the latter (often women) also took up residence in refugee camps in southern Mexico (see also below). Nicaraguan refugees, on the other hand, tended to move south into Costa Rica (PER 1999: 363). This resulted in an estimated 4.5 to 7.5 per cent of Costa Rica's population in the mid-1980s being from outside the country (Diaz-Briquets 1989: 38). Between 1984 and 1997 the number of migrants of Nicaraguan origin in Costa Rica doubled, making up 73 per cent of all foreigners in residence (OIM, 2000). Although some of these immigrants were political refugees, many came to Costa Rica for economic reasons such as greater availability of jobs or lower costs of living (Chant, 1992). By the same token, migration *from* Costa Rica is also noted, especially among Afro-Caribbean males in Limón on the Atlantic coast. Limited occupational mobility among black men in a racially segmented labour market means that overseas migration (usually to work on cruise liners in Miami), is often the only route to enhancing their economic position (McIlwaine,1997; see also Sawyers Royal and Perry, 1995).

Conceptualising international migration

Given the diverse nature of Latin American international migration across space and time, it is, again, unsurprising that numerous conceptual formulations have emerged to explain the phenomenon. Yet while theoretical approaches to international migration have much in common with theories of rural–urban movement insofar as there are neo-classical, structuralist and structuration strands (albeit under different nomenclature), Massey *et al.* (1993:433) note that since 'theories conceptualise causal processes at such different levels of analysis – the individual, the household, the national, and the international – they cannot be assumed, *a priori*, to be inherently incompatible'. Agreement, however, tends to cluster around the notion that 'the conditions that initiate international movement may be quite different from those that perpetuate it across time and space' (ibid.:448). In particular, once migration is established, social networks and cumulative causation become extremely important (see Gregorio Gil, 1998). Aside from the fact that a focus on networks (as with households), circumvents the danger of replacing an 'undersocialised' view of migration in which all actions reflect individual wishes and preferences, with an 'oversocialised view' in which people are seen as passive agents in the migratory process (Boyd, 1989:641), it also allows for an appreciation of the fact that 'migration is a dynamic, developmental process in which decisions made by migrants at one point affect the course and selectivity of migration in later periods' (Durand and Massey, 1992:17). First-stage migration from Mexico to the United States, for example, seems to draw preponderantly from lower-middle income groups of the population (as opposed to the poorest) reflecting the expenses attached to international movement. As costs and risks diminish with the establishment of migrant networks in the USA, and migrant pools are reduced in source areas, income selectivity tends to decline. Moreover, remittances themselves can contribute to raising the class status of families back home (ibid.:17–19; see also below).

In terms of the factors underpinning international migration, labour and earning considerations have received most emphasis. This is perhaps only to be expected given that increasing pressure on employment and incomes in many parts of Latin America during the 1980s and 1990s have been linked with steep rises in international migration, especially from Mexico and other parts of Central America to the United States (Cornelius, 1991; Gledhill, 1995; Roberts, B., 1995). Indeed, while formal job creation seems to have resumed in Mexico from 1996 onwards, this has mainly been concentrated in cities in the West, North and Northern border area, with most 'new' Mexican migration to the USA now occurring from the south of the country (Escobar Latapí, 2000c:10). Even in Peru, which is not a 'traditional' exporter of population, numbers almost tripled to a level of 616,968 between 1989 and 1998, and increasing proportions are not coming back. This has been attributed to the fact that people are finding it increasingly difficult to get jobs in the domestic economy (Aquino Rodríguez, 2000:182 & 191; see also Chapter 8). By the end of 1998, there were just over one million Peruvians living overseas, which represented about 4.5 per cent of the national population (ibid.:183). The economic impulse to migration is such that Mármora (1999:111) argues more generally that this tends to override political or administrative controls. Restrictive legislation has proved unable to stem the flow of people in many cases, and simply leads to hundreds of thousands of undocumented migrants (not to mention greater numbers of deportations).

While employment and earnings differentials have clearly been primary factors in Latin American international mobility, holistic approaches have again proved of most utility in revealing interconnections between different catalysts and motives underpinning international migration, as well as in helping to understand their gender dimensions. The need for such approaches is amply demonstrated by countries such as El Salvador, where somewhere between one-quarter and one-third of the population have been involved in international migration in recent decades, mainly to the USA and Mexico (Bailey and Hane, 1995:178). While the largest flows were prompted by the lead-up to civil war in 1981, Salvadoreans have often been treated as illegal or economic migrants as opposed to refugees (ibid.:171). Yet Bailey and Hane (1995:171) suggest that this dichotomy between refugees and economic migrants fails to capture the complexity of people's movement, especially given the strong interrelations between the political and economic forces impelling movement, and the interractions with gender and educational selectivities that have varied over time.[2] Economic migrants to the USA and Mexico, for example, have traditionally been male, urban and well-educated, whereas those who moved to refugee camps were predominantly female. More recently, there has also been a stream of poorer migrants from rural areas of El Salvador who are targeting the USA and Canada (ibid.:180–3).

Gender dimensions of international migration

As for gender (and age) in international migration, adult men have traditionally figured more prominently in the initial stages, with women and children following afterwards (Durand and Massey, 1992). In the case of Mexico, for example, Wiest (1984:115) points out that male migrants to the USA from the village of Acuitzio del Canje in Michoacán have historically started out as illegal migrants, with women tending to join their husbands and fathers later on a legal basis (see also Boyd, 1989:652). In 1980, the ratio of illegal female to male migrants in the USA was 100:115 (Dória Bilac, 1999:3). Despite the fact that the proportion of men in international migration remained relatively stable during the period 1970-1994, at around 75 per cent of the total flow (Durand *et al.*, 2001:120–1), the differential has narrowed slightly since the passing of the Immigration and Reform Act (IRCA) of 1986 (more commonly known as the Simpson-Rodino bill), which granted amnesty to undocumented Mexican migrants already living in the United States, and also gave some encouragement to family reunification. Around 2 million Mexicans residing in the United States had their status legalised within a very short period of time (Dwyer, 1994: 86).[3]

The maturation of migration streams in general, and family reunification[4] in particular, are not the only motives for female international migrants, however, who now make up almost 50 per cent of international migrants on a world scale (Dória Bilac, 1999:3).[5] While women's migration is more than a function of 'individual decisions guided by rational economic behaviour' (ibid.:7), economic factors, nevertheless have an important part to play. In Peru, for example, there are roughly the same number of female as male international migrants, but the pattern for women to predominate in moves to Europe, and to be underrepresented in those to Asia, is largely attributable to the fact that there are more opportunities for Peruvian women in domestic service in countries such as Spain and Italy (Aquino Rodríguez, 2000:189–90). In a more general review, Hochschild (2000) notes a growing tendency for female international migrants to form part of 'global care chains' stimulated by the rising labour force participation of women in North.[6] This entails a 'pass-down of care' across national borders, such that women from the South end up as working as nannies and domestics in overseas localities, often, in turn, paying someone to look after their own children in their countries of origin (see also below).

While migrant women do not necessarily move without their spouses or children, or with the prime intention of working, they often end up so doing because of links with ethnic enclaves for childcare and jobs (Boyd, 1989:660). Moreover, the North's need for cheap labour usually ensures ready opportunities in 'deteriorated tertiary manufacturing' such as sweatshops, and in low-cost services (Dória Bilac, 1999:8; Moghadam, 1999:306; Pessar, 1994). In southern California, for example, research shows that native or foreign-born Hispanic women make-up a significant component of workers in garments and electronics. In Los Angeles, San Diego and Orange County, for example, employers:

> perceive benefit derived from the presence of large affordable labour pools and comparatively low wage and unionisation rates. All these advantages are associated with the employment of immigrants, particularly those who have recently arrived … and who are undocumented. (Fernández-Kelly and Sassen, 1995:105)

Concluding that women's subordination forms part of wider systems of domination involving class and ethnicity, Fernández-Kelly and Sassen (1995:119) also argue that 'in the age of internationalisation, gender dynamics permeate the reorganisation of production within and across borders'. Interestingly, among Latino migrants (from Mexico, El Salvador and Guatemala) in Los Angeles, gender differentiation in employment appears to be more marked than in other ethnic groups such as the Chinese, Koreans and Filipinos (Wright and Ellis, 2000: 597).

Such patterns hold to a large degree with cross-border migration in Latin America itself. In countries such as Venezuela, local people eschew non-prestigious jobs in prostitution, domestic service and in male agricultural boarding houses, leaving these to Colombian female migrants (Mármora, 1999:103). Similar patterns apply in Argentina where most Bolivian, Chilean and Paraguayan female migrants move into domestic service (Zlotnik, 1999:91)

Notwithstanding the questionable desirability of employment taken by female international migrants, the fact is that they not only increasingly migrate overseas autonomously, but, even in the context of 'family migration', often end up in the labour force. This is argued to counterbalance the construction of migrant women as passive or dependent, revealing instead an 'active image of women in migration processes' (Dória Bilac, 1999:11). In turn, this accords with a 'more dynamic concept of the family group as a structure of relationships between genders and generations, with conflicts, challenges to authority, restructuring and power plays' (ibid.). Moreover, recent evidence from Mexico suggests that growing numbers of Mexican migrants are single, educated women, and that the percentage of Mexican migrant women working in professional and non-manual occupations has risen over time (Escobar Latapí, 2000a:323).

Gender implications of international migration and transnational communities

International migration is generally viewed as economically positive both for sending and receiving countries, but the social and cultural implications are more contested (Appleyard, 1999). One major debate has centred on whether international migration leads to more or less egalitarianism in gender roles and relations. This debate is often complicated by the fact that some international movements are gender-selective, or selective in the early stages, while others involve the migration of family units from the outset. Another critical issue is that research has often ignored the fact that changes in gender in *source* countries are often as, if not more, important than those which arise in destination areas. As summed up by Gutmann (forthcoming) in relation to Mexico:

> Obviously important changes are occurring today in relation to migration from Mexico to *el norte*, including with respect to identities and practices associated with gender and the family. At the same time, Mexico itself is changing as well: modernity in Mexico has its own particularities and it would be a grave error to attribute to migration northward all transformations of this kind in Mexico (see also Hondagneu-Sotelo, 1992).

Bearing these complexities in mind, while a new location clearly has the potential to provide 'a space in which gender relations can be renegotiated' (Willis and Yeoh, 2000:xv), whether this actually occurs, or is to the advantage of women, are other questions entirely. Work on migration from Cochabamba, Bolivia, to Argentina by Balán (1990), for example, reveals that while this is often positive for men, women are prone to suffer a loss of economic independence as a result of difficulties in adapting to a new (more 'developed') country. Moreover, the fact that women might get employment in overseas destinations is not necessarily a guarantee of higher status given that it may not entail substantial changes in gender divisions of labour at home, or in a wider ideological sense (Boyd, 1989:660). This is indicated by Fernández-Kelly's and Sassen's (1995) study of women in the electronics and apparel industry in New York City and Southern California, where their female respondents maintained that while they had greater freedom to go out to work than their mothers and grandmothers, looking after home and children remained women's responsibility. Another study by Pessar (1994) on Dominican female migrants in New York showed that some preferred to remain in the home since this was deemed to raise the social status of the household.

As far as the impacts of male-selective international migration are concerned, views and findings are, again, far from clear-cut. Some studies have shown that men who migrate alone often develop more egalitarian relations with their spouses because in their absence they have to perform their own domestic chores. It is less certain, however, that this persists when they return home, or are joined by their wives overseas (see Alméras, 2000:144; Mirandé, 1997:16–17). Work by Hondagneu-Sotelo (1992) on Mexican immigrant families in the San Francisco Bay area reveals that many of the men who migrated pre-1965 had spent long periods of time with other men in 'bachelor communities' wherein they had learned to do their own household chores. Meanwhile, their wives had been alone for so long that they had become more assertive and independent, often through enlarged roles as a result of the infrequency of remittances (ibid.:401). As a general outcome of these trends, patriarchal relations were modified. This was less the case with post-1965 male migrants, however, whose movements were generally for shorter periods. In these instances, gender divisions of labour tended to remain intact (ibid.). The latter scenario seems also to apply to another case study of male migration from the rural community of Acuitzio del Canje in Michoacán, Mexico. Men who migrated to the USA tended to continue to fulfil their obligations as family breadwinners, with the result that women's dependence on them actually increased (Wiest, 1983). Although women perceived other negative impacts of international migration, such as a lack of companionship and reduced contact of their spouses with children, these were strongly outweighed by the economic benefits (Wiest, 1984: 119). Another outcome was that women were relieved of constant child-bearing, albeit because men felt that frequent pregnancies might indicate that they had lost control of their wives' sexuality (Wiest, 1983:175). On balance, women preferred their migrant husbands to journey to the USA rather than within Mexico, mainly because wages were higher, and because internal migrants tended more commonly to abandon their families (ibid.: 169).

Yet family cohesion may also be undermined by international migration, with Gledhill (1997a:9) reminding us that: '"flexible labour markets" and high international mobility of capital can have patently disruptive effects on families and communities' (see also Pearson, 2000c:14). International migration has often split households and led to high levels of *de jure* as well as *de facto* female household headship, a tendency exacerbated by the fact that war and violence in many countries have created large numbers of widows (Acosta-Belén and Bose, 1995:25; Datta and McIlwaine, 2000; Sawyers Royal and Perry, 1995:219–20). As mentioned earlier, another phenomenon is the growing tendency for women engaging in overseas migration to leave their children behind at home, although this is not as common in Latin American countries as it is for some in Southeast Asia such as the Philippines. Where separations do occur, however, women have to find new ways not only of keeping in contact with their children, but also of re-negotiating and legitimising their maternal roles. The work of Hondagneu-Sotelo and Avila (1997) on Latina nannies in Los Angeles, for example, shows that while women feel guilty about not being with their children, they justify their migration decisions with the notion that in providing for their children they are being good mothers. Hochschild (2000:134), citing the work of Parrenas (2001), maintains that these become 'transnational families for whom obligations do not end but bend'.

Finally, it is important to point out that while migration can be a stressful process for all adult female migrants, for those who move overseas principally to accompany and/or join husbands, and who may not be particularly well integrated in the host society, the prospect of mental disorders has been noted, especially where women lack language and support networks and/or are confined to low-prestige occupations (Paltiel, 1993:141). Similarly, adolescent girls in transnational communities may find themselves caught in a 'culture conflict between parental and societal norms, making their lives more stressful and their development and identity formation more difficult' (ibid.). This is not to say that migrant men escape traumas of their own. As described by Napolitano (2000) for Latino male migrants in San Francisco, men suffer from intermittent, low-status employment, being away from their families and sleeping rough, with a common outcome being dependency on drink.

Gender dimensions of migrant links with source areas

Having noted that long-term migration can fragment households, there has also been considerable discussion in the literature of ties retained with kin in home areas. As Klak (1999:120) notes in relation to Central America, not all people leave for good, with many seeing 'opportunities for employment and education in North Atlantic countries as part of a multidimensional international strategy to make ends meet and advance economically'. Interactions between source and destination localities often endure across time and distance, therefore. They can also comprise substantial monetary transfers even if the value of these is hard to determine, with official data tending only to record bank transfers, leaving money and goods sent by post or with relatives and friends unaccounted (ibid.). This point is elaborated in detail in the regional review by Waller Meyers (1998), in which she notes the wide range of Non-Bank Financial Institutions (NBFI) administering money orders, telegraphic transfers, courier services and so on through which Latin American migrants remit money back home. Whereas bank transfers carry a high cost of about 20 per cent (OIM, 2000), the money transmitted through NBFIs is generally lower, at around half this level. Bearing in mind the difficulties of establishing precise amounts, in 1990 an estimated $5.46 billion US in remittances was sent back to the Latin American and Caribbean region (Waller Meyers, 1998:11). As for what this represented to migrants, it equated to around 6 to 16 per cent of their household income (ibid.:1), and to recipients, up to three-quarters of household income (ibid.:6).

In terms of more specific examples, the aggregate value of migrant remittances to the Dominican Republic in the mid-1980s amounted to nearly as much foreign exchange as that generated by the country's sugar industry, and represented about 5–7 per cent of GDP (Klak, 1999; Sørensen, 1985). In Peru, a total of US$450 million was sent back from Japan in 1998, making overseas earnings from this destination alone the third biggest earner of foreign exchange after gold and copper (Aquino Rodríguez, 2000:194). In Mexico, where 'Mexican researchers have tended towards sins of omission and US investigators towards sins of commission' (Durand and Massey, 1992:11), migrant remittances injected an estimated two billion dollars into the Mexican economy in 1994 (ibid.:12). In 1995, this doubled to four billion dollars, representing 1–2 per cent of the Mexican economy and making labour exports the third largest generator of foreign exchange in the country after oil and tourism (Waller Meyers, 1998:9) By 1999, remittances amounted to 5.9 billion dollars. In Central America, too, the amount of remittances grew during the 1980s alongside the increase in overseas migration (see earlier). In 1999, 1.7 billion dollars were sent back to the region, with 65 per cent of this amount being accounted for by El Salvador (OIM, 2000).

The use and implications of remittances

While the amount of money sent home varies between migrants, and often decreases over generations, many households in Latin America are in receipt of remittances from more than one relative (Waller Meyers, 1998:1). In turn, remittances often represent a vital component of household livelihoods and testify to the importance of situating the analysis of households within their broader social networks.

For the Middle American region, Klak (1999:120) notes a variety of positive outcomes of migrant transfers, with money used for basic needs, the education of children, building or improving housing, and establishing small businesses. Sometimes, as in the Dominican Republic, return migrants transfer skills acquired in the USA to ownership and management positions back home (ibid.). Indeed, 90.3 per cent of business owners in the Dominican Republic are people who have lived abroad (Waller Meyers, 1998:11). For the most part, however, expenditure is weighted more towards consumption than productive investment, a pattern which has met with criticism insofar as it raises demand for imports. In El Savador, for example, the US$400–$600 which households receive in migrant remittances annually is generally stored at home (through lack of bank accounts) or spent on consumption (ibid.:2; see also Boyd, 1989:651; Durand *et al.*, 1996). Research on the Mexican community of Acuitzio del Canje in Michoacán indicates that a lack of local commercial infrastructure and labour market results in the pattern whereby

> a good portion of migrant earnings never circulates in the village of origin, but is spent on consumer durables in the United States or urban centres in Mexico. Those earnings that are returned to the village leave it and the region quickly and with little in the way of multiplier effects at the local or even regional level. (Wiest, 1984:126)

Wiest observes, in turn, that migration tended to lower rather than raise the overall productivity of the source community, with land being used less intensively or abandoned altogether, and an outflow of the most skilled and educated members of the community (ibid.:131). Despite the limited use of remittances for productive investment, however, ECLAC data suggest that proportions of income spent on consumption do not vary much between households which receive remittances and those which do not (Waller Meyers, 1998:8).

Gender and remittances

In some communities, such as in the Dominican Sierra, which has been a long-standing source of out-migration of young people to the USA, de la Brière *et al.* (1997) suggest that how money is spent – for smoothing out income in times of crisis (the 'insurance model') or contributions to household assets that will later be inherited (the 'investment model') – is often determined by a combination of gender and by the intention of migrants to return (or not). Female migrants, male migrants with non-migrant brothers, and migrants who move permanently to the USA are more likely to send money to help households in the place of origin, regardless of the latter's investment behaviour. Alternatively, male migrants, younger migrants, men with brothers who have migrated, and women with no brothers tend only to send remittances with a view to these being placed in investments that they will ultimately benefit from through inheritance.

Gender is also a significant variable in international remittances insofar as female-headed households (mainly *de facto* rather than *de jure* – see Chapter 7) are disproportionately represented among those with overseas migrant members. For example, on the basis of ECLAC data for El Salvador, where 55 per cent of households receive remittances, 47.5 per cent of receiving households are female-headed, compared with 32.2 per cent of non-receivers. In Guatemala the respective figures are 38.2 per cent and 24.7 per cent (Waller Meyers, 1998:6). Since women often remain dependent on men as providers, this could help to explain the skew towards consumption (ibid.:7). Indeed, Wiest's study of international migration from Mexico indicates that despite improvements in incomes of households with migrant men, little of this is used to set up home-based enterprises such as small shops. This is mainly because of the threat to men's peace of mind from their wives having 'too much public exposure and too much independence and power' (Wiest, 1984:118).

When it comes to economic and other linkages between migrant source and destination areas *within* Latin American nations, however, the gender dimension differs insofar as women have traditionally been the main movers. As noted earlier in the chapter in connection with the selectivity of female rural–urban migration flows, young women are often sent by their parents to towns in the expectation that they will remit some of their wages. Not only does this usually turn out to be the case, but women also provide, often for several years, non-monetary transfers such as food and clothing (see Radcliffe, 1985, 1990b on Peru; also Moßrucker, 1997). Women migrants tend also to keep in more regular contact with relatives in source areas, make more frequent visits, and return home for significant events such as the birth of their first child, as in Guanacaste, Costa Rica (Chant, 1992). This accords with a more general global pattern of women sending money more regularly, and a larger share of their income, despite earning less than men (Bullock, 1994:18). In turn, as suggested by Alicea's (1997) work on Puerto Rican transnational communities in the US, these play a vital part in developing and maintaining kin-based networks.

Conclusion

The continued gender selectivity of most population movements within and from Latin America is in many respects a resounding confirmation of the fact that men's and women's lives remain marked by difference. Whether the gender selectivity of migration should necessarily be regarded as problematic, however, is not easy to assess. In some cases, the benefits to individuals are perceived to outweigh the drawbacks, whereas in others, the process has divided families and caused major difficulties and vulnerabilities. What is fairly certain, however, is that the historical legacy of gender-selective migration has contributed to creating conditions for the reformulation of gender roles, relations and identities which, in connection with related changes in family structures and labour markets, may well yield further transformations in future. The main role for policy-makers might best be situated in attempts to safeguard the 'victims' of migration-induced social and economic fragility, by ensuring that women and men alike are guaranteed access to basic resources such as income, employment and shelter, whether in rural or urban areas. While this is conceivably possible nationally, however, across borders it is infinitely more difficult.

Even if the pace of rural–urban migration within Latin American countries shows signs of waning, it is unlikely that there will be a dramatic reduction in overseas mobility. This is partly because of the self-perpetuating dynamic of migrant networks, and partly because demand for immigrant workers looks set to continue, not only in the United States (see Frey, 2000) but also in the leading economies in the region, where maintaining a competitive edge is key to survival in a globalising world. Although in places such as Mexico declining population growth and some employment recovery since the late 1990s may well depress the supply of overseas migrants, on-going restructuring could counteract this trend. Not only did the outbreak of crisis and early neoliberal adjustment prompt increases in labour migration from Mexico to the USA, but, as Escobar Latapí (2000a:339) reminds us,

> restructuring is not a once-only event. The new model of economic growth in Mexico, the US and elsewhere implies a higher degree of mobility of capital and labour and this is itself a vital factor in a new period of more intense international migration.

Whether increasing transnationalism, and especially the influence of the United States, can contribute to improving men's and women's lives in Latin America itself and in the Latin American diaspora will depend very much on whether twenty-first-century global capitalism finds itself able to survive with or without a 'human face', and whether issues of gender equality come to constitute an integral feature. The possibility of 'utopian' or 'dystopian' outcomes, will, as argued by Gutmann (forthcoming), be ultimately a matter for women and men themselves to resolve.

10 CONCLUSION
Looking to the Future

SYLVIA CHANT

Introduction

One of the main concerns in this final chapter is not to reiterate the conclusions reached at the end of each thematic discussion in the book, but to offer a brief résumé of a more general nature as to the extent to which gender inequalities in Latin America have changed over the last few decades. The other key objectives are to suggest ways in which research and policy on gender in Latin America dating from the late twentieth century might best move forward in the twenty-first.

Gender inequalities in Latin America: continuity or change?

Recognising that change rarely goes in one direction, and that inequality not only manifests itself in different ways but has consequences of different weight for different individuals, women in Latin America would seem to have gained a lot of ground in the last few decades. While gains in one sphere are often tempered by a maintenance of the *status quo* and/or losses in others, many Latin American women at the start of the twenty-first century have a stronger political voice, greater access to education and employment, more support from state, civil society and international infrastructure to advance their interests, and greater scope to negotiate their personal, conjugal and/or domestic lives. The main 'costs' of these gains revolve around the fact that women in Latin America today shoulder larger burdens of labour and responsibility than in the past (and often under more precarious conditions), and that men have been rather slower than women to adjust to gendered changes in the home, the labour market and public policy. Although the majority of men have retained their comparative advantage over women in most domains, some men have become so alienated by assumed (as well as actual) increases in women's attainment, autonomy and power, that they feel they are 'losing out'. The consequences, as we have seen, can range from physical violence both within and beyond the home, to taking refuge in drugs or alcohol, to the financial and emotional neglect and/or abuse of partners and children. Indeed, despite some evidence that *machismo* is on the wane, there are various instances in which this powerful complex of male power and superiority is rearing its head as signs of a new, more egalitarian gender regime struggle tentatively into the twenty-first century. One of the biggest challenges in the coming decades will be for men and women to negotiate their way conjointly through the often difficult moments of transition generated by current economic, political, demographic and social trends. This is all the more essential given the increasing fragility of many people's livelihoods, and the waning ability of public institutions to underpin these in any appreciable manner. One possible route towards greater solidarity between men and women is to embrace the idea that changes in the gendered distribution of capabilities and entitlements do not need to be viewed as a 'zero sum game' (Cornwall, 2000:25). Instead, the personal and societal gains made by women, together with a blurring of divisions between male and female spheres, have potential for allowing 'gender scripts' to be rewritten in such a way that they benefit men and women alike. While some women and men in Latin America are exploring ways of doing this on their own terms, state, civil society and international organisations can do much to aid the process.

Useful directions for policy

Feminist activism within and beyond Latin America has been crucial in inspiring initiatives to create greater awareness of, and sensitivity to, gender in various aspects of legislation and policy in the region in recent decades. It is doubtful that without purposeful gender-aware interventions, particularly on the part of governments, the same progress could have been made in respect of diminishing gender inequalities. As Molyneux (2000:40) notes:

> States have served at times to undermine patriarchal relations and redress gender inequalities. As purveyors of new rights for women and as vehicles of social policy, states have acted in certain ways to equalise the gender order and to remove some of the more striking forms of injustice.

Notwithstanding the difficulties of establishing whether different state gender interventions have necessarily arisen out of specific concerns for women, or have been developed as instruments to further other and/or more general goals (ibid.:40 *et seq.*), the fact is that a number of issues stand out as in need of more dedicated attention. In relation to the above discussion, for example, one of the most important is to find ways to galvanise men's commitment to the struggle for more 'gender-fair' development in the region.

Working with men

Although the notion of bringing men into Gender and Development (GAD) policy and programmes is still in its infancy at a global level, it is increasingly recognised that, without men, gender relations cannot be effectively addressed, and in turn that initiatives for women are unlikely to work and/or be sustainable in the long term (see Chant and Gutmann, 2000; Cornwall, 2000; Cornwall and White, 2000; Lancaster, 1992; Sweetman [ed], 2001). It is instructive to note that, while there have been few initiatives pertaining to men and masculinity in Latin America thus far, the majority of these have taken the form of small-scale group projects around violence, health and sexuality, and have evolved under the wing of feminist politics (see de Keijzer, 1998; Hernández and Campanile, 2000; ILANUD, 1996:3; Montoya Tellería, 1998; Sternberg, 2001; also below).

For the most part, however, initiatives for gender in Latin America, as elsewhere in the world, have overwhelmingly targeted women, and, in the sphere of poverty alleviation programmes, generally more 'visible' groups of women such as female-headed households (see Chapters 3 and 7). Attempts to strengthen women's abilities to support their children independently in Latin America have been welcomed in a number of circles, although one of the major problems (as discussed in Chapter 7) is that women continue to be identified as the primary carers of children, and often end up bearing greater responsibility as a result. The greater inclusion of men in such programmes could not only ease women's burdens, but also lead to less isolation and marginalisation among men at a time when they appear to be suffering major dilemmas over changing gender roles and identities. The legislative bedrock for shared parenting and family responsibilities is already in place in many parts of the region, with Family Codes in Cuba, Mexico and El Salvador *inter alia*, dictating that both men and women should take responsibility for financial provision, housework and childcare (CRLP 1997:102 & 160). Yet the very fact that the 'male breadwinner/ female mother-housewife' model continues to be such a powerful normative ideology means that measures for more effective monitoring and enforcement of legal prescriptions are necessary, if greater cooperation in household responsibilities is to be achieved (see Arriagada 1998: 97; Engle, 1997:31).

While there has been little public discussion thus far of 'new roles' for men within family life, some imaginative proactive approaches to redressing gender imbalances are beginning to emerge. In Costa Rica, for example, plans are being mooted to include men in programmes of gender 're-socialisation' (see Chant 2000, 2002b). We discussed in Chapter 4 how the new Law for Responsible Paternity might be regarded by men as punitive in the first instance, although the longer term effects could be as positive for them as they are likely to be for women and children. Indeed, evidence suggests that social policy initiatives geared to 'bringing men (back) in' to family life may not be as difficult as anticipated, given a growing body of research revealing men's deeply-held concerns about their primary kin relationships. In Guatemala, for example, focus groups have shown that men express a profound sense of paternal responsibility, even if in practice, some are not in contact with their children (see Engle and Alatorre Rico 1994:4; also Chapters 1 & 7). The idea that men should cultivate their skills as parents is likely to benefit from strategies along the lines of those advocated by international organisations such as UNICEF (1997:33), which include the 'identification of culturally acceptable and positive images of men and women that can potentially demonstrate a balance of roles and responsibilities between men and women'.

Given long-term grassroots experience in the countries in which they work, local NGOs are likely to have particular expertise to offer in finding effective strategies to work with men. For example, Puntos de Encuentro, the Nicaraguan feminist and youth centre (see Chapter 5), has involved men from the very beginning of its foundation in 1991. According to two of its longest-serving members, Teresita Hernández and Verónica Campanile (2000:56), the inclusion of men (along with the organisation's focus on generational issues):

> does not, for us, represent a contradiction, but rather reflects our conceptual and theoretical starting/standpoints. For many, feminism implies a radical perspective from and for women only, while gender is less threatening and could include men; we therefore start from a 'feminist gender' perspective. Within this perspective, power relations and domination between people are the principal basis of analysis and action.... Not only must we analyse the power relations between men and women but also between adults and young people, heterosexuals and homosexuals, dominant cultures and oppressed, and between rich and poor among others.

Working with difference

Puntos de Encuentro works with the concept of 'diversity with equity', which acknowledges people's multiple identities (Hernández and Campanile, 2000:56). This, again, has been much rarer in state and international agency interventions. Despite lip service in global and national Gender and Development (GAD) circles about the need to work with different constituencies at the grassroots, in practice, 'marginal' groups such as the elderly, lesbians, and indigenous women are often excluded in the interests of satisfying 'majority' concerns (see Coates, 2001; Jolly, 2000). If we accept that gender is so enmeshed in other identities that it almost impossible to treat it in its own right (El-Bushra, 2000; Moore, 1994b), it is equally clear that gender often acts to intensify the discrimination, marginalisation, and subordination which people suffer on account of other social divisions. Aside from finding ways in which gender policies and programmes can be more sensitive to difference in practice, space also needs to be made for demands from the most 'silenced' groups (who are often those with the greatest need for change) to emerge from the grassroots. As Jolly (2000:85) suggests, while many GAD programmes still work only with women, the focus could be shifted away from the simple distinction between women and men towards groups of the population most marginalised by gender norms, or those who lack power. With reference to people marginalised by their sexual orientation, Jolly contends that

> Queer initiatives do have some advantages over more traditional development: their small scale, unofficial nature, and activist element may mean they stand more hope of being reclaimed and controlled by local people (ibid.:86).

Working with global movements and institutions

While local, grassroots input is clearly vital to effective strategies for gender equality, it would be foolish to ignore that engagement with international movements and institutions can also be beneficial to local, national and regional initiatives. As pointed up by Pearson (2000c) and Sweetman (2000) amongst others, 'globalisation' is not just about economics, but also about social concerns.

Historically, support from the international women's movement and activities surrounding the UN Decade for Women (1975–85), helped, *inter alia*, to make visible women's issues and thereby 'put pressure on Latin American governments to improve their record on women's rights and equality' (Molyneux, 2000:63). Thanks largely to the UN Decade, support for women has also become institutionalised in one form or another throughout Latin America (see Chapter 2). Clearly there are major debates about the nature of international, as well as national, machineries for women, not to mention concerns about the ways in which 'global incorporation of gender issues into the NGO and development agenda ... reflects a Western imperialist bias and indicates opposition to appropriate local social relations and practices' (Pearson, 2000c:16; see also Kabeer, 1999). While it is also necessary to exercise caution regarding the scope and effectiveness of gender initiatives in a world increasingly dominated by market forces, international activities and international mandates such as those arising from the successive UN Platforms for Action for Women (see UNDAW, 2000) can be helpful in promoting and/or providing strategically useful tools for feminist movements to advance demands for gender equality at regional and national levels.[1] At the very least, the sharing of experiences in international conferences and encounters is often instructive and illuminating for initiatives within national boundaries.

In turn, it is important that gender initiatives do not confine themselves to 'traditional' realms such as population, health and violence, but tackle issues of economic globalisation which are increasingly framing constraints and opportunities in everyone's lives. Although the 'logic of the market' has traditionally taken little explicit account of gender – or of social justice more generally – there are persuasive arguments as to why gender inequality can work to the detriment of economic efficiency and to the creation of wealth (see Elson and Gideon, 1997b; Moser *et al.*, 1993; Moser and McIlwaine, 2000; UNDP, 1995; cf. Seguino, 2000). Through dialogue with international as well as national institutions, much more could be done to ensure not only that women are spared further suffering from neoliberal orthodoxies, but that they find ways of negotiating 'decent livelihoods' in the context of current global economic change. As Pearson notes (2000c:15–16), the IMF and the World Bank are currently engaged in a proposed Global Standard for Social Policy which recognises the 'interconnectedness between production and reproduction', and which also acknowledges that economic policy cannot continue to be limited to the formal employment sector (see Chapter 8). The proposed Global Standard aims to ensure that all women and men will have access to secure and sustainable livelihoods and decent working conditions, along with access to basic social services, social protection and social integration (ibid.:16). Notwithstanding that much is likely to be lost in translation between principle and practice, this does not detract from the importance of maintaining pressure, from national and international quarters, on the arbiters of world economic policy (see Acosta, 1994). In order to do this most effectively, Elson (1998) suggests a comprehensive strategy built around gender-aware empirical research, the transformation of conceptual tools (rather than the integration of women into existing paradigms), the mobilisation of women outside the policy process, and the building of coalitions with 'sympathetic insiders' (ibid.:168).

Useful directions for research

As suggested above, effective representations to policy-makers require good research and theory. As a starting point it is clear that some important gaps need to be filled in terms of who (and what) is researched in respect of gender in Latin America. As identified at the beginning of the book, certain groups such as men (both gay and straight), lesbian women and subordinated ethnic groups have received less attention than *mestizo* women in the gender literature. It is apparent that research also needs to move in the direction of sub-groups such as elderly women and men, who are a growing presence in Latin America, and who have gendered needs that vary significantly from the generations below them. At the same time, we need to know more about the male and female youth who are benefiting increasingly from rising levels of education, and who arguably possess greater possibilities for transforming aspects of gender which have long worked to the detriment of everyone but the most privileged.

While the growing amount of research on men in Latin America has helped to ance out a female bias in earlier research and greatly enhanced our understanding gender in the region, future research may also benefit from more sustained work with women and men conjointly. Issues such as intra-family relations and divisions of labour and sexuality and reproductive health, for example, are likely to be better illuminated where negotiations over gender are explored first-hand, as well as by proxy, through the fieldwork process. Although the particular strategies necessary to do this clearly need to be elaborated in accordance with the nature and sensitivity of different types of research, mixed focus group discussions have proved a useful tool in exploring issues around gender and the family (see Chant, 2002b on Costa Rica). Similarly, while long adopted as a research practice among anthropologists in the region, extended periods of participant observation involving residence in the households of informants have been shown to be illuminating in studies of men and masculinities insofar as they have provided a means by which to evaluate disjunctures (and consonances) between normative discourses and everyday life (see Gutmann, 1996 on Mexico; Lancaster, 1992 on Nicaragua).

Other directions for research which could expand the basis of knowledge of gender in Latin America as a whole include more gender research in countries where there has been relatively little to date, and more directly comparative fieldwork within the region. This, as with the other priorities identified, will clearly require resources which might ideally be freed up by international cooperation over debt and the relaxation of constraints on public sector spending. Other sources could come through greater international collaboration in research and research funding.

Beyond this, since gender research not only in Latin America but elsewhere in the world has arguably been over-concerned with the realms of the political, the material and the pragmatic, it is perhaps time to complement and enrich this work by more dedicated investigation of domains such as the emotional, the psychological and the sexual. This is the view advanced by El-Bushra (2000:61) on the basis of her long-term experience of working with the Africa-focused NGO, ACORD:

> 'Gender' should be seen not as a politically correct ideology, but as an integral element in a wider search for a deep understanding of human behaviour, which concerns itself with physical and emotional needs, perceptions, motivations, relationships and structures. Concepts such as 'identity', 'agency' and 'power' describe how human beings struggle to carve out acceptable lives for themselves in the constraints imposed by their historical positions, their social roles, and their personal attributes.

The spirit and message of this statement are much wider than the geographical context in which it was born. In the increasingly globalising world of which Latin America is a part, the possibility of adapting such principles to advance the interests of the most marginalised groups of women and men within the region cannot, and should not, be ruled out.

NOTES

FOREWORD

1 PROGRESA is the Programme for Education, Health and Food, and operates through the transfer of funds in cash and through health and education services to the poorest families in the country. Women – housewives, mothers, wives – are the beneficiaries of the programme.
2 See, notably, the work by Brígida García and Orlandina de Oliveira, 1994, *Trabajo Femenino y Vida Familiar*, México, D.F.:El Colegio de México.
3 González de la Rocha, Mercedes and Grinspun, Alejandro, 2001, 'Private Adjustments: Households, Crisis and Work', in Grinspun, A. (ed), *Choices for the Poor: Lessons From National Poverty Strategies*, New York: United Nations Development Programme.
4 See García, Brígida and de Oliveira, Orlandina, op. cit.
5 Benería, and Roldán, 1987.
6 Safa, Helen, 1995a.

CHAPTER 1

1 Levels of education among men have also risen in the last few decades, but comparatively speaking levels of female education have risen more, as evidenced by closing gaps in male/female literacy and educational enrolments. These trends are discussed in more detail in Chapters 4 and 8.
2 The UNDP's Gender-related Development Index (GDI) is calculated on the basis of gender disaggregation of the same measures used to compute the Human Development Index (HDI) – notably health, literacy, education and income – and is effectively the HDI adjusted for gender inequality in the country. As can be seen from Table 1.1, the ranking of GDI scores for Latin America is broadly in line with that of HDI values, which to some extent is only to be expected. For example, where a large proportion of the population are literate or have high levels of educational enrolment, it is more likely that women as well as men will be reached by these benefits. By the same token, disparities between HDI and GDI scores are in some cases inflated, especially where countries have higher overall levels of income (see Bardhan and Klasen, 1999 for a detailed discussion). Whereas the GDI focuses on the impact of gender inequality on human development, the Gender Empowerment Measure (GEM) measures equity in *agency* (Table 1.2). The GEM has been computed for fewer countries (70) than the GDI (143), and is based on political representation (seats in parliament held by women), occupational status (women's share of administrative, managerial, professional and technical jobs), and GDP per capita. Among the criticisms levelled at the GEM is that it is too narrowly focused on national political structures and the formal economy (ibid.).
3 The front cover of the last volume in this list (Nash and Safa, [eds], 1986) actually gives the editors as Nash, Safa and contributors.

4 It is perhaps interesting to note that Eva Perón did not have children before she died of ovarian cancer at the age of 33. This said, it is rumoured that she had a termination before her marriage to Juan Perón (see Craske, 1999).

5 In the book of the same name, Chaney (1979) also maintained that being a woman in politics involved proving oneself as a *supermadre* (literally 'supermother'), by ensuring that maternal duties were not relegated to second place, but were carried out with even more care than usual.

6 In discussing what is signified by *machismo* in a range of cultural and geographical contexts outside, as well as within, Latin America, Cornwall and Lindisfarne (1994:16) observe that 'its meanings multiply exponentially'.

CHAPTER 2

1 The notion of 'engendering' owes much to Sonia Alvarez's seminal work on Brazil (Alvarez, 1990).

2 Increasing the numbers of women representatives is a goal of CEDAW (Convention on the Elimination of All Forms of Discrimination Against Women) and was reiterated at the 1995 Fourth World Conference for Women in Beijing.

3 Virginia Vargas, personal communication to Nikki Craske, August 1999 (see also Vargas, 2002).

4 For a more detailed discussion see Molyneux (1985, 1998).

5 Foweraker and Landman (1997) have placed great emphasis in the Latin American case of the gap between rights in law and rights in practice: extending formal rights is not always translated into rights in practice. On the whole, however, their analysis is not from a gender perspective.

6 For a fuller treatment of these issues in the Latin American context, see Molyneux (2001: Chapter 7).

7 Argentine politician Gracial Fernández Meijide commented that although women are still expected to 'clean up' politics, she personally refuses to take on the role of 'Mrs Mop' (Craske, 1999:200).

8 This has been a common theme in my fieldwork when speaking with women from different backgrounds and with different agendas.

9 Alberto Fujimori, president of Peru 1990–2000, engaged in populist and authoritarian politics (see Crabtree, 2000) and the election in December 1998 of ex-coup instigator, Hugo Chávez, in Venezuela also gave rise to concern (see Dávila, 2000; for an alternative view see Gott, 2000).

10 Despite this, the majority of PPF members were young, single, childless and without previous political experience. These characteristics made it easier for them to become 'delegates of Eva Perón' (Bianchi, 1993:704).

11 See Radcliffe (2002:153 *et seq.*) on how Andean state discourses saw Indian culture as an obstacle to development and promoted their assimilation into 'advanced' *mestizo* society. In particular she notes that indigenous women were seen as the greatest 'problem'.

12 A similar evening for men was a flop: see BBC reports for 10 and 17 March 2001 (http://news.bbc.co.uk/hi/english/world/default.stm).

13 While not strictly a military regime, Cuba has been governed by the same man, Fidel

Castro, without elections since 1959.

14 States that embraced the Doctrine of National Security with its emphasis on anti-subversive strategies were Argentina (1976–82), Brazil (1964–85), Chile (1973–89) and Uruguay (1973–84). Central American states also engaged with some aspects of National Security Doctrine in 1980s.

15 Whether we are in a phase of transition, consolidation or democratisation is a moot point (see Agüero, 1998). Whilst the region is now in its longest period of sustained civilian rule, there is considerable debate over the quality of democracy (see Agüero and Stark [eds] 1998; Cammack, 1994, Diamond *et al* [eds] 1999). Here the term democratisation is preferred to denote a dynamic process of change.

16 In 1997 these were contested in the Inter-American Court of Human Rights: Report No. 28/98, Case 11.625, María Eugenia Morales de Sierra. See http://www.cidh.oas.org/annualrep/97eng/97ench3Lan.htm. Deere and León (2001a:49) note that this was changed in 1998.

17 This is much less the case than in the past, but remains an issue in some more conservative cities such as Puebla and Guadalajara in Mexico (see also Chapter 7).

18 For one of the most comprehensive discussions of gender and citizenship in Latin America, see Molyneux (2001: Chapter 7; see also Molyneux and Craske, 2002).

19 There is great debate over the extent to which rights are, or can be, universal (see for example Foweraker and Landman, 1997; Freeman, 1995 for discussions).

20 In the ICESCR socio-economic rights are 'aspirational'.

21 It is worth noting that in the early days of international agreements such as the ICCPR and the ICESCR, there was a limited understanding of gender discrimination but the approach was to add women into the existing formula rather than question its basic structure (see Molyneux and Craske, 2002:12–14).

22 Women were denied the vote on the grounds that women had little experience outside the domestic arena (*el hogar*) and that their interests had not been disassociated from those of the male members of the family (Tuñón, 1987:184 gives the full Spanish text).

23 Although Paraguay was late in enfranchising women it is worth noting that Switzerland did not extend the vote to women until 1971.

24 Currently one of the most controversial areas in the battle for new rights is in relation to reproductive issues (Jelin, 1996; see also Chapter 4).

25 Interview with Nikki Craske, July 1999.

26 For a case study of the development of such a law, see Johnson (2002). See also Chapter 5 this volume.

27 Virginia Vargas, personal communication to Nikki Craske, August 1999.

28 These reports are available on the United Nations website, http://www.un.org/womenwatch/ daw/cedaw/reports.htm

29 Examples include the PRI and PRD (*Partido de la Revolución Democrática*/Party of the Democratic Revolution) in Mexico; the Party for Democracy, the Christian Democrats and the Socialist Party in Chile; *Acción Democrática* (Democratic Action) in Venezuela; Costa Rica's PUSC (*Partido Unido Social Cristiano*/Social Christian Unity Party); El Salvador's FMLN (*Frente Farabundo Martí para la Liberación Nacional*/Martí Farabundo Front for National Liberation); Nicaragua's FSLN (*Frente Sandinista para la Liberación Nacional*/Sandinista Front for National Liberation), and Paraguay's *Partido Colorado* (Colorado Party) and *Partido Revolucionario Febrerista* (Revolutionary Febrerista Party) (Htun, 1998). These quotas vary from 20 to 40 per cent.

30 Interview with Haydee Birgin, Buenos Aires, August 1995.

31 See footnote 7.

32 Rosalia Arteaga Serrano de Córdova de Fernández was Acting President and Head of Cabinet in Ecuador in 1997.

33 It is impossible to provide a full list here: for further information see the Women Members of Governments by Country website: http://hjem.get2net.dk/Womeningovernments/Ministers_by_Country.htm.

34 All details from Women Members in Governments website (see note 33): there was no mention of a female defence minister.

35 The term 'gender' has not always been accepted in the region. In the run-up to the Beijing Conference in 1995 there were rumours that the Conference was going to endorse five genders: male, female, gay, lesbian and transsexual. This was perceived by some as attack on traditional family values. In the end, no such endorsement occurred but it illustrated the antipathy, indeed fear, towards the term among some people in the region (see also Chapter 6).

CHAPTER 3

1 In the case of Chile, this process began in the 1970s.

2 Cornia (2001:1) notes that during the 1980s there was an average undertaking of six adjustment programmes per country in Latin America with the assistance of the BWI. A few undertook between nine and fourteen.

3 Chile's social costs declined under the post-Pinochet *Concertación* governments (Mesa-Lago, 1997:498, Table 1).

4 Where an index of zero indicates absolute equality among households and 100 implies perfect inequality.

5 González de la Rocha (2001:299) observes that in Guatemala attempts to understand poverty from a Mayan perspective were dismissed by the government.

6 Spending on education is similarly skewed (Helwege, 2000: 198).

7 Benería and Mendoza (1995:56) describe the Honduran and Nicaraguan SFs, which are based on the Bolivian model, as focused on the following: alleviation of social costs of adjustment, including poverty; employment generation; infrastructure repair; mechanism for decentralisation; and integrating the poor into the development process.

8 Not all SFs in Latin American countries followed exactly the same format. Mexico's PRONASOL; for example, did not include an employment programme, focusing instead on providing community services, and was not directly externally funded.

9 Lloyd-Sherlock (2000:110) notes that traditional welfare services in Latin America were already skewed towards the 'more highly-paid, privileged and powerful occupations' and argues that the non-contributing public subsidises social security through their taxes, given that workplace contributions are rarely sufficient to cover the payments (ibid.: 111).

10 Razavi (1999:430) echoes the point, noting that women's programmes in SFs are geared towards education while there is little consideration of agricultural growth strategies, for example.

11 According to the official *Mujeres en Solidaridad* pamphlet published by PRONASOL's Communications Office, 1991.

12 The programme was also different in that it was not targeted at the 'new poor' but at the 20 per cent living in extreme poverty. As Yaschine (1999:53) points out: 'Given that the government recognises a 40 per cent incidence of poverty this would not be benefiting the

other 20 per cent living in poverty.'

13 During my trip to observe the pre-electoral conditions in May 2000, poor women in the Huasteca region of Mexico were asked about their perceptions of PROGRESA. They understood it as a 'women's programme' since it dealt with 'their' issues, while PROCAMPO, the agricultural project, was for men since that dealt with production (Craske: fieldnotes, May 2000).

14 Human rights organisations are outside the scope of this chapter but under authoritarian rule, human rights abuses were commonplace and in response small groups of people organised, first to search for the detained and disappeared, and then to protest against abuses. In some cases, such as the *Madres* in Argentina, or the *Dignas* in El Salvador, they gained national and international recognition and have helped shape the post-authoritarian settlement (see also Chapter 2).

15 Molyneux (forthcoming) points to a number of characteristics of social capital: it conforms to ideas about decentralisation; it is compatible with ideas about working with communities; it is in line with ideas about communities being more efficient than states; it is sympathetic to ideas of the virtues of self-help and, finally, it is seen as a way of reducing state costs.

16 The landless peasant movement in Brazil is a notable exception (see Stephen, 1997) and Fisher (1993) also discusses a movement in rural Paraguay. The Zapatista movement in Chiapas, Mexico, is another notable organisation but it is a moot point as to whether this constitutes a social movement.

17 This was the case in the late 1980s in the neighbourhoods where I carried out my fieldwork.

18 In the context of Chile, Schild (1994:62) observes that for most women participation was directly linked to need but that for some it was 'a growing need to do something ' as a response to political repression.

19 Kaplan (1982) coined this term in analysing women's protests during strikes in Barcelona in 1919–20. It has been used by many looking at women's participation in Latin America.

20 Although it is not explicitly stated, Lind's arguments appear to suggest a lack of social capital in Ecuador and Mexico. Whether there remains greater social capital in Peru after the corruption and authoritarianism of Fujimori is a moot point.

21 See Alvarez (1998:306–8) on the 'NGOisation' of feminist groups.

22 This aspect of social movements as a learning place/experience is repeated often in the many case-study accounts of social movements across the region: see, for example, Alvarez (1990), Jaquette [ed] (1994), Radcliffe and Westwood [eds] (1993).

23 Benedita da Silva's life story is recounted in Benjamin and Mendonça (1997).

24 In my fieldwork in Mexico in the early 1990s two women in a small group of twenty chose to 'suspend' their membership due to their husbands' physical violence and threats, which appeared to be exacerbated by their participation.

25 Trade union membership has declined in the regions, particularly during the early years of restructuring, and therefore offers less of a political education for men than previously (see Chapter 8). It should also be remembered that in many countries unions were closely tied to the state apparatus. Nevertheless, they have offered some kind of introduction to the political world. Political parties likewise have traditionally been dominated by men, though this is changing.

26 In many agencies, women's empowerment is seen as a 'development tool' and an effective mechanism for reducing poverty (Razavi, 1999:418). Barrig (1997), however, warns of the depoliticisation of the feminist agenda should it become too institutionalised (see also Craske, 1998).

27 See Foweraker and Landman (1997: especially Chapter 2) for a discussion of this individual–collective paradox in relation to citizenship.

28 Lind (1997: 14n) comments that Afro-Brazilian women also identify poverty over 'race' in many of their movements.

29 Interviews by Craske with feminist activists in Mexico, Peru and Chile, July–August 1999.

CHAPTER 4

1 Smyth (1994:2) points out that whereas 'birth control' refers to the rights of people to freely regulate the timing, spacing and number of their children, 'population control' refers to policies aimed at controlling the same variables for demographic ends.

2 It is not just the Roman Catholic Church which has been against abortion in Latin America. See for example Molyneux (2001:Chapter 3) for an illuminating discussion of the politics of abortion during Nicaragua's Sandinista regime of the 1980s. Government concerns about the country's labour shortage and fear of political opposition played a major role in denying feminist claims for the right to abortion on demand.

3 Operation Bootstrap was a massive modernisation programme launched by the government of Puerto Rico in 1948. It aimed to industrialise the economy and improve national welfare by attracting private investors through subsidies, tax exemptions, personnel and loan assistance, and the provision of modern transport, energy and communications infrastructure (see Ríos, 1995: 128 *et seq.*).

4 In order to avoid confrontation with the Roman Catholic Church, national affiliates of international organisations such as the International Planned Parenthood Federation (IPPF), have often incorporated the term 'family' in their nomenclature. Aside from 'Profamilia' in Colombia, 'Benfam' in Brazil is another example (Corrêa and Reichmann, 1994:17).

5 As recently as the mid-1970s, the pattern had been different: in 1976, 36 per cent of women in Mexico used the pill, 18.7 per cent the IUD, and only 8.9 per cent sterilisation (CONAPO, 1999b:203–12).

6 As in many other parts of the world, beggars are more likely to be male than female.

CHAPTER 5

1 While neo-natal mortality in general includes death in the immediate aftermath of birth, and therefore often occurs as a result of problems with pregnancy and delivery, the post neo-natal mortality differential is more likely to be a measure of environment and quality of life (Arrossi, 1996:56).

2 Recent data suggest that there are over 100,000 homicides per year in Latin America, compared with 30,000 in the advanced economies (Londoño and Frenk, 2000:24).

3 As of 1994, the Pan American Health Organisation estimated that one-third of the population in Latin America as a whole accessed healthcare through affiliation to a social security institution; a further third was catered for primarily by the public sector, and the remaining third by the private sector (Londoño and Frenk, 2000:34). Although people from different socio-economic strata may use a mixture of services for themselves and family members, the bulk of the population using private services through insurance schemes are on high incomes. It is also predicted that the US-style private model of healthcare will undergo rapid expansion in the coming years (Abel and Lloyd-Sherlock, 2000:6)

4 I am grateful to Anna Coates for this information.

5 Reeves (1998:3) notes for developing regions in general that an estimated 75 per cent of healthcare takes place at the household or community level, and is mainly the domain of women.

CHAPTER 6

1 We do not devote an exclusive section to bisexuality because a) bisexuality *per se* in Latin America is even less documented than homosexuality and lesbianism, and b) because bisexuality is referred to explicitly or implicitly in our discussions of both heterosexuality and homosexuality.
2 See also Laqueur (1990) for post-Foucauldian work on the sexed body in Europe.
3 Hernán Cortés led the conquest of what is present-day Mexico in 1519.
4 Personal comment to Sylvia Chant from Matthias Rohrig Assuncão.
5 The categories of 'respectable madonna' and 'rebarbative whore' are found in many other contexts outside Latin America, past and present (see Scott and Jackson, 1996:3).
6 Extract from speech taken from newspaper article 'Iglesia contra el pecado', by Emilio Mora, *La Nación*, 7 April 1998.
7 Article in the newspaper *El Periódico*, 10 July 2000, entitled 'Juan Pablo II denuncia desfile de homosexuales'.
8 See for example discussions on the website (guategay@hotmail.com), and in the Guatemalan periodical 'for diversity', *Vice Versa*.
9 Prostitution was rife in Cuba during the Batista period, but more or less successfully eliminated by the dedicated efforts of Castro's regime to ban brothels and solicitation, and to re-skill sex workers for other forms of employment (see Abiodun, 2001).
10 Hodge (2001:22) points out that male *jineteros* are men who are not involved in sex with tourists, but 'hustle' in other ways, such as offering tours, selling black market goods, and promoting private restaurants.
11 Personal comment to Sylvia Chant from Carl McLean.
12 Personal comment to Sylvia Chant from Andrew Canessa.
13 Almaguer (1998:537) contrasts 'the rich literature on the Chicana/Latina lesbian experience' with the 'paucity of writings on Chicano gay men'.
14 Chavela Vargas was born in Costa Rica, but migrated to Mexico in the 1950s, where she became a prominent figure in the first wave of the Latin American *rescate del folclor* ('rescue of folklore') movement (Yarbro-Bejerano, 1997:34).
15 Ferris Cox News Service, 23 August 1997 (www.eco.utexas.edu/~archive/chiapas95/1997.08msg00291.html).
16 The law in question was passed in June 1992, and included within its definition of the 'crime of sodomy', anyone inducing, promoting, propagandising or practising cohabitation among people of the same sex. This carried a punishment of up to three years in prison (Thayer, 1997:400).
17 Homosexuals in other parts of Latin America such as Brazil and Argentina also refer to themselves as *entendidos*. The feminine version of this term *entendidas*, is also used by lesbians in Cuba (and Cuban American lesbians) (Arguelles, 1998:206), and, as noted earlier in the text, the name '*Las Entendidas*' was given to Costa Rica's first lesbian group. More specific terms for butch lesbians include *marimacha* ('macho Mary') and *varonilla* ('little male/female'). Other general terms include *maricona* (female version of *maricón* – see earlier), *lesbiana* (lesbian), and *tortillera* (literally, 'pancake maker'). While these latter two terms have often had negative connotations, they have been appropriated and subverted by the lesbian community. For example, one of the Chile's major lesbian organisations (formed in 1991), gave themselves the title '*Lesbianas En Acción*' ('Lesbians in Action') (Rivera Fuentes, 1996b). Another term used in Chile is *cachapera* which derives from *cachapa* or maize pancake, and accordingly has a similar connotation to *tortillera.*
18 Article by Mauricio Herrera Ulloa in *La Nación*, 15 August 1999, based on book *El Sentir Democrático: Estudios Sobre la Cultura Política Centroamericana* edited by Florisabel Rodríguez *et al.*
19 Except in Chile, where male homosexuality is illegal, and Nicaragua, where both

homosexuality and lesbianism are illegal, in the majority of countries in the region (10 out of 19) homosexuality is not specifically mentioned in the law.

20 'Por Primera Vez: Marcha de Gays y Lesbianas', *El Periódico*, 26 June 2000.

CHAPTER 7

1 McCallum's observation relates to Salvador, Brazil, but has widespread resonance throughout Latin America, not to mention other parts of the world (see Chant, 1997a; Fonseca, 1991; Olavarría and Parrini, 1999).

2 The growth in female-headed households is also noted on a global scale (see Chant, 1997a:69). Although there is often as much intra- as inter-regional diversity, Latin America as a whole is usually estimated to have 'intermediate' levels of female household headship, the highest levels being in the Caribbean, and the lowest in South Asia, the Middle East and North Africa (ibid.:70 *et seq.*).

3 It is important to note that the termination of informal unions is often under-recorded.

4 While it is undoubtedly the case that access to employment enhances women's scope to head their own households, there is not necessarily a direct or consistent relationship, especially outside Latin America (see Chant, 1997a). Even within Latin America, the work by Cerrutti and Zenteno (1999:72) on Mexican urban areas reveals that, despite a significant rise in female labour force participation between 1988 and 1997, only a negligible increase in the proportion of households headed by women took place during this period.

5 The legal prescription that men and women should share responsibilities for housework and childcare is increasingly widespread in Latin America.

CHAPTER 8

1 While the figures for Panama, Argentina and Venezuela pertain to 15–24-year-olds, for Uruguay 14-year-olds are also included.

2 Explicit deregulation refers to the formal abandonment or erosion of legislation, whereas implicit deregulation relates to the 'inadequate implementation or systematic bypassing' of regulations (Standing, 1989:1077).

3 Elson (1999:614) stresses the need for caution when interpreting upward trends in female labour force participation. In part, she argues, this is a 'statistical artefact' insofar as an unknown proportion of the rise is due to improvements in accounting for women's economic activity over time.

4 Construction is an important generator of employment for men possessing few skills or qualifications, with around 85 per cent of workers in the Costa Rican building industry being unqualified (Sandoval García, 1997:45–7).

5 The relocation of export processing firms to Third World countries during the 1960s and 1970s was referred to as part of the 'New International Division of Labour' (NIDL), because it took an increasing amount of the global production of consumer goods into the South. This distinguished it from the 'Traditional International Division of Labour' in which the South's role was limited to the export of primary products (Pearson, 1998:171–2; also Fröbel *et al.*, 1980).

6 Argentina has three main national pension funds, each of which requires at least 15 years of contributions from workers (see Lloyd-Sherlock, 1997).

7 Citing the World Bank's *World Development Report* of 1998, Pearson (2000c:17n) characterises

the 'knowledge economy' as involving the 'increasing displacement of physical labour (usually men's) and manually dextrous and docile labour (usually women's – required in sectors such as micro-electronics assembly, garments, food production, data entry and tele-services), with technically trained and qualified labour, predominantly male'.

8 This is not always the case, however. Thomas's study (1995b) of Grameen Bank clones in Latin America found that in respect of generating employment the biggest returns came from lending to men in industrial production, since when women expanded the scale of production they often used unpaid family labourers rather than waged workers.

CHAPTER 9

1 López *et al* (1993) use figures derived from the 1990 Mexican census which relate to recent migrants, being those whose place of residence was different in 1990 from 1985.

2 See also Aguirre (1994) for a detailed review of post-1959 emigration from Cuba, in which the political interests of the US and Cuban authorities have played a critical role in determining levels of migration, and its public and popular meanings and representations.

3 Although the bill was supposed to stop the flow of migrants, apprehensions by the Border Patrol actually rose from just under 900,000 in 1989 to over 1.2 million in 1993, with about 95 per cent of those detained being Mexican (Dwyer, 1994: 86).

4 In Boyd's detailed review of family and personal networks in international migration, she makes the point that, for the most part, families as defined in immigration policies refer to legally married couples and their biological offspring. However, given the coexistence of consensual unions and links with extended kin among migrant populations, 'This definition of family may not fully reflect the kin group that is the unit of adaptive strategies' (Boyd, 1989:648).

5 On a world scale 48 per cent of all international migrants were female in 1990, although they already made up nearly 47 per cent in 1965. In Latin America, which is very close to the world average, the gain in female migrants was slightly greater over this period: from 45.58 per cent in 1965 to 48.56 per cent in 1990 (Zlotnik, 1999:81, Table 2).

6 In the 'First World' as a whole, the labour force participation of mothers with children of six years or less has risen dramatically in the last few decades to an estimated 65 per cent today, compared with only 15 per cent in 1950 (Hochschild, 2000:140).

CHAPTER 10

1 The twelve critical areas of the Platform for Action arising out of Beijing in 1995, for example, are all relevant to women in Latin America in one form or another. These are: (i) women and poverty, (ii) education and training of women, (iii) women and health, (iv) violence against women, (v) women and armed conflict, (vi) women and the economy, (vii) women in power and decision-making, (viii) institutional mechanisms for the advancement of women, (ix) human rights of women, (x) women and the media, (xi) women and the environment, and (xii) the girl-child (see UNDAW, 2000; also DFID, 2000).

BIBLIOGRAPHY

Abel, Christopher and Lloyd-Sherlock, Peter (2000) 'Health Policy in Latin America: Themes, Trends and Challenges', in Lloyd-Sherlock, Peter (ed) *Healthcare Reform and Poverty in Latin America* London: Institute of Latin American Studies, 1–20.

Abiodun, Nehanda (2001) 'Havana's Jineteras', *NACLA: Report on the Americas,* 34: 5, 24–5.

Acero, Liliana (1997) 'Conflicting Demands of New Technology and Household Work: Women's Work in Brazilian and Argentinian Textiles' in Mitter, Swasti and Rowbotham, Sheila (eds) *Women Encounter Technology: Changing Patterns of Employment in the Third World* London: Routledge, 70–92.

Acevedo, Claudia (2000) 'El Espiral que se Genera y Regenera', *Identidades: Lesbianas Guatemaltecas en Su Diversidad* (Guatemala), 1, 10–11.

Acosta, Gladys (1994) 'Feminism and the New World Order' in Küppers, Gaby (ed) *Compañeras: Voices From the Latin American Women's Movement* London: Latin America Bureau, 167–72.

Acosta-Belén, Edna and Bose, Christine (1995) 'Colonialism, Structural Subordination and Empowerment: Women in the Development Process in Latin America and the Caribbean' in Bose, Christine and Acosta-Belén, Edna (eds) *Women in the Latin American Development Process* Philadelphia: Temple University Press, 15–36.

Agüero, Felipe (1998) 'Conflicting Assessments of Democratisation: Exploring the Faultlines' in Agüero, Felipe and Stark, Jeffrey (eds) *Fault Lines Of Democracy in Post-Transition Latin America* Miami: North South Center, University of Miami, 1–20.

Agüero, Felipe and Stark, Jeffrey (eds) (1998) *Fault Lines of Democracy in Post-Transition Latin America* Miami: North South Center, University of Miami.

Aguirre, B.E. (1994) 'Cuban Mass Migration and the Social Construction of Deviants', *Bulletin of Latin American Research*, 13:2, 155–83.

Alba, Francisco (1989) 'The Mexican Demographic Situation' in Bean, Frank; Schmandt, Jürgen and Weintraub, Sidney (eds) *Mexican and Central American Population and US Immigration Policy* Austin: University of Texas Press, 5–32.

Alicea, Marixsa (1997) '"A Chambered Nautilus": The Contradictory Nature of Puerto Rican Women's Role in the Construction of a Transnational Community', *Gender and Society*, 11:5, 597–626.

Almaguer, Tomás (1998) 'Chicano Men: A Cartography of Homosexual Identity and Behaviour' in Nardi, Peter and Schneider, Beth (eds) *Social Perspectives in Lesbian and Gay Studies: A Reader* London: Routledge, 537–52.

Alméras, Diane (2000) 'Equitable Social Practices and Masculine Personal History: A Santiago Study', *European Journal of Development Research*, 12:2, 139–56.

Alvarez, Sonia (1990) *Engendering Democracy in Brazil* Princeton: Princeton University Press.

Alvarez, Sonia (1997) 'Contradictions of a "Women's Space" in a Male-Dominated State: The Political Role of the Commissions of the Status of Women in Postauthoritarian Brazil' in Staudt, Kathleen (ed) *Women, International Development and Politics: The Bureaucratic Mire* Philadelphia: Temple University Press, 59–100.

Alvarez, Sonia (1998) 'Latin American Feminisms "Go Global": Trends of the 1990s and Challenges for the New Millennium' in Alvarez, Sonia; Dagnino, Evelina and Escobar, Arturo (eds) *Cultures of Politics/Politics of Cultures: Re-visioning Latin American Social Movements* Boulder: Westview, 293–324.

Amis, Philip (1995) 'Making Sense of Urban Poverty', *Environment and Urbanisation*, 7:1, 145–7.

Amuchástegui Herrera, Ana (1998) 'Saber o No Saber Sobre el Sexo: Los Dilemas de la Actividad Sexual Femenina para Jóvenes Mexicanos' in Szasz, Ivonne and Lerner, Susana (eds) *Sexualidades en México: Algunas Aproximaciones desde la Perspectiva de las Ciencias Sociales* México DF: El Colegio de México, 107–35.

Anzaldua, Gloria (1990) 'Bridge, Drawbridge, Sandbar or Island: Lesbians-of-Color Hacienda Alianzas' in Albrecht, Lisa and Brewer, Rose (eds) *Bridges of Power: Women's Multicultural Alliances* Philadelphia: New Society, 216–31.

Appleyard, Reginald (1999) 'Migración Internacional y Desarrollo: Una Relación por Resolver', *Revista de la Organización Internacional para las Migraciones en América Latina*, Edición Especial (July) (www.oim.web.cl).

Aquino Rodríguez, Carlos (2000) 'International Migration and Human Resource Development in Peru in the 90s' in Kimura, Michio and Hayase, Yasuko (compilers) *Proceedings of the International Workshop on International Migration and Human Resources Development in the APEC Member Economies* Tokyo: Institute of Developing Economies, JETRO, 181–97.

Arce, Leda and Escamilla, Zaira (1996) 'Mujer, Trabajo y Stress', *Revista Costarricense de Psicología*, 25, 21–8.

Archetti, Eduardo (1996) 'Playing Styles and Masculine Virtues in Argentine Football' in Melhuus, Marit and Stølen, Kristi Anne (eds) *Machos, Mistresses and Madonnas: Contesting the Power of Latin American Gender Imagery* London: Verso, 34–55.

Arenas de Mesa, Alberto and Montecinos, Verónica (1999) 'The Privatisation of Social Security and Women's Welfare: Gender Effects of the Chilean Reform', *Latin American Research Review*, 34:3, 7–37.

Arguelles, Lourdes (1998) 'Crazy Wisdom: Memories of a Cuban Queer' in Darder, Antonia and Torres, Rodolfo (eds) *The Latino Studies Reader: Culture, Economy and Society* Oxford: Blackwell, 228–39.

Arias, Omar (2000) *Are All Men Benefiting from the New Economy? Male Economic Marginalisation in Argentina, Brazil and Costa Rica* Washington DC: World Bank, LCSPR (www.worldbank.org/external/lac).

Arias, Rosario and Rodríguez, Marisela (1998) '"A Puro Valor Mexicano": Conotaciones del Uso del Condón en Hombres de la Clase Media de la Ciudad de México' in Lerner, Susana (ed) *Varones, Sexualidad y Reproducción* México DF: El Colegio de México, 319–39.

Arizpe, Lourdes (1982a) 'Women and Development in Latin America and the Caribbean', *Development Dialogue*, 1/2, 74–84.

Arizpe, Lourdes (1982b) 'Relay Migration and the Survival of the Peasant Household' in Safa, Helen (ed) *Towards a Political Economy of Urbanisation in Developing Countries* Oxford: Oxford University Press, 19–46.

Arriagada, Irma (1998) 'Latin American Families: Convergences and Divergences in Models and Policies', *CEPAL Review*, 65, 85–102.

Arrossi, Silvina (1996) 'Inequality and Health in Metropolitan Buenos Aires', *Environment and Urbanisation*, 8:2, 43–70.

Asthana, Sheena (1994a) 'Economic Crisis, Adjustment and the Impact on Health' in Phillips, David and Verhasselt, Yola (eds) *Health and Development* London: Routledge, 50–64.

Asthana, Sheena (1994b) 'Primary Health Care and Selective PHC: Community Participation in Health and Development' in Phillips, David and Verhasselt, Yola (eds) *Health and Development* London: Routledge, 182–96.

Avila, José Luis and Tuirán, Rodolfo (2000) *Resultados del Estudio Binacional México–Estados Unidos Sobre Migración* México DF: Consejo Nacional de Población (www.conapo.gob.mx/presente/cap06.htm).

Baca, Epifanio (1985) *Economía Campesina y Mercados de Trabajo: El Caso del Sur Oriente* Cuzco: Centro Bartolomé de las Casas.

Baden, Sally (1993) *The Impact of Recession and Structural Adjustment on Women's Work in Developing Countries* Sussex: Institute of Development Studies, Bridge Report No. 2.

Baden, Sally and Goetz, Anne Marie (1997) 'Who Needs [Sex] When You Can Have [Gender]?', *Feminist Review*, 53, 3–25.

Badia, Monica (1999) *The Chilean 'Social Integration' Approach to Poverty Alleviation: The Case of the Programme for Female Heads of Households* Hertford: Employment Studies Paper 25, University of Hertfordshire Business School.

Bailey, Adrian and Hane, Joshua (1995) Population in Motion: Salvadorean Refugees and Circulation Migration', *Bulletin of Latin American Research*, 14:2, 171–200.

Balán, Jorge (1990) 'La Economía Doméstica y las Diferencias entre los Sexos en las Migraciones Internacionales: Un Estudio Sobre el Caso de los Bolivianos en Argentina', *Estudios Migratorios Latinoamericanos*, 5:15/16, 269–94.

Balderston, Daniel and Guy, Donna (1997) 'Introduction' in Balderston, Daniel and Guy, Donna (eds) *Sex and Sexuality in Latin America* New York: New York University Press, 1–6.

de Barbieri, Teresita (1999) 'Cambio Sociodemográfico, Políticas de Población y Derechos Reproductivos en Mexico' in Ortiz-Ortega, Adriana (ed) *Derechos Reproductivos de las Mujeres: Debates sobre Justicia Social en México* México DF: Universidad Autónoma Metropolitana, Unidad Xochimilco/EDAMEX, 101–45.

de Barbieri, Teresita and de Oliveira, Brígida (1989) 'Reproducción de la Fuerza de Trabajo en América Latina: Algunas Hipótesis' in Schteingart, Martha (ed) *Las Ciudades Mexicanas en la Crisis*, México DF: Editorial Trillas, 19–29.

Bardhan, Kalpana and Klasen, Stephan (1999) 'UNDP's Gender-related Indices: A Critical Review', *World Development*, 27:6, 985–1010.

Barker, Gary and Lowenstein, Irene (1997) 'Where the Boys Are: Attitudes Related to Masculinity, Fatherhood and Violence Toward Women among Low-Income Adolescent and Young Adult Males in Rio de Janeiro, Brazil', *Youth and Society*, 29: 2, 166–96.

Barrientos, Stephanie (1997) 'The Hidden Ingredient: Female Labour in Chilean Fruit Exports', *Bulletin*

of Latin American Research, 16:1, 71–81.
Barrientos, Stephanie; Bee, Anna; Matear, Ann and Vogel, Isabel (1999) *Women and Agribusiness: Working Miracles in the Chilean Fruit Export Sector* Houndmills, Basingstoke: Macmillan.
Barrientos, Stephanie and Perrons, Diane (1999) 'Gender and the Global Food Chain: A Comparative Study of Chile and the UK' in Afshar, Haleh and Barrientos, Stephanie (eds) *Women, Globalisation and Fragmentation in the Developing World* Houndmills, Basingstoke: Macmillan, 150–73.
Barrig, Maruja (1997) 'De Cal y de Arena: ONGs y Movimiento de Mujeres en Chile'. Mimeo. Lima.
Bastos, Santiago (1999) 'Concepciones del Hogar y Ejercicio del Poder: El Caso de los Mayas de la Ciudad de Guatemala' in González de la Rocha, Mercedes (ed) *Divergencias del Modelo Tradicional: Hogares de Jefatura Femenina en América Latina* México DF: Centro de Investigaciones y Estudios Superiores en Antropología Social, 37–75.
Batley, Richard (1997) 'Social Agency Versus Global Determination in Latin American Urban Development', *Third World Planning Review*, 19:4, 333–46.
Battersby, Christine (1998) *The Phenomenal Woman: Feminist Metaphysics and the Patterns of Identity* Cambridge: Polity Press.
Baylies, Carolyn (1996) 'Diversity in Patterns of Parenting and Household Formation' in Bortolaia Silva, Elizabeth (ed) *Good Enough Mothering? Feminist Perspectives on Lone Motherhood* London: Routledge, 76–96.
Beales, Sylvia (2000) 'Why We Should Invest in Older Women and Men: The Experience of HelpAge International', *Gender and Development* (Oxfam), 8:2, 9–18.
Beall, Jo (1995) 'In Sickness and in Health: Engendering Health Policy for Development', *Third World Planning Review*, 17:2, 213–22.
Beck, Ulrich and Beck-Gernsheim, Elisabeth (1995) *The Normal Chaos of Love* Cambridge: Polity.
Becker, Charles and Morrison, Andrew (1997) 'Public Policy and Rural–Urban Migration' in Gugler, Josef (ed) *Cities in the Developing World: Issues in Theory and Policy* Oxford: Oxford University Press, 124–38.
Becker, Gary (1976) *The Economic Approach to Human Behaviour* Chicago: Chicago University Press.
Becker, Gary (1981) *Treatise on the Family* Cambridge, Massachusetts: Harvard University Press.
Bee, Anna and Vogel, Isabel (1997) 'Temporeras and Household Relations: Seasonal Employment in Chile's Agro-Export Sector', *Bulletin of Latin American Research*, 16:1, 83–95.
Beetham, David (1995) 'What Future for Economic and Social Rights?', *Political Studies*, 43, 41–60.
Benería, Lourdes (1991) 'Structural Adjustment, the Labour Market and the Household: The Case of Mexico' in Standing, Guy and Tokman, Victor (eds) *Towards Social Adjustment: Labour Market Issues in Structural Adjustment* Geneva: International Labour Organisation, 161–83.
Benería, Lourdes and Mendoza, Breny (1995) 'Structural Adjustment and Social Emergency Funds: The Cases of Honduras, Mexico and Nicaragua', *European Journal of Development Research*, 7:1, 53–76.
Benería, Lourdes and Roldán, Marta (1987) *The Crossroads of Class and Gender: Industrial Homework, Subcontracting and Household Dynamics in Mexico City* Chicago: University of Chicago Press.
Benjamin, Medea and Mendonça, Maisa (1997) *Benedita da Silva: An Afro-Brazilian Woman's Story of Politics and Love* Monroe: Food First Books.
Berry, Albert (1997) 'The Income Distribution Threat in Latin America', *Latin American Research Review*, 32:2, 3–40.
Berthel y Jiménez, Lylia (1995) (ed) *La Mujer de la Tercera Edad: Perspectivas y Necesidades* México DF: Nacional Coordinadora para la IV Conferencia Mundial sobre la Mujer.
Bertranou, Fabio (2001) 'Pension Reform and Gender Gaps in Latin America: What Are the Policy Options?', *World Development*, 29:5, 911–23.
Beuchler, Judith (1986) 'Women and Petty Commodity Production in La Paz, Bolivia' in Nash, June and Safa, Helen (eds) *Women and Change in Latin America* Massachusetts: Bergin and Garvey, 165–88.
Bianchi, Susana (1993) 'Las Mujeres en El Peronismo (Argentina, 1945–55)' in Duby, Georges and Perrot, Michelle (eds) *Historia de las Mujeres Vol V: El Siglo XX* Madrid: Taurus, 696–707.
Bieber, Judy (1998) 'Postmodern Ethnographer in the Backlands: An Imperial Bureaucrat's Perceptions of Post-Independence Brazil', *Latin American Research Review*, 33:2, 37–72.
Bliss, Katherine Elaine (2001) 'The Sexual Revolution in Mexican Studies: New Perspectives on Gender, Sexuality and Culture in Modern Mexico', *Latin American Research Review*, 36:1, 247–68.
Blofield, Merike and Haas, Liesl (2001) 'Religion, Political Institutions and Coalition Politics: Reforming Laws on Women's Rights in Chile', Mimeo, Department of Political Science, Western Michigan University.
Blue, Ilona (1996) 'Urban Inequalities in Mental Health: The Case of São Paulo', *Environment and Urbanisation*, 8:2, 91–9.
Blumberg, Rae Lesser (1989) 'Towards a Feminist Theory of Development' in Wallace, Ruth (ed) *Feminism and Sociological Theory* Newbury Park: Sage, 161–99.
Blumberg, Rae Lesser (1995) 'Gender, Microenterprise, Performance, and Power: Case Studies from the

Dominican Republic, Ecuador, Guatemala, and Swaziland' in Bose, Christine and Acosta-Belén, Edna (eds) *Women in the Latin American Development Process* Philadelphia: Temple University Press, 194–226.

Blumberg, Rae Lesser with García, María Pilar (1977) 'The Political Economy of the Mother–Child Family: A Cross-Societal View' in Leñero-Otero, Luís (ed) *Beyond the Nuclear Family Model* London: Sage, 99–163.

Bolis, Monica (1993) 'Characteristic Treatment of Violence against Women in Latin American Legislation' in Gómez Gómez, Elsa (ed) *Gender, Women and Health in the Americas* Washington DC: Pan American Health Organisation, 237–43.

Boltvinik, Julio and Hernández Laos, Enrique (2000) *Pobreza y Distribución del Ingreso en México* México DF: Siglo Veintiuno Editores.

Borja, Jaime (1993) 'Barbarización y Redes de Endoctrinamiento en los Negros: Cosmovisiones en Cartagena, Siglos XVII y XVIII' in Ulloa, Astrid (ed) *Contribución Africana a la Cultura de las Américas* Bogotá: Proyecto BioPacífico/ICAN, 241–54.

Bose, Christine and Acosta-Belén, Edna (1995) 'Introduction' in Bose, Christine and Acosta-Belén, Edna (eds) *Women in the Latin American Development Process* Philadelphia: Philadelphia University Press, 1–11.

Bose, Christine and Acosta-Belén, Edna (eds) (1995) *Women in the Latin American Development Process* Philadelphia: Philadelphia University Press.

Boserup, Ester (1970) *Women's Role in Economic Development* London: George Allen and Unwin.

Bouvard, Marguerite Guzmán (1994) *Revolutionising Motherhood: The Mothers of the Plaza de Mayo* Wilmington: Scholarly Resources.

Bradshaw, Sarah (1995a) 'Women's Access to Employment and the Formation of Women-headed Households in Rural and Urban Honduras', *Bulletin of Latin American Research*, 14:2, 143–58.

Bradshaw, Sarah (1995b) 'Female-headed Households in Honduras: Perspectives on Rural–Urban Differences', *Third World Planning Review*, 17:2, 117–31.

Brenes, Haydée (1999) 'Experiences Related to Promoting Child Health in Costa Rica' in UNICEF Costa Rica (ed) *Nuestro Derecho a Nutrición y Salud en Costa Rica* San José: UNICEF Costa Rica, 63–9.

de la Brière, Bénédicte; de Janvrey, Alain; Lambert, Sylvie and Sadoulet, Elisabeth (1997) *Who Do Migrants Remit? An Analysis for the Dominican Sierra* Washington DC: International Food Policy Research Institute, Food Consumption and Nutrition Division Discussion Paper No. 37.

Bromley, Ray (1997) 'Working in the Streets of Cali, Colombia: Survival Strategy, Necessity or Unavoidable Evil?' in Gilbert, Alan in association with Hardoy, Jorge and Ramírez, Ronaldo (eds) *Urbanisation in Contemporary Latin America: Critical Approaches to the Analysis of Urban Issues* Chichester: John Wiley, 59–77.

Bromley, Ray (1997) 'Working in the Streets of Cali, Colombia: Survival Strategy, Necessity or Unavoidable Evil?' in Gugler, Josef (ed) *Cities in the Developing World: Issues, Theory and Policy* Oxford: Oxford University Press, 124–38.

Brown, Cynthia J., Pagán, José A. and Rodríguez-Oreggia, Eduardo (1999) 'Occupational Attainment and Gender Earnings Differentials in Mexico', *Industrial and Labour Relations Review*, 53:1, 123–35.

Browner, C.H. (1989) 'Women, Household and Health in Latin America', *Social Science and Medicine*, 28:5, 461–73.

Bruce, Judith (1994) 'Reproductive Choice: The Responsibilities of Men and Women', *Reproductive Health Matters*, 4, 68–70.

Bruce, Judith and Dwyer, Daisy (1988) 'Introduction' in Dwyer, Daisy and Bruce, Judith (eds) *A Home Divided: Women and Income in the Third World* Stanford: Stanford University Press, 1–19.

Bruce, Judith and Lloyd, Cynthia (1992) *Finding the Ties that Bind: Beyond Headship and the Household* New York/Washington DC: Population Council/International Center for Research on Women.

Brydon, Lynne and Chant, Sylvia (1989) *Women in the Third World: Gender Issues in Rural and Urban Areas* Aldershot: Edward Elgar.

Budowksi, Monica (2000) 'Lone Motherhood in Costa Rica: A Threat for Society or a Chance for Change?'. Revised draft of paper delivered for publication of the Proceedings of the symposium 'Order, Risk and Catastrophe', Bern, 11–13 October 1999.

Budowski, Monica and Guzmán, Laura (1998) 'Strategic Gender Interests in Social Policy: Empowerment Training for Female Heads of Household in Costa Rica'. Paper prepared for the International Sociological Association, XIV World Congress of Sociology, Montreal, 26 July – 1 August.

Budowski, Monica and Rosero Bixby, Luis (forthcoming) 'Fatherless Costa Rica? Child Acknowledgement and Support Among Lone Mothers', *Journal of Comparative Family Studies.*

Buffington, Rob (1997) 'Los Jotos: Contested Visions of Homosexuality in Modern Mexico' in Balderston, Daniel and Guy, Donna (eds) *Sex and Sexuality in Latin America* New York: New York University Press, 118–32.

Bullock Susan (1994) *Women and Work* London: Zed.§

Bulmer-Thomas, Victor (1996) 'Conclusions' in Bulmer-Thomas, Victor (ed) *The New Economic Model in Latin America and its Impact on Income Distribution and Poverty* Houndmills, Basingstoke: Macmillan in association with the Institute of Latin American Studies, University of London, 296–327.

Bunster-Burotto, Ximena (1986) 'Surviving Beyond Fear: Women and Torture in Latin America' in Nash, June and Safa, Helen (eds) *Women and Change in Latin America* South Hadley, Massachusetts: Bergin and Garvey, 297–325.

Busby, Cecilia (2000) *The Performance of Gender: An Anthropology of Everyday Life in a South Indian Fishing Village* London: The Athlone Press.

Butler, Judith (1990) *Gender Trouble: Feminism and the Subversion of Identity* London: Routledge.

Butler, Judith (1993) *Bodies That Matter: On the Discursive Limits of 'Sex'* New York: Routledge.

Butler, Judith (1999) *FETSALUD. Nicaragua: The Federation of Health Workers* London: One World Action.

Butterworth, Douglas and Chance, John (1981) *Latin American Urbanisation* Cambridge: Cambridge University Press.

Buvinic, Mayra (1995) *Investing in Women* Washington DC: International Center for Research on Women.

Buvinic, Mayra and Gupta, Geeta Rao (1997) 'Female-headed Households and Female-maintained Families: Are They Worth Targetting to Reduce Poverty in Developing Countries?', *Economic Development and Cultural Change*, 45: 2, 259–80.

Buvinic, Mayra; Valenzuela, Juan Pablo; Molina, Temistocles and González, Electra (1992) 'The Fortunes of Adolescent Mothers and their Children: The Transmission of Poverty in Santiago, Chile', *Population and Development Review*, 18:2, 169–97.

Cammack, Paul (1994) 'Democratisation and Citizenship In Latin America' in Parry, Geraint and Moran, Michael (eds) *Democracy and Democratisation* London: Routledge, 174–95.

Cañadell, Rosa (1993) 'Chilean Women's Organisations: Their Potential for Change', *Latin American Perspectives*, 20:4, 43–60.

Carrier, Joseph (1995) *De los Otros: Intimacy and Homosexuality Among Mexican Men* New York: Columbia University Press.

Carvajal, Manuel and Geithman, David (1985) 'Income, Human Capital and Sex Discrimination: Some Evidence from Costa Rica, 1963 and 1973', *Journal of Economic Development*, 10:1, 89–115.

Castells, Manuel (1997) *The Power of Identity* Oxford: Blackwell.

Caulfield, Sueann (1997) 'The Birth of Mangue: Race, Nation and Politics of Prostitution in Rio Janeiro 1850–1942' in Balderston, Daniel and Guy, Donna (eds) *Sex and Sexuality in Latin America* New York: New York University Press, 86–100.

Caulfield, Sueann (2000) *In Defense of Honor: Sexual Morality, Modernity and Nation in Early Twentieth-Century Brazil* Durham: Duke University Press.

Centro de Educación y Comunicación Popular (CANTERA) (1997) *Identidades Masculinas* Managua: CANTERA.

Centro de Información y Asesoría en Salud (CISAS) (1997) 'Adjusting Health Care: The Case of Nicaragua' in Hill, Eleanor (ed) *Development for Health* Oxford: Oxfam, 86–9.

Centro Legal para Derechos Reproductivos y Políticas Públicas (CRLP) (1997) *Mujeres del Mundo: Leyes y Políticas que Afectan sus Vidas Reproductivas: América Latina* New York: CRLP.

Centro Nacional para el Desarrollo de la Mujer y la Familia (CMF) (1996) *Plan Para la Igualdad de Oportunidad entre Mujeres y Hombres (PIOMH) 1996–1998* San José: CMF.

Centro Nacional para el Desarrollo de la Mujer y la Familia (CMF) (1997) *Mujeres, Pobreza y Políticas Públicas* San José: CMF.

Cerrutti, Marcela (2000a) 'Intermittent Employment Among Married Women: A Comparative Study of Buenos Aires and Mexico City', *Journal of Comparative Family Studies*, 31:1, 19–43.

Cerrutti, Marcela (2000b) 'Economic Reform, Structural Adjustment and Female Labour Force Participation in Buenos Aires, Argentina', *World Development*, 28:5, 879–91.

Cerrutti, Marcela and Zenteno, René (1999) 'Cambios en el Papel Económico de las Mujeres entre las Parejas Mexicanas', *Estudios Demográficos y Urbanos* (El Colegio de México), 15:1, 65–95.

Chaney, Elsa (1979) *Supermadre: Women in Politics in Latin America* Austin: University of Texas Press.

Chant, Sylvia (1984) 'Household Labour and Self-Help Housing in Querétaro, Mexico', *Boletín de Estudios Latinoamericanos y del Caribe*, 37, 45–68.

Chant, Sylvia (1985) 'Single-parent Families: Choice or Constraint? The Formation of Female-headed Households in Mexican Shanty Towns', *Development and Change*, 16:4, 635–56.

Chant, Sylvia (1991) *Women and Survival in Mexican Cities: Perspectives on Gender, Labour Markets and Low-income Households* Manchester: University of Manchester Press.

Chant, Sylvia (1992) 'Migration at the Margins: Gender, Poverty and Population Movement on the Costa Rican Periphery' in Chant, Sylvia (ed), *Gender and Migration in Developing Countries* London: Belhaven, 49–72.

Chant, Sylvia (1994) 'Women's Work and Household Survival Strategies in Mexico, 1982–1994: Past

Trends, Current Tendencies and Future Research', *Bulletin of Latin American Research*, 13:2, 203–33.

Chant, Sylvia (1996a) *Gender, Urban Development and Housing* New York: United Nations Development Programme.

Chant, Sylvia (1996b) 'Women's Roles in Recession and Economic Restructuring in Mexico and the Philippines', *Geoforum*, 27:3, 297–327.

Chant, Sylvia (1997a) *Women-headed Households: Diversity and Dynamics in the Developing World* , Houndmills, Basingstoke: Macmillan.

Chant, Sylvia (1997b) 'Women-headed Households: Poorest of the Poor? Perspectives from Mexico, Costa Rica and the Philippines', *IDS Bulletin*, 28:3, 26–48.

Chant, Sylvia (1998) 'Households, Gender and Rural–Urban Migration: Reflections on Linkages and Considerations for Policy', *Environment and Urbanisation*, 10:1, 5–21.

Chant, Sylvia (1999a) 'Women-headed Households: Global Orthodoxies and Grassroots Realities' in Afshar, Haleh and Barrientos, Stephanie (eds) *Women, Globalisation and Fragmentation in the Developing World* Houndmills, Basingstoke: Macmillan, 91–130.

Chant, Sylvia (1999b) 'Youth, Gender and "Family Crisis" in Costa Rica', report to the Nuffield Foundation, London, Award no. SGS/LB/0223 (October).

Chant, Sylvia (1999c) 'Population, Migration, Employment and Gender' in Gwynne, Robert and Kay, Cristóbal (eds) *Latin America Transformed: Globalisation and Modernity* London: Edward Arnold, 226–69.

Chant, Sylvia (2000) 'Men in Crisis? Reflections on Masculinities, Work and Family in Northwest Costa Rica', *European Journal of Development Research*, 12:2, 199–218.

Chant, Sylvia (2002a) 'Women, Men and Household Diversity' in McIlwaine, Cathy and Willis, Katie (eds) *Challenges and Change in Middle America: Perspectives on Development in Mexico, Central America and the Caribbean* Harlow: Pearson Education, 26–60.

Chant, Sylvia (2002b) 'Whose Crisis? Public and Popular Reactions to Family Change in Costa Rica' in Abel, Christopher and Lewis, Colin (eds) *Exclusion and Engagement: Social Policy in Latin America* London: Institute of Latin American Studies, University of London, 349–77.

Chant, Sylvia and Gutmann, Matthew (2000) *Mainstreaming Men into Gender and Development: Debates, Reflections and Experiences* Oxford: Oxfam.

Chant, Sylvia and McIlwaine, Cathy (1995) *Women of a Lesser Cost: Female Labour, Foreign Exchange and Philippine Development* London: Pluto.

Chant, Sylvia and Radcliffe, Sarah (1992) 'Migration and Development: The Importance of Gender' in Chant, Sylvia (ed) *Gender and Migration in Developing Countries* London: Belhaven, 1–29.

Chávez, Eda (1999) 'Domestic Violence and HIV/AIDS in Mexico' in Foreman, Martin *AIDS and Men: Taking Risks or Taking Responsibility?* London: Panos Institute/Zed, 51–63.

Cheetham, Jacquie and Alba, Wendy (2000) 'Community Research on Older Women in the Dominican Republic', *Gender and Development* (Oxfam), 8:2, 66–73.

Chickering, A. Lawrence and Salahdine, Mohamed (1991) 'Introduction' in Chickering, A. Lawrence and Salahdine, Mohamed (eds) *The Silent Revolution: The Informal Sector in Five Asian and Near Eastern Countries* San Francisco: International Center for Economic Growth, 1–14.

Chinchilla, Norma (1994) 'Feminism, Revolution and Democratic Transition in Nicaragua' in Jaquette, Jane (ed) *The Women's Movement in Latin America: Participation and Democracy* Boulder: Westview, 177–98.

Chuchryk, Patricia (1989) 'Subversive Mothers': The Opposition to the Military Regime in Chile' in Charlton, Ellen; Everett, Jana and Staudt, Kathy (eds) *Women, the State and Development* Albany: State University of New York Press.

Chuchryk, Patricia (1994) 'From Dictatorship to Democracy: the Women's Movement in Chile' in Jaquette, Jane (ed) *The Women's Movement in Latin America: Participation and Democracy* Boulder: Westview, 65–108.

Cicerchia, Ricardo (1997) 'The Charm of Family Patterns: Historical and Contemporary Patterns in Latin America' in Dore, Elizabeth (ed) *Gender Politics in Latin America: Debates in Theory and Practice* New York: Monthly Review Press, 118–33.

Claramunt, María Cecilia (1997) *Casitas Quebradas: El Problema de la Violencia Doméstica en Costa Rica* San José: Editorial Universidad a Distancia.

Clark, Fiona C. and Laurie, Nina (2000) 'Gender, Age and Exclusion: A Challenge to Community Organisations in Lima, Peru', *Gender and Development* (Oxfam), 8:2, 80–8.

Clark, Mary (1997) 'Transnational Alliances and Development Policy in Latin America: Nontraditional Export Promotion in Costa Rica', *Latin American Research Review*, 32:2, 71–97.

Clarke, Colin and Howard, David (1999) 'Cities, Capitalism and Neoliberal Regimes' in Gwynne, Robert and Kay, Cristóbal (eds) *Latin America Transformed: Globalisation and Modernity* London: Edward Arnold, 305–24.

Clendinnen, Inga (1995) *Aztecs: An Interpretation* Cambridge: Cambridge University Press.

Coates, Anna (2001) 'Health, Reproduction and Identity: Indigenous Women of Chiapas, Mexico', PhD thesis in preparation, Gender Institute, London School of Economics.

Cobián, Eduardo and Reyes, Sara (1998) *Percepciones Masculinas de las Necesidades y Servicios de Planificación Familiar y Salud Reproductiva: Un Estudio Cualitativo en Chimbote* New York: Population Council, Documentos de Trabajo No.17.

Coe, Gloria and Hanft, Ruth (1993) 'The Use of Technologies in the Health Care of Women: A Review of the Literature' in Gómez Gómez, Elsa (ed) *Gender, Women and Health in the Americas* Washington DC: Pan American Health Organisation, 195–207.

Colaboración Area Legal (1997) 'Pulso Legislativo: Nuevos Proyectos de Ley', *Otra Mirada* (Centro Nacional para el Desarrollo de la Mujer y la Familia, San José), 1:2, 51.

Colectivo Mujer–Es Somos (CMS) (1997) *Saliendo del Closet* (2nd edition) Guatemala City: CMS.

Collier, Jane; Rosaldo, Michelle and Yanagisako, Sylvia (1997) 'Is There a Family? New Anthropological Views' in Lancaster, Roger and di Leonardo, Micaela (eds) *The Gender/Sexuality Reader* New York: Routledge, 71–81.

Comisión Económica para América Latina (CEPAL) (1994) 'El Sector Informal Urbano desde la Perspectiva de Género: El Caso de México'. Paper presented at workshop 'El Sector Informal Urbano desde la Perspectiva de Género', México DF, 28–29 November.

Comisión Económica para América Latina y el Caribe (CEPAL) (1995) *Statistical Yearbook for Latin America and the Caribbean 1994* Santiago de Chile: CEPAL/United Nations.

Comisión Económica para América Latina y el Caribe (CEPAL) (1998) *Social Panorama of Latin America* Santiago de Chile: CEPAL/United Nations.

Comisión Económica para América Latina y el Caribe (CEPAL) (2000) *The Challenge of Gender Equity and Human Rights on the Threshold of the Twenty-First Century*, report to the Eighth Session of the Regional Conference on Women in Latin America and the Caribbean, 8–10 February, Lima.

Comisión Económica para América Latina y el Caribe (CEPAL) (2001), *Panorama Social de América Latina*, Santiago de Chile: CEPAL.

Congreso de la República (1997) *Tipificación del Delito de Discriminación (Propuestas de Ley)* Guatemala City: Congreso de la República.

Consejo Nacional de Población (CONAPO) (1999a) *Situación Demográfica de México, 1999* Mexico DF: CONAPO.

Consejo Nacional de Población (CONAPO) (1999b) *IV Informe de Avances del Programa Nacional de Población 1995–2000* Mexico DF: CONAPO.

Cook, Rebecca (1993) 'International Law and Women's Health' in Gómez Gómez, Elsa (ed) *Gender, Women and Health in the Americas* Washington DC: Pan American Health Organisation, 244–51.

Cooper Tory, Jennifer (1990) 'La Re-estructuración Productiva y el Empleo de la Mujer en México: Lineamientos para su Estudio' in Ramírez Bautista, Elia and Dávila Ibáñez, Hilda (eds) *Trabajo Femenino y Crisis en México* México DF: Universidad Autónoma Metropolitana, Xochimilco, 171–82.

Corcoran-Nantes, Yvonne (1990) 'Women and Popular Urban Social Movements in São Paulo, Brazil', *Bulletin of Latin American Research*, 9:2, 249–64.

Corcoran Nantes, Yvonne (1993) 'Female Consciousness or Feminist Consciousness? Women's Consciousness Raising in Community-Based Struggles in Brazil' in Radcliffe, Sarah and Westwood, Sallie (eds) *'Viva': Women and Popular Protest in Latin America* London: London, 136–55.

Cordera Campos, Rolando and González Tiburcio, Enrique (1991) 'Crisis and Transition in the Mexican Economy' in González de la Rocha, Mercedes and Escobar, Agustín (eds) *Social Responses to Mexico's Crisis of the 1980s* San Diego: Center for US–Mexican Studies, 155–93.

Cornelius, Wayne (1991) '"Los Migrantes de la Crisis": The Changing Profile of Mexicn Migration to the United States' in González de la Rocha, Mercedes and Escobar, Agustín (eds) *Social Responses to Mexico's Crisis of the 1980s* San Diego: Center for US–Mexican Studies, 155–93.

Cornia, Giovanni Andrea (2001) 'Social Funds in Stabilisation and Adjustment Programmes: A Critique', *Development and Change,* 32:1, 1–32.

Cornwall, Andrea (1994) 'Gendered Identities and Gender Ambiguity among Travestis in Salvador, Brazil' in Cornwall, Andrea and Lindisfarne, Nancy (eds) *Dislocating Masculinity: Comparative Ethnographies* London: Routledge, 111–32.

Cornwall, Andrea (1998) 'Beyond Reproduction: Changing Perspectives on Gender and Health', *Bridge Development and Gender In Brief* (Institute of Development Studies, Sussex), 1–2 November.

Cornwall, Andrea (2000) 'Missing Men? Reflections on Men, Masculinities and Gender in GAD', *IDS Bulletin*, 31:2, 18–27.

Cornwall, Andrea and Lindisfarne, Nancy (1994) 'Dislocating Masculinity: Gender, Power and Anthropology' in Cornwall, Andrea and Lindisfarne, Nancy (eds) *Dislocating Masculinity: Comparative Ethnographies* London: Routledge, 1–47.

Cornwall, Andrea and White, Sarah (2000) 'Introduction. Men, Masculinities and Development: Politics, Policies and Practice', *IDS Bulletin*, 31:2, 1–6.

Côrrea, Sonia with Reichmann, Rebecca (1994) *Population and Reproductive Rights: Feminist Perspectives from the South* London: Zed.

Coveney, Lal; Jackson, Margaret; Jeffreys, Sheila; Kay, Leslie and Mahony, Pat (1984) *The Sexuality Papers: Male Sexuality and the Social Control of Women* London: Hutchinson.

Crabtree, John (2000) 'Populisms Old and New: the Peruvian Case', *Bulletin of Latin American Research*, 19:2, 163–76.

Craske (1993) 'Women's Political Participation in Colonias Populares in Guadalajara, Mexico' in Radcliffe, Sarah and Westwood, Sallie (eds) *'Viva': Women and Popular Protest in Latin America* London: 112–35.

Craske, Nikki (1994) *Corporatism Revisited: Salinas and the Reform of the Popular Sector*, Research Paper No. 37, Institute of Latin American Studies, University of London.

Craske, Nikki (1998) 'Remasculinisation and the Neoliberal State in Latin America' in Randall, Vicky and Waylen, Georgina (eds) *Gender, Politics and the State* London: Routledge, 100–20.

Craske, Nikki (1999) *Women and Politics in Latin America* Cambridge: Polity.

Craske, Nikki (2000a) *Continuing the Challenge: The Contemporary Latin American Women's Movement(s)* Liverpool: Research Paper 23, Institute of Latin American Studies, University of Liverpool.

Craske, Nikki (2000b) 'Beyond Rights: Reflections on Motherist Politics in Latin America', Mimeo, Institute of Latin American Studies, University of Liverpool.

Craske, Nikki (forthcoming) 'Gender and Sexuality in Latin America' in Swanson, Philip (ed) *A Companion to Latin American Studies* London: Edward Arnold.

Csörnyei, Claudia and Palumbo, Silvia (1996) 'Las Lunas y Las Otras' in Reinfelder, Monika (ed) *Amazon to Zami: Towards a Global Lesbian Feminism* London: Cassell, 152–60.

Cubitt, Tessa (1995) *Latin American Society* (2nd edition) Harlow: Longman.

Cubitt, Tessa and Greenslade, Helen (1997) 'Public and Private Spheres: The End of Dichotomy' in Dore, Elizabeth (ed) *Gender Politics in Latin America: Debates in Theory and Practice* New York: Monthly Review Press, 52–64.

Curto de Casas, Susana Isabel (1994) 'Health Care in Latin America' in Phillips, David and Verhasselt, Yola (eds) *Health and Development* London: Routledge, 234–48.

Daines, Victoria and Seddon, David (1994) 'Fighting for Survival: Women's Responses to Austerity Programs' in Walton, John and Seddon, David *Free Markets and Food Riots: The Politics of Global Adjustment* Oxford: Blackwell, 57–96.

Darcy de Oliveira, Rosiska (1998) *In Praise of Difference: The Emergence of a Global Feminism* New York: Rutgers University Press.

Datta, Kavita and McIlwaine, Cathy (2000) '"Empowered Leaders"? Perspectives on Women Heading Households in Latin America and Southern Africa', *Gender and Development* (Oxfam), 8:3, 40–9.

Dávila, Luis (2000) 'The Rise and Fall of Populism in Venezuela', *Bulletin of Latin American Research*, 19:2, 223–38.

Dávalos López, Enrique (1998) 'La Sexualidad en los Pueblos Meso–Americanos Prehispánicos. Un Panorama General' in Szasz, Ivonne and Lerner, Susana (eds) *Sexualidades en México: Algunas Aproximaciones desde la Perspectiva de las Ciencias Sociales* México DF: El Colegio de México, 71–106.

Department for International Development (DFID) (2000) *Poverty Elimination and the Empowerment of Women* London: DFID.

Deere, Carmen Diana and León, Magdalena (2001a) *Empowering Women: Land and Property Rights in Latin America* Pittsburgh: University of Pittsburgh Press.

Deere, Carmen Diana and León, Magdalena (2001b) 'Institutional Reform of Agriculture under Neo-liberalism: The Impact of Women's and Indigenous Movements', *Latin American Research Review*, 36:2, 31–64.

Deighton, Jane; Horsely, Rossana; Stewart, Sarah and Cain, Cathy (1983) *Sweet Ramparts: Women in Revolutionary Nicaragua* London: War on Want/Nicaragua Solidarity Campaign.

Deutsch, Sandra McGee (1991) 'Gender and Socio-Political Change in Twentieth Century Latin America', *Hispanic American Historical Review*, 71:2, 251–306.

Diamond, Larry; Hartlyn, Jonathan; Linz, Juan and Lipset, Seymour Martin (eds) (1999) *Democracy in Developing Countries: Latin America* Boulder: Lynne Rienner.

Díaz, Margarita and Rogow, Debbie (1995) 'El Colectivo: Un Colectivo Femenista de Salud y Sexualidad Femenina en Brasil', *Calidad/Quality/Qualité* (Population Council), 6, 1–24.

Diaz-Briquets, Sergio (1989) 'The Central American Demographic Situation: Trends and Implications' in Bean, Frank; Schmandt, Jürgen and Weintraub, Sidney (eds) *Mexican and Central American Population and US Immigration Policy* Austin: University of Texas Press, 33–64.

Dickenson, John; Gould, Bill; Clarke, Colin; Mather, Sandra; Prothero, Mansell; Siddle, David; Smith, Clifford and Thomas-Hope, Elizabeth (1996) *A Geography of the Third World*, 2nd edn London: Routledge.

Dietz, Mary (1998) 'Context Is All: Feminism and Theories of Citizenship' in Phillips, Anne (ed) *Feminism and Politics* Oxford: Oxford University Press, 378–400.

Dierckxsens, Wim (1992) 'Impacto del Ajuste Estructural Sobre la Mujer Trabajadora en Costa Rica' in Acuña-Ortega, Marvin (ed) *Cuadernos de Política Económica* Heredia: Universidad Nacional de Costa Rica, 2–59.

Dobles Oropeza, Ignacio (1998) 'Algunos Elementos Sobre la Violencia en la Familia en Costa Rica: Un Estudio Nacional en Sectores Urbanos' in Rodríguez, Eugenia (ed) *Violencia Doméstica en Costa Rica: Mas Allá de los Mitos* San José: FLACSO Sede Costa Rica, Cuaderno de Ciencias Sociales 105, 31–52.

Dore, Elizabeth (1997) 'The Holy Family: Imagined Households in Latin American History' in Dore, Elizabeth (ed) *Gender Politics in Latin America: Debates in Theory and Practice* New York: Monthly Review Press, 101–17.

Dória Bilac, Elizabete (1995) 'Gender, Family and International Migrations', *IOM Latin American Migration Journal*, 13:1, 3–20.

Draibe, Sonia Miriam and Arretche, Marta Teresa (1995) 'Involving Civil Society: Brazil' in Raczynski, Dagmar (ed) *Strategies to Combat Poverty in Latin America* Washington, DC; IADB/CIEPLAN, 87–143.

Dresser, Denise (1991) *Neopopulist Solutions to Neoliberal Problems: Mexico's National Solidarity Programme* San Diego: Center for US–Mexican Studies, University of California.

Drogus, Carol Ann (1997) 'Private Power or Public Power: Pentecostalism, Base Communities, and Gender' in Cleary, Edward and Stewart-Gambino, Hannah (eds) *Power, Politics and Pentecostals in Latin America* Boulder: Westview, 55–75.

Dunkerley, James (1993) *The Pacification of Central America: Political Change in the Isthmus, 1987–1993* London: Verso.

Durand, Jorge; Kandel, William; Parrado, Emilio and Massey, Douglas (1996) 'International Migration and Development in Mexican Communities', *Demography*, 33:2, 249–64.

Durand, Jorge and Massey, Douglas (1992) 'Mexican Migration to the United States: A Critical View', *Latin American Research Review*, 27:2, 3–42.

Durand Jorge; Massey, Douglas and Zenteno, René (2001) 'Mexican Immigration to the United States: Continuity and Change', *Latin American Research Review*, 35:1, 107–27.

Durham, Eunice (1991) 'Family and Human Reproduction' in Jelin, Elizabeth (ed) *Family, Household and Gender Relations in Latin America* London/Paris: Kegan Paul International/UNESCO, 40–63.

Dwyer, Augusta (1994) *On the Line: Life on the US–Mexico Border* London: Latin America Bureau.

Ehrenfeld Lenkiewicz, Noemí (1989) 'El Ser Mujer: Identidad, Sexualidad y Reproducción' in de Oliveira, Orlandina (ed) *Trabajo, Poder y Sexualidad* México DF: El Colegio de México, 383–97.

Ekblad, Solvig (1993) 'Stressful Environments and their Effects on the Quality of Life in Third World Cities', *Environment and Urbanisation*, 5:2, 125–34.

El-Bushra, Judy (2000) 'Rethinking Gender and Development Practice for the Twenty-first Century' in Sweetman, Caroline (ed) *Gender in the 21st Century* Oxford: Oxfam, 55–62.

Elmendorf, Mary (1977) 'Mexico: The Many Worlds of Women' in Giele, Janet Zollinger and Smock, Audrey Chapman (eds) *Women: Roles and Status in Eight Countries* New York: John Wiley, 127–72.

Elshtain, Jean, B. (1998) 'Antigone's Daughters' in Phillips, Anne (ed) *Feminism and Politics* Oxford: Oxford University Press, 363–77.

Elson, Diane (1998) 'Talking to the Boys: Gender and Economic Growth Models' in Jackson, Cecile and Pearson, Ruth (eds) *Feminist Visions of Development* London: Routledge, 155–70.

Elson, Diane (1999) 'Labour Markets as Gendered Institutions: Equality, Efficiency and Empowerment Issues', *World Development*, 27:3, 611–27.

Elson, Diane (ed) (1991) *Male Bias in the Development Process* Manchester: Manchester University Press.

Elson, Diane and Çağatay, Nilufer (2000) 'The Social Content of Macroeconomic Policies', *World Development,* 28:7, 1347–64.

Elson, Diane; Fauné, María Angélica; Gideon, Jasmine; Gutiérrez, Maribel; López de Mazier, Armida and Sacayón, Eduardo (1997) *Crecer con la Mujer: Oportunidades para el Desarrollo Ecónomico Centroamericano* San José: Embajada Real de los Países Bajos.

Elson, Diane and Gideon, Jasmine (1997a) 'Análisis de Género de la Economía de Nicaragua' in Elson, Diane; Fauné, María Angélica; Gideon, Jasmine; Gutiérrez, Maribel; López de Mazier, Armida and Sacayón, Eduardo *Crecer con la Mujer: Oportunidades para el Desarrollo Ecónomico Centroamericano* San José: Embajada Real de los Países Bajos, 253–306.

Elson, Diane and Gideon, Jasmine (1997b) 'Preocupaciones de Género y Cuestiones Económicas. Las Economías Centromericanas como Estructuras de Género: Un Estudio Comparativo' in Elson, Diane; Fauné, María Angélica; Gideon, Jasmine; Gutiérrez, Maribel; López de Mazier, Armida and Sacayón, Eduardo *Crecer con la Mujer: Oportunidades para el Desarrollo Ecónomico Centroamericano* San José: Embajada Real de los Países Bajos, 307–38.

Elson, Diane and Pearson, Ruth (1981) 'Nimble Fingers Make Cheap Workers', *Feminist Review*, 7, 87–107.

Engle, Patrice L. (1995) 'Father's Money, Mother's Money, and Parental Commitment: Guatemala and

Nicaragua' in Blumberg, Rae Lesser; Rakowski, Cathy; Tinker, Irene and Monteón, Michael (eds) *Engendering Wealth and Well-Being: Empowerment for Global Change* Boulder: Westview, 155–79.
Engle, Patrice L. (1997) 'The Role of Men in Families: Achieving Gender Equity and Supporting Children' in Sweetman, Caroline (ed) *Men and Masculinity* Oxford: Oxfam, 31–40.
Engle, Patrice L. and Alatorre Rico, Javier (1994) *Taller Sobre Paternidad Responsable* New York/Washington DC : Population Council/International Center for Research on Women.
Engle, Patrice and Breaux, Cynthia (1994) *Is There a Father Instinct? Fathers' Responsibility for Children* Washington/New York: International Center for Research on Women/The Population Council.
Ennew, Judith, (1986) 'Mujercita and Mamacita: Girls Growing Up in Lima', *Bulletin of Latin American Research*, 5:2, 49–66.
Epstein, Edward (2000) 'Changing Latin American Labour Relations amidst Economic and Political Liberalisation', *Latin American Research Review*, 35:1, 208–18.
Escobar Latapí, Agustín (1998) 'Los Hombres y Sus Historias: Reestructuración y Masculinidad en México', *La Ventana* (Universidad de Guadalajara), 122–73.
Escobar Latapí, Agustín (2000a) 'Low-skill Emigration from Mexico: Current Situation, Prospects and Methodological Controversies' in Kimura, Michio and Hayase, Yasuko (compilers) *Proceedings of the International Workshop on International Migration and Human Resources Development in the APEC Member Economies* Tokyo: Institute of Developing Economies, JETRO, 317–54.
Escobar Latapí, Agustín (2000b) 'El Mercado de Trabajo de Guadalajara: Clase, Género y Edad, 1987–1996' in Instituto Tecnológico de Estudios Superiores de Occidente (ITESO) *Jalisco Diagnóstico y Prospectiva (Sociedad, Política y Economía)* México DF: ITESO.
Escobar Latapí, Agustín (2000c) 'Employment Trends in Mexico: Reversing a 15-year Loss?' Mimeo. Guadalajara: Centro de Investigaciones y de Estudios Superiores en Antropología Social.
Escobar Latapí, Agustín; Bean, Frank and Weintraub, Sidney (1999) *La Dinámica de la Emigración Mexicana* México DF: Centro de Investigaciones y Estudios Superiores en Antropología Social/Editorial Miguel Angel Porrúa.
Escobar Latapí, Agustín and González de la Rocha, Mercedes (1995) 'Crisis, Restructuring and Urban Poverty in Mexico', *Environment and Urbanisation*, 7:1, 57–76.
Escobar Latapí, Agustín; González de la Rocha, Mercedes and Roberts, Bryan (1987) 'Migration, Labour Markets, and the International Economy' in Eades, Jeremy (ed) *Migrants, Workers, and the Social Order* London: Tavistock, 42–64.
Espada Calpe, José María (2001) 'Políticas Sexuales: Cambios y Permanencias en la Sexualidad y la Afectividad en España'. Paper for Postgraduate Seminar 'Introdction to Masculinities and Feminism', Sociology IV, Universidad Complutense de Madrid.
Esquivel, Gerardo; Larraín, Felipe and Sachs, Jeffrey (2001) 'Central America's Foreign Debt Burden and the HIPC Initiative', *Bulletin of Latin American Research*, 20:1, 1–28.
Ewig, Christina (1999) 'The Strengths and Limits of the NGO Women's Movement Model: Shaping Nicaragua's Democratic Institutions', *Latin American Research Review*, 34:3, 75–102.
Fachel Leal, Ondina and Fachel, Jandrya (1998) 'Aborto: Tensión y Negociación entre lo Femenino y lo Masculino' in Lerner, Susana (ed) *Varones, Sexualidad y Reproducción* México DF: El Colegio de México, 308–18.
Falabella, Gonzalo (1997) 'New Masculinity: A Different Route', *Gender and Development* (Oxfam) 5:2, 62–4.
Faulkner, Anne and Lawson, Victoria (1991) 'Employment versus Empowerment: A Case Study of the Nature of Women's Work in Ecuador', *Journal of Development Studies*, 27:4, 16–47.
Fauné, María Angélica (1997) 'Costa Rica: Las Inequidades de Género en el Marco de la Apertura Comercial y la Reestructuración Productiva: Análsis a Nivel Macro, Meso, Micro' in Elson, Diane; Fauné, María Angélica; Gideon, Jasmine; Gutiérrez, Maribel; López de Mazier, Armida and Sacayón, Eduardo (1997) *Crecer con la Mujer: Oportunidades para el Desarrollo Ecónomico Centroamericano* San José: Embajada Real de los Países Bajos, 51–126.
Feijoó, María del Carmen (1999) 'De Pobres Mujeres a Mujeres Pobres' in González de la Rocha, Mercedes (ed) *Divergencias del Modelo Tradicional: Hogares de Jefatura Femenina en América Latina* México DF: Centro de Investigaciones y Estudios Superiores en Antropología Social, 155–62.
Feijoó, María del Carmen (2001) *Nuevo País, Nuevo Pobreza* Buenos Aires: Fondo de Cultura Económica.
Feijoó, María del Carmen and Gogna, Monica (1990) 'Women in the Transition to Democracy' in Jelin, Elizabeth (ed) *Women and Social Change in Latin America* London: Zed, 79–114.
Feijoó, María del Carmen with Nari, Marcela María Alejandra (1994) 'Women and Democracy in Argentina' in Jaquette, Jane (ed) *The Women's Movement in Latin America: Participation and Democracy* Boulder: Westview, 109–29.
Ferguson, Bruce and Maurer, Cresencia (1996) 'Urban Management and Environmental Quality in South America', *Third World Planning Review*, 18:2, 117–54.

Fernández, Oscar (1992) 'Qué Valores Valen Hoy en Costa Rica?' in Villasuso, Juan Manuel (ed) *El Nuevo Rostro de Costa Rica* Heredia: Centro de Estudios Democráticos de América Latina.

Fernández-Kelly, María Patricia (1983) 'Mexican Border Industrialisation, Female Labour Force Participation and Migration' in Nash, June and Fernández-Kelly, María Patricia (eds) *Women, Men and the International Division of Labour* Albany: State University of New York Press, 205–23.

Fernández-Kelly, María Patricia and Sassen, Saskia (1995) 'Recasting Women in the Global Economy: Internationalisation and Changing Definitions of Gender' in Bose, Christine and Acosta–Belén, Edna (eds) *Women in the Latin American Development Process* Philadelphia: Temple University Press, 95–124.

Figueroa, Juan Guillermo (1998a) 'Algunos Elementos para Interpretar la Presencia de los Varones en los Procesos de Salud Reproductiva', *Revista de Cadernos de Saúde Pública* (Ministério de Saúde, Sáo Paulo), 14:1, 87–96.

Figueroa, Juan Guillermo (1998b) 'Fecundidad, Anticoncepción y Derechos Reproductivos' in García, Brígida (ed) *Mujer, Género y Población en México* Mexico DF: El Colegio de México/Sociedad Mexicana de Demografía, 61–102.

Figueroa, Juan Guillermo (1999) 'Derechos Reproductivos y el Espacio de las Instituciones de Salud: Algunos Apuntes sobre la Experiencia Mexicana' in Ortiz-Ortega, Adriana (ed) *Derechos Reproductivos de las Mujeres: Debates sobre Justicia Social en México* México DF: Universidad Autónoma Metropolitana, Unidad Xochimilco/EDAMEX, 147–90.

Figueroa, Juan Guillermo and Rivera, Gabriela (1993) 'Algunas Reflexiones sobre la Representación Social de la Sexualidad Femenina' in González Montes, Soledad (ed) *Mujeres y Relaciones de Género en la Antropología Latinoamericana* México DF: El Colegio de México, 141–67.

Fisher, Jo (1993) *Out of the Shadows: Women, Resistance and Politics in South America* London: Latin American Bureau.

Folbre, Nancy (1991) 'Women on their Own: Global Patterns of Female Headship' in Gallin, Rita S. and Ferguson, Ann (eds) *The Women and International Development Annual Vol. 2* Boulder: Westview, 69–126.

Folch-Lynn, Evelyn; Macorra, Luis and Schearer, Bruce (1981) 'Focus Group and Survey Research on Family Planning in Mexico', *Studies in Family Planning*, 12:12, 409–32.

Fonseca, Claudia (1991) 'Spouses, Siblings and Sex-linked Bonding: A Look at Kinship Organisation in a Brazilian Slum' in Jelin, Elizabeth (ed) *Family, Household and Gender Relations in Latin America* London: Kegan Paul International/Paris: UNESCO, 133–60.

Foote, Nicola (2001) 'Rethinking Race, Gender and Citizenship: Black West Indian Women in Costa Rica, *c.* 1920–1940'. Paper prepared for symposium 'Citizenship, Community and the State', Annual Conference of the Society for Latin American Studies, University of Birmingham, 6–8 April.

Foreman, Martin (1999) *AIDS and Men: Taking Risks or Taking Responsibility* London: Panos.

Forrest, David (1999) 'Sex, Lenin and the Pinguero: Maleness and Scarcity in Socialist Cuba', Gender Institute Seminar 'Masculinities in Question', London School of Economics, 10 February.

Forsythe, Nancy; Korzeniewicz, Roberto Patricio and Durrant, Valerie (2000) 'Gender Inequalities, Economic Growth and Structural Adjustment: A Longitudinal Evaluation', *Economic Development and Cultural Change*, 48:3, 573–618.

Foucault, Michel (1973) *The Birth of the Clinic* London: Tavistock.

Foucault, Michel (1978) *The History of Western Sexuality*, Vol.1 Harmondsworth: Penguin.

Foweraker, Joe (1989) 'Popular Movements and the Transformation of the System' in Cornelius, Wayne; Gentleman, Judith and Smith, Peter (eds) *Mexico's Alternative Political Futures*, San Diego: Center for US–Mexican Studies, University of California, 109–30.

Foweraker, Joe (1999) 'Grassroots Movements, Political Activism and Social Development: A Comparison of Chile and Brazil', Mimeo, UNRISD, Geneva.

Foweraker, Joe and Landman, Todd (1997) *Citizenship Rights and Social Movements: A Comparative and Statistical Analysis* Cambridge: Cambridge University Press.

Fraga, Juan Carlos Alfonso and Alvarez Suárez, Magda (1998) 'Rol Masculino y Disminución de la Fecundidad: El Caso Cubano' in Lerner, Susana (ed) *Varones, Sexualidad y Reproducción* México DF: El Colegio de México, 369–90.

Franco, Jean (1998) 'Defrocking the Vatican: Feminism's Secular Project', in Alvarez, Sonia; Dagnino, Evelina and Escobar, Arturo (eds) *Cultures of Politics, Politics of Cultures: Re-visioning Latin American Social Movements* Boulder: Westview, 277–89.

Franco, Jean (2001) 'Bodies in Contention', *NACLA: Report on the Americas,* XXXIV: 5, 41–4.

Freeman, Michael (1995) 'Are There Collective Human Rights?', *Political Studies*, XLIII, 25–40.

Freston, Paul (1997) 'Charismatic Evangelicals in Latin America: Mission and Politics on the Frontiers of Protestant Growth' in Hunt, Stephen; Hamilton, Malcolm and Walter, Tony (eds) *Charismatic Christianity: Sociological Perspectives* Houndmills, Basingstoke: Macmillan, 184–204.

Frey, William (2000) 'US Immigration Country Report' in Kimura, Michio and Hayase, Yasuko (compilers) *Proceedings of the International Workshop on International Migration and Human Resources Development in the APEC Member Economies* Tokyo: Institute of Developing Economies, JETRO, 61–77.

Frías, Patricio, Ruiz-Tagle, Jaime (1995) 'Free Market Economics and Belated Democratisation: The Case of Chile' in Thomas, Henk (ed) *Globalisation and Third World Trade Unions* London: Zed, 130–48.

Friedemann, Nina S. de and Arocha, Jaime (1995) 'Colombia' in Minority Rights Group (ed) *No Longer Invsible: Afro-Latin Americans Today* London: Minority Rights Publications, 47–76.

Friedman, Elisabeth Jay (2002) 'Getting Rights for Those Without Representation: The Success of Conjunctural Coalition-Building in Venezuela' in Craske, Nikki and Molyneux, Maxine (eds) *Gender and the Politics of Rights and Democracy in Latin America* Basingstoke: Palgrave, 57–78.

Fröbel, Folker; Heinrichs, Jürgen and Kreye, Otto (1980) *The New International Division of Labour* Cambridge: Cambridge University Press.

Fukuda-Parr, Sakiko (1999) 'What Does Feminisation of Poverty Mean? It Isn't Just Lack of Income', *Feminist Economics*, 5:2, 99–103.

Fuller, Norma (2000) 'Work and Masculinity Among Peruvian Urban Men', *European Journal of Development Research*, 12:2, 93–114.

Funkhouser, Edward (1996) 'The Urban Informal Sector in Central America: Household Survey Evidence', *World Development*, 24:11, 1737–51.

Furedy, Frank (1997) *Population and Development* Cambridge: Polity.

Fuskova-Kornreich, Ilse and Argov, Dafna (1993) 'Lesbian Activism in Argentina: A Recent but Very Powerful Phenomenon' in Hendriks, Aart; Tielman, Rob and van der Veen, Evert (eds) *The Third Pink Book: A Global View of Lesbian and Gay Liberation and Oppression* New York: Prometheus Books, 80–5.

Fuwa, Nobuhiko (2000) 'The Poverty and Heterogeneity Among Female-headed Households Revisited: The Case of Panama', *World Development*, 28:8, 1515–42.

Gafar, John (1998), 'Growth, Inequality and Poverty in Selected Caribbean and Latin American Countries, with Emphasis on Guyana', *Journal of Latin American Studies*, 30:3, 591–617.

Gaio, Janine (1997) 'Women in Software Programming: The Experience of Brazil' in Mitter, Swasti and Rowbotham, Sheila (eds) *Women Encounter Technology: Changing Patterns of Employment in the Third World* London: Routledge, 205–32.

García, Brígida and de Oliveira, Orlandina (1997) 'Motherhood and Extradomestic Work in Urban Mexico', *Bulletin of Latin American Research*, 16:3, 367–84.

García, Brígida and de Oliveira, Orlandina (2000) 'Transformaciones Recientes en los Mercados de Trabajo Metropolitanos de México: 1990–1998'. Mimeo. México DF: El Colegio de México.

Garduno-Rivera, Rafael (2000) Factors that Influence Women's Economic Participation in Mexico. Unpublished dissertation, MSc in Local Economic Development, London School of Economics.

Geldstein, Rosa (1994) 'Working Class Mothers as Economic Providers and Heads of Families in Buenos Aires', *Reproductive Health Matters*, 4, 55–64.

Geldstein, Rosa (1997) *Mujeres Jefas de Hogar: Familia, Pobreza y Género* Buenos Aires: UNICEF–Argentina.

Ghosh, Bimal (1997) 'Migration and Development: Some Selected Issues', *IOM Latin American Migration Journal*, 15:1/3 (www.oim.web.cl).

Giddens, Anthony (1992) *The Transformation of Intimacy: Sexuality, Love and Eroticism in Modern Societies* Cambridge: Polity.

Gideon, Jasmine (1998) 'The Politics of Social Service Provision through NGOs: A Study of Latin America', *Bulletin of Latin American Research*, 17:3, 303–21.

Gideon, Jasmine (2000) 'Gender and Participation in Chile: The Case of Primary Health Care Delivery'. Paper presented at the session 'Politics and Policy in Latin America: Does Gender Still Matter?', Annual Conference of the Society for Latin American Studies, University of Hull, 14–16 April.

Gideon, Jasmine (2002) 'Economic and Social Rights: Exploring Gender Differences in a Central American Context' in Craske, Nikki and Molyneux, Maxine (eds) *Gender and the Politics of Rights and Democracy in Latin America* Basingstoke: Palgrave, 173–98.

Gilbert, Alan (1990) *Latin America* London: Routledge.

Gilbert, Alan (1995a) 'Debt, Poverty and the Latin American City', *Geography*, 80:4, 323–33.

Gilbert, Alan (1995b) 'Globalisation, Employment and Poverty: The Case of Bogotá, Colombia'. Seminar, Geography and Planning Research Series, London School of Economics, 30 November.

Gilbert, Alan (1998) *The Latin American City*, 2nd edition, London: Latin America Bureau.

Gilbert, Alan and Gugler, Josef (1992) *Cities, Poverty and Development: Urbanisation in the Third World* Oxford: Oxford University Press.

Gindling, T.H. (1993) 'Women's Wages and Economic Crisis in Costa Rica', *Economic Development and Cultural Change*, 41:2, 277–97.

Gledhill, John (1995) *Neoliberalism, Transnationalisation and Rural Poverty: A Case Study of Michoacán* Boulder: Westview.

Gledhill, John (1997a) 'The Challenge of Globalisation: Reconstruction of Identities, Transnational

Forms of Life and the Social Sciences'. English translation of keynote address to the XIX Coloquio de Antropología e Historia Regionales 'Fronteras Fragmentadas: Género, Familia e Identidades en la Migración Mexicana al Norte', El Colegio de Michoacán, Zamora, 22 October.

Gledhill, John (1997b) 'The Mexican Contribution to Restructuring US Capitalism: NAFTA as an Instrument of Flexible Accumulation'. Paper presented at the session 'Critique-ing Flexible Labor: Increasing Inequality, Fragmentation and the Possibility for Labor Mobilisation' (American Ethnological Society), 96th Annual Meeting of the American Anthropological Association, Washington DC, 23 November.

Gledhill, John (2000) 'Disappearing the Poor? A Critique of the New Wisdoms of Social Democracy in an Age of Globalisation'. Paper presented to Invited Session 'Global Capitalism, Neoliberal Policy and Poverty' (Society for the Anthropology of North America, Association of Latina and Latino Anthropologists), 99th Annual Meeting of the American Anthropological Association, San Francisco, 16 November.

Gomáriz, Enrique (1997) *Introducción a los Estudios Sobre la Masculinidad* San José: Centro Nacional para el Desarrollo de la Mujer y Familia.

Gomes, Eustáquio (1994) 'Choice or Authorised Crime? An Epidemic of Caesareans and Sterilisations in Brazil' in Panos (ed) *Private Decisions, Public Debate: Women, Reproduction and Population* London: Panos, 69–80.

Gómez-Dantes, Octavio (2000) 'Health Reforms and Policies for the Poor in Mexico', in Lloyd-Sherlock, Peter (ed) *Healthcare Reform and Poverty in Latin America* London: Institute of Latin American Studies, 129–42.

Gómez Gómez, Elsa (1993a) 'Introduction' in Gómez Gómez, Elsa (ed) *Gender, Women and Health in the Americas* Washington DC: Pan American Health Organisation, ix–xix.

Gómez Gómez, Elsa (1993b) 'Sex Discrimination and Excess Female Mortality in Childhood' in Gómez Gómez, Elsa (ed) *Gender, Women and Health in the Americas* Washington DC: Pan American Health Organisation, 25–42.

González de la Rocha, Mercedes (1988) 'Economic Crisis, Domestic Reorganisation and Women's Work in Guadalajara, Mexico', *Bulletin of Latin American Research,* 7:2, 207–23.

González de la Rocha, Mercedes (1991) 'Family Well-being, Food Consumption and Survival Strategies during Mexico's Economic Crisis' in González de la Rocha, Mercedes and Escobar, Agustín (eds) *Social Responses to Mexico's Economic Crisis of the 1980s* San Diego: Center for US Mexican Studies, Contemporary Perspectives Series No.1, 115–27.

González de la Rocha, Mercedes (1994) *The Resources of Poverty: Women and Survival in a Mexican City* Oxford: Blackwell.

González de la Rocha, Mercedes (1995) 'Social Restructuring in Two Mexican Cities: An Analysis of Domestic Groups in Guadalajara and Monterrey', *European Journal of Development Research*, 7:2, 389–406.

González de la Rocha, Mercedes (1997) 'The Erosion of the Survival Model: Urban Responses to Persistent Poverty'. Paper prepared for the UNRISD/UNDP/CDS Workshop 'Gender, Poverty and Well-Being: Indicators and Strategies', Trivandrum, Kerala, 24–27 November.

González de la Rocha, Mercedes (1999a) 'A Manera de Introducción: Cambio Social, Transformación de la Familia y Divergencias del Modelo Tradicional' in González de la Rocha, Mercedes (ed) *Divergencias del Modelo Tradicional: Hogares de Jefatura Femenina en América Latina* México DF: Centro de Investigaciones y Estudios Superiores en Antropología Social, 19–36.

González de la Rocha, Mercedes (1999b) 'Hogares de Jefatura Femenina en México: Patrones y Formas de Vida' in González de la Rocha, Mercedes (ed) *Divergencias del Modelo Tradicional: Hogares de Jefatura Femenina en América Latina* México DF: Centro de Investigaciones y Estudios Superiores en Antropología Social, 125–53.

González de la Rocha, Mercedes (2000) *Private Adjustments: Household Responses to the Erosion of Work* New York: Social Development and Poverty Elimination Division, United Nations Development Programme.

González de la Rocha, Mercedes (2001) 'Guatemala and Uruguay' in Grinspun, Alejandro (ed) *Choices for the Poor: Lessons from National Poverty Strategies* New York: UNDP, 289–301.

González de la Rocha, Mercedes and Escobar, Agustín (1990) 'La Ley y la Migración Internacional: El Impacto de la 'Simpson-Rodino' en una Comunidad en los Altos de Jalisco', *Estudios Sociológicos*, 7, 517–46.

González de la Rocha, Mercedes; Escobar, Agustín and Martínez Castellanos, María de la O. (1990) 'Estrategias versus Conflictos: Reflexiones para el Estudio del Grupo Doméstico en Epoca del Crisis' in de la Peña, Guillermo; Durán, Juan Manuel; Escobar, Agustín and García de Alba, Javier (eds) *Crisis, Conflicto y Sobrevivencia: Estudios Sobre la Sociedad Urbana en México* Guadalajara: Universidad de Guadalajara/CIESAS, 351–67.

Gott, Richard (2000) *In the Shadow of the Liberator* London: Verso.

Grabowski, Richard and Shields, Michael (1996) *Development Economics* Oxford: Blackwell.

Grau, Patricia; Matamala, María Isabel; Meyer, Ruth and Vega, Adriana (1991) *La Salud de las Mujeres Trabajadoras de la Salud* Santiago: GICAMS, Area Salud de la Mujer.

Green, Duncan (1991) *Faces of Latin America* London: Latin America Bureau.

Green, Duncan (1995) *Silent Revolution: The Rise of Market Economics in Latin America* London: Cassell in association with Latin America Bureau.

Green, Duncan (1996) 'Latin America: Neoliberal Failure and the Search for Alternatives', *Third World Quarterly*, 17:1, 109–22.

Green, James, N. (1999) *Beyond Carnival: Male Homosexuality in Twentieth Century Brazil* Chicago: University of Chicago Press.

Greenberg, David (1997) 'Transformations of Homosexuality-based Classifications' in Lancaster, Roger and di Leonardo, Michaela (eds) *The Gender Sexuality Reader* London: Routledge, 179–93.

Gregorio Gil, Carmen (1998) *Migración Femenina: Su Impacto en las Relaciones de Género* Madrid: Editorial NARCEA.

Grosh, Margaret (1994) *Administering Targeted Social Programs in Latin America: From Platitudes to Practice* Washington DC: World Bank.

Grosz, Elizabeth (1994) *Volatile Bodies: Towards a Corporeal Feminism* Indiana: Bloomington University Press.

Grupo Agenda Política de Mujeres Costarricenses (1997) *Agenda Política de Mujeres Costarricenses* San José: Grupo Agenda Política de Mujeres Costarricenses.

Gudmundson, Lowell (1986) *Costa Rica Before Coffee: Society and Economy on the Eve of the Export Boom* Baton Rouge: Louisiana State University Press.

Güendel, Ludwig and González, Mauricio (1998) 'Integration, Human Rights and Social Policy in the Context of Human Poverty' in UNICEF (ed) *Adolescence, Child Rights and Urban Poverty in Costa Rica* San José: UNICEF/HABITAT: San José, 17–31.

Gueri, Miguel; Patterson, Adeline W. and González-Cossio, Teresa (1993) 'Women and Nutrition in the Americas: Problems and Perspectives' in Gómez Gómez, Elsa (ed) *Gender, Women and Health in the Americas* Washington DC: Pan American Health Organisation, 118–30.

Gutiérrez Castillo, Maribel (1997) 'Aspectos de Género de la Economía de El Salvador' in Elson, Diane; Fauné, María Angélica; Gideon, Jasmine; Gutiérrez, Maribel; López de Mazier, Armida and Sacayón, Eduardo *Crecer con la Mujer: Oportunidades para el Desarrollo Ecónomico Centroamericano* San José: Embajada Real de los Países Bajos, 127–71.

Gutmann, Matthew (1996) *The Meanings of Macho: Being a Man in Mexico City* Berkeley: University of California Press.

Gutmann, Matthew (1997) 'The Ethnographic (G)Ambit: Women and the Negotiation of Masculinity in Mexico City', *American Ethnologist*, 24:4, 833–55.

Gutmann, Matthew (1999) 'A Manera de Conclusión: Solteras y Hombres. Cambio e Historia' in González de la Rocha, Mercedes (ed) *Divergencias del Modelo Tradicional: Hogares de Jefatura Femenina en América Latina* México DF: Centro de Investigaciones y Estudios Superiores en Antropología Social, 163–72.

Gutmann, Matthew (forthcoming) 'Dystopian Travels in Gringolandia: Engendering Ethnicity among Mexican Migrants to the US', *Ethnic and Racial Studies*.

Guyer, Jane and Peters, Pauline (1987) 'Introduction', *Development and Change*, 18 (Special issue on 'Conceptualising the Household: Issues of Theory and Policy in Africa'), 197–214.

Gywnne, Robert (1999) 'Globalisation, Neoliberalism and Economic Change in South America and Mexico' in Gwynne, Robert and Kay, Cristóbal (eds) *Latin America Transformed: Globalisation and Modernity* London: Edward Arnold, 68–97.

Gywnne, Robert and Kay, Cristóbal (2000) 'Views From the Periphery: Futures of Neoliberalism in Latin America', *Third World Quarterly*, 21:1, 141–56.

Hamilton, Sarah (1998) *The Two-headed Household: Gender and Rural Development in the Ecuadorian Andes* Pittsburgh: University of Pittsburgh Press.

Haraway, Donna (1989) 'Situated Knowledges: The Science Question and the Privilege of Partial Perspective' *Feminist Studies*, 14, 575–99.

Hardon, Anita (1997a) 'Reproductive Rights in Practice' in Hardon, Anita and Hayes, Elizabeth (eds) *Reproductive Rights in Practice: A Feminist Report on the Quality of Care* London: Zed, 3–14.

Hardon, Anita (1997b) 'A Review of National Family Planning Policies' in Hardon, Anita and Hayes, Elizabeth (eds) *Reproductive Rights in Practice: A Feminist Report on the Quality of Care* London: Zed, 15–21.

Hardon, Anita (1997c) 'Setting the Stage: Health, Fertility and Unmet Need in Eight Countries' in Hardon, Anita and Hayes, Elizabeth (eds) *Reproductive Rights in Practice: A Feminist Report on the Quality of Care* London: Zed, 22–9.

Harris, Olivia (1981) 'Households as Natural Units' in Young, Kate; Wolkowitz, Carol and McCullagh, Roslyn (eds) *Of Marriage and the Market* London: CSE Books, 48–67.

Harris, Olivia (1982) 'Latin American Women: An Overview' in Harris, Olivia (ed) *Latin American Women* London: Minority Rights Group, 4–8.

Harrison, Margaret (1991) 'Mexico City: The Supply of a Primary Health Care Service', *Bulletin of Latin American Research*, 10:2, 329–58.

Hart, Gillian (1997) 'From "Rotten Wives" to "Good Mothers": Household Models and the Limits of Economism', *IDS Bulletin*, 28:3, 14–25.

Hartmann, Betsy (1997) 'Population Control in the New World Order' in Hill, Eleanor (ed), *Development for Health* Oxford: Oxfam, Development in Practice Reader, 80–5.

Harvey, Penelope (1994) 'Domestic Violence in the Peruvian Andes' in Harvey, Penelope and Gow, Peter (eds) *Sex and Violence: Issues in Representation and Experience* London: Routledge, 66–89.

Harvey, Penelope and Gow, Peter (eds) (1994) *Sex and Violence: Issues in Representation and Experience* London: Routledge.

Hattaya, Noriko (1992) 'Urban–Rural Linkage of the Labour Market in the Coffee Growing Zone in Colombia', *The Developing Economies*, 30:1, 63–83.

Heise, Lori L. (1997) 'Violence, Sexuality and Women's Lives' in Lancaster, Roger and di Leonardo, Michaela (eds) *The Gender/Sexuality Reader* New York: Routledge, 411–33.

Heise, Lori L. with Pitanguy, Jacqueline and Germain, Adrienne (1994) *Violence Against Women: The Hidden Health Burden* Washington DC: World Bank, Discussion Paper 255.

Helwege, Ann (2000) 'Growth and Poverty in Latin America', *New Economy*, 7:4, 194–8.

Henthorne, Stephanie (2000) 'Masculinities and Gender in Nicaragua: GAD Agenda Benders, or Men Behaving Nicely?' Unpublished dissertation, MA Social Anthropology of Development, School of Oriental and African Studies, University of London.

Henriques Mueller, María Helena and Yunes, João (1993) 'Adolescence: Misunderstandings and Hopes' in Gómez Gómez, Elsa (ed) *Gender, Women and Health in the Americas* Washington DC: Pan American Health Organisation, 43–61.

Hernández, Teresita and Campanile, Verónica (2000) 'Feminism at Work. A Case Study of Transforming Power Relations in Everyday Life: Puntos de Encuentro' in Royal Tropical Institute *Institutionalising Gender Equality: Commitment, Policy and Practice, A Global Source Book* Amsterdam/Oxford: KIT Publishers/Oxfam, 53–66.

Hernández Espinosa, Guadalupe (2000) 'No Mother's Day For Women Workers: Sex Discrimination in Mexico' in Mirsky, Judith and Radlett, Marty (eds) *No Paradise Yet: The World's Women Face the New Century* London: Panos/Zed, 213–32.

Hochschild, Arlie Russell (2000) 'Global Care Chains and Emotional Surplus Value' in Hutton, Will and Giddens, Anthony (eds) *On the Edge: Living with Global Capitalism* London: Jonathan Cape, 130–46.

Hocquenghem, Anne Marie (1987) *Iconografía Mochica* Lima: Pontificia Universidad Católica del Perú/Fondo Editorial.

Hodge, G. Derrick (2001) 'Colonisation of the Cuban Body: The Growth of Male Sex Work in Havana', *NACLA: Report on the Americas*, 34: 5, 20–8.

Hola, Eugenia and Portugal, Ana María (eds) (1997) *La Ciudadanía a Debate* Ediciones de las Mujeres No. 25, Santiago de Chile: ISIS.

Hollander, Nancy Caro (1996) 'The Gendering of Human Rights: Women and the Latin American Terrorist State', *Feminist Studies*, 22:1, 41–80.

Homedes, Nuria; Paz-Narváez, Ana Carolina; Selva-Sutter, Ernesto; Solas, Olga and Ugalde, Antonio (2000) 'Health Reforms: Theory and Practice in El Salvador', in Lloyd-Sherlock, Peter (ed) *Healthcare Reform and Poverty in Latin America* London: Institute of Latin American Studies, 57–97.

Hondagneu-Sotelo, Pierrette (1992) 'Overcoming Patriarchal Constraints: The Reconstruction of Gender Relations Among Mexican Immigrant Women and Men', *Gender and Society*, 6:3, 393–415.

Hondagneu-Sotelo, Pierrette and Avila, Ernestine (1997) 'I'm Here, But I'm There: The Meanings of Latina Transnational Motherhood', *Gender and Society*, 2:5, 548–71.

Horrocks, Roger (1997) *An Introduction to the Study of Sexuality* Basingstoke: Macmillan

Hossfeld, Karen (1991) 'Introduction' in Working Women Worldwide (ed) *Common Interests: Women Organising in Global Electronics* London: WWW, 13–17.

Howard-Grabman, Lisa (1996) '"Planning Together": Developing Community Plans to Address Priority Maternal and Neonatal Health Problems in Rural Bolivia' in de Koning, Korrie and Martin, Marion (eds) *Participatory Research in Health: Issues and Experiences* London: Zed, 153–63.

Htun, Mala (1998) 'Women's Rights and Opportunities in Latin America: Problems and Practices' *Women's Leadership Conference of the Americas Issue Brief* <www.thedialogue.org/htunrigh.html/#Political Participation>.

Htun, Mala and Jones, Mark (2002) 'Engendering the Right to Participate in Decision-Making: Electoral Quotas and Women's Leadership in Latin America' in Craske, Nikki and Molyneux, Maxine (eds) *Gender and the Politics of Rights and Democracy in Latin America* Basingstoke: Palgrave, 32–56.

Humphrey, John (1997) 'Gender Divisions in Brazilian Industry' in Gugler, Josef (ed) *Cities in the Developing World: Issues, Theory and Policy* Oxford: Oxford University Press, 171–83.

Huntington, Dale (1999) 'Atención Post-Aborto: Una Estrategia para Mejorar la Salud Reproductiva', *Alternativas de Investigación Operativa* (Population Council, Mexico), January, 1–5.

Ibarra, Rosario (1994) 'The Search for Disappeared Sons: How It Changed the Mothers' in Küppers, Gaby (ed) *Compañeras: Voices From the Latin American Women's Movement* London: Latin America Bureau, 116–9.

Instituto Latinamericano de las Naciones Unidas para la Prevención de Delito y Tratamiento del Delincuente (ILANUD) (1996) *Construcción de la Identidad Masculina* San José: Programa Mujer, Justicia y Género, ILANUD.

Instituto Latinoamericano de las Naciones Unidas para la Prevención de Delito y Tratamiento del Delincuente (ILANUD) (1999) *Programa Regional de Capacitación Contra la Violencia Doméstica* San José: ILANUD.

Instituto Mixto de Ayuda Social (IMAS) (1999) *Programa Construyendo Oportunidades* San José: IMAS.

Instituto Mixto de Ayuda Social (IMAS) (2001) *Area Atención Integral para el Desarrollo de las Mujeres. Programas: Creciendo Juntas, Construyendo Oportunidades* San José: IMAS.

Instituto Nacional de las Mujeres (INAMU) (1998) *Maternidad y Paternidad: Dos Caras del Embarazo Adolescente* San José:INAMU.

Instituto Nacional de la Mujeres (INAMU) (2001) *Responsible Paternity Law* San José:INAMU.

Inter American Development Bank (IADB) (1990) *Economic and Social Progress in Latin America 1990 Report: Working Women in Latin America* Washington DC: IADB.

Inter American Development Bank (IADB) (1993) *Economic and Social Progress in Latin America 1993 Report: Human Resources* Washington DC: IADB.

Inter American Development Bank (IADB) (1998) *Economic and Social Progress in Latin America 1998 Report: Facing Up to Inequality in Latin America* Washington DC: IADB.

Inter American Development Bank (IADB) (1999) *Economic and Social Progress in Latin America 1999 Report* Washington DC: IADB.

Inter American Development Bank (IADB) (2000) *Economic and Social Progress in Latin America 2000 Report: Development Beyond Economics* Washington DC: IADB.

International Labour Organisation (ILO) (2001) *Reducing the Decent Work Deficit: A Global Challenge* Geneva: ILO.

International Labour Organisation (ILO) Lima (2000) *2000 Labour Overview* (www.ilolim.org.pe/english/260ameri/publ/2000.special.shtml)

International Planned Parenthood Federation (IPPF) (1993) *Strategic Plan: Vision 2000* London: IPPF.

Izazola, Haydea (2001) 'Mexico City: Individual and Collective Responses to Urban Environmental Deterioration' in UNESCO (ed) *Encyclopedia of Life Support Systems* Oxford: EOLSS Publishers-UNESCO.

Izazola, Haydea; Martínez, Caroline and Marquette, Catherine (1998) 'Environmental Perceptions, Social Class and Demographic Change in Mexico City: A Comparative Approach', *Environment and Urbanisation*, 10:1, 107–18.

Jackson, Cecile (1996) 'Rescuing Gender from the Poverty Trap', *World Development*, 24:3, 489–504.

Jackson, Cecile (2000) 'Men at Work', *European Journal of Development Research*, 12:2, 1–22.

Jaquette, Jane (1994) 'Introduction': From Transition to Participation – Women's Movements and Democratic Politics' in Jaquette, Jane (ed) *The Women's Movement in Latin America: Participation and Democracy* Boulder: Westview, 1–11.

Jaquette, Jane (ed) (1994) *The Women's Movement in Latin America: Participation and Democracy* Boulder: Westview.

Jayawardena, C. (1960) 'Marital Instability in Two Guianese Sugar Estate Communities', *Social and Economic Studies*, 9, 76–100.

Jelin, Elizabeth (1990a) 'Introduction' in Jelin, Elizabeth (ed) *Women and Social Change in Latin America* London: Zed, 1–11.

Jelin, Elizabeth (1990b) 'Citizenship and Identity: Final Reflections' in Jelin, Elizabeth (ed) *Women and Social Change in Latin America* London: Zed, 184–207.

Jelin, Elizabeth (1991) 'Introduction: Everyday Practices, Family Structures, Social Processes' in Jelin, Elizabeth (ed) *Family, Household and Gender Relations in Latin America* London/Paris: Kegan Paul International/UNESCO, 1–5.

Jelin, Elizabeth (1996) 'Women, Gender and Human Rights' in Jelin, Elizabeth and Hershberg, Eric (eds) *Constructing Democracy: Human Rights, Citizenship and Society in Latin America* Boulder: Westview, 177–96.

Jelin, Elizabeth (1997) 'Engendering Human Rights' in Dore, Elizabeth (ed) *Gender Politics in Latin America: Debates in Theory and Practice* New York: Monthly Review Press, 65–83.

Jelin, Elizabeth (ed) (1990) *Women and Social Change in Latin America* London: Zed.

Jelin, Elizabeth (ed) (1991) *Family, Household and Gender Relations in Latin America* London/Paris: Kegan Paul International/UNESCO.

Jenkins, Rhys (1997) 'Structural Adjustment and Bolivian Industry', *European Journal of Development Research*, 9:2, 107–28.

Jiménez, Rodrigo (1996) 'Adios al Patriarca', in ILANUD *Construcción de la Identidad Masculina* San José: ILANUD, Programa Mujer, Justicia y Género, 43–6.

Joekes, Susan (1987) *Women in the World Economy: An INSTRAW Study* Oxford: Oxford University Press.

Jolly, Susie (2000) '"Queering" Development: Exploring Links Between Same-Sex Sexualities, Gender and Development' in Sweetman, Caroline (ed) *Gender in the 21st Century* Oxford: Oxfam, 78–88.

Jordan, Sara and Wagner, Fritz (1993) 'Meeting Women's Needs and Priorities for Water and Sanitation in Cities', *Environment and Urbanisation*, 5:2, 135–45.

Joseph, Alun and Martin-Matthews, Anne (1994) 'Caring for Elderly People: Workforce Issues and Development Questions' in Phillips, David and Verhasselt, Yola (eds) *Health and Development* London: Routledge, 168–81.

Kabeer, Naila (1994) *Reversed Realities: Gender Hierarchies in Development Thought* London: Verso.

Kabeer, Naila (1999) 'Resources, Agency, Achievements: Reflections on the Measurement of Women's Empowerment', *Development and Change*, 30:3, 435–64.

Kabeer, Naila (2000) *The Power to Choose: Bangladeshi Women and Labour Market Decisions in London and Dhaka* London: Verso.

Kabeer, Naila and Joekes, Susan (1991) 'Editorial', *IDS Bulletin*, 22:1 (Special issue: 'Researching the Household: Methodological and Empirical Issues'), 1–4.

Kandiyoti, Deniz (1991) 'Bargaining with Patriarchy' in Lorber, Judith and Farrell, Susan (eds) *The Social Construction of Gender* Newbury Park: Sage, 104–18.

Kanji, Nazneen (1991) 'Structural Adjustment Policies: Shifting the Costs of Social Reproduction to Women', *Critical Health*, 34, 61–7.

Kaplan, Temma (1982) 'Female Consciousness and Collective Action: The Case of Barcelona 1910–18', *Signs: Journal of Women in Culture and Society*, 7:3, 545–66.

Kay, Cristóbal (1999) 'Rural Development: From Agrarian Reform to Neoliberalism and Beyond' in Gwynne, Robert and Kay, Cristóbal (eds) *Latin America Transformed: Globalisation and Modernity* London: Edward Arnold, 272–304.

Kaztman, Rubén (1992) 'Por Qué Los Hombres son Tan Irresponsables?', *Revista de la CEPAL*, 46, 1–9.

de Keijzer, Benno (1998) 'El Varón como Factor de Riesgo' in Population Council *Familia y Relaciones de Género en Transformación: Cambios Transcendentales en América Latina* Mexico City: Population Council/EDAMEX.

Klak, Thomas (1999) 'Globalisation, Neoliberalism and Economic Change in Central America and the Caribbean' in Gwynne, Robert and Kay, Cristóbal (eds) *Latin America Transformed: Globalisation and Modernity* London: Edward Arnold, 98–126.

Koonings, Kees; Kruijt, Dirk and Wils, Frits (1995) 'The Very Long March of History' in Thomas, Henk (ed) *Globalisation and Third World Trade Unions* London: Zed, 99–129.

Korzeniewicz, Roberto Patricio and Smith, William C. (2000) 'Poverty, Inequality and Growth in Latin America: Searching for the High Road to Globalisation', *Latin American Research Review*, 35:3, 7–54.

Kratochwil, K. Hermann (1995) 'Cross-Border Population Movements and Regional Economic Integration in Latin America, *IOM Latin American Migration Journal*, 13:2, 13–21.

Krauskopf, Dina (1998) 'The Rights and Reproductive Health of Urban Adolescents' in UNICEF (ed) *Adolescence, Child Rights and Urban Poverty in Costa Rica* San José: UNICEF/HABITAT: San José, 101–12.

Krohn-Hansen, Christian (1996) 'Masculinity and the Political among the Dominicans: "The Dominican Tiger"' in Melhuus, Marit and Stølen, Kristi Ann (eds) *Machos, Mistresses, Madonnas: Contesting the Power of Latin American Gender Imagery* London: Verso, 108–33.

Kulick, Don (1995) 'Introduction. The Sexual Life of Anthropologists: Erotic Subjectivity and Ethnographic Work' in Kulick, Don and Wilson, Margaret (eds) *Taboo: Sex, Identity and Erotic Subjectivity in Anthropological Fieldwork* London: Routledge, 1–28.

Kulick, Don (1998) 'Fe/male Trouble: The Unsettling Place of Lesbians in the Self-Images of Brazilian Travesti Prostitutes', *Sexualities*, 1:3, 299–312.

Kuznesof, Elizabeth (1989) 'The Family in Latin America: A Critique of Recent Research', *Latin American Research Review*, 24:2, 168–86.

Lagarde, Marcela (1994) 'Maternidad, Feminismo y Democracia' in Grupo de Educación Popular con Mujeres AC (ed) *Repensar y Politizar la Maternidad: Un Reto de Fin de Milenio* México DF: Grupo de

Educación Popular con Mujeres AC, 19–36.

Lancaster, Roger (1992) *Life is Hard: Machismo, Danger and the Intimacy of Power in Nicaragua* Berkeley: University of California Press.

Lancaster, Roger (1997a) 'Guto's Performance: Notes on the Transvestism of Everyday Life' in Balderston, Daniel and Guy, Donna (eds) *Sex and Sexuality in Latin America* New York: New York University Press, 9–32.

Lancaster, Roger (1997b) 'On Homosexualities in Latin America (and Other Places)' *American Ethnologist*, 24: 1, 193–202.

Lancaster, Roger (1998) 'Transgenderism in Latin America: Some Critical Introductory Remarks on Identities and Practice', *Sexualities* 1:3, 261–74.

Langer, Ana; Lozano, Rafael and Bobadilla, José Luís (1991) 'Effects of Mexico's Economic Crisis on the Health of Women and Children' in González de la Rocha, Mercedes and Escobar, Agustín (eds) *Social Responses to Mexico's Crisis of the 1980s* San Diego: Center for US–Mexican Studies, 195–219.

Laqueur, Thomas (1990) *Making Sex: Body and Gender from the Greeks to Freud* Harvard: Harvard University Press.

Larkin, Maureen (1998) 'Global Aspects of Health and Health Policy in Third World Countries' in Kiely, Ray and Marfleet, Phil (eds) *Globalisation and the Third World* London: Routledge, 91–111.

Leach, Fiona (1999) 'Women in the Informal Sector: The Contribution of Education and Training' in Oxfam *Development with Women* Oxford: Oxfam, 46–62.

Lehmann, David (1994) 'Bringing Society Back In: Latin America in a Post Development World'. Draft application for British Academcy Research Fellowship, Centre for Latin American Studies, University of Cambridge.

Lehmann, David (1996) *Struggle for the Spirit: Religious Transformation and Popular Culture in Brazil and Latin America* Cambridge: Polity.

Leiner, Marvin (1994) *Sexual Politics in Cuba: Machismo, Homosexuality and AIDS* Boulder: Westview.

di Leonardo, Michaela and Lancaster, Roger (1997) 'Introduction: Embodied Meanings, Carnal Practices' in Lancaster, Roger and di Leonardo, Michaela (eds) *The Gender Sexuality Reader* London: Routledge, 1–10.

Lerner, Susana (1998) 'Participación del Varón en el Proceso Reproductivo: Recuento de Perspectivas Analíticas y Hallazgos de Investigación' in Lerner, Susana (ed) *Varones, Sexualidad y Reproducción* México DF: El Colegio de México, 9–45.

LeVine, Sarah (in collaboration with Clara Sunderland Correa) (1993) *Dolor y Alegría: Women and Social Change in Urban Mexico* Madison: University of Wisconsin.

Lewis, Nancy Davis and Kieffer, Edith (1994) 'The Health of Women: Beyond Maternal and Child Health' in Phillips, David and Verhasselt, Yola (eds) *Health and Development* London: Routledge, 122–37.

Lind, Amy (1997) 'Gender, Development and Urban Social Change: Women's Community Action in Global Cities', *World Development*, 25:8, 1187–203.

Lister, Ruth (1997) *Citizenship: Feminist Perspectives* Basingstoke: Macmillan.

Lloyd-Sherlock, Peter (1997) *Old Age and Urban Poverty in the Developing World: The Shanty Towns of Buenos Aires* Houndmills, Basingstoke: Macmillan.

Lloyd-Sherlock, Peter (2000) 'Failing the Needy: Public Social Spending in Latin America', *Journal of International Development*, 12:1, 101–19.

Lloyd-Sherlock, Peter (ed) (2000) *Healthcare Reform and Poverty in Latin America* London: Institute of Latin American Studies.

Loáiciga Guillén, María Elena (1997) 'Actitudes y Prácticas Asociadas a la Sexualidad en Adolescentes Guanacastecos con Exito en el Rendimiento Escolar', *Ciencias Sociales* (Universidad de Costa Rica), 73–4, 221–30.

Lock, Margaret (1993) 'Cultivating the Body: Anthroplogy and Epistemologies of Bodily Practice and Knowledge', *Annual Review of Anthropology*, 22, 33–55.

Logan, Kathleen, (1990) 'Women's Participation in Urban Protest' in Foweraker, Joe and Craig, Ann (eds) *Popular Movements and Political Change in Mexico* Boulder: Lynne Reinner Publishers, 59–77.

Lomnitz Adler, Claudio (1992) *Exits from the Labyrinth: Culture and Ideology in Mexican National Space* Berkeley: University of California Press.

Lomnitz, Larissa (1977) *Networks and Marginality: Life in a Mexican Shanty Town* New York: Academic Press.

Lomnitz, Larissa and Pérez-Lizaur, Marisol (1991) 'Dynastic Growth and Survival Strategies: The Solidarity of Mexican Grand-Families' in Jelin, Elizabeth (ed) *Family, Household and Gender Relations in Latin America* London/Paris: Kegan Paul International/UNESCO,123–32.

Londoño, Juan Luis and Frenk, Julio (2000) 'Structured Pluralism: Towards an Innovative Model for Health System Reform in Latin America', in Lloyd-Sherlock, Peter (ed) *Healthcare Reform and Poverty in Latin America* London: Institute of Latin American Studies, 21–56.

López, María de la Paz and Izazola, Haydea (1995) *El Perfil Censal de los Hogares y las Familias en México* Aguascalientes: Instituto Nacional de Estadística, Geografía e Informática.

López, María de la Paz; Izazola, Haydea and Gómez de León, José (1993) 'Characteristics of Female Migrants According to the 1990 Census of Mexico' in United Nations (ed) *Internal Migration of Women in Developing Countries* New York: United Nations, 133–53.

López de Mazier, Armida (1997) 'La Mujer, Principal Sostén del Modelo Económico de Honduras: Un Análisis de Género de la Economía Hondureña' in Elson, Diane; Fauné, María Angélica; Gideon, Jasmine; Gutiérrez, Maribel; López de Mazier, Armida and Sacayón, Eduardo (1997) *Crecer con la Mujer: Oportunidades para el Desarrollo Ecónomico Centroamericano* San José: Embajada Real de los Países Bajos, 215–52.

Lozano, Wilfrido (1997) 'Dominican Republic: Informal Economy, the State and the Urban Poor' in Portés, Alejandro; Dore-Cabral, Carlos and Landoff, Patricia (eds) *The Urban Caribbean: Transition to a New Global Economy* Baltimore: John Hopkins University Press, 153–189.

Lumsden, Ian (1996) *Machos, Maricones and Gays: Cuba and Homosexuality* Philadelphia/London: Temple University Press/Latin America Bureau.

Lungo, Mario (1997) 'Costa Rica: Dilemmas of Urbanisation in the 1990s' in Portés, Alejandro; Dore-Cabral, Carlos and Landoff, Patricia (eds) *The Urban Caribbean: Transition to a New Global Economy* Baltimore: John Hopkins University Press, 57–86.

Macaulay, Fiona (2002) 'Taking the Law into Their Own Hands: Women, Legal Reform and Legal Literacy in Brazil' in Craske, Nikki and Molyneux, Maxine (eds) *Gender and the Politics of Rights and Democracy in Latin America* Basingstoke: Palgrave, 79–102.

Machado, Leda (1988) 'The Participation of Women in the Health Movement of Jardim Nordeste, in the Eastern Zone of São Paulo, Brazil: 1976–1985', *Bulletin of Latin American Research*, 7:1, 47–63.

Machado, Leda (1993) '"We Learned to Think Politically": The Influence of the Catholic Church and the Feminist Movement on the Emergence of the Health Movement in the Jardim Nordeste Area in São Paulo, Brazil' in Radcliffe, Sarah and Westwood, Sallie (eds) *'Viva': Women and Popular Protest in Latin America* London: 88–111.

Machado, María Helena (1993) 'Women and the Health Sector's Labour Market in the Americas: Female Hegemony' in Gómez Gómez, Elsa (ed) *Gender, Women and Health in the Americas* Washington DC: Pan American Health Organisation, 255–62.

Madden Arias, Rose Mary (1996) 'Outraging Public Morality: The Experience of a Lesbian Feminist Group in Costa Rica' in Reinfelder, Monika (ed) *Amazon to Zami: Towards a Global Lesbian Feminism* London: Cassell, 130–7.

Marenco, Leda; Trejos, Ana María; Trejos, Juan Diego and Vargas, Marienela (1998) *Del Silencio a la Palabra: Un Modelo de Trabajo con las Mujeres Jefas del Hogar* San José: Segunda Vicepresidencia.

Mármora, Lelio (1999) 'Los Movimientos Migratorios Internacionales en los Países Andinos', *Revista de la Organización Internacional para las Migraciones en América Latina*, Edición Especial (July), 95–124.

Marqués, Josep Vicent (1980) *Modelos Sexuales y Dominación Masculina* San Sebastián: Editorial Hordago.

Marshall, T. H. (1950) *Citizenship and Social Class* Cambridge: Cambridge University Press.

Martin, C.J. (1996) 'Economic Strategies and Moral Principles in the Survival of Poor Households in Mexico: An Urban and Rural Comparison', *Bulletin of Latin American Research*, 15:2, 193–210.

Martin, Joann (1990) 'Motherhood and Power: The Production of a Women's Culture of Politics in a Mexican Community', *American Ethnologist*, 17:3, 470–90.

Martínez Nogueira, Roberto (1995) 'Devising New Approaches to Poverty in Argentina' in Raczynski, Dagmar (ed) *Strategies to Combat Poverty in Latin America* Washington, DC: IADB/CIEPLAN, 33–85.

Massey, Douglas; Arango, Joaquín; Hugo, Graeme; Kouaouci, Ali; Pellegrino, Adela and Taylor, J.Edward (1993) 'Theories of International Migration: A Review and Appraisal', *Population and Development Review*, 19:3, 431–66.

Massolo, Alejandra (1998a) 'Introducción: Gobierno Municipal y Mujeres: Un Encuentro Posible' in Massolo, Alejandra and Bassols, Dalia (eds) *Mujeres Que Gobiernan Municipios: Experiencias, Aportes y Retos* México DF: El Colegio de México, 13–27.

Massolo, Alejandra (1998b) 'Pluralidad Política y Pluralidad de Género en Favor de Ayuntamientos Democráticos' in Massolo, Alejandra and Bassols, Dalia (eds) *Mujeres Que Gobiernan Municipios: Experiencias, Aportes y Retos* Mexico: El Colegio de México, 31–48.

Matear, Ann (1996) 'Desde la Protesta a la Propuesta: Gender Politics in Transition Chile', *Democratisation*, 3:3, 254–63.

McCallum, Cecilia (1999) 'Restraining Women: Gender, Sexuality and Modernity in Salvador da Bahia, Brazil', *Bulletin of Latin American Research*, 18:3, 275–93.

McClenaghan, Sharon (1997) 'Women, Work and Empowerment: Romanticising the Reality' in Dore, Elizabeth (ed) *Gender Politics in Latin America: Debates in Theory and Practice* New York: Monthly Review Press,19–35.

McIlwaine, Cathy (1993) 'Gender, Ethnicity and the Local Labour Market in Limón, Costa Rica'. Unpublished PhD thesis, Department of Geography, London School of Economics.

McIlwaine Cathy (1997) 'Vulnerable or Poor? A Study of Ethnic and Gender Disadvantage among Afro-Caribbeans in Limón, Costa Rica', *European Journal of Development Research*, 9:2, 35–61.

McIlwaine, Cathy (2001) 'Women, Children and Violence' in Potter, Robert and Desai, Vandana (eds) *The Arnold Companion to Development Studies* London: Edward Arnold, 327–32.

McIlwaine, Cathy (2002) 'Perspectives on Poverty, Vulnerability and Exclusion', in McIlwaine, Cathy and Willis, Katie (eds) *Challenges and Change in Middle America: Perspectives on Mexico, Central America and the Caribbean* Harlow: Pearson Education, 82–109.

Medeiros, A. (1986) *Politics and Intergovernmental Relations in Brazil, 1964–1982* New York: Garland Press.

Mehra, Rekha and Gammage, Sarah (1997) *Employment and Poor Women: A Policy Brief on Trends and Strategies* Washington DC: International Center for Research on Women.

Mehra, Rekha and Gammage, Sarah (1999) 'Trends, Countertrends and Gaps in Women's Employment', *World Development*, 27:3, 533–50.

Melhuus, Marit (1996) 'Power, Value and the Ambiguous Meanings of Gender' in Melhuus, Marit and Stølen, Kristi Ann (eds) *Machos, Mistresses, Madonnas: Contesting the Power of Latin American Gender Imagery* London: Verso, 230–59.

Melhuus, Marit and Stølen, Kristi Anne (1996) 'Introduction' in Melhuus, Marit and Stølen, Kristi Ann (eds) *Machos, Mistresses, Madonnas: Contesting the Power of Latin American Gender Imagery* London: Verso, 1–33.

Méndez-Rivero, Diego (1995) 'Decline of an Oil Economy: Venezuela and the Legacy of Incorporation' in Thomas, Henk (ed) *Globalisation and Third World Trade Unions* London: Zed, 149–65.

Mesa-Lago, Carmelo (1997) 'Social Welfare Reform in the Context of Political Liberalisation: Latin American Cases', *World Development*, 25:4, 497–517.

Miller, Francesca (1991) *Latin American Women and the Search for Social Justice* Hanover: University Press of New England.

Ministerio de Desarrollo Sostenible y Planificación (MINDESP) (2001) *Plan Nacional de Equidad de Género, 2001–2003* La Paz: MINDESP.

Ministerio de Educación Pública (MEP) (1994) *Aspectos Generales Sobre el Uso Indebido de Drogas en Costa Rica* San José: MEP.

Ministerio de Planificación Nacional y Política Económica (MIDEPLAN) (1995) *Estadísticas Sociodemográficas y Económicas Desagregadas por Sexo, Costa Rica, 1980–1994* San José: MIDEPLAN.

Ministerio de Salud (1996) *Perfil Socio Familiar y Laboral de los Recursos Humanos del Sector Público de Salud desde una Perspectiva de Género* Santiago: Ministerio de Salud, Departamento Desarrollo de Recursos Humanos, División de Planificación Estratégica.

Minority Rights Group (ed) (1995) *No Longer Invisible: Afro-Latin Americans Today* London: Minority Rights Group Publications.

Miraftab, Faranak (1994) '(Re)Production at Home: Reconceptualising Home and Family', *Journal of Family Issues*, 15:3, 467–89.

Mirandé, Alfredo (1997) *Hombres y Machos: Masculinity and Latino Culture* Boulder: Westview.

Mitter, Swasti (1997) 'Information Technology and Working Women's Demands' in Mitter, Swasti and Rowbotham, Sheila (eds) *Women Encounter Technology: Changing Patterns of Employment in the Third World* London: Routledge, 19–43.

Moßrucker, Harald (1997) 'Amerindian Migration in Peru and Mexico' in Gugler, Josef (ed) *Cities in the Developing World: Issues, Theory and Policy* Oxford: Oxford University Press, 74–87.

Moguel, Julio (1990) 'National Solidarity Program Fails to Help the Very Poor', *Voices of Mexico*, 25, 24–9.

Moghadam, Valentine (1994) 'Women in Societies', *International Social Science Journal*, 139, 95–115.

Moghadam, Valentine (1995) 'Gender Aspects of Employment and Unemployment in Global Perspective' in Simai, Mihaly; Moghadam, Valentine and Kuddo, Arvo (eds) *Global Employment: An International Investigation into the Future of Work* London: Zed, 111–39.

Moghadam, Valentine (1997) *The Feminisation of Poverty: Notes on a Concept and Trend* Normal: Illinois State University,Women's Studies Occasional Paper No.2

Moghadam, Valentine (1999) 'Gender and Globalisation: Female Labour and Women's Mobilisation', *Journal of World-Systems Research*, 5:2, 298–314.

Molina, Giselle (1993) *Cómo Obtener Protección Legal?* San José: Centro Feminista de Información y Acción.

Molyneux, Maxine (1984) 'Mobilisation Without Emancipation?', *Critical Social Policy* 10,4:7, 59–75.

Molyneux, Maxine (1985) 'Mobilisation without Emancipation? Women's Interests, the State and Revolution in Nicaragua', *Feminist Studies*, 11:2, 227–54.

Molyneux, Maxine (1996) *State, Gender and Institutional Change in Cuba's 'Special Period': the Federación de Mujeres Cubanas* London: Research Paper 43, Institute of Latin American Studies, University of London.

Molyneux, Maxine (1998) 'Analysing Women's Movements', *Development and Change*, 29:2, 219–45.

Molyneux, Maxine (2000) 'State Formations in Latin America' in Dore, Elizabeth and Molyneux, Maxine (eds) *Hidden Histories of Gender and the State in Latin America* Durham: Duke University Press, 33–81.

Molyneux, Maxine (2001) *Women's Movements in International Perspective: Latin America and Beyond* Basingstoke: Palgrave.

Molyneux, Maxine (forthcoming) 'Gender and the Silences of Social Capital: Lessons from Latin America', *Development and Change*.

Molyneux, Maxine and Craske, Nikki (2002) 'The Local, the Regional and the Global: Transforming the Politics of Rights' in Craske, Nikki and Molyneux, Maxine (eds) *Gender and the Politics of Rights and Democracy in Latin America* Basingstoke: Palgrave, 1–31.

Montéon, Michael (1995) 'Gender and Economic Crises in Latin America: Reflections on the Great Depression and the Debt Crisis' in Blumberg, Rae Lesser; Rakowski, Cathy; Tinker, Irene and Monteón, Michael (eds) *Engendering Wealth and Well-Being: Empowerment for Global Change* Boulder: Westview, 39–62.

Montoya Tellería, Oswaldo (1998) *Nadando Contra Corriente: Buscando Pistas para Prevenir la Violencia Masculina en las Relaciones de Pareja* Managua: Puntos de Encuentro.

Moore, Henrietta (1988) *Feminism and Anthropology* Cambridge: Polity.

Moore, Henrietta (1994a) *Is There a Crisis in the Family*? Geneva: Occasional Paper 3, World Summit for Social Development, UNRISD.

Moore, Henrietta (1994b) *A Passion for Difference* Cambridge: Polity.

Moore, Henrietta (1994c) 'The Problem of Explaining Violence in the Social Sciences' in Harvey, Penelope and Gow, Peter (eds) *Sex and Violence: Issues in Representation and Experience* London: Routledge, 138–55.

Moore, Henrietta (1996) 'Mothering and Social Responsibilities in a Cross-Cultural Perspective' in Bortolaia Silva, Elizabeth (ed) *Good Enough Mothering: Feminist Perspectives on Lone Motherhood* London: Routledge, 58–75.

Mora, Germán and Yunes, João (1993) 'Maternal Mortality: An Overlooked Tragedy' in Gómez Gómez, Elsa (ed) *Gender, Women and Health in the Americas* Washington DC: Pan American Health Organisation, 62–79.

Moreno, Wagner (1997) 'Cambios Sociales y el Rol del Adolescente en la Estructura Familiar', *Ciencias Sociales* (Universidad de Costa Rica), 75, 95–101.

Morris, Arthur (1995) *South America: A Changing Continent* London: Hodder and Stoughton.

Morris, Rosalind (1995) 'All Made Up: Performance Theory and the New Anthropology of Sex and Gender', *Annual Review of Anthropology*, 24, 567–92.

Moser, Caroline (1978) 'Informal Sector or Petty Commodity Production: Dualism or Dependence in Urban Development', *World Development*, 6, 135–78.

Moser, Caroline (1982) 'A Home of One's Own: Squatter Housing Strategies in Guayaquil, Ecuador', in Gilbert, Alan in association with Hardoy, Jorge and Ramírez, Ronaldo (eds) *Urbanisation in Contemporary Latin America* Chichester: John Wiley, 159–80.

Moser, Caroline (1989) 'The Impact of Recession and Structural Adjustment at the Micro-level: Low-income Women and their Households in Guayaquil, Ecuador' in UNICEF (ed) *Invisible Adjustment Vol. 2* New York: UNICEF, Americas and Caribbean Regional Office, 137–62.

Moser, Caroline (1992) 'Adjustment from Below: Low-income Women, Time and the Triple Role in Guayaquil, Ecuador' in Afshar, Haleh and Dennis, Carolyn (eds) *Women and Adjustment Policies in the Third World* Houndmills, Basingstoke: Macmillan, 87–116.

Moser, Caroline (1993) *Gender Planning and Development: Theory, Practice and Training* London: Routledge.

Moser, Caroline (1997) *Household Responses to Poverty and Vulnerability Volume 1: Confronting Crisis in Cisne Dos, Guayaquil, Ecuador* Washington DC: World Bank, Urban Management and Poverty Reduction Series No. 21.

Moser, Caroline; Herbert, Alicia and Makonnen, Rosa (1993) *Urban Poverty in the Context of Structural Adjustment: Recent Evidence and Policy Responses* Washington DC: World Bank, Urban Development Division, Transportation, Water and Urban Development Discussion Paper No. 4.

Moser, Caroline and McIlwaine, Cathy (2000) *Urban Poor Perceptions of Violence and Exclusion in Colombia* Washington DC: World Bank.

Muncie, John and Wetherell, Margaret (1995) 'Family Policy and Political Discourse' in

Muncie, John; Wetherell, Margaret; Dallos, Rudi and Cochrane, Allan (eds) *Understanding the Family* Milton Keynes: Open University Press, 39–80.

Muñoz, Eduardo (1997) 'Madres Adolescentes: Una Realidad Negada', *Otra Mirada* (Centro Nacional para el Desarrollo de la Mujer y la Familia, San José), 1:3, 43–5.

van Naerssen, Tom and Barten, Françoise (1999) 'Healthy Cities in Developing Countries: A Programme of Multilateral Assistance' in Simon, David and Närman, Anders (eds) *Development as Theory and*

Practice Harlow: Longman, 230–46.

Napolitano, Valentina (2000) 'Prisms of Belonging and Social Suffering in Transnational Migrant California'. Seminar, Gender Institute, London School of Economics, 8 November.

Nash, June (1980) 'A Critique of Social Science Roles in Latin America' in Nash, June and Safa, Helen (eds) *Sex and Class in Latin America: Women's Perspectives on Politics, Economics and Family in the Third World* New York: Bergin, 1–21.

Nash, June (1986) 'A Decade of Research on Women in Latin America' in Nash, June and Safa, Helen (eds) *Women and Change in Latin America* South Hadley, Massachusetts: Bergin and Garvey, 3–21.

Nash, June (1995) 'Latin American Women in the World Capitalist Crisis' in Bose, Christine and Acosta-Belén, Edna (eds) *Women in the Latin American Development Process* Philadelphia: Temple University Press, 151–66.

Nash, June and Fernández-Kelly, María Patricia (eds) (1983) *Women, Men and the International Division of Labour* Albany: State University of New York Press.

Nash, June and Safa, Helen (eds) (1980) *Sex and Class in Latin America: Women's Perspectives on Politics, Economics and Family in the Third World* New York: Bergin.

Nash, June and Safa, Helen (eds) (1986) *Women and Change in Latin America* South Hadley, Massachusetts: Bergin and Garvey.

Nencel, Lorraine (1996) 'Pacharachas, Putas and Chicas de su Casa: Labelling, Femininity and Men's Sexual Selves in Lima, Peru' in Melhuus, Marit and Stølen, Kristi Ann (eds) *Machos, Mistresses, Madonnas: Contesting the Power of Latin American Gender Imagery* London: Verso, 56–82.

Nye, Robert (1999) 'Introduction: On Why History is so Important to an Understanding of Human Sexuality' in Nye, Robert (ed) *Sexuality* Oxford: Oxford University Press, 3–15.

Oficina de la Primera Dama, Consejo Interinstitucional de Atención a la Madre Adolescente and Instituto Nacional de las Mujeres (1999) *Construyendo Oportunidades: Un Programa de Apoyo para Abrir Caminos a las Adolescentes Embarazadas y Madres* San José: INAMU.

Olavarría, José and Parrini, Rodrigo (1999) 'Los Padres Adolescentes/Jóvenes: Hombres Adolescentes Jóvenes Frente al Embarazo y Nacimiento de un/a Hijo/a: Antecedentes para la Formulación y Diseño de Políticas Públicas en Chile'. Mimeo, Santiago de Chile: FLACSO.

de Oliveira, Orlandina (1991) 'Migration of Women, Family Organisation and Labour Markets in Mexico' in Jelin, Elizabeth (ed) *Family, Household and Gender Relations in Latin America* London/Paris: Kegan Paul International/UNESCO, 101–18.

de Oliveira, Orlandina; Eternod, Marcela; López, María de la Paz and Monroy, Aramely (1995) *Las Familias Mexicanas* México DF: CONAPO, Comité Nacional para la IV Conferencia Mundial de la Mujer.

Organización Internacional para las Migraciones (OIM) (2000) 'Migraciones en Centroámerica: Proceso Puebla - Huracán Mitch: Bases para la Reflexión y Propuestas de Acción', *Revista de la Organización Internacional para las Migraciones en América Latina*, 18:1 (www.oim.web.cl).

Ostermann, Ana Cristina and Keller-Cohen, Deborah (1998) '"Good Girls go to Heaven; Bad Girls..." Learn to be Good: Quizzes in American and Brazilian Teenage Girls' Magazines', *Discourse and Society*, 9:4, 531–58.

Padgug, Robert, A. (1999) 'Sexual Matters: On Conceptualising Sexuality in History' in Parker, Richard and Aggleton, Peter (eds) *Culture, Society and Sexuality: A Reader* London: UCL Press, 15–28.

Palmer, Ingrid (1992) 'Gender, Equity and Economic Efficiency in Adjustment Programes' in Afshar, Haleh and Dennis, Carolyn (eds) *Women and Adjustment Policies in the Third World* Houndmills, Basingstoke: Macmillan, 69–83.

Paltiel, Freda L. (1993) 'Mental Health of Women in the Americas' in Gómez Gómez, Elsa (ed) *Gender, Women and Health in the Americas* Washington DC: Pan American Health Organisation, 131–48.

Paolisso, Michael and Gammage, Sarah (1996) *Women's Responses to Environmental Degradation: Poverty and Demographic Constraints. Case Studies from Latin America* Washington DC: International Center for Research on Women.

Parker, Richard (1997) 'The Carnivalisation of the World' in Lancaster, Roger and di Leonardo, Michaela (eds) *The Gender Sexuality Reader* London: Routledge, 361–77.

Parker, Richard (1999) '"Within Four Walls": Brazilian Sexual Culture and HIV/AIDS' in Parker, Richard and Aggleton, Peter (eds) *Culture, Society and Sexuality: A Reader* London: UCL Press, 253–66.

Parras, Micaela and Morales, María José (1997) 'Reproductive Rights on Paper: Four Bolivian Cities' in Hardon, Anita and Hayes, Elizabeth (eds) *Reproductive Rights in Practice: A Feminist Report on the Quality of Care* London: Zed, 77–94.

Parrenas, Rhacel Salazar (2001) *Servants of Globalisation: Women, Migration and Domestic Work* Stanford: Stanford University Press.

Patel, Vikram; Araya, Ricardo; de Lima, Mauricio; Ludermir, Ana and Todd, Charles (1999) 'Women, Poverty and Common Mental Disorders in Four Restructuring Societies', *Social Science and Medicine*, 49,

1461–71.
Pateman, Carole (1988) *The Sexual Contract* Stanford: Stanford University Press.
Patterson, Sybil (1994) 'Women's Survival Strategies in Urban Areas: CARICOM and Guyana' in Meer, Fatima (ed) *Poverty in the 1990s: The Responses of Urban Women* Paris: UNESCO/International Social Science Council, 117–33.
Paz, Octavio (1959) *El Laberinto de la Soledad* México DF: Fondo de Cultura Económica.
Pearson, Ruth (1986) 'Latin American Women and the New International Division of Labour: A Reassessment', *Bulletin of Latin American Research*, 5:2, 67–79.
Pearson, Ruth (1995) 'Gender Perspectives on Health and Safety in Information Processing: Learning from International Experience' in Mitter, Swasti and Rowbotham, Sheila (eds) *Women Encounter Technology: Changing Patterns of Employment in the Third World* London: Routledge, 278–302.
Pearson, Ruth (1997) 'Renegotiating the Reproductive Bargain: Gender Analysis of Economic Transition in Cuba in the 1990s', *Development and Change*, 28, 671–705.
Pearson, Ruth (1998) '"Nimble Fingers" Revisited: Reflections on Women and Third World Industrialisation in the Late Twentieth Century' in Jackson, Cecile and Pearson, Ruth (eds) *Feminist Visions of Development: Gender Analysis and Policy* London: Routledge, 171–88.
Pearson, Ruth (2000a) 'Rethinking Gender Matters in Development' in Allen, Tim and Thomas, Alan (eds) *Poverty and Development: Into the Twenty-first Century* Milton Keynes/Oxford: Open University Press in association with Oxford University Press, 383–402.
Pearson, Ruth (2000b) 'All Change? Men, Women and Reproductive Work in the Global Economy', *European Journal of Development Research*, 12:2, 219–37.
Pearson, Ruth (2000c) 'Moving the Goalposts: Gender and Globalisation in the Twenty-first Century' in Sweetman, Caroline (ed) *Gender in the 21st Century* Oxford: Oxfam, 10–19.
Peña Saint Martin, Florencia (1996) *Discriminación Laboral Femenina en la Industria del Vestido de Mérida, Yucatán* México DF: Serie Antropología Social, Instituto Nacional de Antropología e Historia.
Pérez Sarduy, Pedro and Stubbs, Jean (1995) 'Introduction' in Minority Rights Group (ed) *Afro-Latin Americans Today: No Longer Invisible* London: Minority Rights Publications, 1–17.
Pescatello, Ann (1976) *Power and Pawn: The Female in Iberian Families, Societies and Cultures* Westport, Connecticut: Greenwood Press.
Pessar, Patricia (1994) 'Sweatshop Workers and Domestic Ideologies: Dominican Women in New York's Apparel Industry', *International Journal of Urban and Regional Research*, 18:1, 127–42.
Phillips, Anne (1998) 'Introduction' in Phillips, Anne (ed) *Feminism and Politics* Oxford: Oxford University Press, 1–20.
Phillips, Anne (ed) (1998) *Feminism and Politics* Oxford: Oxford University Press.
Phillips, David and Verhasselt, Yola (1994) 'Introduction: Health and Development' in Phillips, David and Verhasselt, Yola (eds) *Health and Development* London: Routledge, 3–32.
Pineda, Javier (2000) 'Partners in Women-headed Households: Emerging Masculinities', *European Journal of Development Research*, 12:2, 72–92.
Pirelli, Carina (1994) 'The Uses of Conservatism: Women's Democratic Politics in Uruguay' in Jaquette, Jane (ed) *The Women's Movement in Latin America: Participation and Democracy* Boulder: Westview, 131–50.
Pitanguy, Jacqueline and Mello E Souza, Cecilia (1997) 'Codes of Honour: Reproductive Life Histories of Domestic Workers in Rio de Janeiro' in Harcourt, Wendy (ed) *Power, Reproduction and Gender: The Intergenerational Transfer of Knowledge* London: Zed, 72–97.
Pitkin, Kathryn and Bedoya, Ritha (1997) 'Women's Multiple Roles in Economic Crisis: Constraints and Adaptation', *Latin American Perspectives*, 24:4, 34–49.
Pollack, Molly (1989) 'Poverty and the Labour Market in Costa Rica' in Rodgers, Gerry (ed) *Urban Poverty and the Labour Market* Geneva: International Labour Organisation, 65–80.
Portés, Alejandro (1989) 'Latin American Urbanisation During the Years of the Crisis', *Latin American Research Review*, 24:3, 7–44.
Portés, Alejandro and Schauffler, Richard (1993) 'Competing Perspectives on the Latin American Informal Sector', *Population and Development Review*, 19:3, 33–60.
Portugal, Ana María and Matamala, María Isabel (1993) 'Women's Health Movement: A View of the Decade' in Gómez Gómez, Elsa (ed) *Gender, Women and Health in the Americas* Washington DC: Pan American Health Organisation, 269–80.
Potter, George Ann (2000) *Deeper than Debt: Economic Globalisation and the Poor* London: Latin America Bureau.
Potter, Robert; Binns, Tony; Elliott, Jennifer and Smith, David (1999) *Geographies of Development* Harlow: Longman.
Potts, Lydia (1990) *The World Labour Market: A History of Migration* London: Zed.
Prieur, Annick (1996) 'Domination and Desire: Male Homosexuality and the Construction of Masculinity in Mexico' in Melhuus, Marit and Stølen, Kristi Anne (eds) *Machos, Mistresses and Madonnas:*

Contesting the Power of Latin American Gender Imagery London: Verso, 83–107.

Pringle, Rosemary and Watson, Sophie, (1998) ' "Women's Interests" and the Poststructuralist State' in Phillips, Anne (ed) *Feminism and Politics* Oxford: Oxford University Press, 203–23.

Probyn, Elspeth (1995) 'Queer Belongings: The Politics of Departure' in Grosz, Elizabeth and Probyn, Elspeth (eds) *Sexy Bodies: The Strange Carnalities of Feminism* London: Routledge, 1–18.

Programa de Desarrollo de las Naciones Unidas (PNUD) (1998) *Guatemala: Los Contrastes del Desarrollo Humano* Guatemala City: PNUD.

Proyecto Estado de la Nación (PEN) (1998) *Estado de la Nación en Desarrollo Humano Sostenible* San José: Proyecto Estado de la Nación.

Proyecto Estado de la Región (PER) (1999) *Estado de la Región en Desarrollo Humano Sostenible* San José: Proyecto Estado de la Nación.

Puar, Jasbir (1996) 'Nicaraguan Women, Resistance and the Politics of Aid' in Afshar, Haleh (ed) *Women and Politics in the Third World* London: Routledge, 73–92.

Quiroga, José (1997) 'Homosexualities in the Tropic of Revolution' in Balderston, Daniel and Guy, Donna (eds) *Sex and Sexuality in Latin America* New York: New York University Press, 133–51.

Raczynski, Dagmar (ed) (1995) *Strategies to Combat Poverty in Latin America* Washington, DC: IADB/CIEPLAN.

Radcliffe, Sarah (1986) 'Women's Lives and Peasant Livelihood Strategies: A Study of Migration in the Peruvian Andes'. Unpublished PhD dissertation, Department of Geography, University of Liverpool.

Radcliffe, Sarah (1990a) 'Ethnicity, Patriarchy and Incorporation into the Nation: Female Migrants as Domestic Servants in Peru', *Environment and Planning D: Society and Space*, 8, 379–93.

Radcliffe, Sarah (1990b) 'Between Hearth and Labour Market: The Recruitment of Peasant Women in the Peruvian Andes', *International Migration Review*, 24:2, 229–49.

Radcliffe, Sarah (1991) 'The Role of Gender in Peasant Migration: Conceptual Issues from the Peruvian Andes', *Review of Radical Political Economy*, 23:3–4, 148–73.

Radcliffe, Sarah (1992) 'Mountains, Maidens and Migration: Gender and Mobility in Peru' in Chant, Sylvia (ed) *Gender and Migration in Developing Countries* London: Belhaven, 30–48.

Radcliffe, Sarah (1999) 'Latina Labour: Restructuring of Work and Renegotiations of Gender Relations in Contemporary Latin America', *Environment and Planning A*, 31, 196–208.

Radcliffe, Sarah (2002) 'Indigenous Women, Rights and the Nation-State in the Andes', in Craske, Nikki and Molyneux, Maxine (eds) *Gender and the Politics of Rights and Democracy in Latin America*, Houndmills, Basingstoke: Palgrave, 149–72.

Radcliffe, Sarah and Westwood, Sallie (eds) (1993) *'Viva': Women and Popular Protest in Latin America* London: Routledge.

Ramos Escandón, Carmen (1996) 'Demandas de Género y Crisis Política en el México de Hoy' in Luna, Lola and Vilanova, Mercedes (eds) *Desde las Orillas de la Política: Género y Poder en América Latina* Barcelona: Seminario Interdisciplinar Mujeres y Sociedad, Universitat de Barcelona, 117–47.

Ramos, Joseph (1997) 'Neo-liberal Structural Reforms in Latin America: The Current Situation', *CEPAL Review*, 62, 15–37.

Ravallion, Martin (1997) 'Good and Bad Growth: The Human Development Reports', *World Development*, 25:4, 631–8.

Razavi, Shahra (1999) 'Gendered Poverty and Well-being: Introduction', *Development and Change*, 30:3, 409–33.

Reeves, Hazel (1998) 'Health Sector Reform, Poverty and Gender Inequality', *Bridge Development and Gender In Brief* (IDS, Sussex), November, 2–3.

Restrepo, Helen (1993) 'Cancer Epidemiology and Control in Women in Latin America and the Caribbean' in Gómez Gómez, Elsa (ed) *Gender, Women and Health in the Americas* Washington DC: Pan American Health Organisation, 90–103.

Rey de Marulanda, Nohra (1996) 'Prospects for Latin America in the New World Economic Order' in Karlsson, Weine and Malaki, Akhil (eds) *Growth, Trade and Integration in Latin America* Stockholm: Stokholm University, Institute of Latin American Studies, 17–33.

Reyes Zapata; Cuevas Miguel, Laura; Robledo, Cecilia and Tolbert, Kathryn (1999) *Un Sistema de Medición de la Calidad de los Servicios de Salud Sexual y Reproductiva desde una Perspectiva de Género* New York: Population Council.

Rico de Alonso, Ana and López Téllez, Nadia (1998) 'Informalidad, Jefatura Femenina y Supervivencia', *Revista Javeriana* (September), 193–7.

Ríos, Palmira (1995) 'Gender, Industrialisation and Development in Puerto Rico' in Bose, Christine and Acosta-Belén, Edna (eds) *Women in the Latin American Development Process* Philadelphia: Temple University Press, 125–48.

de los Ríos, Rebecca (1993) 'Gender, Health and Development: An Approach in the Making' in Gómez

Gómez, Elsa (ed) *Gender, Women and Health in the Americas* Washington DC: Pan American Health Organisation, 3–17.

Rivas, Patricia (1999) 'Cronología de Políticas de Seguridad Alimentaria y Nutrición en Costa Rica' in UNICEF (ed) *Nuestro Derecho a la Nutrición y Salud en Costa Rica* San José: UNICEF Costa Rica, 74–83.

Rivas Zivy, Martha (1998) 'Valores, Creencias y Significaciones de la Sexualidad Femenina. Una Reflexión Indispensable para la Comprensión de las Prácticas Sexuales' in Szasz, Ivonne and Lerner, Susana (eds) *Sexualidades en México: Algunas Aproximaciones desde la Perspectiva de las Ciencias Sociales* México DF: El Colegio de México, 137–54.

Rivas Zivy, Martha; Amuchástegui Herrera, Ana and Ortiz-Ortega, Adriana (1999) 'La Negociación de los Derechos Reproductivos en México' in Ortiz-Ortega, Adriana (ed) *Derechos Reproductivos de las Mujeres: Debates sobre Justicia Social en México* México DF: Universidad Autónoma Metropolitana, Unidad Xochimilco/EDAMEX, 257–370.

Rivera Fuentes, Consuelo (1996a) 'They Do Not Dance Alone: The Women's Movements in Latin America' in Cosslet Tess; Easton, Alison and Summerfield, Penny (eds) *Women, Power and Resistance* Buckingham: Open University Press, 250–62.

Rivera Fuentes, Consuelo (1996b) 'Todas Locas, Todas Vivas, Todas Libres: Chilean Lesbians 1980–95' in Reinfelder, Monika (ed) *Amazon to Zami: Towards a Global Lesbian Feminism* London: Cassell, 138–51.

Roberts, Bryan (1994) 'Informal Economy and Family Strategies', *International Journal of Urban and Regional Research*, 18:1, 6–23.

Roberts, Bryan (1995) *The Making of Citizens: Cities of Peasants Revisited* London: Edward Arnold.

Roberts, Kenneth (1985) 'Household Labour Mobility in a Modern Urban Economy' in Standing, Guy (ed) *Labour Circulation and the Labour Process* London: Croom Helm, 358–81.

Roberts, Kenneth (1995) 'Neoliberalism and the Transformation of Populism in Latin America: The Peruvian Case', *World Politics*, 48:1, 82–116.

Roberts, Penelope (1991) 'Anthropological Perspectives on the Household', *IDS Bulletin*, 22:1, 60–64.

Robles Berlanga, Héctor with Artís, Gloria, Salazar, Julieta and Muñoz, Laura (2000) '*¡....Y Ando Yo en el Campo! Presencia de la Mujer en el Agro Mexicano*' México DF: Procaduría Agraria.

Rodríguez, Eugenia (1994) '"Titiya Bea los Que Me Han Echo": Estupro e Incesto en Costa Rica (1800–1850)' in Molina Jiménez, Ivan and Palmer, Steven (eds) *El Paso de la Cometa: Estado, Políticas Sociales y Culturas Populares en Costa Rica (1800–1950).* San José: Ediotorial Porvenir/Plumsock Mesoamerican Studies, 19–45.

Rodríguez, Eugenia (1998) '"Matrimonios Felices": Cambios y Continuidades en las Percepciones y en las Actitudes Hacia la Violencia Doméstica en el Valle Central de Costa Rica, 1750–1930' in Rodríguez, Eugenia (ed) *Violencia Doméstica en Costa Rica: Mas Allá de los Mitos* San José: FLACSO Sede Costa Rica, Cuaderno de Ciencias Sociales 105, 9–30.

Rodríguez, Eugenia (2000) *Hijas, Novias y Esposas: Familia, Matrimonio y Violencia Doméstica en el Valle Central de Costa Rica 1750–1850* Heredia: Editorial Universidad Nacional.

Rodríguez, Florisabel; Castro, Silvia and Espinosa, Rowland (eds) (1999) *El Sentir Democrático: Estudios Sobre la Cultura Política Centroamericana* San José/Heredia: Asociación Programa Centroamericano para la Sostenibilidad/Editorial Fundación UNA.

Rodríguez, Lilia (1994) 'Barrio Women: Between the Urban and the Feminist Movement', *Latin American Perspectives*, 21:3, 32–48.

Rothstein, Frances Abrahamer (1995) 'Gender and Multiple Income Strategies in Rural Mexico: A Twenty-Year Perspective' in Bose, Christine and Acosta-Belén, Edna (eds) *Women in the Latin American Development Process* Philadelphia: Temple University Press, 167–93.

Rubin, Gayle (1984) 'Thinking Sex', in Vance, Christine *Pleasure and Danger: Exploring Female Sexuality* London: Routledge and Kegan Paul.

Rudolf, Gloria (1999) *Panama's Poor: Victims, Agents and Historymakers* Gainesville: University Press of Florida.

Ruiz, Vicki and Tiano, Susan (eds) (1987) *Women on the US–Mexico Border: Responses to Change* Boston: Allen and Unwin.

Ruz, Mario Humberto (1998) 'La Semilla del Hombre: Notas Etnológicas acerca de la Sexualidad y Reproducción Masculinas entre los Mayas' in Lerner, Susana (ed) *Varones, Sexualidad y Reproducción* México DF: El Colegio de México, 193–221.

Sacayón Manzo, Eduardo Enrique (1997) 'Guatemala: Perfíl Económico con una Perspectiva de Género' in Elson, Diane; Fauné, María Angélica; Gideon, Jasmine; Gutiérrez, Maribel; López de Mazier, Armida and Sacayón, Eduardo *Crecer con la Mujer: Oportunidades para el Desarrollo Ecónomico Centroamericano* San José: Embajada Real de los Países Bajos, 173–215.

Safa, Helen (1990) 'Women and Industrialisation in the Caribbean' in Stichter, Sharon and Parpart, Jane (eds) *Women, Employment and the Family in the International Division of Labour* Houndmills, Basingstoke: Macmillan, 72–97.

Safa, Helen (1992) 'Development and Changing Gender Roles in Latin America and the Caribbean' in Kahne, Hilda and Giele, Janet (eds) *Women's Work and Women's Lives: The Continuing Struggle Worldwide* Boulder: Westview Press, 69–86.

Safa, Helen (1995a) *The Myth of the Male Breadwinner: Women and Industrialisation in the Caribbean*. Boulder: Westview.

Safa, Helen (1995b) 'Economic Restructuring and Gender Subordination', *Latin American Perspectives*, 22:2, 32–50.

Safa, Helen (1999) *Women Coping With Crisis: Social Consequences of Export-Led Industrialisation in the Dominican Republic* Miami: North-South Agenda Paper No 36, North-South Center, University of Miami.

Safilios-Rothschild, Constantina (1990) 'Socio-economic Determinants of the Outcomes of Women's Income-Generation in Developing Countries' in Stichter, Sharon and Parpart, Jane (eds) *Women, Employment and the Family in the International Division of Labour* Houndmills, Basingstoke: Macmillan, 221–8.

Salas, José Manuel (1998) 'Algunos Apuntes sobre la Violencia Doméstica Desde la Perspectiva de los Hombres' in Rodríguez, Eugenia (ed) *Violencia Doméstica en Costa Rica: Mas Allá de los Mitos* San José: FLACSO Sede Costa Rica, Cuaderno de Ciencias Sociales 105, 53–68.

Salessi, Jorge (1995) 'The Argentine Dissemination of Homosexuality, 1890–1914' in Bergman, Emilie and Smith, Paul J. (eds) *Entiendes? Queer Readings, Hispanic Writings* Durham: Duke University Press, 49–91.

Sánchez-Ayéndez, Melba (1993) 'Women as Primary Support Providers for the Elderly: The Case of Puerto Rico' in Gómez Gómez, Elsa (ed) *Gender, Women and Health in the Americas* Washington DC: Pan American Health Organisation, 263–8.

Sandoval García, Carlos (1997) *Sueños y Sudores en la Vida Cotidiana: Trabajadores y Trabajadoras de la Maquila y la Construcción en Costa Rica* San José: Universidad de Costa Rica, Colección Instituto de Investigaciones Sociales.

Satterthwaite, David (1993) 'The Impact on Health of Urban Environments', *Environment and Urbanisation*, 5:2, 87–111.

Sawyers Royal, Kathleen and Perry, Franklin (1995) 'Costa Rica' in Minority Rights Group (ed) *Afro-Latin Americans Today: No Longer Invisible* London: Minority Rights Publications, 215–24.

Sayavedra, Gloria (1997) 'Fulfilling Providers' Preferences: Four Mexican States' in Hardon, Anita and Hayes, Elizabeth (eds) *Reproductive Rights in Practice: A Feminist Report on the Quality of Care* London: Zed, 95–111.

Scheffer, Mario and Marthe, Marcelo (1999) 'Men in Prison in Brazil' in Foreman, Martin (ed) *AIDS and Men: Taking Risks or Taking Responsibility?* London: Panos Institute/Zed, 144–56.

Scheper-Hughes, Nancy (1997) 'Lifeboat Ethics: Mother Love and Child Death in Northeast Brazil' in Lancaster, Roger and di Leonardo, Micaela (eds) *The Gender Sexuality Reader* London: Routledge, 82–8.

Schifter, Jacobo (1998) *Lila's House: Male Prostitution in Latin America* New York: Hayworth.

Schifter, Jacobo and Madrigal, Johnny (1996) *Las Gavetas Sexuales del Costarricense y el Riesgo de la Infección con el VIH* San José: Editorial IMEDIEX.

Schild, Verónica (1994) 'Recasting "Popular" Movements: Gender and Political Learning in Neighbourhood Organisations in Chile', *Latin American Perspectives*, 21:2, 59–80.

Schild, Verónica (1998) 'New Subjects of Rights? Women's Movements and the Construction of Citizenship in the "New Democracies"' in Alvarez, Sonia; Dagnino, Evelina and Escobar, Arturo (eds) *Cultures of Politics, Politics of Cultures: Re-visioning Latin American Social Movements* Boulder: Westview, 93–117.

Schirmer, Jennifer (1993) 'The Seeking of Truth and the Gendering of Consciousness: The CoMadres of El Salvador and the CONAVIGUA Widows of Guatemala' in Radcliffe, Sarah and Westwood, Sallie (eds) *'Viva': Women and Popular Protest in Latin America* London: Routledge, 30–64.

Schmink, Marianne (1984) 'Household Economic Strategies', *Latin American Research Review*, 19:3, 87–101.

Scobie, Jane (2000) 'Growing Old in the South: The Impact of Gender on the Lives of Poor People', *Social Development Newsletter* (Department for International Development, UK), 8:1, 6–9.

Scott, Alison MacEwen (1986a) 'Women in Latin America: Stereotypes and Social Science', *Bulletin of Latin American Research*, 5:2, 21–7.

Scott, Alison MacEwen (1986b) 'Industrialisation, Gender Segregation and Stratification Theory' in Crompton, Rosemary and Mann, Michael (eds) *Gender and Stratification* Cambridge: Polity, 154–89.

Scott, Alison MacEwen (1986c) 'Women and Industrialisation: Examining the "Female Marginalisation" Thesis', *Journal of Development Studies*, 22:4, 649–80.

Scott, Alison MacEwen (1990) 'Patterns of Patriarchy in the Peruvian Working Class' in Stichter, Sharon and Parpart, Jane (eds) *Women, Employment and the Family in the International Division of Labour* Houndmills, Basingstoke: Macmillan, 198–220.

Scott, Alison MacEwen (1994) *Divisions and Solidarities: Gender, Class and Employment in Latin America* London: Routledge.

Scott, Alison MacEwen (1995) 'Informal Sector or Female Sector? Gender Bias in Labour Market Models' in Elson, Diane (ed) *Male Bias in the Development Process*, 2nd ed, Manchester: Manchester University Press, 105–32.

Scott, Sue and Jackson, Stevi (1996) 'Sexual Skirmishes and Feminist Factions: Twenty-Five Years of Debate on Women and Sexuality' in Jackson, Stevi and Scott, Sue (eds) *Feminism and Sexuality: A Reader* Edinburgh: Edinburgh University Press, 1–31.

Secretaría de Gobernación (1996) *Alianza para la Igualdad: Programa Nacional de la Mujer, 1995–2000* México DF: Secretaría de Gobernacíon.

Seguino, Stephanie (2000) 'Gender Inequality and Economic Growth: A Cross-Country Analysis', *World Development*, 28:7, 1211–30.

Selby, Henry; Murphy, Arthur and Lorenzen, Stephen (1990) *The Mexican Urban Household: Organising for Self-Defence* Austin: University of Texas Press.

Sen, Amartya (1987) *Gender and Cooperative Conflicts* Helsinki: World Institute for Development Economics Research.

Sen, Amartya (1991) 'Gender and Cooperative Conflicts' in Tinker, Irene (ed) *Persistent Inequalities: Women and World Development* New York: Oxford University Press, 123–49.

Sen, Gita (1999) 'Engendering Poverty Alleviation: Challenges and Opportunities', *Development and Change*, 30:3, 685–92.

Sen, Kasturi (1994) *Ageing: Debates on Demographic Transition and Social Policy* London: Zed.

Sennott-Miller, Lee (1993) 'Older Women in the Americas: Problems and Potential' in Gómez Gómez, Elsa (ed) *Gender, Women and Health in the Americas* Washington DC: Pan American Health Organisation,104–17.

Shallat, Lezak (1994) 'Rites and Rights: Catholicism and Contraception in Chile' in Panos (ed) *Private Decisions, Public Debate: Women, Reproduction and Population* London: Panos, 149–62.

Sheahan, John (1997) 'Effects of Liberalisation Programs on Poverty and Inequality: Chile, Mexico and Peru', *Latin American Research Review*, 32:3, 7–37.

Sifuentes Jáuregui, Ben (1997) 'Gender without Limits: Transvestism and Subjectivity in *El Lugar sin Límites*' in Balderston, Daniel and Guy, Donna (eds) *Sex and Sexuality in Latin America* New York: New York University Press, 44–61.

Skeldon, Ronald (1990) *Population Mobility in Developing Countries* London: Belhaven.

Smyke, Patricia (1994) *Women and Health* London: Zed.

Smyth, Ines (1994) *Population Policies: Official Responses to Feminist Critiques* London: London School of Economics, Global Governance Discussion Paper 14.

Solo, Julie (1999) 'Hacía Dónde Vamos? Camino al Futuro', *Alternativas de Investigación Operativa* (Population Council, Mexico), January, 18–19.

Solórzano, Irela; Abaunza, Humberto and Bradshaw, Sarah (2000) 'Evaluación de la Campaña "Violencia Contra las Mujeres: Un Desastre que los Hombres Sí Podemos Evitar"'. Mimeo, Managua: Puntos de Encuentro.

Sørensen, Nina (1985) 'Roots, Routes and Transnational Attractions: Dominican Migration, Gender and Cultural Change' in Peek, Peter and Standing, Guy (eds) *State Policies and Migration: Studies in Latin America and the Caribbean* London: Croom Helm, 173–205.

de Soto, Hernando (1989) *The Other Path: The Invisible Revolution in the Third World* New York: Harper and Row.

Stacey, Judith (1997) 'The Neo-Family-Values Campaign' in Lancaster, Roger and di Leonardo, Michaela (eds) *The Gender/Sexuality Reader* New York: Routledge, 432–70.

Standing, Guy (1989) 'Global Feminisation through Flexible Labour', *World Development*, 17:7, 1977–95.

Standing, Guy (1999) 'Global Feminisation through Flexible Labour: A Theme Revisited', *World Development*, 27:3, 583–602.

Staudt, Kathleen, (1987) 'Programming Women's Empowerment: A Case from Northern Mexico' in Ruiz, Vicki and Tiano, Susan (eds) *Women on the US–Mexican Border: Responses to Change* Winchester: Allen and Unwin, 155–73.

Staudt, Kathleen (ed) (1997) *Women, International Development and Politics: The Bureaucratic Mire* Philadelphia: Temple University Press.

Stavans, Ilán (1998) 'The Latin Phallus' in Darder, Antonia and Torres, Rudolfo (eds) *The Latino Studies Reader: Culture, Economy and Society* Oxford: Blackwell, 228–39.

Stavig, Ward (1995) '"Living in Offense of Our Lord": Indigenous Sexual Values and Marital Life in the Colonial Crucible', *Hispanic American Historical Review*, 75: 4, 598–622.

Steiner, Henry and Alston, Philip (1996) *International Human Rights in Context: Law, Politics and Morals* Oxford: Clarendon Press.

Stephen, Lynn (1997) *Women and Social Movements in Latin America: Power From Below* Austin: University of Texas Press.

Stern, Claudio (2000) 'El Embarazo Adolescente' in Valdés, Luz María (ed) *Población, Reto del Tercer Milenio: Curso Introductorio a la Demografía* México DF: Universidad Autónoma Nacional de México/Editorial Miguel Angel Porrua, 90–6.

Sternbach, Nancy Saporta; Navarro Aranguren, Marysa; Chuchryk, Patricia and Alvarez, Sonia (1992) 'Feminisms in Latin America: From Bogotá to San Bernardo' in Escobar, Arturo and Alvarez, Sonia (eds) *The Making of Social Movements in Latin America* Boulder: Westview Press, 207–39.

Sternberg, Peter (2000) 'Challenging Machismo: Promoting Sexual and Reproductive Health with Nicaraguan Men', *Gender and Development* (Oxfam), 8:1, 89–99.

Sternberg, Peter (2001) 'Challenging Machismo to Promote Sexual and Reproductive Health: Working with Nicaraguan Men' in Sweetman, Caroline (ed) *Men's Involvement in Gender and Development Policy and Practice: Beyond Rhetoric* Oxford: Oxfam, 59–67.

Stetson, Dorothy McBride and Mazur, Amy (eds) (1995) *Comparative State Feminism* Thousand Oaks: Sage.

Stevens, Evelyn (1965) 'Mexican Machismo: Politics and Value Orientations', *Western Political Quarterly*,18:4, 848–57.

Stevens, Evelyn (1973) 'Marianismo: The Other Face of Machismo in Latin America' in Pescatello, Ann (ed) *Female and Male in Latin America* Pittsburg: University of Pittsburg Press, 89–102.

Stevenson, Linda (1999) 'Gender Politics in the Mexican Democratisation Process: Electing Women and Legislating Sex Crimes and Affirmative Action, 1988–97' in Domínguez, Jorge and Poiré, Alejandro (eds) *Toward Mexico's Democratisation: Parties, Campaigns, Elections and Public Opinion* New York: Routledge, 24–56.

Stewart, Frances (1995) *Adjustment and Poverty: Options and Choices* London: Routledge.

Stichter, Sharon (1990) 'Women. Employment and the Family: Current Debates' in Stichter, Sharon and Parpart, Jane (eds) *Women, Employment and the Family in the International Division of Labour* Houndmills, Basingstoke: Macmillan, 11–71.

Stolcke, Verena (1991) 'The Exploitation of Family Morality: Labour Systems and Family Structure on São Paulo Coffee Plantations 1850–1979' in Jelin, Elizabeth (ed) *Family, Household and Gender Relations in Latin America* London/Paris: Kegan Paul International/UNESCO, 69–100.

Stolcke, Verena (1995) 'Invaded Women: Sex, Race and Class in the Formation of Colonial Society' in Wilson, Fiona and Frederikson, Bodil Folke (eds) *Ethnicity, Gender and the Subversion of Nationalism* London: Frank Cass, 7–21.

Stølen, Kristi Anne (1996) 'The Power of Gender Discourses in a Multi-Ethnic Community in Rural Argentina' in Melhuus, Marit and Stølen, Kristi Ann (eds) *Machos, Mistresses, Madonnas: Contesting the Power of Latin American Gender Imagery* London: Verso, 159–83.

Streicker, Joel (1995) 'Policing Boundaries: Race, Class and Gender in Cartagena, Colombia', *American Ethnologist*, 22, 54–74.

Sufía, Rosa María Martina (1992) 'Mujer y SIDA en México: El Riesgo de Ignorar', *Boletín Editorial del Colegio de México*, 42, 9–13.

Sundari Ravindran, T.K. (1997) 'Research on Women's Health: Some Methodological Issues' in Hill, Eleanor (ed) *Development for Health* Oxford: Oxfam, 14–22.

Sweetman, Caroline (2000) 'Editorial' in Sweetman, Caroline (ed) *Gender in the 21st Century* Oxford: Oxfam, 2–9.

Sweetman, Caroline (ed) (2001) *Men's Involvement in Gender and Development Policy and Practice* Oxford: Oxfam.

Szasz, Ivonne (1998) 'Los Hombres y la Sexualidad: Aportes de la Perspectiva Feminista y los Primeros Acercamientos a su Estudio en México' in Lerner, Susana (ed) *Varones, Sexualidad y Reproducción* México DF: El Colegio de México, 137–62.

Szirmai, Adam (1997) *Economic and Social Development* Hemel Hempstead: Prentice Hall.

Taylor, Lucy (1998) *Citizenship, Participation and Democracy: Changing Dynamics in Chile and Argentina* Basingstoke: Macmillan.

Thayer, Millie (1997) 'Identity, Revolution and Democracy: Lesbian Movements in Central America', *Social Problems*, 44: 3, 386–407.

Thomas, Jim (1995a) *Surviving in the City: The Urban Informal Sector in Latin America* London: Pluto Press.

Thomas, Jim (1995b) 'Replicating the Grameen Bank: The Latin American Experience', *Small Enterprise Development*, 6:2, 16–26.

Thomas, Jim (1996) 'The New Economic Model and Labour Markets in Latin America' in Bulmer-Thomas, Victor (ed) *The New Economic Model in Latin America and its Impact on Income Distribution and Poverty* Houndmills, Basingstoke: Macmillan, in association with the Institute of Latin American Studies, University of London, 79–102.

Thomas, Jim (1997) 'The Urban Informal Sector and Social Policy: Some Latin American Contributions to the Debate'. Paper presented at Workshop for the Social Policy Study Group, Institute of Latin American Studies, University of London, 28 November.

Thomas, Jim (1999) 'El Mercado Laboral y el Empleo' in Crabtree, John and Thomas, Jim (eds) *El Perú de Fujimori* Lima: Universidad del Pacífico, 255–96.

Tiano, Susan (1990) 'Maquiladora Women: A New Category of Workers' in Ward, Kathryn (ed) *Women Workers and Global Restructuring* Ithaca, New York: ILR Press, Cornell University, 192–223.

Tiano, Susan (2001) 'From Victims to Agents: A New Generation of Literature on Women in Latin America', *Latin American Research Review*, 36:3, 183–203.

Tielman, Rob and Hammelburg, Hans (1993) 'World Survey on the Social and Legal Position of Gays and Lesbians' in Hendriks, Aart; Tielman, Rob and van der Veen, Evert (eds) *The Third Pink Book: A Global View of Lesbian and Gay Liberation and Oppression* New York: Prometheus Books, 249–340.

Tironi, Eugenio and Lagos, Ricardo (1991) 'The Social Actors and Structural Adjustment', *CEPAL Review*, 44, 35–50.

Thorner, Alice and Ranadive, Jyoti (1992) 'Working Class Women in an Indian Metropolis: A Household Approach' in Saradamoni, K. (ed) *Finding the Household: Methodological and Empirical Issues* New Delhi: Sage, 143–62.

Tokman, Victor (1989) 'Policies for a Heterogeneous Informal Sector in Latin America', *World Development*, 17:7, 1067–76.

Tokman, Victor (1991) 'The Informal Sector in Latin America: From Underground to Legality' in Standing, Guy and Tokman, Victor (eds) *Towards Social Adjustment: Labour Market Issues in Structural Adjustment* Geneva: International Labour Organisation, 141–57.

Tokman, Victor (1992) *Beyond Regulation: The Informal Sector in Latin America* Boulder: Lynne Rienner.

Tokman, Victor and Klein, Emilio (1996) *Regulation and the Informal Economy: Microenterprises in Chile, Ecuador and Jamaica* Boulder: Lynne Rienner.

Townsend, Janet; Zapata, Emma; Rowlands, Jo; Alberti, Pilar and Mercado, Marta (1999) *Women and Power: Fighting Patriarchies and Poverty* London: Zed.

Trotz, Alissa (1996) 'Gender, Ethnicity and Familial Ideology in Georgetown, Guyana: Household Structure and Female Labour Force Participation Reconsidered', *European Journal of Development Research*, 8:1, 177–99.

Tuman, John (2000) 'Labour Markets and Economic Reform in Latin America: A Review of Recent Research', *Latin American Research Review*, 35:3, 173–87.

Tuñón, Enriqueta (1987) 'La Lucha Política de la Mujer Mexicana por el Derecho al Sufragio y sus Repercusiones' in Ramos Escandón, Carmen (ed) *Presencia y Transparencia: La Mujer en la Historia de México* México DF: El Colegio de México, 181–9.

Tuyuc, Rosalina (1994) 'From Grief Comes Strength: Indigenous Women's Resistance' in Küppers, Gaby (ed) *Compañeras: Voices From the Latin American Women's Movement* London: Latin America Bureau, 111–5.

United Nations (UN) (1995) *The World's Women 1995: Trends and Statistics* New York: UN.

United Nations (UN) (1997) *Demographic Yearbook 1995* New York: UN.

United Nations (UN) (2000) *The World's Women 2000: Trends and Statistics* New York: UN.

United Nations Centre for Human Settlements (UNCHS) (1996) *An Urbanising World: Global Report on Human Settelements* New York: Oxford University Press.

United Nations Children's Fund (UNICEF) (1997) *Role of Men in the Lives of Children: A Study of How Improving Knowledge About Men in Families Helps Strengthen Programming for Children and Women* New York: UNICEF.

United Nations Children's Fund (UNICEF) (1998) *The State of the World's Children 1988* Oxford: Oxford University Press.

United Nations Development Programme (UNDP) (1995) *Human Development Report 1995* New York: Oxford University Press.

United Nations Development Programme (UNDP) (1997) *Human Development Report 1997* New York: Oxford University Press.

United Nations Development Programme (UNDP) (1998) *Human Development Report 1998* New York: Oxford University Press.

United Nations Development Programme (UNDP) (2000) *Human Development Report 2000* New York: Oxford University Press.

United Nations Division for the Advancement of Women (UNDAW) (2000) *Women 2000: Gender Equality, Development and Peace for the 21st Century* New York: UNDAW.

United Nations Economic Commission for Latin America and The Caribbean (ECLAC) (1994) *Social Panorama of Latin America* Santiago: ECLAC.

United Nations International Committee on Integrated Rural Development for Asia and the Pacific (UNIRDAP) (1995) 'New Challenges: Cairo International Conference on Population and Development', *Poverty Alleviation Initiatives*, 4:2, 8–13.

Valdés, Teresa and Gomáriz, Enrique (1995) *Latin American Women: Compared Statistics* Madrid/Santiago de Chile: Instituto de la Mujer/FLACSO.

Valverde, José Manuel (1998) 'Recent Urbanisation and Quality of Life of Adolescents at High Social Risk' in UNICEF (ed) *Adolescence, Child Rights and Urban Poverty in Costa Rica* San José: UNICEF/ HABITAT, 49–64.

Vance, Irene (1985) 'More than Bricks and Mortar: Women's Participation in Self-Help Housing in Managua, Nicaragua' in Moser, Caroline and Peake, Linda (eds) *Women, Human Settlements and Housing* London: Tavistock, 139–65.

Vargas, Virginia (2002) 'The Struggle by Latin American Feminisms for Rights and Autonomy' in Craske, Nikki and Molyneux, Maxine (eds) *Gender and the Politics of Rights and Democracy in Latin America* Basingstoke: Palgrave, 199–221.

Varley, Ann (2000) 'Women and the Home in Mexican Family Law', in Dore, Elizabeth and Molyneux, Maxine (eds) *Hidden Histories of Gender and the State in Latin America* Durham: Duke University Press, 238–61.

Varley, Ann and Blasco, Maribel (2000a) 'Intact or In Tatters? Family Care of Older Women and Men in Urban Mexico', *Gender and Development* (Oxfam), 8:2, 47–55.

Varley, Ann and Blasco, Maribel (2000b) 'Exiled to the Home: Masculinity and Ageing in Urban Mexico', *European Journal of Development Research*, 12:2, 115–38.

Venguer, Tere; Fawcett, Gillian; Verbon, Ricardo and Pick, Susan (1998) *Violencia Doméstica: Un Marco Conceptual para la Capacitación del Personal de Salud* Mexico City: Population Council.

Vernon, Ricardo (1999) 'Anticoncepción de Emergencia en Ecuador y México', *Alternativas de Investigación Operativa* (Population Council, Mexico), January, 13–15.

Villareal, Magdalena (1996) 'Power and Self-Identity: The Beekeepers of Ayuquila' in Melhuus, Marit and Stølen, Kristi Ann (eds) *Machos, Mistresses, Madonnas: Contesting the Power of Latin American Gender Imagery* London: Verso, 184–206.

Vincent, Susan (1998) 'Gender Ideologies and the Informal Economy: Reproduction and the "Grapes-of-Wrath Effect" in Mata Chico, Peru', *Latin American Perspectives*, 25:2, 120–39.

Vincenzi, Atilio (1991) *Código Civil y Código de la Familia* San José: Lehmann Editores.

Vivian, Jessica (1995) 'How Safe are "Social Safety Nets"? Adjustment and Social Sector Restructuring in Developing Countries', *European Journal of Development Research,* 7:1, 1–25.

Viveros, Mara (1998a) 'Quebradores y Cumplidores: Biografías Diversas de la Masculinidad' in Valdés, Teresa and Olavarría, José (eds) *Masculinidades y Equidad de Género en América* Latina Santiago: FLAC-SO-Chile, 36–55.

Viveros, Mara (1998b) 'Dionisos Negros: Sexualidad. Corporalidad y Ordén Racial en Colombia'. Paper presented at the Session 'Is there a Latin American Sexuality', XXI Congress of the Latin American Studies Assosication, Chicago, 24–26 September.

Viveros, Mara (1999) 'Esterilización Masculina, Dinámicas Conyugales y Ambitos de Poder: Un Estudio de Caso Colombiano' in Scavone, Lucila (ed) *Género y Salud Reproductiva en América Latina* Cartago: Libro Universitario Regional, 153–179.

Wade, Peter (1993) *Blackness and Race Mixture: The Dynamics of Racial Identity in Colombia* Baltimore: John Hopkins University Press.

Wade, Peter (1994) 'Man the Hunter: Gender and Violence in Music and Drinking Contexts in Colombia' in Harvey, Penelope and Gow, Peter (eds) *Sex and Violence: Issues in Representation and Experience* London: Routledge, 115–37.

Walby, Sylvia (1985) 'Theories of Women, Work and Unemployment' in The Lancaster Regionalism Group (ed) *Localities, Class and Gender* London: Pion, 145–60.

Waller Meyers, Deborah (1998) *Migrant Remittances to Latin America: Reviewing the Literature* Washington DC: The Tomás Rivera Policy Institute.

Walton, John and Shefner, Jonathan (1994) 'Latin America: Popular Protest and the State' in Walton, John and Seddon, David (eds) *Free Markets and Food Riots: The Politics of Global Adjustment* Oxford: Blackwell, 97–134.

Ward, Kathryn and Pyle, Jean (1995) 'Gender, Industrialisation, Transnational Corporations and Development: An Overview of Trends and Patterns' in Bose, Christine and Acosta-Belén, Edna (eds) *Women in the Latin American Development Process* Philadelphia: Temple University Press, 37–64.

Warnes, Anthony (1994) 'Socio-economic Change and the Health of Elderly People: Future Prospects for the Developing World' in Phillips, David and Verhasselt, Yola (eds) *Health and Development* London: Routledge, 156–67.

Wartenburg, Lucy (1999) 'Vulnerabilidad y Jefatura en los Hogares Urbanos Colombianos' in González de la Rocha, Mercedes (ed) *Divergencias del Modelo Tradicional: Hogares de Jefatura Femenina en América Latina* México DF: Centro de Investigaciones y Estudios Superiores en Antropología Social, 77–96.

Waylen, Georgina (1993) 'Women's Movements and Democratisation in Latin America', *Third World Quarterly*, 14:3, 573–87.

Waylen, Georgina (1994) 'Women and Democratisation: Conceptualising Gender Relations in Transition

Politics', *World Politics*, 46, 327–54.
Weeks, Jeffrey (2000) *Making Sexual History* Cambridge: Polity Press.
Westwood, Sallie (1996) '"Feckless Fathers": Masculinities and the British State' in Mac An Ghaill, Maírtín (ed) *Understanding Masculinities: Social Relations and Cultural Arenas* Buckingham: Open University Press, 21–34.
Whitley, Paul (2000) 'Economic Growth and Social Capital', *Political Studies*, 48, 443–66.
Wiest, Raymond (1983) 'Male Migration, Machismo, and Conjugal Roles: Implications for Fertility Control in a Mexican Municipio', *Journal of Comparative Family Studies*, XIV:2, 168–81.
Wiest, Raymond (1984) 'External Dependency and the Perpetuation of Temporary Migration to the United States' in Jones, Richard C. (ed) *Patterns of Undocumented Migration: Mexico and the United States* Totowa, New Jersey: Rowman and Allanheld, 110–35.
Wiest, Raymond (1998) 'A Comparative Perspective on Households, Gender and Kinship in Relation to Disaster' in Enarson, Elaine and Morrow, Betty Hearn (eds) *The Gendered Terrain of Disaster: Through Women's Eyes* Westport, Connecticut: Praeger, 63–79.
Willis, Katie (1993) 'Women's Work and Social Network Use in Oaxaca City, Mexico', *Bulletin of Latin American Research*, 12:1, 65–82.
Willis, Katie (2000) '"No es Fácil pero es Posible": The Maintenance of Middle Class Women-headed Households in Mexico', *European Review of Latin American and Caribbean Studies*, 69, 29–45.
Willis, Katie and Yeoh, Brenda (2000) 'Introduction' in Willis, Katie and Yeoh, Brenda (eds) *Gender and Migration* Cheltenham: Edward Elgar, xi-xxi.
Willmott, Ceri (2002) 'Constructing Citizenship in the Poblaciones of Santiago, Chile: The Role of Reproductive and Social Rights' in Craske, Nikki and Molyneux, Maxine (eds) *Gender and the Politics of Rights and Democracy in Latin America* Basingstoke: Palgrave, 124–48.
Willott, Sara and Griffin, Christine (1996) 'Men, Masculinity and the Challenge of Long-term Unemployment', in Mac An Ghaill, Maírtín (ed), *Understanding Masculinities: Social Relations and Cultural Arenas* Buckingham: Open University Press, 77–92.
Wilson, Fiona (1995) 'Questioning Race and Gender in Colonial Peru' in Wilson, Fiona and Frederikson, Bodil Folke (eds) *Ethnicity, Gender and the Subversion of Nationalism* London: Frank Cass, 22–32.
Wilson, Gail (2000) *Understanding Old Age: Critical and Global Perspectives* London: Sage.
Wolf, Eric (1959) *Sons of the Shaking Earth* Chicago: Chicago University Press.
World Bank (1980) *World Development Report 1980* New York: Oxford University Press.
World Bank (1990) *World Development Report 1990* New York: Oxford University Press.
World Bank (1995) *World Development Report 1995* New York: Oxford University Press.
World Bank (1996) *World Development Report 1996* New York: Oxford University Press.
World Bank (1999) *World Development Report 1999* New York: Oxford University Press.
World Bank (2000a) *World Development Report 1999/2000* New York: Oxford University Press.
World Bank (2000b) *World Development Report 2000/2001* New York: Oxford University Press.
Wright, Richard and Ellis, Mark (2000) 'The Ethnic and Gender Division of Labour Compared Among Immigrants to Los Angeles', *International Journal of Urban and Regional Research*, 24:3, 583–600.
Yanagisako, Sylvia and Collier, Jane (1987) 'Toward a Unified Analysis of Gender and Kinship' in Collier, Jane and Yanagisako, Sylvia (eds) *Gender and Kinship: Essays Toward a Unified Analysis* Stanford: Stanford University Press, 14–50.
Yarbro-Bejerano, Yvonne (1997) 'Crossing the Border with Chabela Vargas: A Chicana Femme's Tribute' in Balderston, Daniel and Guy, Donna (eds) *Sex and Sexuality in Latin America* New York: New York University Press, 33–43.
Yaschine, Iliana (1999) 'The Changing Anti-Poverty Agenda: What Can the Mexican Case Tell Us?', *IDS Bulletin*, 30:2, 47–60.
Yashar, Deborah (1995) 'Civil War and Social Welfare: The Origins of Costa Rica's Competitive Party System' in Mainwaring, Scott and Scully, Timothy (eds) *Building Democratic Institutions: Party Systems in Latin America* Stanford: Stanford University Press, 72–99.
Yudelman, Sally (1989) 'Access and Opportunity for Women in Central America: A Challenge for Peace' in Ascher, William and Hubbard, Ann (eds) *Central American Recovery and Development: Task Force Report to the International Commission for Central American Recovery and Development* Durham: Duke University Press, 235–56.
Zabaleta, Marta (1986) 'Research on Latin American Women: In Search of Our Political Independence', *Bulletin of Latin American Research*, 5:2, 97–103.
Zlotnik, Hania (1999) 'Women in Migration' in Pontificial Council for the Pastoral Care of Migrants and Itinerant People (ed) *Migration at the Threshold of the Third Millennium: Proceedings, World Congress on the Pastoral Care of Migrants and Refugees* Rome: Vatican, 79–100.

INDEX